BORODIN
Stalin's Man in China

BORODIN

Stalin's
Man
in
China

Dan N. Jacobs

HARVARD UNIVERSITY PRESS

CAMBRIDGE, MASSACHUSETTS, AND LONDON, ENGLAND   1981

Library of Congress Cataloging in Publication Data

Jacobs, Daniel Norman, 1925-
    Borodin, Stalin's man in China.

    Bibliography: p.
    Includes index.
        1. Borodin, Mikhail Markovich, 1884-1951.
2. Revolutionists—Russia—Biography. 3. Revolutionists—China—Biography. 4. China—Politics and government—1912-1949. 5. Communism—China—History.
I. Title
DK268.B65J32   947.084′2′0924 [B]   80-24636
ISBN 0-674-07910-8

To all those who have dreamed and
struggled to make a better world

And to four who have made one:
Jan and Maggie, Ken, and Susan

Prologue

Among the famous of the world some stars burn brightly and constantly. Others shoot quickly into view, burn with high intensity, and then disappear as suddenly as they appear. Such shooting stars are often quickly forgotten, but in the brief period of their luminescence they obscure all other lights. For good or for ill, such stars, such men, dominate their time and place. Such a man was Mikhail Markovich Borodin in the China of 1926–27.

In the mid-1920s, newspaper headlines around the world warned of the march of revolution across China. The national revolutionary armies of the Kuomintang were on the move from their capital in Kwangtung province. Almost everywhere they were hailed as liberators and heroes; opposition dissolved as one town after another greeted them with crimson banners and exploding firecrackers. By the end of 1926, these forces had unexpectedly taken half of China and had moved the capital from Canton north to the Yangtze sister cities of Wuchang, Hankow, and Hangchow, called, collectively, Wuhan.

Six hundred miles downstream in Shanghai, Western imperialism's capital in China, British colonial newspapers spewed vicious editorials against the Wuhan "Bolsheviks," spread rumors of commissars involved in debauches and of parades of naked Chinese virgins, and urged intervention by the British government. Globe-trotting, sensationalist reporters descended on Shanghai from New York, Paris, and Berlin to find out what was really happening in China. Some of the more conscientious, adventurous, and sober among them left the bar of the International Hotel long enough to take the risky packet trip upriver to Wuhan, to observe that area firsthand and to interview the alleged instigator of the mischief then afoot in China: Borodin.

To the Shanghai colonials, the filter through which most opinions about China passed to the West, everything in China was comfortably in hand until Borodin and his aides appeared. The same wild rumors that were spread about developments in Wuhan were projected onto Borodin. In the absence of fact, grandiose fabrications were devised, which to this day partially cloud the truth. The silence that Borodin maintained about himself facilitated the manufacture of such fables. But what could have been more unbelievable than the truth? The Chinese revolution was being piloted to victory by a Chicago schoolmaster, born a shtetl Jew in the tsar's Pale, and now in the service of international communism.

Contents

Illustrations *(following page 152)*

Borodin in Chicago, around 1917.

Fanya and Borodin.

Bordin's 1919 visa.

Seeing off Chiang Kai-shek on the Northern Expedition, 1926.

Borodin at luncheon, Wuhan, 1927.

Fanya and the new women of China, Canton, 1925.

Borodin in Canton, 1925.

Borodin with broken arm, Wuhan, 1927.

Borodin shooting grouse in the Gobi Desert, 1927.

The Sugar Palace, Moscow.

Borodin back in Moscow, 1927.

BORODIN
Stalin's Man in China

The primary consideration in the transliterations used in this volume has been easy recognition, not rigid adherence to particular systems. "Sovetnik" (adviser), which comes from the same root as Soviet, is spelled without the "i" so as to differentiate between the service performed and the regime.

Out of the Pale

Borodin, the Bolshevik conqueror of half of China, was born in the Pale, that part of western Russia to which the tsars sought to restrict their Jewish subjects. There had been Jews in Russia since the diaspora that followed the destruction of the first temple. Occasionally they played a vital role in Russian life, but always they were outsiders. This was particularly so in the nineteenth century, after Poland had been partitioned by Russia, Prussia, and Austro-Hungary. Russia took the eastern part of the country, with its one million Jews. From then on, successive tsars were obsessed by the need to deal with the "Jewish problem," to keep the Jews in the old Polish lands and to prevent them from infiltrating into the rest of Russia.

Jews were not permitted to settle where other Russians did. They were not granted equal citizenship in the empire, were excluded from public office, and were restricted in occupation and land ownership. They were subjected to special taxation, to police harassment and extortion, and to terms of military service that were sometimes twenty-five years long. Despite such state-imposed hardships, however, remarkably few Jews left Russia. The Jewish community continued to grow and by 1880 numbered about four million. But in 1881, after the assassination of Tsar Alexander II (in which no Jews were directly involved), the government, to excuse itself for economic failures and to alleviate growing pressures for progress and reform, began to blame the Jews for whatever went wrong. Within a month after Alexander's assassination, the regime unleashed a series of pogroms in the south. Hundreds of thousands of Jews fled Russia. By the end of the decade, more than a million had gone; by the end of the century, two million.

Despite the mass flight out of Russia, however, many Jews stayed on, though they dreamed of escaping from the hard, bitter life of the *shtetlech* and ghettoes of the tsar's kingdom. For some, the way of escape was through assimilation; for others, it was through Jewish nationalism, both Zionist and non-Zionist. Still others placed their hopes in socialism. Each of a number of socialist groups had its special appeal. But the one with the greatest impact on Russian Jewry was the General Jewish Workers' Union, or the Bund, which originated in Vilna in 1897.

The Bund had been founded by intellectuals, who, while not ready to abandon their Jewish identity, nevertheless were dedicated to the goals of traditional Marxist socialism. But when the Bund's original leaders were jailed or exiled, they were replaced by less ideologically oriented men, mostly workers, who were more directly concerned with day-to-day problems and were increasingly attracted to Jewish nationalism. The Bund's increased attention to improving wages and working conditions, and its Jewish-nationalist orientation, angered orthodox Marxists, who blasted the Bund for its bourgeois positions. But there were two aspects of the Bund that other socialists grudgingly admired, utilized, and sought to emulate: the Bund's skill at organizing and smuggling. The Bund membership came largely from Jewish artisans, who had for generations been organized in guilds, which gave the Jewish worker an organizational experience largely alien to his gentile counterpart. And the Bund's adeptness at whisking illegal persons and materials in and out of the country came from those Jews in the Pale who for a century had lived by smuggling whatever was in demand across Russia's frontiers. The Bund's smuggling operation became the best and most professional among the socialists.

In 1900, the Bund was recognized as the largest social-democratic organization in Russia. At the congress of the Second International in Paris in that year, eleven of the thirty Russian delegates represented the Bund, by far the largest single Russian delegation. The Bund had the enthusiastic support of the Jewish working class, whose political consciousness it helped to develop. This was the most attractive movement for an adventurous Jewish youth emerging from the ghetto and shtetl. It was the one Borodin joined when he reached sixteen.

Borodin's life before the Bund is cloaked in obscurity; any records, if they ever existed, have long since been destroyed by war, revolution, and repression. The picture is further obscured by the Bolshevik dogma that it is not the individual (Lenin and Stalin excepted, of course) but the mass that is significant—and by Borodin's reticence about himself. His taciturnity about his youth and indeed about any phase of his public or private existence was noted by many who were in close contact with him at various stages of his life. There were occasions when, from bitterness or a desire for recognition, he seemed to let the mask slip, but we cannot be sure if the "real" Borodin was being revealed. Still, it was not just the requirements of party or position that made him closemouthed. It was his nature. In any case, Borodin's penchant for silence heightened the mystery that surrounded him and it increased party regard for him; he could be relied upon, among other things, to keep secrets.

What little is known of Borodin's childhood comes largely from the limited accounts he provided when he became a subject of general popular interest. In 1926 he told V. Rait, who later wrote a number of brief biographical statements about Borodin, that he was born Mikhail Markovich Gruzenberg in Yanovichi, in Vitebsk province, on July 9, 1884, moved to Latvia when he was three, and attended Russian schools. These spare facts are the basis for most Soviet accounts of Borodin's early life. In 1971 Borodin's son Norman, writing in a monthly supplement to an obscure journal,[1] filled in the lacunae a bit. He related that his father, while still very young, became a riverboatman, floating logs down the western Dvina from the Vitebsk area to Dvinsk and then on to Riga. Later he decided to remain in the Latvian capital. During the day he worked at the port and in the evening went to a Russian school, preparing to enter a polytechnical institute.

Such are the "hard" facts available on Borodin's childhood and youth (even they are somewhat contradictory). Questions arise: Why was Borodin so reticent? Were even the few facts that Borodin gave Rait and others about himself true? But to raise the questions is not to answer them. As Borodin said many years later on several occasions when asked to contribute details about his life: What good are facts?

It is reasonable to assume that Borodin was born in 1884 in Yanovichi, one of those hundreds of Pale villages whose tiny population—mostly Jewish—seemed to sleep away the generations. The market town of Vitebsk was twenty miles away. A thriving river port of 48,000 people, Vitebsk was on a main railroad line that led east to Smolensk, west to Riga, and north to Pskov. But as Mark Chagall, who was born in Vitebsk three years after Borodin, has demonstrated in his paintings, Vitebsk was provincial and backward. How much more so Yanovichi?

By the time he reached maturity, Borodin had learned to speak Russian without an accent and discuss Russian classical literature with enough sophistication at least to impress non-Russian intellectuals. Russian sources—fed by Borodin—emphasize that Borodin attended "Russian" schools. But, as his son indicates, this probably took place only after he went to Riga as a young man. Although there is no proof that Borodin had been a *kheder* boy or had studied the five books of Moses, it can in the circumstances be assumed that he had more than passing contact with these. Yiddish was his native language, and the shtetl was his cultural milieu. As an adult, Borodin cut himself off from the language and tradition to which he was born. Like many Russian Jews who aspired to the intelligentsia, he disparaged his heritage: Yiddish, the Bible, the synagogue, all represented a history of sectarianism and superstition that had become inimical. The future lay in the Russian language, in Marx and socialism.

But from one important aspect of his tradition Borodin did not isolate himself: the veneration of education. Again and again Borodin exhibited respect for education as a vehicle of personal and societal liberation. In supplying biographical material, Borodin never failed to mention that he had attended a Russian "university" before the revolution. He never identified the university; indeed, if he was exposed to higher education in Russia at all it was probably at one of those schools established by Jews for Jewish youths who passionately desired a secular education, but who could not by reason of prejudice gain admission to the established institutions. If the United States, Borodin did attend a university for a short period, and possibly he matriculated briefly in an evening law school and took courses in literature.

He graduated from none of these programs, yet repeatedly claimed to be a university graduate.

For those, like Borodin, in transition between the ghetto and the world outside, membership in the Bund provided support. Like other socialist groups, it voiced concern for all proletarians and yearned to join with all mankind in the struggle for equality and justice. The Bund also represented a special brand of Jewish social democracy. But when, at the turn of the century, it was "captured" by the Jewish masses, socialist idealism increasingly took second place to economic and Jewish national concerns. More than a few young Bundist intellectuals and semi-intellectuals became disenchanted with their organization. What they wanted was not immersion in the "crass materialism" and "narrow nationalism" they saw materializing in the Bund, but a sharpening of the battle to overthrow the tsarist tyranny. They sought not adjustment and reform but revolution to wipe out once and for all the stupidity, inequities, and cruelty that characterized the regime and to participate in an effort to improve the conditions of life, not just for their fellow Jews but for all men. For those who aspired to such a revolutionary future, it seemed necessary to seek an army other than the Bund, one less bogged down in the here and now.

There was no dearth of groups that beckoned to the disenchanted Bundist intellectuals. Some joined the Social Revolutionaries, whose enthusiastic acceptance of terrorism gave them high standing among Jewish intellectuals and workers alike. But, despite their name, the Social Revolutionaries were not a Marxist party. And in the ghetto, among the "liberated," entranced by their first exposure to so-called science, dedicated to intellectual matters as well as to revolution, it was Marx with his new Bible who appealed. And among the Marxists, to those most dedicated to daring action and revolution, it was Vladimir Ilyich Lenin who captured the imagination.

By 1903, Lenin was recognized in revolutionary circles for his determination and acumen. In exile in Siberia at the end of the 1890s, during sleepless nights when he paced back and forth in his cabin or took long walks in the deep snow, Lenin worked out his principles of revolutionary organization. They called for a tightly knit, centrally controlled group of professional revolutionaries whose chief initial activity would be publication and dissemination of an underground national newspaper. To create a revolution, Lenin held, one must develop revolutionary consciousness—an awareness of how bad things were, confidence that one did not stand alone and that something could be done—and the newspaper was to be the focal point for developing that consciousness.

When he returned from exile, Lenin did not at first share the gathering socialist hostility against the Bund. He concentrated on establishing his own organization. In fashioning the apparatus for smuggling his newspaper into Russia from abroad, Lenin recognized that the Bund's well-established routes and techniques could be of assistance. For a while he used the Bund, but shortly he too turned against it. In 1903 at the Second Party Congress, he came out squarely against the Bund, as did most of the social democrats assembled there. Whether Borodin left the Bund as a result of the latter's growing stress on economic and national concerns or because of its drift away from the mainstream of social democracy can only be surmised. It is plausible that he may have been influenced by the Kishinev pogrom of April 1903, in which hundreds of Jews were killed and which was followed by antisemitic outbreaks all over southern Russia. The pogroms conceivably made clear to Borodin what the social-democratic *Iskra* had been saying in its editorials: the Jews, no matter how well organized, were helpless by themselves. They had to cooperate with others and participate as individuals in the general social-democratic movement.

Whatever the reason, sometime in 1903 Borodin decided to leave the Bund and join Lenin. Doubtless he was welcome because, in late 1903, there were perhaps less than a hundred revolutionaries in all of Russia—indeed in all of Europe—who counted themselves members of Lenin's Bolshevik faction of the Russian Social Democratic Labor Party (RSDLP). If Borodin came to Lenin early in 1903, prior to the Second Party Congress but after Lenin had attacked the Bund, he would have been welcomed by Vladimir Ilyich as evidence of the soundness of his arguments and indication of their success in attracting support, and as an ally in the battle to win over Jewish workers. But if Borodin joined him later in the year, when Lenin's support was melting away, how much more welcome as one who swam against the tide? In any event, Borodin was one of the few Lenin loyalists during the disintegration of Lenin's group following the party congress and during the 1904 battle to build a new party organization—a struggle in which Lenin worked himself to the verge of nervous collapse.

Borodin would also have been attractive to Lenin because of his youth—he was only nineteen. Lenin was constantly seeking young followers, leaders-to-be of the new generation. Moreover, Borodin by 1903 had already had three years of experience with the Bund, and his knowledge of boats and the Riga waterfront, which was a hotbed of smuggling, were potentially useful as well. To the extent that Borodin possessed organizing and smuggling skills, he significantly increased his usefulness to Lenin. Moreover, Borodin came from the "Northwest," where Lenin had previously had few contacts. In that area of the empire there were Lithuanians, Latvians, Estonians, Finns, as well as Russians, all of whom had to be reached. And though Borodin's Jewish origin kept him from being the model agent in that part of the tsar's empire, he was familiar with the area and he spoke German (the *lingua franca* of the Baltics) as well as Latvian. And he was available.

For a variety of reasons, then, Lenin welcomed, valued, and could make use of Borodin. In mid-1904, he was ordered to Switzerland by Lenin on "party instructions."[2] It was a time when Lenin, in exile, was gathering followers around him to evaluate them and to form them into a new organization—his own. Borodin, arriving in Switzerland in the second half of 1904, did not remain there for long. On January 10, 1905, the electrifying news reached the Bolsheviks in exile that on the preceding Sunday, tsarist troops had fired on a workers' demonstration in the Winter Palace Square in St. Petersburg, killing and wounding hundreds. Ostensibly the workers had come to the palace to petition the tsar for relief from economic hardships and to protest the unsuccessful war against Japan. Historians continue to disagree whether the demonstration was intended as a peaceful act or a provocation designed to elicit an attack. But to the revolutionaries, as to many other Russians, the meaning of "Bloody Sunday" was clear: the regime, petitioned by its suffering and unarmed subjects, had responded brutally by opening fire. Time could indicate that the powerful stabilizing myth of the tsar as father-protector of the Russian people was largely vaporized by the events of January 9, 1905; with the myth went much of the tsar's authority.

In Switzerland, revolutionaries rushed to tell one another the Petersburg news. Lenin's wife Krupskaya recalled: "We sought each other's company. But hardly a word was spoken—we were all so excited. We sang the revolutionary funeral march *You Have Fallen in the Struggle*—with grim set faces. The realization came over everyone in a wave that the revolution had begun, that the shackles of faith in the tsar had been torn apart."[3] Lenin's first move after he had absorbed the staggering news of Bloody Sunday was to learn all he could about the situation inside Russia. Newspaper accounts were fragmentary and superficial; he needed to know what was happening. Lenin might have returned home, but for whatever reason—fatigue, fear of failure, instinctive caution, the need to organize further before he moved, the belief that the revolutionary hour had not yet come—he did not. But others soon did. The party school Lenin had been conducting broke up, and most of those in training, along with a wide variety of other resident revolutionaries, hurried back to Russia to participate in the great events they anticipated. To many of those returning, Lenin gave instructions and promised to see them before long in Russia.

Borodin, like all the exiles, was energized by the portent of Bloody Sunday. His dreams had materialized. The prospect of immediate revolution was at hand, and now was the time for action. Borodin was one of the first to return to Russia, leaving Switzerland before the end of January and carrying credentials as Lenin's agent and instructions to the party in Riga. When Borodin arrived, the Latvian capital had already experienced revolutionary outbreaks, as had other urban centers. The six months before Bloody Sunday had witnessed numerous demonstrations in Riga accompanied by widespread strike activity. The events of January 9 in front of the Winter Palace had brought thousands more of all classes, bourgeoisie as well as workers and students, into the streets. In some areas factory workers clashed with soldiers and police. In others the police needed no serious provocation to fire into the crowds. During the second ten days of January 1905, scores were killed and wounded in Riga and hundreds arrested. But by early February, when Borodin arrived, the situation had calmed down and an uneasy peace had returned.

It is unclear exactly what role the Bolsheviks played in the January events in Riga, but of necessity it was minor since their local organization was all but nonexistent. Prior to 1905 Lenin knew very little about the social democrats in Latvia; what he did know concerned only the activities of the strongest social-democratic organization in the area: the Bund. Not until mid-1905, apparently, did Lenin begin to focus on Latvia. Increasingly, his articles noted and discussed Riga events, largely drawn from information supplied by Borodin. But Borodin's commission in Riga and the scope of his activities were far wider than those of a mere correspondent. In going to Riga as Lenin's agent, Borodin was returning to a situation he knew well. During the course of 1905 he worked vigorously and successfully to organize and develop the weak movement he found there. Within six months, he turned the Bolsheviks into a politically significant if not the leading social-democratic organization in Riga.

In so doing, Borodin discovered his greatest asset: the ability to work effectively with people of differing backgrounds and ideologies. Borodin was not then, nor would he ever become, an insensitive fanatic. He lacked the fanatic's ability to suspend judgment; he was able to see merit in other points of view and flaws in his own. It was a defect in the ideal Leninist; but in the Riga of 1905, as at other times and places, it was an advantage to be able to work not only with Bolsheviks but also with others who shared roughly similar objectives.

As 1905 wore on, sectarian differences among the various revolutionary forces had dimmed, particularly in the provinces. In Riga, as elsewhere, forces that ranged from anarchists to liberal Constitutional Democrats (Kadets) moved toward one another. And in the Latvian capital, Borodin was instrumental in bringing this about. Although he belonged to none of the three principal groups with which he worked—the Latvian social democrats, the Russian workers, and the Bund—he established rapport with each. He spoke Latvian, *and* he offered crucially important credentials as a leading Russian social democrat. Although the Latvian social democrats were more Latvian than social democratic, they realized that they could accomplish their nationalistic goals only by cooperation with Russian revolutionaries. To the Russian workers in Riga who felt isolated among the Latvians, Borodin could speak in Russian as one who valued and appreciated Russian culture and as the agent of a leading Russian revolutionary party. To the Bundists, Borodin, perhaps both handicapped and advantaged by his previous Bund membership, could speak in Yiddish as one who understood Bund problems and had himself been subject to antisemitism.

At this time, it was the Bund that most strongly resisted the idea of revolutionary unity in Riga. But the July 1905 pogroms convinced the Bund that effective opposition to the tsar was imperative and that it could not organize this alone. Although a loose Federative Committee of the leading reform and revolutionary forces had, in one form or another, existed in Riga since January 1905 (possibly even before), a broad-spectrum organization, ranging from liberals leftward, was effectively constituted only in July of that year. From July to October the Federative Committee had approximately sixty members, including representatives of the Bund, the Latvian social democrats, Mensheviks, Bolsheviks, the Social Revolutionaries, Kadets, "antiwar" groups, and several other factions, mostly established on a national basis.[4] There were three Bolsheviks on the Riga Federative Committee: P. A. Kobozev, S. Z. Rozovsky, and M. M. Borodin, who was one of its three secretaries.

During the summer and fall of 1905, the sparks of revolution were everywhere. The tsar held on, but his authority was questioned widely—by bankers as well as cabdrivers, by ballerinas as well as steelworkers. Demonstrations, mutinies, and strikes erupted by the hundreds, terminating in a paralyzing general strike that began with the railroads and spread until it brought the national economy to a halt. The regime seemed close to collapse. But Nicholas II, ordinarily not prone to compromise, was prevailed upon by his chief minister, Witte, to issue the October Manifesto, offering vague concessions designed to split the left from its liberal supporters. It succeeded notably.

Most men who take to the streets in defiance of authority do so impulsively rather than in planned response to a challenge. But as quickly as mass passions flare, they usually subside. By October 1905, many who had energetically opposed the tsar's regime began to have second thoughts. The promises of the October Manifesto were well-timed and appealing; the alliance of radicals and liberals began to crumble. The liberals, partly afraid of what they had done, partly pleased, were willing to accept the tsar's "concessions." But the radicals were not. For them, the revolution had yet to be accomplished. It was more necessary than ever to push on, since victory seemed so near.

Among the radicals, however, particularly among social democrats, there was sharp disagreement over how to proceed. Some wanted to see how the October Manifesto worked out before taking further revolutionary action; they hoped to accomplish their goals by relying on mass organization and popular pressure, which had just proved successful. To Lenin, however, this was nonsense. The enemy was on the run, and now was the time to increase the tempo of the attack. The revolution would come from militant activism, led by himself, not from waiting to see what might develop.

In Riga, beginning in October, the differences between the Leninist and other radical positions were fought out in a series of mass meetings in which the "Opposition" was often represented by S. Klevansky, freshly arrived from Siberian exile. Klevansky, destined to become a noted Bundist orator, was a powerful speaker. Against Klevansky, representing the Bolsheviks and advocating immediate and further revolutionary activity, was pitted Borodin. Though the latter was no orator of Klevansky's caliber, he was apparently the Bolsheviks' best man for that job. According to Bolshevik sources, the Klevansky–Borodin debates focused on such slogans as "fighting alliance," proposed by the Bolsheviks, and "legalization," proposed by their opponents.[5] Borodin stressed the need to cement revolutionary ties, to strengthen the underground, to prepare to fight. Klevansky emphasized mass organization and the necessity to enlist large numbers of workers to press the tsar into broader reform.

Whether the debates raged around these or other issues, the Bolsheviks conceded that Klevansky carried the masses. Even if

Borodin had been a more accomplished speaker, it is unlikely that he could have altered the results significantly, for Klevansky's position of reconciliation and procrastination responded to the popular mood in late 1905. But the decline in Bolshevik popularity did not weaken Borodin's position in Bolshevik circles. What was happening in Riga was not unique; events were moving in the same direction almost everywhere in Russia. Borodin had achieved status by his Riga activities and he was able to maintain it.

Toward the end of 1905, Borodin, from Lenin's point of view, was one of the major Riga figures and one of the rising young Bolsheviks. When a meeting of Bolshevik leaders was called for December to plan the next phase of the revolution, Borodin was among the list of delegates whom Lenin summoned.

2

The 1905 Revolution

Lenin finally reached St. Petersburg in November 1905. By then the "Days of Freedom" that followed the October Manifesto were in full swing. Next to the period between the February and October revolutions of 1917, the weeks after the October Manifesto were the freest modern Russia has ever known.

On the left, the revolutionary organizations began to emerge from underground. The various forces (though the Bolsheviks less than others) pushed the development of new organizations, suitable to the open operations that seemed in the offing. There was a race to see which left-wing newspaper could first begin legal publication, with the Bolshevik *Novaya zhizn* (New Life) put out by Maxim Litvinov and Leonid Krassin winning out over Trotsky's *Nachalo* (Beginning). But even at the moment that the new freedom was proclaimed, the government was moving to curtail it.

By splitting the opposition, the October Manifesto had reduced the pressure on the tsarist forces, giving them time to regroup. Measures were taken in November and December to ensure the loyalty of the army. The police were strengthened. And, as had been done before, scapegoats were found to siphon off the discontent of the masses. Pogroms were renewed, particularly in the south.

In Petersburg the moment for urban mass involvement had passed. But in Moscow there was still determination in some circles to take revolutionary action. In that city a strike began in December; however, the following day, the local Bolshevik-Menshevik committee was arrested en masse. In spite of this, several thousand workers set up barricades in the streets. But noth-

ing came of it. The railroads continued to run. Loyal troops—
the dread Semyenovsky Regiment—were brought in to replace
the local garrisons suspected of sympathy with the revolution.
After the Semyenovsky Regiment appeared, continuing resistance was confined mostly to the Presnya working-class district.
By December 20, twelve days after it had begun, the Moscow
uprising had petered out. The howling revolutionary wind, contained by the October Manifesto, had now become a more man-
ageable zephyr.

The December events in Moscow, when the workers insisted
on moving to the barricades (events that Lenin later considered
the most momentous aspect of 1905), were not anticipated by
the top Bolshevik leadership. Lenin had scheduled for early December not a revolution, but a party meeting in Tammerfors.
Finland. At the moment the Moscow outbreak occurred, leading
Bolsheviks from all over Russia were headed for Finland. Information about the Tammerfors conference is limited. Krupskaya
noted:

> What a pity the minutes of this conference have been lost! The en-
> thusiasm that reigned there! The revolution was in full swing, and
> the enthusiasm was tremendous. Every comrade was ready for a
> fight. In the intervals we learned to shoot. One evening we attended
> a Finnish torchlight meeting, and the solemnity of it fully harmon-
> ized with the temper of the delegates. I doubt whether anyone who
> was at that conference could ever forget it.[1]

Certainly Borodin never did. At Tammerfors there was almost
universal belief that the revolution was just around the corner.
And there he was, alongside Bolshevik leaders from all over
Russia, discussing revolutionary actions of the immediate past
and planning to exploit the revolutionary moment just ahead.
Tammerfors had to be a heady potion for a twenty-one-year-old,
reinforced by his selection by Lenin to serve on the conference
presidium. Though he was only a Bolshevik backbencher at
Tammerfors, just being there must have brought him great satisfaction.

In later years, Borodin would benefit from the prestige of having been at Tammerfors—and from the people he met there.
Borodin had known Lenin in Switzerland; he probably met

Krupskaya there too. It is also likely that he had previously met other prominent Bolsheviks, such as S. A. Lozovsky. The latter had also been in exile in Switzerland in 1904 and played an important role at Tammerfors; much later, he would be with Borodin at a critical moment halfway around the world. But Borodin certainly had not previously met the young Georgian Koba-Ivanovich-Djugashvili, later known as Stalin, who, before Tammerfors, had never been beyond his native Caucasus. Stalin was five years Borodin's senior, but their local leadership roles placed them in roughly equivalent positions at the conference. If anything, Borodin's position was stronger. He knew more people. He was far more experienced in many ways than Stalin and, by comparison, more sophisticated. Ordinarily, Stalin's quiet, provincial characteristics might not have appealed to Borodin. But Borodin was young—and it was his first revolutionary gathering, as it was Stalin's. Circumstances may have forced Borodin and Stalin together at Tammerfors. Of course they met there and a few months later would meet again, on which occasion there would be no doubt that they were closely identified.

The Tammerfors conference lasted from December 12 through the 17th, in the midst of the Moscow uprising and before the latter had aborted. The conference passed a resolution calling for the immediate organization of an armed uprising throughout Russia, and then adjourned so the delegates could return to their revolutionary posts. Borodin made his way back to Riga as speedily as he could. By the time he got there, it was clear that the December uprising was not going to ignite revolution. But nevertheless the belief persisted that the revolution could not be far off. Borodin picked up his party responsibilities. In March he attended the spring conference of the Latvian social-democratic organization, where discussions were held on affiliating with the Russian social democrats. Other of his activities between January and April 1906, like those of most revolutionaries at the time, are conjectural. Almost a decade later, Borodin reminisced about his exploits with the "Forest Brotherhood," a Latvian Robin Hood group that engaged in hit-and-run raids against the tsar's forces and was distinguished by its marksmanship. Some who knew Borodin in 1905–06 and were familiar with the operation of the Brotherhood denied his participation. Indeed, it seems unlikely that Borodin was a partisan: it was not his style; he was an organization man, not a guerrilla fighter. Moreover, he was a Jew, and most Baltic guerrilla groups were antisemitic. On the other hand, the situation in the Baltic area was fast becoming desperate. The Latvian peasants had stepped up their burnings and lootings in 1906. Punitive expeditions sent out by the government engaged rebellious peasants in pitched battles in which hundreds were killed. In the mopping-up operations that followed, arrests and executions were widespread. In Riga there were roadblocks at almost every corner. Cossacks and police spread their nets wide in search of revolutionaries. Anyone arousing the least suspicion was likely to be stopped and searched. While arrests and executions were less frequent in the city than in the countryside, they were numerous.

In the circumstances, Borodin was forced underground. It may have been difficult for Borodin to avoid involvement with the Forest Brotherhood, or it may have been that the youthful Borodin, with the energizing vapors of revolution pervading the land, craved action. In any event, when the Unity Congress of the Russian Social Democratic Labor Party, attended by both Bolsheviks and Mensheviks, opened in Parlor D of the huge Peoples' House in Stockholm on April 10, 1906, Borodin, using the party name of Vanyushin, was there as the lone voting representative of the Riga Bolsheviks.

From the very beginning at Stockholm the atmosphere was tense. The Bolsheviks were assertive and aggressive; the Mensheviks, uncertain and defensive. At the last general party congress in 1903, the split between the two had been regretted by most partisans on both sides. But by this time Bolsheviks and Mensheviks had come to view one another with deep suspicion and moved toward and around one another slowly and guardedly. The verbal battles, the incessant squabbling, the fierce jockeying for position, which was to characterize the Stockholm "Unity" Congress, became evident at the opening meetings of the credentials committee. Its stormy sessions witnessed repeated presentations by delegates seeking accreditation as the representatives of often nonexistent local organizations, as both sides maneuvered to increase their numbers. After four days, slightly over a hundred delegates had been seated, the majority of them Mensheviks. After the months-long struggle Lenin had conducted for a Bolshevik majority, his minority position was a bitter pill to swallow.

Lenin was discouraged, but he was not about to give up; on point after point, he insisted on his position. He usually lost, and sometimes he backed down to preserve an appearance of unity, but his positions were for the most part clear and decisive, certainly far less cluttered than those of the opposition. He was a dynamic, self-assured leader. Although the opposition had the votes to defeat Lenin and used them, it feared him; and many of its members were attracted to him, seemingly against their better judgment and against their will.

At Stockholm, Borodin remained a relatively unknown local committeeman. His experiences in 1905, while intense, had been largely limited to the Riga area. His previous contact with the leaders present at the Stockholm congress had been minimal. On the only occasion he stood for election, he was defeated, receiving only six votes, an undistinguished performance even among the Bolsheviks. Borodin's primarily local identification and orientation were further indicated by the occasions when he spoke out at the congress. There were only two: the first, to express opposition to the Mensheviks on the agricultural question, a position based on Latvian experience; second, to comment on the application of the Latvian social democrats to establish a formal relationship with the RSDLP. It was the latter issue that most heavily involved Borodin's participation on the floor of the congress. Representing the Riga organization of the Bolsheviks and having attended the March conference of the Latvian social democrats, Borodin was an obvious choice to handle the floor discussion for the Bolsheviks, even though the plays were called by Lenin.

The Bolsheviks, as internationalists, opposed the idea of national parties. But facts were facts: Lenin was obliged to recognize that a chief motivation for revolutionary involvement was nationalism. Many supported "revolution" not primarily because of commitment to a Marxist concept of historical development, but because they wanted national independence. Only a party indifferent to its own interests could disregard this. Thus the position had been established by the Bolsheviks that national parties were to be permitted, but only if they were based on "territory" and not "nationality." The party of the Latvian social democrats did not fit that criterion, however; theirs was clearly a party based on nationality.

Borodin disputed first the name the Latvian social democrats proposed for their party: Social Democracy of the Latvian Krai (SDLK). Autonomous parties were to be permitted within the RSDLP, Borodin said, only when distinctive cultural and life styles in those areas lent themselves to the formation of such organizations. But in the case of the Latvian krai (territory), there was such a conglomeration of life styles within a single culture that the designation of all as "Latvian" was ridiculous. He asserted that if, as the Latvians stated, the principal reason for having their own party was that its work could be carried on in their own language, then what should be done about the language requirements of the Jews, Lithuanians, Germans, and Estonians, as well as other language groups who lived in the Latvian krai and who were to be included in the jurisdiction of the SDLK? Moreover, as Borodin pointed out, the krai included Kurland province, Lifland province, parts of Vitebsk, Kovno, and Novgorod provinces and, in at least three of these, the culture and life styles, as well as the language, were those of Russia, not Latvia. Accordingly, Borodin proposed that the name of the organization should be Social Democracy of the *Baltic* Krai, which was totally unacceptable to the Latvian nationalists.

The principle was an important one and Borodin argued for it strongly, reflecting a lifelong experience with Latvian domination. The opposition did itself no good by its disingenuousness as it sought to mask its nationalistic bias. When the vote came on Borodin's proposal to change the name of the Latvian affiliate, it was very close: 26 votes for his proposal, 27 against, with large numbers of delegates abstaining. A recount was demanded. This time a few more delegates voted, the vote changing to 27–30, but it was still against Borodin and the Bolsheviks. A large number of delegates failed to vote, indicating the ticklishness of the subject for Mensheviks as well as Bolsheviks. Borodin was obviously correct that the SDLK did represent national bias, and the name-change amendment carried the maximum force of his argument. He came close to winning with it. But, if he could not win on that score, he could not win on any. Rapidly his other proposals to limit the autonomy of the Latvian party were voted down. When the Latvians thought they might lose a particular point, they said they could not accept the revision without further "consultations" at home. Since the majority of the congress wanted unity, wanted the Latvian social democrats in the RSDLP, the Latvians got their way and were admitted to the RSDLP virtually on their own terms.

Although, according to the records of the congress, Borodin was voted down on the Latvian issue at least six times, it was no political embarrassment to him. The Bolsheviks simply didn't have the votes. Lenin's proposals, by and large, fared little better; on the contrary, they usually did worse. Borodin's role at the congress, even on the losing side, could only advance his revolutionary career. This Stockholm congress, the first general meeting since 1903, was more representative than the earlier assemblage and had many more revolutionaries in attendance. With the exception of Trotsky, who was in prison after the December uprising, and Martov, all of the greats of Russian social democracy were in attendance: Lenin, G. V. Plekhanov, P. B. Axelrod, F. L. Dan. As at Tammerfors, the contacts Borodin had with the revolutionary luminaries must have gratified and exhilarated him as well as advance his career. But even more significant, though a score of years would pass before this would become apparent, were the contacts made with the Bolsheviks who came to prominence in 1917. At the congress, in the halls of the People's House, in the Bristol Hotel where most of the Bolshevik delegates stayed, at the Swedish workers' restaurant where most of them ate, Borodin consorted with future Bolshevik greats: M. I. Kalinin, later titular head of the Soviet government; M. V. Frunze, destined to become one of the leaders of the revolution and the civil war; K. E. Voroshilov, future marshal of the Red Army; A. S. Bubnov, member of the first Politburo and chairman of a party commission that came to be vitally linked with Borodin's fate two decades later.

Even more important for Borodin's future, during most of the sessions at Stockholm he not only sat next to Stalin, but most of the time voted with him. In the eighteen recorded votes at the congress in which Borodin participated, he voted with Lenin eleven times, but with Stalin fourteen times. On the vital issues of nationalization of land, participation in the Duma elections in the Caucasus, and the Menshevik resolution on armed uprising, Borodin and Stalin voted together and differently from Lenin. Stalin and Borodin had been together at Tammerfors in December. It seems likely that, as local committeemen appearing at the center of the movement for the first time, they were drawn together then. Now at Stockholm they met again, sat next to each other at most sessions, and voted together. These contacts in 1905–06, when neither man was in the front ranks of the Bolshevik leadership, help to explain much about Borodin's fate in later decades.

When the Stockholm congress ground to an end on April 25, 1906, Mikhail Markovich Borodin could take satisfaction in his party position, even though he remained outside the inner circle of Bolshevik leadership. He was young, still only twenty-one; he had performed effectively as a party organizer and representative; he had been summoned to a major party conference, where he had been named to its presidium, and to a congress where he had been the party spokesman in an important if not crucial debate; he had met and was known by Lenin and a score of other top social democrats. Borodin's future in Bolshevik ranks seemed extremely promising—and so Borodin must have viewed it himself. The past year had developed an appetite for power that he doubtless believed would be gratified in the near future. The revolution he so badly wanted was close at hand—or so the congress held—and he was to be an integral part of it. Not only liberation but position as well lay just ahead. There was to be hard work and danger, but Borodin was ready. Within four months of the end of the Unity Congress, however, Borodin was out of Russia, soon out of Europe—and out of the revolutionary scene.

3

The New World

Though Borodin, like Lenin and his fellow Bolsheviks, left Stockholm convinced that the revolution was imminent, the tsar had other ideas. Repression, already evident in the closing months of 1905, now picked up force. Under the direction of the tsar's new first minister, P. A. Stolypin, an able administrator with previous experience in brutally suppressing opposition, the screws were tightened. Repressive measures dubbed the *stolypinshchina* after their author, spread throughout the country.

Rebels, revolutionaries, and others, many of whom had suffered at the tsar's hands before and feared for their lives, fled abroad by the thousands. But others, likely targets of the tsar's wrath, couldn't or didn't leave; one of those was Borodin. When he returned to Riga from Stockholm in May, he discovered that the Latvian situation was too hot for him. The Okhrana—the tsarist secret police—were after him and the underground offered little protection. Borodin fled to Petersburg. But he was no safer there than in Riga; like thousands of others he was gathered up by the *stolypinschchina.*

There was a pattern in the handling of revolutionaries arrested at that time. Picked up in July or August, they were kept in prison until September and then given the choice of going east to Siberia or west to Europe. Like most, Borodin chose foreign rather than domestic exile, and in early October he arrived in London. He placed an ad in the *Daily Telegraph* offering "to give Russian lessons in exchange for English."[1] In the advertisement Borodin, surrendering to his greatest vanity, described himself as a young Russian "with university education." He could have been following the example of Lenin who, when in

London in 1902, placed a notice in the *Atheneum* under the name of Richter offering to exchange Russian instruction for English. Or he may have been using the *Telegraph* to contact other refugees—or both. Whatever the case, the British became suspicious of Borodin's "active role among immigrant groups." Two Scotland Yard detectives interviewed him, and, after the legal amenities had been observed, he was promptly sent on his way, out of England—and still further west. By early 1907, Borodin was in Boston.

Within a little over six months, Borodin had been actively engaged in revolution, forced underground and flushed out of it, sent to prison, and deported from two countries. Now he crossed the Atlantic, in steerage like the hundreds of thousands of others who came from Russia at the time, and passed through the gates of America into its streets "paved with gold." For the average Russian Jew who came to the United States, America was the land of the future. Frequently he despised its furious pace, its unfamiliar, and often noxious sights, sounds, and smells, the crowded yet impersonal conditions of its ghetto life. Was it for this that he had abandoned the fresh mushrooms and sour cream, the aroma of new-mown hay, the close family and community life of Russia, albeit tsarist Russia? While some Russian Jews, like other immigrants, might dream of making their fortune and then returning to the old country, the majority knew that for them this was impossible. For better or worse, their future was in America; for the most part, they and their children quickly embarked on making a living and becoming Americanized.

But for Borodin, who was not the average Russian Jew, the situation was different. He had not come to the United States because tsarist oppression had made life unbearable. He had not crossed the Atlantic to find a haven and to seek opportunity. He wanted to remain in Russia, to help destroy the system and create a better and freer society. Borodin left Russia because he had been ordered out. As he stood at the ship's rail staring out at the unending expanse of water, being carried farther from Russia and closer to America, he must have pondered his future. Shouldn't he, like most of those around him, turn his back on the world he knew: on Russia, on tsarist oppression, on his dreams of revolution? Shouldn't he throw himself into the life of the new country? There, after all, were the freedom and opportunity he had sought for Russia and for himself. But Borodin entertained such thoughts only in moments of weakness. He did not seriously consider surrendering his goals and the revolution in which they had become enmeshed. The fulfillment of 1905 in Riga, of Tammerfors, of Stockholm, the imminent promise of being at the forefront of a great liberating movement that would free not only Russia but all men—these one did not readily give up. One is attached more to such ideals and dreams than to a nostalgic longing for sour cream and mushrooms.

Though Borodin's commitment to revolution in Russia remained strong, Boston provided few opportunities for a newly arrived Russian immigrant to express his revolutionary fervor. In America, like most other immigrants, Borodin was faced by a more immediate concern: earning his daily bread. Little is known of how Borodin made his way during the first months in the United States. Perhaps he was already working "on the farms in the summer, in factories in the winter," as he later described his activities in America, though in making such a statement he may well have been trying to establish his proletarian qualifications. On several occasions he claimed to have been engaged with the Carnegie Institution in Boston, but only once did he specifically identify the project he had worked on. In 1922, when he was under arrest, he said that he had "attended" the Carnegie Nutrition Institution that was carrying out experiments in conjunction with the Harvard Medical School.

The use of the word "attended" seems to have been another attempt to identify himself with the world of learning. Harvard did have several contracts with the Carnegie Institution to do nutrition research, but none of these involved a school that Borodin could have attended. It is more likely that, if Borodin was involved with the Carnegie at all (institution records do not support his claim), it was as a paid subject in experimental research. (At this time, the Carnegie Institution of Washington was also underwriting a history of Russian immigration to the United States, under the direction of S. A. Goldenweiser, whose father had been Tolstoy's friend and counselor and who would one day become a distinguished member of the U.S. Civil Service Commission. Goldenweiser, himself a recent immigrant, had several native respondents to assist him. It is conceivable, but unlikely, that Borodin was one of these.)

In any event, Borodin was not in Boston, not to mention Harvard, for long. By early 1908 he had moved to Chicago. He was following the call of revolution, and Chicago was the center of socialism in America. But what Borodin found first in Chicago was not revolution but a teenaged wife, Fanya Orluk, who came from Vilna. When Fanya became pregnant, the pressure increased to find steady employment. But what job could a man whose chief qualification was ex-revolutionary expect to find in an alien, unrevolutionary land? He might have tried his hand as a riverboatman on the Chicago or the Mississippi, as he had on the Dvina, but that was hardly an alternative for a recent Russian-Jewish immigrant. He might have turned to peddling or worked in a sweatshop, like many other Jewish newcomers, but he lacked the background—and the inclination. He wanted a profession more intellectual, more "respectable," less painful to his socialist and personal sensibilities. Certainly he was not without pride yet he had no marketable skills.

In late summer of 1908, Borodin appeared on the campus of Valparaiso University in Valparaiso, Indiana, to commence his American university career. We may wonder where he got the funds to go to college. But he didn't need much, because even by 1908 standards an education at Valparaiso was not expensive. A twelve-week quarter cost $30, including food, lodging, and tuition, and if you paid in advance the charges were even less.

Valparaiso had been purchased for a few hundred dollars in 1873 by two Ohioans, H. B. Brown and O. P. Kinsey, who still controlled it at the time of Borodin's matriculation. They ran the place as a commercial venture. But to succeed they had to offer potential students the education they wanted at a price they could pay. They kept prices low by growing food on their own land, purchasing in quantity, using student labor, eliminating such frills as physical education, and taking a personal interest in every facet of the economic and academic administration of the institution. Instruction was available at almost any level, beginning with elementary school, and a student could matriculate in any quarter.

The education offered at Valparaiso was not of a superior sort, and critics frequently found fault with it. But Valparaiso survived repeated examinations in the press and elsewhere—and, as its reputation spread by word of mouth and frequent ads in the popular magazines, it prospered and grew. During its heyday in 1900–1912, it averaged over five thousand students a year and was, next to Harvard, the largest educational institution in America. In fact, probably to Borodin's amusement and perhaps satisfaction, it was sometimes called "Little Harvard." Out of its 1900–1912 student body came two governors, a member of the Court of International Justice at the Hague, Dr. Reuben L. Kahn (who devised the Kahn test for symphilis), Lieutenant-General Walter Bedell Smith, Lowell Thomas—and Borodin.

Borodin, who was registered in various classes at Valparaiso as M. Grosenberg, M. G. Grosenberg "of Russia," and Grossenberg "of St. Petersburg," took Rhetoric I, Phonography I (Pitman's shorthand system), and Elocution I during his first term. However, phonography was the only course that lasted for the entire twelve weeks—and the only course for which he received a grade, 89, (80 being passing), and credit. During the second term Borodin took Phonography II and Typewriting I. Again, Borodin received credit only for phonography, just passing with an 80. In the third term Borodin took a single course, civil government and, after reporting sick at the end of the third week, never returned to class.

Several conclusions can be drawn from Borodin's Valparaiso experience. That he took practical business courses indicates his concern to prepare himself quickly to support his wife and coming child. That he was able to pass shorthand indicates that he already had a good command of English. That the classes met daily indicates that he was resident in Valparaiso during the time. That he carried such a light load—one could take as many or as few courses as one chose—suggests that he held down a job on the outside, as most students at Valparaiso did (perhaps on the university farm).

The mainline of the Chicago Northern went directly through the campus, and many a night Borodin must have heard the whistle of the evening expresses going west to Chicago, east to Cleveland, and probably wished he was aboard—and wondered what he was doing in Valparaiso. It was a far cry from Riga and Petersburg, from the significant, rewarding, and exciting activity of revolution, to this northern Indiana hamlet, known chiefly for having the highest elevation in the state. Time seemed scarcely to move there, yet time had caught up with Borodin. He had always been "the youngest," only sixteen when he joined the Bund, only twenty when he was sent by Lenin to Russia to become one of the leaders of revolutionary Riga. At twenty-one he had been a member of a party conference and a party congress, full of experience though still a revolutionary wunderkind. But now he was twenty-four, married, about to become a father, with no steady job and no revolution in the offing.

But Borodin was not the only one at Valparaiso in this predicament. No one else in America had been so high in the revolutionary hierarchy as he, but there were others no longer so young, fresh from Russia, victims of its oppression and stirred by the events of 1905, eager to make their way in the new world, yet unable to turn their backs completely on the old. Borodin met some of them and they talked about Russia, revolution, socialism, and about making a living. With two of them, Hyman Bolotin and Henry Krasnow,[2] Borodin established relationships that would continue in Chicago and for as long as he remained in the United States.

Borodin's departure from Valparaiso in early 1909 coincided with the birth of his son Frederick. When Borodin walked down to the station of the Chicago Northern, only a few hundred yards from the campus, his university training came to an end. Though he would later frequently allude to other university experiences and his friends thought he had studied literature or the law, there is no evidence that he did.

The Chicago in which Borodin took up residence in 1909 was Sandburg's churning ugly giant, marked by great industrial achievement but also by great ruthlessness and cruelty. It claimed to be the fourth largest city in the world, having doubled its population in fifteen years. But if Chicago was first in energy and optimism, it may have been first as well in human misery and poverty. By the thousands, the immigrants from Italy and Greece and Russia had been funneled into its streets through the ports of New York, Boston, and Baltimore. After

1900, they came in more rapidly than ever before. They had little money, few skills, almost no knowledge of the city and its language or ways. Families crowded into the smallest spaces, using every inch. If an entire family lived in a single room, and still couldn't make ends meet, it would take in boarders. People lived in cellars and attics. A closet was a room, a room an apartment, and an apartment a mansion. Men worked twelve to thirteen hours a day for $6 or $7 a week and were thankful to have a job. Smallpox and consumption, white slavery, and organized crime were as close as one's next-door neighbor.

Those who lived in Chicago's ghettoes were desperately in need of help. Lonely, homesick, ignorant, gullible, their inadequacies and longings made them victims of the con men and panderers who preyed upon the immigrant. Still, in the depths of the city were places where the newly arrived could go—to meet with others recently from their homeland, to learn about the customs of the new country, and perhaps to gain some of the skills necessary to cope with it. These were the settlement houses. The immigrants of the 1890s and the first decade of the twentieth century had good reason to be grateful for such places, Borodin perhaps more than most.

In Chicago the most important settlement house was Hull House, named after the man who had previously lived in the original building but identified throughout its existence with its leader, the unconquerable Jane Addams. Hull House, at the corner of Polk and Halstead, was in the middle of the Bulgarian and Italian neighborhoods; nearby were the pushcarts of the Russian Jews in Maxwell Street, as well as groups of Irish, Greeks, and Poles living cheek-by-jowl but nonetheless suspicious of one another—not greatly different from what had been the case in Europe.

All were welcome at Hull House. Its Immigrants' Protective League maintained waiting rooms at the railroad stations, staffed by foreign-language speakers, to welcome new arrivals to Chicago and to invite them to Hull House. There the newly arrived could find entertainment, social activities, and such services as kindergartens, day nurseries, and the well-baby clinics that practiced preventive medicine—a startling innovation. Perhaps more important, Hull House offered courses on American customs, citizenship, and English and helped in finding jobs.

Hull House was not only open to all comers, but to all ideas as well. Although it was reformist, not revolutionary—Walter Lippman once attacked it for that reason—it provided an open forum for advocates of liberal, radical, or revolutionary causes. As a consequence, whenever there were bombings in Chicago, Hull House was always suspected as the instigator of the crime and of harboring the guilty. As late as the 1930s, Hull House was viewed by some as the "most dangerous place" in the United States.[3] Most of the fear and abhorrence that adhered to Hull House was attributable to its concern with and protection of the foreign-born. Although Jane Addams herself was hardly a radical (by present standards, she was hardly even a liberal on domestic issues), there is no doubt that she idealized the refugees from foreign political oppression—particularly the Russian Jews. Hull House received the children of the victims of the Kishinev pogrom with loving arms; was horrified by the scarred back of girls who had been whipped by cossacks; cherished the memory of the girl who returned to Kiev so that she could bring food to her imprisoned revolutionary brother. The Russians she had seen in Chicago, Jane Addams wrote, belong to "the noble company of martyrs."[4]

Inevitably, Hull House was an early stopping point for Borodin in Chicago. Perhaps it was there that he chose his American occupation—teaching—and there that he taught his first class, English for foreigners. He began with four students. At precisely what point Borodin decided to become a teacher probably not even he was aware. Few immigrants to America knew how they were going to support themselves when they got there. Most of those without skills, or skills in demand, stumbled into jobs; it may very well have been that Borodin, coming to Hull House at a time when Russians were pouring into the city in the wake of the *stolypinschchina*, responded to a real demand for English-language teachers.

Becoming a teacher of English had various attractions for Borodin. Education would help others do what he sought to accomplish for himself, to adapt to a secular society and prosper within it. Nor did teaching violate his intellectual and socialist sensibilities. It wasn't like leading the revolution in Riga, but it was at least temporarily acceptable and a man had to earn a living. As a teacher, Borodin did well. He was able to communicate with his students and they apparently liked him.[5] His classes grew and he soon had many students.

Though teaching at Hull House was gratifying, he saw no future there. The staff consisted, for the most part, of well-to-do "all-American" college graduates, who worked for little more than their keep. Whatever else he may have been, Borodin was an immigrant whose heart and roots were elsewhere and who could not become part of the regular Hull House corps. Moreover, he and his family needed more income than the classes at Hull House could provide. In the ghetto's great demand for English instruction, Borodin saw an opportunity. During the summer he convinced his Valparaiso friend Henry Krasnow—and possibly one or two others—to start a night school of their own. As the model Borodin and Krasnow would take Valparaiso, which had impressed them with its easy admission, inexpensive tuition, and courses designed to meet the practical needs of its students. But their school was to have one advantage over Valparaiso. It would be located not in the Indiana cornfields but in the Chicago ghetto, where the students lived and worked and where they could attend classes in the evening. And the new school would be staffed by immigrants who had "adjusted" to America and could understand the problems of the students.

Finances, of course, were a concern, since neither of the partners had money. Still, the capital investment would not be great: a month's rent plus the cost of a blackboard, some used tables and chairs. Borodin and his family, who needed a place to stay anyway, could live in the back. In September 1909, Borodin and Krasnow opened their school in an eight-room flat at Roosevelt and Newberry roads in the middle of the Russian Jewish section. Classes, offered at both the primary and secondary levels, met three times a week. The fee was $2 per course per term. The first class had forty students and the number soon grew.[6]

Borodin must have received considerable satisfaction from the opening of his school. Six months in Chicago—and now his own school! He still continued to teach at Hull House, needing the income, but the financial future looked a good deal more promising than it had in the spring. If, at those odd moments when he had the time, he castigated himself for wandering from the path of revolutionary idealism, he could console himself that it was better than starving.

Although Borodin and Krasnow had considerable early success with their new school, two years later they ran into difficulties. The Triangle Shirtwaist Company catastrophe in New York, in which 146 workers (mostly young girls) lost their lives because management had locked the workroom doors to prevent unauthorized rest breaks and thus kept the women from escaping when a fire broke out, sparked a renewed drive for unionization. And the efforts were as vigorous in Chicago as in Manhattan. Workers by the thousands went out on strike. Strikes meant no wages and, since most of Borodin's students were workers, most could not pay their tuition. At one point during this period, of Borodin's 130 students only 40 were paying.

The Borodin-Krasnow so-called preparatory school was not the only institution of its type in the neighborhood. Advertisements in Jewish and Russian papers in Chicago at the time indicate at least two others. One of these, the Progressive Preparatory School, also located on 12th Street, was operated by Borodin's Valparaiso acquaintance, Hyman Bolotin. Faced with financial problems, Bolotin sold out to Borodin and Krasnow. The two schools merged and in 1912, when the labor unrest receded, the partners moved their school to 1206 North Hoyne, at the corner of Division Street, nearer the center of the "little ghetto." Shortly thereafter Krasnow, well along in his medical training, stopped participating in the school. Borodin, who had used various spellings of his family name Gruzenberg, now dropped the first part of the name, in the spirit of adapting to America, and called his institution the Berg Progressive Preparatory School. The new location provided more space and better equipment. Both he and his institution seemed well established.

Though busy with his school, Borodin did not forget Russia and the revolution. Since his was essentially a night school, he had time during the day to pursue other interests. Borodin had come to Chicago because of its reputation as the center of socialism in America; when he arrived he hoped to engage himself in

the struggle for socialist advancement. But, if Borodin anticipated finding Chicago an embattled outpost of the international
revolution, eager to welcome him as a comrade-in-arms, he was
destined for disappointment. If he had expected to find Chicago
a source of support for the Russian revolution, he was equally
disappointed.

At the beginning of the twentieth century, socialism in
America was enjoying its most hopeful years, borne along on the
progressive tide that was sweeping the country. Ida Tarbell,
Lincoln Steffens, and Upton Sinclair had begun to reveal the
seaminess and misery of the growing American working class.
The public was shocked. Many saw the cause of all the suffering
in capitalism—and the answer, socialism, though there was no
agreement on what socialism was or how it was to be gained.
Nevertheless, by 1912 there were over a thousand socialist office-
holders in the United States, including 56 mayors.

But American socialism, as Borodin was to discover, was more
American than socialist. Closer to the tradition of Henry George
and Edward Bellamy than to Marx, it was not revolutionary. It
drank deeply of the waters of populism. It was often anti-intel-
lectual and individualistic. By and large, its leaders cared little
for ideology, and though in future years many of them would
hail Marx, they knew little about him. Regardless of the strain
of socialism to which they belonged, it was the American experience, the American past, and the American future that dominated their understanding and determined their viewpoint.
Unhappily for Borodin, too, American socialism had an antiforeign bias or, at best, an indifference to the foreign-born—particularly those from southern and eastern Europe. The American socialist movement in the first decade of the twentieth
century showed little interest in recruiting from among this most
recent group of immigrants. If the newcomer could speak English and was willing to adapt to the existing organization, he
could join. But the Socialist Party stood squarely against the establishment of special sections for the foreign-born. It was not
just a matter of potential organizational rivalry; it involved a
basic dislike and distrust of foreigners.

Of all the immigrant groups, the most scorned at Socialist
Party headquarters were the Russians because all Russian im-

migrants were thought to be Jews. Whenever an appeal for help came from Russian sources to the Socialist Party in Chicago, it was automatically sent to the *Forward,* the Yiddish socialist newspaper in New York. Russian socialists thus worked under the double prejudice of being seen not only as foreign but also as Jewish. Between 1905 and 1912, the number of Russians in Chicago more than doubled. However, in 1909, when Borodin came to Chicago from Valparaiso, there was no organized body of Russian socialists in the city. In 1908, a call had gone out from the east for the formation of a national Russian socialist organization, and a "convention" met in New York, attended by several Chicagoans. A central committee of the Union of Russian Social Democratic Organizations in America was elected and a monthly journal, the *Russko-Amerikanskii Rabochii,* was started to which, in the 1920s, Borodin claimed he had contributed. (There are no extant copies of this journal.) But the central committee soon lost momentum and disbanded, and the *Rabochii* ceased publication.[7]

Although there was no permanent organization of Russian socialists in Chicago when Borodin arrived, there was no dearth of *ad hoc* "progressive" groups. There were social revolutionaries, social democrats, the Hand of Aid to the Russian Revolution, and even one association called the Society of Russian Workers, which was open to all except Jews. As it happened, most of the same people were in all of the groups, and the latter mostly existed only on paper, met infrequently, and, when they did, accomplished nothing. The first "permanent" Russian social-democratic organization in Chicago was organized at Hull House on August 21, 1909, as the Russian Socialist Branch of the Ninth Ward. It had ten members and though within three months its membership had doubled, it, like its predecessors, accomplished little.

However, late in 1909 or early 1910, one Michael Altshuler appeared on the scene. Altshuler, a mysterious figure with a detailed knowledge of Chicago socialism, claimed to have played a major role in the development of its Russian component. But other than in two articles that he inspired in 1912 in the *Chicago Daily Socialist,* an English-language "establishment" socialist newspaper, there is no other reference to Altshuler in the literature. It is noteworthy that Altshuler shared with Borodin a common first name, year of birth, and age of joining the RSDLP. The name Altshuler—"old teacher" in German and Yiddish—would have pleased Borodin's fancy. Actually, the name comes from the Jewish community of Prague, where one who attended the old ("alte") synagogue ("shul") was called "altshuler." But it is unlikely that Borodin would have known that. Probably Borodin would have used a pseudonym to protect his school and income, particularly since the articles were appearing in the English-language socialist press. Though other details that Altshuler gives of his life differ significantly from those of Borodin's life, the account does have something in common with another Borodin cover story. We can surmise that Borodin and Altshuler were the same person.

When Altshuler-Borodin came across the Ninth Ward Branch, it was all but inactive. Coaxing the secretary into calling a meeting, he tried to spur the eight who showed up into action, but they were apathetic or at least suspicious of this stranger who offered to build an organization that would "spread over the entire land." They doubted that the Ninth Ward Branch had sufficient numbers to accomplish anything but, if he wanted to try, he was welcome.[8] Altshuler worked hard at organizing, and when the Ninth Ward group next met in February 1910 fifty comrades were present. As a result of that meeting, a propaganda bureau consisting of Altshuler as secretary, plus two or three other activists, was set up and the publication of a newspaper, the *sine qua non* of Leninist tactics, was authorized. The paper *Prizyv* (The Call) came out the following month and lasted for one issue.

Altshuler and his activists were determined to increase the social-democratic following as quickly as possible. The major Russian liberal emigré group at the time was the Russian Social Economics Club. Organized in the fall of 1909 at Hull House, by early 1910 the club had over a hundred members, was growing quickly, and was at the center of the Russian socialist colony. Its members were "intensely interested" in the struggle in Russia and received many Russian publications. The propaganda bureau, again following a Leninist prescription, decided to take it over and did.

But simultaneously with the successful efforts to infiltrate the Social Economics Club, a struggle developed within the Ninth Ward Branch between the propaganda bureau and the rest of the membership. There was obvious unhappiness among the older members of the organization over the way the propaganda people had moved in, first taking over the leadership of the existing group and then of the Social Economics Club. There were other points of contention as well: in imitation of the battles then raging among Russian social democrats in Europe, the conflicts focused on the issue of fundraising but had deeper implications. In the spring of 1910, the Ninth Ward organization held a number of meetings, plays, and picnics in order to raise money. None of these activities brought in more than $100 at a time, but there were several of them and the treasury grew. At this point, a dispute erupted over which social-democratic faction in Russia was to benefit from the funds that had been collected. The propaganda-bureau group, which consisted of only five or six members, wanted to turn the money over to Lenin's organization; the others sought to direct the funds to the Mensheviks. The differences could not be resolved; in June the bureau withdrew from the Ninth Ward Branch and established itself as a separate organization. From then until 1917, the Ninth Ward group would be known as the First Russian Social-Democratic Branch. (Numbers two and three had existed briefly in 1910.)

In the months to follow, the First and Fourth branches reached an accommodation but without reconsolidation. During 1912 and 1913, interest in socialism was at a low level as the spirit of nonpartisanship ran high in Chicago's Russian colony. In 1914, however, socialist activity, though not partisanship, increased and the Bolshevik-inclined Fourth Branch, which had struggled along throughout 1911, 1912, and 1913, came into its own. In 1911, it had lost its lease and, lacking funds to hire a meeting hall, had arranged for lectures in private homes at which, more than once, no one showed up. But by early 1914 the Fourth Branch had thirty-eight members. During one six-month period, it sponsored eleven free lectures with an average attendance of forty, and five mass meetings were attended by an average of two hundred and fifty persons. It was at this time that the

Fourth Branch moved into new headquarters at 1206 North Hoyne, the same small building in which Borodin's school was located. It is likely that the offices were shared.

Borodin's socialist activities in Chicago occurred within the parameters described above. He was a member of the Socialist Party, but only nominally. His political activities were wholly concerned with the Russian situation. His identification was specifically with the Bolshevik-leaning Fourth Branch, where he was a frequent speaker and one of the prime movers of that group, if not its guiding force. But if Borodin was a political activist with Leninist leanings during his first years in America, he as well as the other leaders of the Fourth Branch gradually came to the conclusion that, if the group were to develop a following, it could not maintain a Leninist exclusionist orthodoxy. And, far away from Lenin, that apostle of partisanship and of splitting, there was decreasing will to do so. Though the organization embraced members deeply dedicated to Russia, who would return there to participate and die in the revolution and the civil war, there was a reluctant realization that Lenin's tactics were vitiating support for the revolutionary movement.

Borodin himself grew angry at those who, as he saw it, were constantly dividing the movement by their intransigence. On the eve of World War I, he told Mark Khinoy, who was also a member of the Fourth Branch, that he had become a "bitter" opponent of Lenin, of his organization and tactics.[9] Perhaps "bitter" was too strong a word, but there is no doubt that Borodin decreasingly followed a Leninist line. Whether the lessening of Borodin's partisanship was brought about because of disillusionment with Lenin's splitting tactics, or because of the debilitating effect of the New World on ideology—a lower East Side socialist saying was that "It is difficult to be a socialist in America"—or by the temper of the times and the destructive factional experience in the Ninth Ward, or because he was by disposition a conciliator unsuited to uncompromising partisanship, the fact is that as Borodin's sojourn in America lengthened, he drew further away from Bolshevism. As his erstwhile partner Krasnow recalled, "during his residence in America, Mr. Berg was not a party man, but rather was interested in all phases of the Russian revolutionary movement."[10] Increasingly, while in Chicago, Borodin participated in a wide variety of Russian-oriented activities, socialist and nonsocialist, attacking the tsarist system. But, more and more, he took part not as a fierce partisan of one faction or another, but as one who could cooperate with others whose ideology was not precisely the same as his.

4

On the Brink of Decision

B y the autumn of 1914 Borodin had been out of Russia for over seven years and a resident of Chicago for five. Like other immigrants, he had had to make profound adjustments, and he made them with moderate success. The school he had cofounded was beginning to prosper. It was relocated again, in the north-west direction in which the earlier Russian Jewish settlers, prod-ded by fresh waves of migrants, were moving. Borodin had more room there for his school and for his family, soon to be increased by a second child. His school would never make Borodin rich. He charged only $15 for a six-month course. But it was well at-tended, had considerable influence among Chicago's Russian Jews (of whom there were almost a quarter million by this time), and continued to grow.

In an October 1914 advertisement the school appeared as both "Michael Berg's Preparatory School" and "The Progressive Preparatory School, Director, M. Gruzenberg." Borodin's name and the consolidation of Bolotin's Progressive Preparatory School with his own were still in the works. The school at the time was located at 2058 West Division Street. In another adver-tisement two years later in the *Daily Jewish Courier,* three loca-tions were ascribed to the Progressive Preparatory School: 2058 West Division, 1637 West 12th, and 2317 West 12th. In 1914, for the first time, Borodin and the school were listed in the *Lakeside Directory,* Chicago's general registry. In late 1915, he had a tele-phone installed at the Division Street branch. And a year later he had one put in at 1637 West 12th. By 1916, the "graduating" class of the Progressive Preparatory School had grown so large that Borodin had to hire a hall to satisfy the request for tickets.

As the Progressive Preparatory School became a fixture on the near northside and the newcomers became more sophisticated, a demand developed for courses beyond "English for Foreigners," though this remained the most heavily patronized offering of the school. The more well-established immigrants, and their sons and daughters, now wanted more American education. They wanted to finish high school and go on to college. Borodin extended his offerings to include American history, civics, literature, and, in 1916–1917 as an innovation, a class in psychology. Obviously Borodin could no longer teach all the courses, though apparently he did expand his personal offerings to include literature. Almost from the beginning, his wife Fanya had helped out. Over the years others, some of whom went on to make names for themselves elsewhere, were hired: "Dr." Kennedy later taught economics at the University of Chicago; "Dr." Karp served on the faculty of the School for Social Services in New York, and W. E. Rodriguez became a Chicago councilman who, from time to time, addressed meetings and graduations at the school.

Increasingly, the premises at 2058 West Division came to be known simply as "Berg's" and formed the center of community social and socialist activities. It was more than just a school. A dance class was started; public lectures on such writers as Shaw and Ibsen were scheduled; and a variety of cultural as well as social and political organizations met there. In the last years of the second decade of the twentieth century, the school played a meaningful role in the Russian community of Chicago, and its director was widely recognized for the service he was providing. He was well known and, according to a friend, an important figure.[1] But Borodin was not satisfied. Although his discontents were not one-dimensional, they had a particular focus: Russia and revolution.[2] He did not really expect to recreate those glorious days in 1905 at the barricades, but he could not forget them. Part of him remained in Riga, Tammerfors, and Stockholm— with the revolution.

Borodin kept his hand in Russian socialist activities, perhaps as much out of habit as conviction. But he could not let go of his dreams, which were probably no longer so much of liberation as of involvement and glory and power. Maybe, like Trotsky, he had concluded that America was the "foundry in which the fate of man is to be forged."[3] But though what happened in his school, in Chicago, in America, was not unimportant to him, for real interest, real importance, Russia was foremost.

The outbreak of World War I in the late summer of 1914 brought consternation to the European socialist camp. The never-united socialists broke down into three chief groups: using Lenin's terms, the "social patriots" who, their socialist internationalism quickly proving weaker than their ties to the motherland, moved to support national war efforts; the "social pacifists" who, in the face of great difficulties, were convinced that the war was between capitalist powers and that socialists could support neither side; and Lenin's faction, which proposed that the war be turned into a class struggle by the simple expedient of convincing the French and German soldier-workers to turn their guns around and fire at their bourgeois officers instead of at one another. Of the three groups, the social patriots had by far the greatest number of supporters. Lenin's group, as usual, stood alone. And even within it there was no unity. Increasingly Lenin's "own" intellectuals, who had replaced the local committeemen of 1905 and 1906 in leadership positions among the Bolsheviks, took issue with his positions, particularly with his divisive tactics.

In Chicago, the various stances that characterized international socialism had their local followings. Adherents fought fiercely among themselves and, according to an observer in 1915, they argued "insanely" over Lenin.[4] In Chicago, as in the United States generally, there were special factors that colored the dispute. In 1915 and 1916, the United States was not yet at war. Isolationist sentiment was strong, and it was easier to be a socialist pacifist in New York or Chicago than in wartime Paris, London, or Berlin. In the early phases of the war, particularly among the socialist rank and file, if any side was favored, it was the German, for midwestern socialism in Wisconsin, Illinois, Missouri, and Ohio had strong German roots. Moreover, there was the traditional American hostility to the English: for Colonel McCormick's influential *Chicago Tribune*, 1776 was only yesterday. And among Russians, Poles, Lithuanians, and other migrants from Russia, the feeling persisted that only the defeat of the tsar would improve the lot of their countrymen. Still, there was little advocacy of American intervention on behalf of the kaiser. American socialism was generally pacifist.

To Lenin, now in Zurich, even more than usually isolated because of his position on the war, the reports of strong antiwar sentiment emanating from the United States made it appear a fertile ground for recruitment. Lenin sent at least one agent to the United States in 1915, for that purpose: the aristocratic and mercurial Alexandra Kollontai, who visited Chicago in October. Kollontai, the daughter of a tsarist general, descendant of Ukranian aristocracy, was a rebel even within the socialist movement, jumping from one faction to another almost as quickly as she moved from one sleeping partner to another. When she was finally tamed, and then only ideologically, it was by age and the cohorts of Stalin. After the revolution, women's liberation and free love became her crusade. She was the apostle of the "drink of water" theory (sexual intercourse should be of no greater consequence than drinking a glass of water); and, though Stalin got her out of several scrapes, she offended his revolutionary puritanism. But during World War I she had ideologically moved closer to Lenin, and while she did not join the Bolsheviks until 1917, she was prepared to be his eyes, ears, and voice even before that date.

In the early fall of 1915 Kollantai arrived in New York, assigned by Lenin to raise funds, to have his brochure "Socialism and War" translated, published, and distributed, and to make contacts. Lenin instructed Kollantai *"everywhere to see local Bolsheviks (even if only for five minutes), 'to refresh memories' and to put them in contact with us."*[5] Kollantai was in the United States for four and a half months, crossed the country twice, visited 80 cities and made 123 speeches, mostly against the war. She spent five days in Chicago during the second half of October 1915, where she met with Borodin and eventually informed Lenin, who had known where Borodin was for several years, of the fact. But the meeting apparently had no effect upon Borodin's politics. It would be dramatic to be able to say that in 1915, having met Kollontai as she traveled through Chicago, Borodin reestablished close contact with Lenin, followed party orders, and returned to Russia in 1918 at Lenin's command. But that is not the way it happened. The meeting with Kollontai led to no exchange of messages between Borodin and Lenin. Borodin continued to pursue an independent path, especially after the outbreak of revolution in Petrograd in February 1917.

Although the overthrow of the tsarist regime in 1917 came as a shock to almost everyone, there had been ample harbingers of its approach. It had been forecast for years, and as military defeat, political ineptitude, poverty of resources, and hunger undermined the authority of tsarism, the deteriorating situation inside Russia was clear. Still, when the cossacks winked at the rioters rushing on the Petrograd bakeries that February day and the tsar was actually deposed, the shock was prodigious. In many circles, of course, the enthusiasm was also enormous.

The excitement and euphoria that February 1917 generated among tens of millions of Russians of all classes, at home and abroad, can never be adequately put to paper. In the United States, Trotsky wrote, "gatherings, extraordinary for their size and enthusiasm, were held wherever there were Russians. In New York—not only the Russian immigrants, but their children, who knew hardly any Russian, came to these meetings to breathe-in the reflected joy of the revolution."[6] The *Forward* editorialized on March 18: "What a day we are living through! What a golden day!" and two days later asserted in a banner headline that troubles were over. To some, however, the end of tsarism signaled not the end of trouble, but a call to action. The tsar was out, but it was far from clear who was to be in. Many exiles who had awaited this moment for years hastened to Petrograd, now the center of the international revolution. In Zurich, Lenin concocted scheme after scheme that might get him to Russia. In New York, Trotsky prevailed upon the Swedish consul-general to issue papers permitting him to return home.

However, unlike the peregrinating Trotsky or the unbaggaged Lenin, Borodin—who had lived in the United States for a decade, had a business, a wife, and two children, aged eight and one—felt he was in no position to pick up stakes and go marching off to the revolution. For Lenin and Trotsky their course was clear. Borodin certainly thought of taking the next boat to Petrograd—the dreamed-of moment was at hand—but he had acquired interests in the New World which were not easily cast aside. Still, the desire for involvement was strong.

In March, he announced the founding of an Enlightenment Society with headquarters in his Division Street school. The society immediately scheduled lectures on the meaning of February. "Berg's" became the scene of "revolutionary evenings" and presentations such as "The Motive Force and Perspectives of the Russian Revolution."[7] In April, the Society for Aid to the Russian Revolution was organized in a meeting at the Hotel Sherman. Its principal purpose was to help "Russians in America who desire to perfect themselves in different trades and professions, so that they may apply their knowledge and ability in Russia."[8] Borodin was one of the founders and when, at the first meeting, bitter disagreement arose as to whether the Provisional Government that had taken power after the tsar's fall or the shadow soviet organization lurking in the background was to be supported by the society, Borodin was appointed chairman of a "commission" to attempt a reconciliation.

In Chicago, as in Russia, the task of trying to reconcile the two positions proved too much. The society split in two. The minority, who were for the soviets and immediate socialist revolution, kept the original name. The majority, 42 of 60 members, reformed as the Friends of Russian Democracy, elected Borodin as president and his friend Krasnow as recording secretary. Thus in the first months following the February Revolution in Petrograd, a supportive movement had developed in Chicago, had split over the issue of backing the Provisional Government or taking a more radical course—and Borodin had emerged as the leader of the former choice. The meager membership of the Society for Aid to the Russian Revolution and the Friends of Russian Democracy indicates all too clearly that few people in Chicago wanted to become personally involved in the struggle over Russia's future. But far greater numbers, even after the initial excitement at the tsar's overthrow had faded, were eager to become vicariously identified with the new Russia.

When in May 1917 the Provisional Government appointed Boris Bakhmetiev as its first ambassador to the United States, immigrant groups throughout the country were eager to greet him and display their approval of the overthrow of Nicholas II. Arrangements were made for him to visit Chicago on the first weekend in August and elaborate plans for the visit were drawn up. Ambassador Bakhmetiev and his party would be received by representatives of the mayor and chamber of commerce and the leading lights of the Russian community. But the plans also called for a mass meeting, to be held in the auditorium of Douglas Park on Saturday evening, at which "the people" would be present. Borodin was appointed chairman of that event.

The meeting at Douglas Park was to enable the average Russian immigrant to meet the representatives of the new government. Borodin and the organizers of the rally wanted to bring together as many elements as possible of the local Russian community. This was a heavy order because the national, religious, and political animosities that had developed in the Russian empire over centuries had been imported into Chicago's ghettoes. And now they would come together in one meeting hall. Fights were already commonplace in Douglas Park on Saturday nights, and this meeting could produce a major row. Borodin, at his best in getting disparate groups to work together, ultimately succeeded in inveigling representatives of thirty-eight organizations, ranging from the radical left to the conservative right, to serve on his committee. He knew these groups had little in common. Certainly they didn't all support the Provisional Government; nor were they equally enthusiastic about the overthrow of the tsar. Borodin had a formidable task, but he was confident he could hold things together, at least through the meeting.

But whereas Borodin's immediate aim was limited, others resolved to use the occasion for their own purposes; this was a golden opportunity to revile the past and shape the future. Those most bent on exploiting the affair, whatever the risks, were members of the radical Society for Aid to the Russian Revolution. The society attacked Borodin personally. In an open letter to the Friends of Russian Democracy, of which Borodin was the president, the society demanded: "Is it true that in preparing the celebration for the visiting delegation you work with all elements including priests and representatives of the Black Hundreds?"[9] Borodin struck back in the press, accusing the society of fostering disunity, but the latter continued to snipe away, charging the Friends of Russian Democracy and Borodin with publicly attacking fellow socialists.

In spite of these difficulties, Borodin persisted in seeking to attract as broad a spectrum as possible to the rally. An article in the *Russkaya pochta* (Russian Post) of July 14 reported a preparatory meeting, organized by the Friends of Russian Democracy, attended by fifteen groups including the parish of the Holy Archangel Mikhail, the St. Mikhail Brotherhood, the parish of the Holy Trinity, and the Russian National Club[10]—scarcely a conclave to set a Bolshevik, a Menshevik, or even a liberal heart aflutter. As the great day drew near, more meetings were held. Manifestos were issued, and articles publicizing the visit appeared in the general press. The *Chicago Tribune* reported that a sixty-piece band had been hired and that Douglas Park auditorium was to be adorned with decorations honoring "all parts" of Russia.

In the general press there was little hint of the discord among those planning to attend the Saturday meeting. Everything appeared well-organized and peaceful. But the Russians in Chicago knew better, as did Ambassador Bakhmetiev. Early in July in New York, Bakhmetiev, having survived an establishment welcome at Carnegie Hall during which Teddy Roosevelt, for reasons unrelated to Russia, had punched Samuel Gompers in the face, found himself on the following day at a bitterly split people's meeting at Madison Square Garden. Only the intervention of the New York police and the determined efforts of a detachment of Russian sailors who happened to be there quieted the riotous audience sufficiently to allow the proceedings to go on. Bakhmetiev's statement to the press the next day, suggesting that German agents had caused the disturbance, could not disguise the national antipathies that persisted thousands of miles from their origin or how badly split even "progressive" Russians were over the future of the revolution.

The Bakhmetiev entourage pulled into the station in Chicago on Friday morning, August 3, 1917. It was greeted by an official delegation, sent to the Congress Hotel, and ushered through a succession of uneventful and decorous tours, parades, meetings, and banquets. On Saturday afternoon, part of the Russian Jewish population of Chicago heard reassurances from Bakhmetiev on the place of Jews in the new Russia. Afterwards a reception at the Congress Hotel was attended by two hundred Jewish luminaries. From the hotel, Bakhmetiev was taken to Douglas Park for the mass meeting. There are several accounts of events at the auditorium that Saturday night, August 4, including those from both involved and uninvolved sources. All agree that it started peaceably enough with the playing of the "Star Spangled Banner," but before it was over, reported the *Chicago Tribune*, it was as if revolutionary Petrograd had been transported to Chicago.[11]

After the playing of the national anthem, Krasnow, the committee secretary, addressing the audience in Russian (as did subsequent speakers), made a few opening remarks and turned the gavel over to the chairman, "Mr. Berg." Borodin greeted the delegation "in the name of the revolution and progressive organizations." He spoke of freedom, of democratic ideals, of the plight of the exiles; his remarks brought forth loud shouts of approval. Then he proposed a standing tribute to "fighters for liberty" and, as all rose, the band struck up the "Revolutionary Funeral March," followed by the revolutionary song of the Bund.

Borodin next introduced Mark Khinoy, representing the Social-Democratic Party Organizational Committee. He was followed by "Comrade" Mills who spoke for the Bund. Both were received politely. After more music, Comrade K. Jurgelionis, supposedly representing the Lithuanian social democrats, rose to speak. It was at this moment that the bombshell hit the proceedings. Whereas Krasnow, Borodin, Khinoy, and Mills had couched their remarks in terms intended to keep the thirty-eight groups in harmony, Jurgelionis had no such intent. "In the name of the workers of Lithuania and Russia," he launched a heated diatribe against the Catholic Church, linking it with rich landowners as the enemy of the workers and peasants. As "handclapping interspersed with hisses came from various parts of the house," Borodin, "wearing an anxious look," moved to the rostrum to remind Jurgelionis that there were priests present. What was he trying to start, a riot? But Jurgelionis, whom the Bolshevik *Novyi mir* (New World) account said presented the only uncensored remarks at the entire meeting, now revealed that he was speaking for the "Lithuanian Workers' Soviet."[12]

Refusing to be silenced, Jurgelionis assailed exploiters everywhere. Again Borodin came forward to plead with him, but Jurgelionis persisted in his attacks on all who did not share the Bolshevik line. When he finished, on the stage and in the audience, except for a few scattered handclaps, there was stony silence; everyone sat still, waiting for the next move. After a moment, pandemonium broke loose: cheering, applause, hissing, booing, foot stamping, then shoving and fist fights. The mass meeting threatened to become a mass riot. Only the opportune presence of a large number of mostly Irish Chicago police, who had not understood a word of what had been said and who were milling around, also waiting for something to happen, managed to restore order.[13] But the "unity" of the assembly was broken. Bakhmetiev, whom the crowd had come to cheer, was quickly introduced by Borodin. He spoke briefly to a quiet audience, and shortly thereafter the rally adjourned.

Borodin was grievously disappointed. His conciliation efforts had failed. What he had expected the mass meeting to lead to, probably even he didn't know. But it had been a chance to be involved. There was a revolution in Russia and he wasn't there; at least he could lead its welcoming in Chicago. The rally—the committee work preceding it, the melding of diverse groups, the organization—at times must have created the illusion of being part of the revolution. But whatever the *Tribune* may have written about Petrograd's being transported to Chicago, it was a pale, a very pale, reverberation of revolution, and Borodin knew it.

In the late summer of 1917, when the Bakhmetiev delegation came to Chicago, Borodin's position on the revolution in Russia was clearly not the Bolshevik one. He accepted the Provisional Government, or at least its Washington representatives, and he did not favor pushing the socialist revolution now. But in autumn, important events were to occur that would catch Borodin in their net: the storming of the Winter Palace by the Bolsheviks on November 7, 1917, the overthrow of the Provisional Government, and the establishment of the Lenin regime.

The dramatic fact of Bolsheviks in power had an explosive effect on Russians everywhere. Half a world away in the United States, it had been possible for many to be wishy-washy about the Provisional Government; Lenin's seizure of power allowed no such indecision. The Provisional Government had been just what its name stated: provisional. There had been little pressure to commit oneself for it or against it, except in the most general sense. It was transitional, pointing to the future. But the Leninist regime would be the future. It demanded a definite commitment.

When the news of February 1917 had reached Borodin, he was elated. He wanted desperately to return to Russia and the revolution—or did he? A decade in Chicago had left its mark upon him. And he was beset by doubts. Would the revolution succeed? It hadn't in 1905. Was this only another skirmish, or was it the real thing? If he returned, where did he belong in the revolution? His greatest glory had been with the Bolsheviks. But he was no longer in that camp; indeed, he had openly opposed it. What about the Bund? He had outgrown it; history had passed it by. The anarchists? Borodin knew many of them in Chicago and found them impractical. The Mensheviks? Although he had grown close to them in recent years, he could not forget how he had despised their indecisiveness and irresolution in 1905 and 1906. Part of Borodin's dilemma was solved by the Bolshevik seizure of power in November 1917. It now became increasingly apparent that if you were to play an active role in the continuing revolution in Russia, it would have to be on the Bolshevik side. If you wished to travel the main track, it perforce would be aboard the Lenin express.

Borodin's imagination, moreover, was piqued and his ambitions whetted by the reputations being quickly won by those already on board. As late as July 1917, Lenin was virtually unknown except in Russian socialist circles; when cited in the general press, he was described as a "pacifist agitator." Now he had become almost a household name. Trotsky, Bukharin, and Kollontai had achieved newspaper prominence. A year earlier, all three had been in the United States; two had not even been Bolsheviks. Now they were governing and changing Russia, as Borodin had dreamed of doing much of his life. He was one of many tempted to hasten to the scene of action. The American and immigrant press were filled with stories, often embellished, of great battles taking place, of great transformations in Russia. Thousands felt that they should, even must, go back regardless of the consequences. History was being made. Their dream of dreams was being both realized and endangered. Family, security, position—none of these should stand in the way.

Borodin resolved to return to Russia and the revolution. In August 1917 he had met the representatives of the Provisional Government in Douglas Park. In the months following he kept in contact with some of them. And, as they made their decisions to go with or against the Bolsheviks, to remain in the United States or return to Russia, he shared their dilemma. He contacted the few leaders of the fledgling Bolshevik apparat in New York, and in particular the Finn, Santeri Nuorteva, who encouraged the uncertain to cast their lot with the Bolsheviks. Nuorteva established contacts between potential returnees and Petrograd, and did what he could to facilitate their journey back to Russia.

In June 1918 Borodin, plagued by doubts but no longer able to resist the compelling appeals of idealism, fame, and fortune, left wife and sons and boarded the train for New York. There he obtained transit documents as second secretary to the railroad expert Yuri Lomonsov, who had served on Ambassador Bakhmetiev's staff and had now also elected to join the Bolsheviks. Soon Borodin was on one of the comparatively few passenger ships still traversing the U-boat-infested Atlantic, the Norwegian *Bergensfjord* bound for Oslo. Within the month he was back in Russia.

5

Back in the Fray

When Borodin left the United States in July 1918, he hardly knew what to expect in Russia. Though he had established contact with the new regime and had been encouraged to return, the pressure to make the voyage was largely self-generated. He was not seriously concerned that his straying from the Leninist path would hamper him. Many who were now close to Lenin had had strong differences with the Bolshevik leader during the interrevolutionary years. But he was concerned about the role he would play. Would his achievements of the past be remembered? When he left America's shores, the excitement of his mission and then the dangers of the journey pushed his anxieties into the background. But the closer he came to his revolutionary home, the more persistent they became.

Borodin made a very swift journey to Moscow. Touching land in Belgium on July 19, he continued to Oslo by sea. There he received a transit visa that took him as far as Stockholm where the Soviet *polpred* (diplomatic agent) V. V. Vorovsky supplied him with papers to proceed to Moscow. The route that Borodin followed was probably through Tallinn and Petrograd. Given the wartime conditions in late July–early August 1918, it could not normally have been a speedy trip. So it is impressive that, by August 20, when we next learn about Borodin, he had reached Moscow, "founded" a short-lived Russian-American friendship society, and had seen Lenin.

When Borodin arrived in Moscow, Lenin was eager for information from the outside world. The revolution was going badly. A renewed German offensive seemed imminent. The entire Volga region was in danger of falling to the Whites. The British were moving again in the north. There were reports of peasant attacks on Red forces in several provinces. In Moscow the workers, exhausted and hungry, had lost interest in the revolution. The Bolsheviks were quarreling among themselves, often over such prime revolutionary concerns as who was to receive the most desirable apartment or the choicest rug from the storehouse of confiscated valuables. Lenin believed the revolution could be kept alive only if it spread quickly to the capitalist West. As he told the workers of Moscow's Sokolniki district:

> Comrades, we are in a very difficult position, but we must overcome every difficulty and hold fast the banner of socialist revolution we have raised aloft. The workers of the world are looking hopefully towards us. We can hear their cries: "Hold on a little longer. You are surrounded by enemies, but we shall come to your aid, and by our joint effort we shall finally hurl the imperialist vulture over the precipice."[1]

Any newcomer to Moscow, comrade or not, might be invited to Lenin's Kremlin office, seated in one of the overstuffed grandfather chairs, and asked questions about conditions abroad. Thus, within days of his arrival in Moscow, Borodin had an audience. Long-lost disciple, intelligent, perceptive, enthusiastic supporter of the revolution, Borodin surely represented the vanguard of fresh forces Lenin hoped would come from the West to reinforce his beleaguered garrisons. Out of their meeting came Lenin's decision to write a letter to the workers of America seeking to enlist support for the revolution. And Borodin was to deliver the message.

Borodin must have had first and second thoughts about returning so soon to America. But these were submerged by the elation of being back in the revolution, received and accepted by Lenin, and having been given what seemed a most significant mission. In the next few weeks, Lenin, though besieged by crises, found time to write his lengthy "Letter to American Workers," which began "Comrades! A Russian Bolshevik who took part in the 1905 Revolution, and who lived in your country for many years afterwards, has offered to convey my letter to you."[2] (Whether Lenin knew about Borodin's post-1906 non-Bolshevik relationships is a moot point. Probably so, but he was anxious to embrace the man that Borodin had been and was eager to be again.) In long and angry passages Lenin unleashed his fury at the imperialists who opposed peace conversations with the Germans. He protested the lies being spread about the Soviets in the English, French, and American press. Certainly the Bolsheviks had committed mistakes, but "for every hundred mistakes we commit, and which the bourgeoisie and their lackeys (including our own Mensheviks and Right Social Revolutionaries) shout about to the whole world, 10,000 great and heroic deeds are performed."

Lenin, in fleeting deference to realities, conceded that "we know that help from you will probably not come soon . . . We know that although the European proletarian revolution has been maturing very rapidly lately, it may, after all, not flare up within the next few weeks." But then, looking ahead, he concluded:

> We are now, as it were, in a besieged fortress, waiting for the other detachments of the world socialist revolution to come to our relief. These detachments *exist,* they are *more numerous* than ours, they are maturing, growing, gaining more strength the longer the brutalities of imperialism continue. Slowly but surely the workers are adopting communist, Bolshevik tactics and are marching toward the proletarian revolution, which alone is capable of saving dying culture and dying mankind.
>
> In short, we are invincible, because the world proletarian revolution is invincible.[3]

This is the message of apprehension and faith that Borodin was to take to the American workers. But before the details of Borodin's return to the United States could be completed, Lenin was shot. On the evening of August 30, Fanya Kaplan, a Right Social Revolutionary, attacked him as he was leaving the Mikhelson plant where he had been addressing the workers. In the uncertainty over Lenin's survival, Borodin's return to the United States was delayed, but by mid-September he was on his way to Scandinavia en route to America.

He never made the trip. For some reason his orders were changed. Perhaps it was because Borodin was reluctant to return to America so soon after leaving it; or he may have sensed certain dangers in returning to the United States—his departure had not gone unnoticed; or perhaps the Bolsheviks decided that

Borodin was needed in Scandinavia and someone else could deliver the letter. In any case, he was instructed to find a replacement to carry Lenin's message to the American proletariat. Borodin, whose presence on such business was clearly illegal, shopped around in Stockholm and then went to Oslo. There he found his man: P. I. Travin.

Travin, whose party name was Sletov, had participated in the 1905 revolution in Riga and then, threatened by the *stolypinshchina*, had migrated to the United States. There he lived for the next decade working, among other things, as an IWW organizer. In August 1918 he made a return pilgrimage to the site of revolution and had just arrived in Oslo. According to his own fanciful and not always consistent accounts (recorded on several occasions four decades after the incidents involved), he was wandering the streets when suddenly he heard a voice cry out in English, "Mr. Sletov!" He turned and saw Borodin. Although Borodin was now bearded, and Travin had never seen him so, Travin immediately recognized his old friend "Kirill" (Borodin's 1905 name). They congratulated each other on their unexpected meeting, and Borodin invited Travin to his room where he told him at length how happy he was to see him after so long a time (they had not met in the United States), ending meaningfully: "You are very necessary to us."

Borodin told Travin to stay in the room while he returned to Stockholm for a few days, his unstated purpose being to check on whether *polpred* Vorovsky would agree that the mission to America should be entrusted to Travin. Three days later, having secured Vorovsky's tentative approval, Borodin returned to Oslo, told Travin that Vorovsky wanted to see him, and that same night left again for Stockholm. Fearful lest both of them be picked up by the police, Borodin set up a rendezvous in the Swedish capital and told Travin to follow him the next day. In Stockholm, Borodin took Travin to meet Vorovsky. After a lengthy interview, Vorovsky "ordered" Travin to return to the United States. The *polpred* removed from the office safe three typewritten copies of the "Letter to American Workers," each signed by Lenin, and har.ded them over to the newly enlisted agent, along with copies of the Constitution of the RSFSR and the text of a note from the Soviet government to President Wil-

1ed the new agent over to Borodin, who was to
1is way.

v documents, Borodin and Travin traveled to
:re the former sought to make arrangements for
rip to the United States. But he had no luck. By
can immigration officials had begun to crack
down, as concern about the import of revolution increased.
Borodin didn't have the documents, visas, or letters to get Travin legally on board a ship to New York. So they devised a scenario wherein Travin impersonated an unemployed American
sailor, stranded in Denmark by the blockade, the Great War still
not having ended. Travin then went to the American consulate
armed with an AFL identification card that Borodin had somehow obtained and, in bitter tones, told the consul how desperately he wanted to leave sinking Europe and get back to the
good old USA. The consul provided him with the necessary
papers. Three days later on the *Prince Olaf,* employed as a ship's
carpenter, he was on his way to New York.

Finding a vessel and getting on board was not the end of Travin's difficulties, for when he arrived in New York, immigration
authorities refused to admit him. According to his own account,
he jumped overboard and swam to shore. Wringing wet, he entered the first drugstore he could find and telephoned John
Reed, the Bolshevik-sympathizing American journalist who had
recently returned from Moscow with instructions to establish an
American communist party. Reed then took over the job of dis-
seminating the "Letter." Travin returned to Europe via Latin
America shortly after the first of the year. (Travin subsequently
engaged in engineering-technical work. Imprisoned during the
Stalin period, he survived the camps and was rehabilitated, as
the frequent publication of his recollection of the "Letter" incident indicates.)

Borodin, having sent Travin off, remained in Scandinavia
where he served as a jack-of-all-intelligence-trades, his chief assignment being to dispatch men, money, and propaganda
abroad. To do this he needed other Travins. He was so engaged
when, in November, he intercepted Carl Sandburg, the future
biographer of Lincoln and poet of the American heartland, sitting on a park bench outside Oslo's Grand Hotel. Sandburg,

who had at one time been an organizer for the socialists in
cago, a man with "known bolshevist friends," was Europe
correspondent for the Newspaper Enterprise Association. He
initially had difficulty obtaining a passport because of his old as-
sociations. He noted in a letter at the time that to improve his
chances of receiving documents, he had kept away from the "Socialist and I.W.W. bunch" for a time, though he still saw John
Reed, whom he admired greatly, a couple of times. But at length
the passport was granted, and Sandburg left for the Continent,
arriving at Bergen on October 14.[4]

Sandburg's task was to report on European developments as
seen from Scandinavia. On November 1, he wrote that Stockholm and Eastern Europe "are all such a blur and a chaos now
that nothing in the future seems much of a certainty."[5] It was at
this point that Borodin offered to supply Sandburg with information that would help clarify the blur and chaos. Sandburg
accepted the offer, probably unaware of Borodin's motives, and
Borodin proceeded to make himself useful to Sandburg in this
and other ways. Sandburg, ever the cultural conservative,
quickly tired of Europe. He wrote his wife from Stockholm two
weeks after he had arrived: "I look forward to when I can go
home . . . I have seen enough sophistication and ignorance to last
me a good while."[6] As Sandburg prepared to leave, Borodin put
the question: Would Sandburg be willing to take "Rus" (meaning Bolshevik) pamphlets, books, and newspapers into the
United States? The answer was yes, and when Sandburg arrived
in New York at the end of December, he had quantities of such
material in his luggage.

But it was not only propaganda that Sandburg carried. He
also had a $10,000 check drawn on a New York bank and 400
Norwegian kroner, all given to him by Borodin. But at the last
moment, Sandburg evidently had had second thoughts about
the check and informed the American ambassador at Oslo of it
but not of the other items.[7] As a result, when he arrived in New
York on December 25 he was greeted by an official search committee, which took custody not only of the check but also of the
suitcases carrying the Soviet literature. Evidently, however,
Sandburg managed to conceal the 400 kroner, which Borodin
had asked him to deliver to Fanya in Chicago. Military Intelli-

gence detained Sandburg, refused to release his luggage, and not until a month had elapsed, and Sandburg consented to the government's keeping the literature and using it as they saw fit, were charges against him dropped.

As for the $10,000, Santeri Nuorteva, who was nominally the representative in New York of the short-lived Finnish People's Republic, but really of the Lenin government, claimed that it was meant for him. In presenting his case, Nuorteva wrote:

> Some time last summer I asked Mr. Berg, who at that time was the Secretary of Professor Lomonosov, the head of the Russian Railway Commission, and who went to Russia, to ask my Finnish friends in Moscow to send me some funds in order to carry on the publicity work which I had been engaged in in the interest of bringing out the truth about conditions in Finland and incidentally in Russia ... I had been expecting some funds through that channel for a long time, and when pressed for an explanation Mr. Sandburg admitted to me that Mr. Berg, who is now in Christiana [Oslo], was the man who brought the drafts for me.

When Sandburg informed the American ambassador in Norway that he had been approached by Borodin, the latter was clearly compromised in the eyes of the Norwegian government. Oslo, however, did not take action against him until another incident some six weeks later, when an attempt to transfer funds to the newly established Soviet agency in New York misfired. The Norwegian government then ordered Borodin to leave the country. Three other agents departed with him, whereupon the American Embassy informed the U.S. Secretary of State: "With the departure of these men, the driving force of the Bolshevik movement in Norway is eliminated."[8]

Though Borodin's performance in Scandinavia in the late fall and early winter of 1918–19 was no unblemished triumph, it was not without its successes. Though he had twice failed to transmit funds to the New World, other shipments and messages may have slipped through. According to Scotland Yard, he had succeeded in smuggling funds, as well as orders, persons, and information in and out of Scandinavia on numerous occasions. He had operated successfully in the underground and proved himself as a recruiter. To Moscow his successes overshadowed his failures as he returned to the capital from Norway. His reputation was further strengthened because he returned with secret Swedish government documents given him by a member of the Reichstag, whom he had personally recruited.[9] By the time he reached Moscow, Borodin had won Bolshevik recognition as an effective agent. Six months back from America, he was not dissatisfied with his role.

The Moscow of winter 1918–19 to which Borodin now returned was besieged by hunger, famine, cold, fears of a White offensive in the spring, and the possibility of increased Allied intervention, now that World War I had ended. Men and horses died in the street of hunger and disease. Sleds containing uncovered horseflesh were pulled along while drivers wildly waved whips in an unsuccessful effort to beat off hordes of starving crows. The small ventilating windows that Russian hotel rooms have could not be left open lest crows force their way in to devour any scraps of food to be found. Even among the privileged Bolsheviks in the Hotel National, bread and sugar were nonexistent, though small luxuries were occasionally available from couriers, returned officials, and visitors from the West. The kitchen was heated only at mealtime and, if the potatoes and soup were not eaten soon enough, they froze.

Still, the period was not entirely without hope for the revolutionaries. The regime had survived the perils of the preceding summer. Believers listened wide-eyed as the glories of the future were described. News of the collapse of Germany and the Austro-Hungarian Empire and of the mounting series of revolutionary outbreaks in Central Europe suggested that the sparks from the Russian conflagration were at last about to ignite all of Europe. Lenin concluded that the time had come for a Third International to spur the revolution.

On January 24, the Soviet government broadcast an invitation to revolutionary groups throughout the world to send delegates to an international congress. But the radius of the broadcast was limited, few listeners were in a position to respond, and the Bolsheviks were unprepared vigorously to support the new organization. Nevertheless, on March 2, 1919, a congress was convened in the Kremlin. Only one or two delegates arrived from the West. Most of Europe's leftists and radicals were unaware of the congress until it had ended. But the congress was held, and its Russian sponsors had sought delegates from many quarters to represent the international working class. Russian-born returnees from abroad were utilized to represent the countries where they had spent their exile. Prisoners of war who had joined the Bolsheviks upon release were appointed delegates of their home countries. More than one fellow traveler who happened to be in Moscow at the time found himself appointed to the congress to repesent his—or even some other—country. Few of the delegates represented political parties.

The chief purpose of the congress was to disseminate word of the coming worldwide revolution. But though the principal aim of the congress was propaganda, that was not its only goal. Even at this First Congress, harbingers were present that the new Communist International (Comintern, known even more briefly as the CI) was destined to become primarily an agency not for spreading the revolution, but for maintaining Russian control over the international movement. Angelica Balabanoff, the Russian-Italian revolutionary, who was the chief of the CI's secretariat, soon realized that power was vested not in her international secretariat, but in a "secret" Russian party committee, which aimed at the creation of parties under Soviet control. The Bolsheviks wanted "a docile sect, dependent for its very existence upon the Comintern."[10] Although Borodin was in Moscow during the First Congress of the CI, and his future would be affected greatly by its outcome, he was not a delegate; other former residents in America had priority. But he was attached to the secret Bolshevik party committee, which Balabanoff recognized as controlling the congress and the new organization. And G. Y. Zinoviev, the chairman of the secret committee, used him to communicate decisions to the delegates, Balabanoff, and the rest of the secretariat, and to run various errands.

Once the CI had been formed, however, there were more important uses for Borodin than as message bearer from Zinoviev. If the objective of the recent congress was to be fulfilled, its declarations and instructions had to be spread abroad and agents had to be recruited to carry out the CI's purposes abroad. But when the congress concluded in the spring of 1919, Russia was closed off from the rest of the world by a highly effective Allied blockade, drawn up to prevent the spread of communism to the West. Some radio messages occasionally got through, but the infant wireless was unsatisfactory for either secret or public communication. The mails were blocked, and it was perilous even to attempt to reach the West. The casualty rate among couriers was almost prohibitively high; often, less than one out of three succeeded and many were executed when apprehended. But, if messages and instructions were to get through, if the international proletariat was to be aroused and organized, it had to be via courier agents. That is how Borodin was seen in the Kremlin.

In April 1920 Borodin was dispatched on what was to become an extensive, controversial, and adventurous expedition, during which he would visit a dozen countries on two continents, carrying out party missions under challenging and often dangerous circumstances. By the time he returned to Moscow, his exploits had made him almost a legend in top party circles.

6

Comintern Agent

Initially there was little effort by the new leaders in Moscow to distinguish between Comintern and Soviet foreign policy objectives. The goal of both was to spread the revolution. Only later did Lenin perceive that the interests of the international revolution and of Russia might not always coincide and that there might be value in at least a pretense of separate identities. But in 1919 an agent sent abroad to arrange diplomatic relations with an existing government could have, along with the usual responsibilities, a mission to establish a local communist party devoted to ovethrowing that same government.

So it was when Borodin left Moscow soon after the First Comintern Congress had dissolved in early March. It was essential to spread abroad, as widely and quickly as possible, the word and instructions of the CI. The CI was designed to exploit the critical situation in Europe in the late winter of 1918–19. Realizing the revolutionary potential, a revolutionary regime was established in Budapest on March 21 by Bela Kun, a convert to the revolution while a war prisoner in Russia. During the first week in April, a Red government was set up in Bavaria. Liaison must be established with the revolutionary situation developing in the West.

That Borodin's trip was originally conceived as wide-ranging can be deduced from Borodin's appointment by Lenin as Soviet consul to the Mexican government. For some time Lev Karakhan, the number-two man in the Comissariat of Foreign Affairs, had cultivated the Mexican acting consul-general in Moscow. He played upon the hatred the Mexican revolutionary government felt for its neighbor to the north, particularly after President Wilson had ordered U.S. cavalry into Mexico in pursuit of Pancho Villa in 1916. Karakhan told the consul-general that Soviet Russia and the Carranza government had much in common, sharing a contempt for imperialism and the United States. He convinced the consul-general to place the passport-issuing facilities of the consulate at Russian disposal and, specifically, to issue a Mexican diplomatic passport to a Soviet representative appointed by Lenin, enabling him to visit Central and South America. The representative was Borodin.

On April 12, Borodin's Mexican passport was visaed by a U.S. consul in Moscow. On April 17, he received his appointment from Lenin. On April 18, 1919, loaded down with heavy suitcases, and accompanied by an attaché of the Mexican consulate in Moscow to ease his way, he left Moscow for the West. Borodin's first port-of-call was Germany. The need for a courier to reach that revolution- and violence-racked country was as great as the dangers involved. The Spartakist uprising of January had been bloodily quelled and its two communist leaders, Rosa Luxembourg and Karl Liebknicht, executed. Moscow's man in Berlin, the obnoxious but effective Karl Radek, had managed to stay free until February; now he too was in prison.

With the German communist leadership crippled, and Radek incapacitated for the time being, Moscow was anxious to reach disoriented "locals," particularly after the news of the Bavarian April uprising had reached the Soviet capital. Moreover, the CI was determined to make Berlin the headquarters for its activities in the West. Borodin's mission was to deliver materials and instructions to Berlin, as well as funds to set up CI machinery. His stay in Germany was short, particularly since the revolutionary uprising in Munich was suppressed soon after his arrival in Berlin, followed by a general round-up of communists.

Quickly leaving Germany, Borodin with his heavy suitcases next went to Switzerland, where he deposited 500,000 Romanov rubles, presumably to be used for CI and other purposes, in the Federal Bank of Geneva. In Switzerland he also attended the Women's International Conference for Permanent Peace, which met in Zurich, May 14 to 18. At the meetings, according to a Scotland Yard report, he contacted several of the delegates and handed over some packets to at least one member of the U.S.

delegation. Although the delegate's name was not mentioned in the report, it is interesting to note that the conference was presided over by Borodin's old Chicago acquaintance, Jane Addams. It seems likely that he contacted her in Zurich, and it may be that he used or attempted to use Addams in May 1919, just as he had employed another Chicagoan, Carl Sandburg, as a courier's courier half a year earlier. In her memoirs, Jane Addams complains that in Europe she was constantly under surveillance of the secret service and oppressed by the efforts of miltary intelligence "to get something on" her. She felt freer in "neutral Switzerland," where she met Borodin.[1]

By mid-July Borodin had reached Holland and given instructions to local sympathizers. On the 14th of that month, still heavily laden with baggage, he left for the United States. The bags that Borodin lugged about Europe have been the subject of some controversy over the past half-century. Borodin doubtless brought valuables to the Western hemisphere in support of Bolshevik causes. The Russian Soviet Government Bureau in New York, to which he had attempted to dispatch funds when in Scandinavia, still needed them. Money was required to strengthen the budding pro-Moscow movement in the United States and to create Bolshevik parties elsewhere in the Western hemisphere. What is less clear is what these valuables were and what happened to them. Three decades later, a one-time CI colleague of Borodin, Manabendra Nath Roy, whom Borodin had personally brought into the party and who was once his proudest recruit, wrote that Borodin had told him "the whole story." According to Roy, Borodin was assigned by Karakhan to smuggle tsarist jewels worth a million rubles ($500,000) into the United States. The jewels were sewn into the lining of two bulky leather suitcases and the suitcases then filled with blueprints.

Reaching Holland, Borodin took passage on a Dutch vessel bound for Curacao, hoping to divert suspicion from the first objective of his journey to the New World: the United States. But when the ship reached the Caribbean, it was stopped by American customs officers and its passengers, including Borodin, were brought to Port-au-Prince, Haiti, and searched. Borodin had, Roy continued, prepared for such an eventuality by bringing with him a young demobilized Austrian officer of aristocratic background, who, "frustrated, disillusioned, and embittered," had decided to abandon Europe and migrate to South America "in quest of peace in the solitude of some remote hacienda." With a bonafide passport and no previous espionage involvement, he would presumably be less subject to suspicion than Borodin. Faced with the imminent confiscation of the jewels, Borodin handed them over to the Austrian, with the instruction that, as soon as the coast was clear, he was to deliver them to Borodin's wife Fanya in Chicago. Several days later, Borodin "managed to escape," reached Jamaica in a sailing vessel, and from there went to New York.

Judging from other sources, Roy's tale would appear to be less than fully accurate. Borodin did leave Holland on a Dutch vessel that may very well have been bound for Curacao, but it stopped at the island of Hispaniola where Borodin went ashore to seek passage to New York. But Borodin realized that even though he managed to obtain a U.S. visa, his chances, as an English-speaking Russian with Mexican papers, of getting the jewels past U.S. customs were remote. Accordingly, he asked the Austrian, whom he had met aboard the vessel and found sympathetic, to help the cause by taking the bags, the secret contents of which Borodin apparently did not reveal, past customs for him and bringing them to Chicago as soon as he could.

In late August 1919 Borodin visited the U.S. consul-general in Santo Domingo and told him that he was an employee of the Mexican consulate, on his way to Mexico City with sealed documents from the Mexican consul-general in Moscow destined for the Mexican foreign office. However, he first wanted to visit his wife and children in Chicago. The consul-general, suspicious of anyone coming from Moscow, wired Washington recommending a "most careful" examination of Borodin when he reached New York. On September 7, Borodin arrived in New York harbor abroad the *S. S. Huron*. The message from the consul-general in Santo Domingo was heeded and Borodin was detained at Ellis Island pending investigation.

At this point the story is picked up by Jacob Spolansky, a U.S. federal agent. The Russian-born Spolansky had also been a Hull House habitué, at one time had published a Russian newspaper in Chicago, and knew Borodin quite well. In 1918, Spolansky had been inducted into army intelligence and was now a member of the Bureau of Investigation, predecessor of the FBI.[2] Special agent Spolansky was sent to interrogate Borodin. He searched Borodin's baggage thoroughly and questioned him. But he discovered little except that Borodin was anxious to visit his wife and family. The Bureau of Investigation decided to allow Borodin to go to Chicago and remain there briefly, but ordered Spolansky to keep a close check on him. As soon as Borodin was released, his first stop was the office of D. H. Dubrowsky, a dentist associated with the Russian Soviet Government Bureau in New York. Borodin told Dubrowsky that he had been given diamonds in Moscow to deliver to the United States, that he did not have them with him, but that Dubrowsky could expect delivery in the near future.[3]

Shortly thereafter Borodin left for Chicago where he was met at the depot by Spolansky, who reminded him that his visa was only good for a short visit—and that he should "keep in touch." Borodin was in Chicago the third and fourth weeks in September. If one of his purposes in returning to Chicago was to participate in the founding of an American communist party, he was late by several weeks. The founding—actually of two communist parties and, for a while in 1920, three—had taken place in late August and early September in a heated, brawling atmosphere from which emerged the Communist Party of America, representing chiefly Russian elements, and the Communist Labor Party of the "native-born."

Borodin saw many of his old colleagues in Chicago. Even though he was under surveillance, there was no reason to avoid them, since old-time Chicagoan Spolansky, who had been at the founding congress of the Communist Party of America, knew who the radicals, old and new, were. Borodin probably tried to recruit some of them for the CI, as he did Spolansky. Just before he left the United States he told the latter, "there's a great opportunity for a man like you" in Soviet Russia. But Borodin had two other important reasons for being in Chicago. One was to see his family. It had been over a year since he had left for Russia. He must have missed his wife and sons, now ten and four, and sometimes wondered what he was doing so far away in Moscow, Berlin, or Santo Domingo, slipping across borders, on constant guard against detection. Like many other revolutionaries, he cared about his family, though they did not come before the revolution.

Borodin's other reason for returning to Chicago was to recover the diamonds when they reached there. But they had not arrived, and he must now depart. His wife and boys had expected, or at least hoped, to go with him. Fanya had already applied for passports for the three of them. But Borodin was traveling fast. He still had calls to make—who knew how many dangers lay ahead, and who had ever heard of a secret agent with a dumpy wife and two children in tow? More important, Fanya had to stay behind to receive the diamonds when they arrived. He told Fanya to contact him or L. K. Martens, the head of the Russian Soviet Government Bureau in New York, the moment they came. Those diamonds would plague Borodin for years to come and eventually would jeopardize his standing in party circles. Even when they were reassured about them, tall tales would continue to circulate elsewhere about "Borodin's diamonds." For a period Borodin himself may not have known what happened to them. According to Dubrowsky, the dentist, Borodin approached him in Red Square on May Day, 1920, and asked Dubrowsky to testify that he had received a quarter of a million dollars worth of diamonds. Dubrowsky would do no such thing, for though he had received a bag of diamonds two weeks after Borodin's visit, they turned out to be worth only $12,000. Evidently, Dubrowsky, like Borodin and others who would become Borodin's enemies, accepted that fact that this bag held Borodin's diamonds. And Borodin was now in trouble, for how had $500,000 worth of diamonds suddenly shrunk to a packet worth less than a fortieth as much? The answer that would ultimately develop was that these were probably not the same diamonds, but jewels dispatched through another channel.

Another story surrounding the jewels is that they were pawned to Eamon De Valera, the Irish leader and future prime minister and president.[4] In this account, many of whose details were confirmed in debate in the Dail in 1948 and two years later by the Irish Government Information Bureau, Martens, the chief Soviet agent in New York, received a packet of jewels (Borodin's?) that he was supposed to sell in order to support Soviet activities. Unable to market them, he approached De Valera, as one revolutionist to another, offering to hand over the jewels, worth many times the amount asked, as security for a loan of $20,000. De Valera agreed, made the loan, and transmitted the jewels to his colleague, Harry Boland. Just before Boland died in 1922, he instructed his mother and sister to keep the diamonds until a republic was created in Ireland. When the Irish Constitution was established in 1938, Boland's sister handed the jewels back to De Valera, who on at least one occasion asked the Russians to redeem them. It was not until 1948, however, after the transaction of three decades earlier had become a *cause célèbre* in the Irish general election of that year, that the Soviets agreed to repay the loan—on a noninterest basis—in exchange for the gems.

Still another Borodin jewel story came from the one-time left-wing socialist and cofounder of the Communist Party of America, Louis Fraina. In Russia and Germany in the early years of the twenties Borodin and Fraina were very close. On one occasion, according to an FBI interrogation of Fraina thirty years later, Borodin told Fraina about the attempt to smuggle the jewels into the United States and said that, faced with disclosure, he had thrown them into New York harbor where they presumably still rested.

Although Borodin did not leave Chicago with Fanya, the boys, or the diamonds in September 1919, he did not leave alone. Traveling with him was a young Chicago socialist of Mexican descent, Raphael Mallen. Borodin had business in Mexico. Because he didn't speak Spanish, he felt that he needed a cicerone and Mallen had been recommended to him for that purpose by an old Chicago acquaintance. With Mallen at his side, Borodin arrived in Mexico City later in September. His tasks: to assess Mexico's revolutionary potential, to organize a communist party, and to establish diplomatic relations between Soviet Russia and Mexico.

There were more than a few American socialists in Mexico City at the time. Some were adventurers, others had gone there to escape the World War I draft. Linn Gale, who founded *Gale's Magazine,* later to become the socialist party organ in Mexico, was there for the draft reason; so were Charles Phillips and

Irwin Granick (the real name of Mike Gold). When Borodin went to Mexico, Martens had given him the names of Phillips and Gold. But Borodin was cautious. He had been under surveillance in the United States and he might be here. Moreover, Martens' contacts were not always reliable and his information not always accurate. Borodin put Mallen to work scouting out the situation.

One of the leading Mexico City newspapers was *El Heraldo de Mexico*. It aspired to be a quality newspaper and hired first-rate writers, artists, and even poets. For the growing colony of Americans, it had an English-language section edited by Manuel Gomez, from Chicago. Shortly after he arrived in Mexico, Borodin sent Mallen to the editorial offices of *El Heraldo* to talk with Gomez and Gold, who was also on the staff. A casual reading of the English section of *El Heraldo,* whose policy was completely different from that of the rest of the paper, should have satisfied Borodin as to its leanings: entire articles were lifted from the communist-sponsored *Soviet Russia Today* and sympathy for revolutionary socialism was unmistakable. But Borodin had sent Mallen to find out how the editors felt: about socialism, Soviet Russia, and so forth. Mallen's feelers led him to believe that Gomez and Gold were trustworthy. He told them he had a very important friend who would like to meet them. Could they come to the Ritz for lunch with him right now? Gomez and Gold thought the circumstances, the request, and its urgency were rather strange, but they went. There, at the Ritz, in luxury accommodations that Borodin had engaged on his arrival, Mallen introduced them to "Mr. Alexandrescu," a Chicago businessman, traveling on a Rumanian passport, in Mexico for an indefinite stay. Borodin—Mr. Alexandrescu—was clearly nervous. He impressed Gomez as "one of the most cautious men I have ever known, and one of the most secretive, given to talking in whispers and looking around."[5] But Borodin was soon satisfied that he could trust Gold and Gomez as much as anyone, and he told them a little about his real identity and his goals in Mexico. They, in turn, began introducing this stranger, who identified himself as the "personal emissary" of Lenin in the New World, to their own small socialist coterie.

Socialism in Mexico was, in spite of that country's revolutionary involvement, only weakly developed. Not only was the entire country affected by Yanqui economic imperialism, but even its socialist movement was mostly American in membership and origin. M. N. Roy indicated the condition of Mexican socialism when he described one of its chief occasions: a socialist baptism conducted in Yiddish. A Mexican working-class father, a socialist sympathizer, was determined that his newborn son not be baptized, believing that the priestly blessings would permanently enslave the boy. But his wife was adamant. In an attempt to satisfy both, the socialist party executive committee and other local American radicals converted a room into a private chapel and appointed one of their comrades as priest. He recited blessings in Yiddish, and the socialist claque responded with shouts of "Amen" and "Long Live the Revolution!" The child was christened Karl Marx Flores. The mother was satisfied and the movement chalked up another victory.[6]

What there was of socialism in Mexico had become increasingly leftist under the influence of the October Revolution. By August 1919 preparations were underway for holding a congress and establishing a socialist party. Most of the impetus for starting the party had come from Americans, but the chief mover— and financier—was not an American but an Indian, a Brahman, the previously mentioned M. N. Roy. Roy, two years Borodin's junior, had been a passionate nationalist, dedicated to ousting the British from his homeland. With the outbreak of World War I, he became convinced of the liberating mission of Germany. Germany, he was certain, would provide the Indian nationalists with weapons to overcome the British Raj. In 1914, Roy went to the Dutch East Indies, anticipating a load of munitions to be delivered there, but came away empty-handed. The following year he traveled to China on a similar, equally futile mission. Then back to the East Indies, to Japan, and across the Pacific, hoping to reach Germany through the United States, to make a personal plea for support. Roy arrived in the United States prior to the latter's entry into the war and was able to convince the German representatives there to support him with funds, which they did quite liberally. Using German money, while waiting for an action plan to be put into effect, Roy attended Stanford University for several months. There he met an American girl, whom he married in 1917 in a New York City jail, when he was arrested in a roundup of Indians, following the U.S. declaration of war. Released from jail, Roy went to Mexico, where he continued to be so generously supported by the German government that even after Germany's defeat he was still in comfortable financial condition. Part of the money Roy received from the Germans was spent on living well and on building his influence; the rest he spent on radical causes.

When Roy arrived in Mexico in 1917, he was no Marxist. In his writings in 1918 and early 1919 there is no hint of Marxist influence. But because there was no appreciable group of Indian nationals in Mexico City and the English-speaking Roy knew no Spanish, he drifted into the company of radical Americans, most of whom were already socialists when they had come to Mexico. Under their tutelage, Roy moved enthusiastically in that direction. Now they were considering forming a party in support of the October Revolution. And Roy was on hand to provide the driving impetus of the convert—and the money. The founding congress of the Socialist Party of Mexico convened in Mexico City on August 25 and remained in session until September 4, with its sponsor, Roy, as chairman. Almost immediately upon its opening, a quarrel broke out between liberals and conservatives, and the congress split, establishing two minuscule parties. Roy became the head of the more conservative Socialist Party of Mexico.

Such was the condition of Mexican socialism when Borodin arrived in Mexico City, nervous and nearly broke. Nevertheless, he rented a huge suite, albeit in a hotel that had seen better days. As Lenin's personal representative and "the first emissary of the Communist International to the New World," he couldn't stay in a flea bag. But without money even for lodging or food, he needed funds badly. Phillips and Gold pointed him toward Roy. As Roy told the story, Borodin, using the name Brantwein, received Roy in his luxury suite attired in a black silk dressing gown. Roy was impressed by the style and affluence of the Bolshevik agent. But when they went to a restaurant for dinner Borodin, before ordering, asked if Roy could pay. When Roy said yes, Borodin proceeded to order lavishly. Later Borodin strengthened the impression of his impecuniousness—and nervousness—when he visited Roy's home in the suburbs. Arriving at night by taxi, Borodin jumped out of the cab, ran into Roy's house, and anounced that he had not paid the driver, since he feared being silhouetted in the glare of the taxi's headlights while counting out the change. Roy paid the bill.

When Borodin saw the elegant quarters Roy was occupying, he decided these were indeed suitable quarters for a representative of Lenin's. And having been told by Gomez and Gold that Roy and his wife were most hospitable, Borodin surmised that if he complained about his hotel room, Roy would invite him to move in—which he did. On the following day Roy arrived at the Ritz to help Borodin move out. While they were so engaged, Borodin mentioned to Roy that he was, unfortunately, still short of funds. Roy paid the hotel bill. The relationship between Borodin and Roy was, at the time, one in which Borodin quite frankly exploited Roy. But this was soon to change into one in which, as Roy would later recall, he learned much from Borodin, and Borodin from him. "In the beginning I was the gainer."[7]

Borodin soon realized that Roy was not only the answer to his financial dilemma but also the key to fulfillment of his mission to Mexico. Roy was the secretary-general of the local socialist party; he was also on excellent terms with the Mexican government, with which Borodin hoped to establish diplomatic relations. He was, as well, highly intelligent and an experienced and dedicated revolutionary, though only a recent and superficial convert to socialism. He was well worth cultivating and capturing for the Leninist cause. During the weeks and months that followed, Borodin spent many days with Roy discussing subjects ranging from Shakespeare to Washington's retreat across Long Island, on all of which Borodin seemed to be an expert. But mostly they spoke of the march of history, of revolution, and of Hegel, Marx, and Lenin. Roy, along with others in his circle, was tremendously impressed by this man of "extraordinary intellect and encyclopedic knowledge,"[8] as Gomez described him. Borodin "initiated me in the intricacies of Hegelian dialectics as the key to Marxism," said Roy. "My lingering faith in the special genius of India faded as I learned from him the history of European culture."[9] Roy recalled the months spent in Mexico under Borodin's tutelage, with instruction beginning after dinner and continuing late into the night, as "the most memorable period of my life."[10] Borodin proselytized so effectively that Roy's interest in the Indian revolution began to take second place to the call of the international workers' revolution. Later when the Russian wanted Roy to lead the revolutionary movement in India, he hesitated, partly because his interests were no longer so parochial.

That Roy and Gomez describe Borodin's intellectual qualities and attainments in such terms as extraordinary and encyclopedic comes largely as a surprise. No one before had ever endowed him with such superlatives, and one might discount these remarks as inspired by the aura that enveloped Borodin in romantic retrospect. Yet so many who knew Borodin in the 1920s described him similarly that they cannot be lightly dismissed. As a teacher, Borodin's self-education may have advanced rapidly in Chicago. His desire to become a member of the intelligentsia may have driven him further than the bare records suggest. In teaching civics and literature he seems to have absorbed and integrated the material he taught. Now among small groups, as he sought to impress and convert, he wove together his experience and his knowledge of government and literature with the teachings of Marx and Lenin. By the testimony of dozens, he did it with a skill and dedication that were to attain epic proportions.

Not long after the two men met, Borodin proposed that Roy's socialist organization should become the Mexican Communist Party. Roy assented and they promptly drew up plans for a founding congress. Roy recalled that Borodin was tremendously excited at the prospect. As the day for the opening of the formal congress grew near, he and Roy drafted greetings to the congress from the Executive Committee of the Comintern. Supposedly coming from Moscow, these greetings were the highlight of the congress. Borodin was aware of the impact of "personal greetings" from Moscow, and it was not the last time he would compose them on the spot.

Once the new party had been officially founded, Borodin wanted to inform the Comintern at once. Through Roy's contacts with the Mexican foreign ministry, which used its legation in Amsterdam to inform the West European bureau of the CI,

Moscow was informed that Borodin had established "the first communist party outside Russia." Shortly thereafter, Borodin wrote the history of the founding of the new party.

In the course of the continuing Borodin-Roy relationship, Borodin raised the subject of diplomatic relations with Mexico. They decided that Roy would arrange a dinner party to which President Carranza would be invited and at which Borodin would be present. Carranza, whose anti-Americanism had made hin favor Germany during the war, felt isolated when Germany fell. Although he was not eager to undertake adventures that might attract hostile U.S. attention, he was not opposed to exploratory talks with fellow anti-imperialists. During the dinner, Borodin demonstrated that wide-ranging knowledge and conversational skill that had impressed Roy and would be often noted in the decade ahead. He emphasized the sympathy Moscow now had with the peoples of Latin America in their struggle against the scourge of imperialism. He proposed that a Latin American bureau of the Comintern be established in Mexico, with Roy at its head.

As Roy viewed it, Carranza saw in Borodin's proposal the "prospect of his dream of a Latin American League being realized in different form." Carranza may have been tempted to reach for the bait, but the position of his government was perilous. Recognition of the Soviet government might have brought the U.S. army across the border again. Government support of a Comintern agency would almost certainly do so. However, Carranza did authorize Borodin to transmit his regards to Lenin, and he made the resources of the Mexican foreign office available to Borodin for this and other purposes. Later, just before Borodin left Mexico, he had an audience with the Mexican foreign minister who told him that he hoped soon to establish *de jure* relations with Russia and to exchange ambassadors. This was not all that Borodin had hoped for, and he realized that such sentiments, especially as expressed to a departing "diplomat," were tenuous. But for the beleaguered Bolshevik regime, a pariah among nations, even this vague expression was a breakthrough. Borodin and Moscow recognized it as such.

Whereas Borodin had been apprehensive and perhaps somewhat disheartened when he arrived in Mexico City, he was now buoyed up by success. He sent Moscow properly modest, but nonetheless glowing, reports of his achievements. But if Borodin had reason for a more optimistic outlook, he was still disturbed by the missing jewels. Their continued absence took the bloom off his triumphs. He knew Moscow would hold him responsible. Borodin had told Fanya to notify him as soon as the suitcases arrived. Every day he went to the post office to pick up his mail, and though there were letters from Fanya, none contained the news that he was waiting for. Instead they told Borodin how bad the family's situation had becme since he left. On one occasion Borodin had Roy send Fanya $500 from his German funds. Borodin also persuaded Roy to send $10,000 to Martens in New York, to support the Soviet Bureau there. Thus, although the jewels were missing, Borodin was still helping to fund Soviet activities in North America. His ability to do so in the circumstances further augmented his growing reputation in Moscow.

What happened to the gems? While in Mexico Borodin sent two, perhaps three, agents to Hispaniola. (Roy mentions that Borodin located an old party member, who was a sailor and an "iron-willed anarchist," to undertake the mission. Since this description fits neither of the two men whom Gomez said were sent on the expedition, it is possible that three searchers were dispatched.) One of these was Raphael Mallen, who had come to Mexico City with Borodin from Chicago. But when, after more than a month, Mallen had not returned, Borodin asked Gomez if he would take a trip on party business. Gomez, eager to be of service to the newborn party (he would be a delegate to the Sixth Congress of the CI in 1928), agreed. Borodin thereupon told Gomez the story of his having handed a suitcase full of compromising "blueprints" to a "German" shipboard companion, who had apparently taken them to Haiti. Borodin instructed Gomez to proceed first to Havana, since there was no direct line from Vera Cruz to Port-au-Prince, and there to check all sailings from Havana to New York to see if Mallen's name was on any of the lists. If it was, Borodin was to be notified at once. But if no trace of Mallen was found, Gomez was to tour the hotels of Havana looking for him; if this failed, he was to go on to Haiti.

Borodin gave Gomez an address in the hills behind Port-au-

Prince. There he was to present himself as the agent of Mr. Alexandrescu and collect the blueprints. If there were difficulties, Gomez was to tell the "German" that the safety of his relatives in Europe depended on the return of the baggage to its rightful owner. To emphasize his determination, he gave Gomez a gun and told him to use it if necessary. Gomez went to Havana and, finding no trace of Mallen, proceeded to Port-au-Prince. He arrived in a driving rain, took a cab up the hill to a district now called Petionville, and knocked at the door of the address given by Borodin. A German-speaking woman opened the door. When Gomez said that he had come from Mr. Alexandrescu, she immediately called out to a man inside. He came out in a fury, went to a closet, and pulled out a suitcase. He opened it to reveal a false bottom that had been ripped open, plus some blueprints. He closed the suitcase, handed it to Gomez, and told him to get out, saying, as Gomez recalled forty years later, "I've had one person here already, and when I tried to do Mr. Alexandrescu a favor, he never told me that he was giving me something with a false bottom that could get me into trouble." Gomez was delighted to take the suitcase (only one piece of luggage is mentioned) and leave. The torn secret compartment did not concern him, since Borodin had mentioned only blueprints, not diamonds.

Gomez returned to Havana at once and, while waiting for the boat to leave for Vera Cruz, again examined the New York passenger lists. This time he found Raphael Mallen's name on the list of a Ward Line vessel scheduled to depart for New York on the following day. Gomez went to the boat and waited for Mallen to arrive. As Mallen boarded the ship, Gomez stopped him and asked him where he was going. When Mallen replied New York, Gomez said no, he had to return to Mexico City. Gomez cabled Borodin that he was returning with both baggage and Mallen.[11] When Gomez arrived, he was met at the station by an ebullient Borodin, accompanied by Roy. Anticipating that the jewels were there, Borodin was overjoyed. He promised Gomez a champagne dinner. Gomez called it "an amazing reception."

But as soon as Borodin had returned to Roy's house and discovered that there were no diamonds in the suitcase, his exhilaration turned to despair and anger. He searched Gomez and

Mallen. Finding nothing, he ordered Mallen into the sitting room where he began haranguing him, threatening him with "murder, torture, every conceivable thing." But Mallen insisted he knew nothing of the diamonds. He had gone to see the "German," but the false bottom, the man's attitude, the secrecy, the mystery of the whole thing, frightened him and he decided to return to the United States as quickly as possible. Borodin finally decided, apparently, that Mallen didn't have the diamonds and knew nothing about them. Mallen was free to leave. Borodin still bought Gomez the champagne dinner, with Roy's money, but it was not the happy occasion that Roy and Gomez and Borodin had anticipated.

The time had come for Borodin to move on. It was December, and weeks earlier Borodin had been ordered to return to Moscow, or so he told Roy. He had delayed until the Mexican Communist Party had been founded and Gomez had returned. Now he could wait no longer. Borodin told Roy he was leaving for Europe and instructed him to follow soon. They would meet in Berlin and proceed together to Moscow. In the meantime, Borodin had business in Spain, and he asked Gomez to accompany him to Madrid as his interpreter.

In December 1919 Borodin and Gomez boarded a Spanish Line vessel in Vera Cruz bound for Spain. In Seville, Barcelona, Madrid, and other cities, Borodin, whose coffers had apparently now been replenished by Moscow, sought to contract sympathizers and to hatch a Spanish communist party. Apparently he knew little about communists or potential communists in Spain. He asked Gomez to pore over the Spanish press in search of names appearing in contexts indicating that they were prospects. Having compiled a list, Gomez was to visit these persons, screen out the poorer prospects, and introduce the remainder to Borodin. In this way Borodin met a number of Spanish socialists and anarchists, mostly trade unionists, including the redoubtable Angel Pestaña who, apparently at Borodin's initiative, attended the next Comintern congress.

By now—it was late January or early February 1920—Borodin had received instructions to proceed to Amsterdam for a meeting of the West European bureau of the Comintern. He left Gomez behind to organize a communist movement in Spain. He gave him a little money and promised more when he reached Berlin. The money was sent. At this point, Borodin took a cattle boat to Holland, which only eight months before had been his last port of call en route to America. In Amsterdam he was to represent Russian interests at the West European bureau conference scheduled for early February.

The conference, arranged by S. J. Rutgers, a gentle Dutch anarchist who had spent many years in Indonesia and had lived in Brooklyn during World War I, was doomed from the outset. It was as completely infiltrated by the police as had been the First Congress of the Russian social democrats in Minsk a quarter century earlier. At least one of the delegates, Louis Fraina, was able to reach Amsterdam only through the aid—passport, funds, and "guidance"—of an agent who worked for both Scotland Yard and American intelligence. On the second day of the conference, Borodin, who had just arrived, either suspicious or acting on his normally cautious instincts, checked the adjoining apartment and found the Dutch police with a dictaphone, putting down the proceedings of the conference. Borodin rushed back into the meeting to blurt out what he had discovered, but the police arrived as soon as he did and all of the delegates were arrested. Those without passports were deported; those having them were told to leave Holland at once. But Borodin, Fraina, Rutgers, James T. Murphy, a working-class radical who was one of the numerous British delegates, the Dutch astronomer Anton Pannopoek, the British union leader Fred Willis, the suffragette Elizabeth Pankhurst, and a few others determined to continue the conference.

They hid out in Amsterdam for a few days and then proceeded to Rutgers' house at Amersfoort, which was only a few yards from the local military barracks. Here the work of the conference was completed. The decisions reached were radical ones abjuring the gradual gaining of power by parliamentary means or through union conquests. Power must be seized by a revolutionary working class.

The delegates' efforts were fruitless, for in April the Executive Committee of the Comintern in Moscow dissolved the West European bureau and rendered its decisions null and void. In the months since the First Congress of the Comintern, Moscow's aims for the CI had changed. Its chief function was no longer to spread the revolution, but to control the revolutionary forces throughout the world. The new relationship between Moscow and foreign parties was indicated in a riddle circulated a few years later among U.S. radicals: "Why is the CPUS like Brooklyn Bridge? Because it stands suspended between cables—from Moscow." It became apparent to Moscow that the West European bureau with its unreconstructed syndicalists and other "wildmen"—few of those at the Amsterdam conference were card-carrying members of any party—could not be easily controlled, particularly from a Moscow whose communications with the outside world were tenuous at best. Accordingly, the West European bureau had to be disbanded and its radical judgments, no longer in favor, repudiated.

Although Amsterdam-Amersfoort was an aborted conference, it did not diminish Borodin's reputation. On the contrary, Borodin had occupied a position of importance as the designated representative of Russian communism at an international meeting of representatives from Western Europe, the United States, and Asia. Although Rutgers was the presiding official, Borodin, fresh from the New World, represented the authority of the revolution. His personal position was reinforced by his recent exploits and by his discovery of the police and dictaphone in the adjoining room. If he was not the dominating figure in Amsterdam, he became such by the time the conference reconvened at Amersfoort.

With the meeting adjourned, many of those present planned to make their way to Moscow for the forthcoming Second Congress of the Comintern. But it was first necessary to slip out of Holland, whose security forces were on the lookout for Borodin, Rutgers, and the others. To facilitate their escape, the delegates broke up into groups of twos and threes. In Borodin's group were Murphy and Fraina. All three were English-speaking and Borodin's German would help them all reach Berlin, their first objective.

Twenty years later, when the war against Hitler brought Russia and Britain closer together and invited the telling of tales of earlier cooperation between Russians and Englishmen, Murphy recalled how the three, fearful of being detected going East, having passports but no vias, decided to walk across the Dutch frontier. They left Amersfoort before dawn and tramped across the silent Dutch flatlands hour after hour, seeing little but clumps of woods and windmills. Occasionally they came across a house or a village, which they skirted. Finally, late at night, they arrived at the shop of a blacksmith to whom they had been given a document of introduction. While they remained in the black-smith's one-room-combination smithy and living quarters, the smith went off in search of someone who could smuggle them across the frontier. The uproar in Amsterdam about the local exploits of the Bolshevik conspirators had so increased border precautions that it was difficult to find anyone willing to under-take the mission. After three days, however, a carter arrived with a wagon filled with hay. With Borodin, Fraina, and Murphy concealed under the hay, the journey to the frontier was re-sumed. Twenty-four hours later, having gone partly by wagon and partly by walking through forests and swamps and moors, they arrived in Germany. There, taking leave of their guide, they again walked to the nearest railroad station, where they boarded what proved to be the last train to Berlin from the West before the general strike of February 1920.

During their journey Murphy got to know Borodin quite well. Like others who had observed Borodin in small group settings, Murphy was greatly impressed by the latter's grasp of world history and literature. Because of Borodin, said Murphy, he came to trust "intellectuals." He had found a man of erudition in whom he could place confidence, a man who daily risked all for the cause. In evaluating Borodin, as he came to know him both on the march to Germany and on subsequent occasions, Murphy wrote that "of all the so-called 'emissaries' of Lenin I have known, I know of none more expert and capable than he in win-ning the confidence and regard of the people to whom he was sent."[12] For Borodin, steadily gaining confidence in his ability, winning disciples had become almost second nature.

Berlin in the late winter of 1920 was a tense city. Hunger, un-employment and inflation were widespread and would grow worse. But even more prevalent were disillusionment and inde-cision. Few favored the status quo, but there was little agree-ment on an alternative course. Attempts at left-wing revolution had failed; the right would soon fail too. Neither left nor right nor center could gain effective control. The stage was set for the decade of chaos that would eventually bring Hitler to power.

Though the communists could not seize control of Berlin, they could use the freedom of the German capital to further a multitude of their enterprises. The strong left-wing orientation of the workers provided them with protection. The loosening of old norms had led to the remarkable blossoming of the arts that would characterize Weimar Germany. And in the great intellectual salons of the day, communists and communist causes found adherents. No less flourishing than the salons were the narrow alleys of Berlin's demiworld where purloined or forged passports and identification papers were available and where smuggling, money-changing, and other illegal services could be contracted for on a discreet basis. Berlin offered a wide variety of facilities suitable for Comintern activities. When the West European bureau in Amsterdam was dissolved because it could not be controlled, Moscow designated Berlin, where it could more readily set up and control its apparat under its own Moscow-appointed agents, and where it already had considerable experience, as the base for Western operations. During the next decade, Berlin would be the center of CI activities in the West, the first port of call for those moving out to Europe, the last stop for those returning to the Soviet Union.

In Berlin, Borodin received orders to return to Moscow as quickly as possible. He and the party "transportation specialists" surveyed the possible routes. The Swedish route, they felt, was precluded both by a British circular on Borodin, issued by the Home Office in December 1919, which listed him as a dangerous international agent, and by his prior actions there. The way through Poland, where Bolsheviks were being shot on sight, was too risky to chance. The northern route was ruled out by the presence of ice, which reinforced the Allies' blockade. Borodin even considered hiring an airplane to be piloted by German officers who were sympathetic to National Bolshevism (a concept flirted with during this period by both Germans and Russians that called for an alliance of right and left against the center). But this too proved unfeasible; Borodin was forced to wait. Meanwhile he, Fraina, and Murphy stayed together at a rooming house that catered to the left. They were impatient to be on their way.

Roy, who by now had reached Berlin from Mexico and who had been placed by Borodin in a luxury hotel, recalled that he spent much of his time in the literary-political salons that were so popular in Berlin. Here Roy had met Karl Kautsky, Alex Hilferding, and the almost blind Edward Bernstein, all significant figures of the socialist past but anathema to Lenin. Roy knew he wasn't supposed to associate with them, and Borodin reminded him, but since they were prominent figures in the history of his newfound faith, he couldn't pass them up. Borodin also was not immune from salon hopping, according to Roy. He remembered that Borodin personally introduced him into the leftist salon of the film star Erna Morena, where, he said, everyone knew Borodin and his exploits, magnified in the telling. As for Murphy and Fraina, who were not the salon type, they and Borodin spent time together visiting various trade-union headquarters and observing street clashes between workers and troops. Borodin's interests were wide, and he wanted to keep both Roy, his prized recruit, and the others, who were rapidly becoming his devotees, happy. Accordingly, he offered entertainment to taste.

Thus weeks passed as Borodin and the rest waited for a route to open so that they could move on to Moscow. In April, Pilsudski advanced against the Ukraine in a gamble to expand newly recreated Poland. In the confusion that followed, Borodin saw a chance to slip back through Poland into Russia. Telling Murphy, Fraina, and Roy that the road was dangerous and that he had to travel quickly and alone if he were to have any chance to get through, he left them behind in Berlin. Whether he went through Poland, which certainly would have been foolhardy, or by another route, by early May Borodin had reached Moscow.

7

Apparatchik

When Borodin reached Moscow in the spring of 1920, he had been away for over a year. In that time, he had crossed, mostly illegally, numerous borders dozens of times. Ever since he had left the United States two years before, he had lived a strenuous, and dangerous life, under constant threat of apprehension by border guards, security police, and intelligence agents. Now that he was back in Moscow, he might have expected a period of rest and relaxation. But it was not to be. By their own standards, Bolsheviks could not rest until the grave. For complicated emotional and historical reasons, Leninists believed rest only gave the enemy a chance to seize the initiative. Moreover, Russia's tactical situation in May 1920 did not lend itself to relaxation.

A harsh winter had already left the country weakened by starvation, plague, and rising discontent when, on April 26, the Polish general Jozef Pilsudski proclaimed his intention of taking the Ukraine. By May 8, he had advanced as far as Kiev. The Bolshevik forces, intent upon countering the White army of General Denikin in the northwest, were unprepared for an attack from Poland. It was a gloomy cast of delegates that gathered in April and May for the much-postponed Second Congress of the Comintern.

In the year since his departure, Borodin's reputation had grown apace. Reports of his exploits and successes, coming when the fires of revolution were burning low at home, only magnified his accomplishments. In some eyes, he was Borodin the magnificent, one who skipped across impassable borders as easily as others crossed Red Square, establishing parties and gathering disciples as he went. When he was pointed out, many said:

"There goes a great man." He was in favor with Lenin, who sent for him upon his arrival in Moscow, questioned him about his activities, and praised him. In the Russian capital at the time, in many places to mention that you knew Borodin was to guarantee immediate attention. But Borodin's enhanced reputation, though gratifying to his ego, also invited opposition. Within the struggle for Soviet power, struggles for personal position also took place. Borodin's successes attracted not only admiration but jealousy. And he was vulnerable: he had once been a Bundist; he had not been a steadfast Leninist in Chicago; he had not returned to Russia until a year and a half after the February Revolution, well after the Bolsheviks had seized power. In 1918, these had not been of primary importance, but with increased internal rivalry and an endangered revolution, such transgressions against orthodoxy had become a peril. Borodin was vulnerable not only because of the past but also because of more recent events. True, he had achieved notable successes on his trip to the New World. But he had not completely fulfilled all his charges—and where were the jewels? Borodin hadn't absconded with them. It might even be accepted that he didn't know where they were. But was it responsible to give $500,000 ($250,000? $25,000?) to a total stranger (the shipboard convert)?

As soon as Borodin arrived in Moscow, he was debriefed by various Comintern people, in addition to Lenin. His reports, which had preceded his return, had been read, studied, and admired, grudgingly or otherwise. He commented in what would soon be regarded as his typical "world historical" style on what he had observed, not only in the United States, Mexico, and Spain but also in Holland and in critically important Germany. In the information-starved Kremlin, Borodin, who seemed to have all the latest information, was a highly valued resource. At this point, on the eve of the Second Congress, his next assignment seemed obvious. With many of the delegates to the congress either recruited by him or personally acquainted with him through his recent sojourns in the West, his presence at the congress was needed. He was not a delegate, if only because he had no constituency either outside or inside Russia. But Mexican, Spanish, and Indian delegates had been personally enlisted by him. They looked to him for guidance in the ways of Moscow, and Moscow looked to him to provide that guidance. Others as well had become acquainted with him in Amsterdam and Berlin; for them too he represented the authority of the revolution—he was their adviser and confessor.

One of Borodin's next steps was to arrange for "his people" to see Lenin. He set up an appointment for Roy the third day after the latter arrived in Moscow, and for Fraina and Murphy soon after they arrived. Borodin, in their presence, phoned Lenin's secretary for the appointments; they were impressed by Borodin's easy access to Lenin and Lenin's willingness to see them on short notice. They were not aware that the entire procedure had been set up in advance. For Lenin, this was an opportunity to judge these "revolutionaries" rounded up from all over the world. Once the appointments were made, it was Borodin's task to shepherd the delegates at the meetings, suggesting appropriate behavior, discussing what Lenin might say, and indicating topics the delegates might want to raise. After the interview, Borodin would question the visitors. What had they thought of Lenin? What had Lenin said? It was up to Borodin to discern anything about the visitors' reactions which should be reported to his CI superiors. Thus, in addition to being adviser and confessor, Borodin was also informer.

Although superintending the delegates was now Borodin's chief duty, it was not his only one. Lenin had written important position papers for the congress, and they were not being translated into English to his satisfaction. Borodin was called in on the work, which was fateful. For if translating for Lenin was a one-time effort for Borodin, the documents he helped to translate would largely shape his future. As he faced the forthcoming congress of the International, Lenin was deeply concerned about his revolutionary message. The longed-for revolutions in the West had either not developed or had failed. The revolutionary situation that had existed at the end of the Great War had passed, and the new situation required new tactics.

Lenin had to explain the new scene to the delegates. He sought to do so in a pamphlet " 'Left-Wing' Communism: An Infantile Disease," written in April and May 1920. Lenin told the communist parties of the West—particularly those of Germany and Britain—that they must accommodate the latest developments. They had learned to attack; now they must learn to retreat. When necessary, they must compromise, accepting the discipline of the altered circumstances. When direct attack would not succeed, other approaches must be used. To recognize "only one road, only the direct road, that will not permit tacking, maneuvering, compromising" would be a mistake; indeed, it had already done harm.

Closely identified with the strategy for the developed countries which Lenin set forth in " 'Left-Wing' Communism" was another for the national liberation movement, outlined in the collateral "Preliminary Draft Theses on the National and Colonial Questions." In it Lenin emphasized that the first priority for communists, from whatever country, had now become the "struggle of the world bourgeoisie against the Soviet Russian Republic." Only the victory of the Soviet system could assure salvation for colonial peoples. Soviet Russia needed their help in undermining international capitalism since Russia's continued survival was essential to their future.

" 'Left-Wing' Communism" and the "Draft Theses" were vastly important to Lenin. He had written them for the congress and he wanted to get them into delegates' hands as quickly as possible. But Lenin had written in Russian, which was understood by few of the delegates. Accordingly, he gave Karl Radek, the number-two man in the CI, the job of translation. As usual, English presented the biggest problem. Lenin's dissatisfaction with the work of the usual translators led Radek to turn to Borodin. But Borodin's efforts with " 'Left-Wing' Communism" proved no more satisfactory. Lenin told Borodin either to do a better job or to organize a group that could. Borodin chose the latter alternative. But getting a translation pleasing to Lenin was difficult, particularly because he kept changing the text. On the eve of the opening of the congress, Lenin sent a telegram to Kamenev, Borodin, and Radek, in that order, instructing them to reread the texts of " 'Left-Wing' Communism" in English and in French to make sure that alterations in the original were correctly reflected in the other versions.

This telegram of July 17, besides indicating the company Borodin was keeping in the upper echelons of the CI, also showed the importance Lenin attached to the announcement that new tactics were needed for the burgeoning communist parties of the world. In many ways " 'Left-Wing' Communism" is the most powerful pamphlet Lenin ever wrote. It has been used by the international movement as a basic training manual for over fifty years. Murphy called it "one of the most profound pieces of writing on revolutionary theory in relation to questions of strategy and tactics ever written and it has probably influenced my own political development more than any other book in the armoury of revolutionary Socialism and Communism."[1] Seemingly, it had no less influence on Borodin. Its message of adjustment and accommodation was one he understood and acted upon—too well, his detractors would later charge.

The Second Congress of the Comintern had two chief objectives. The first was to separate the dependable comrades from the chaff of anarchists, vague leftists, socialists, and others who had been brought to Moscow's side by the revolution, but who could not be relied upon to follow Moscow's orders. The second objective was to impose upon the movement the strategy developed in " 'Left-Wing' Communism"—that immediate world revolution was unlikely and that revolutionary forces must prepare for the long haul. When it actually convened, the congress opened in circumstances that made the conservatism of the new Leninist views seem premature to many revolutionaries. Suddenly the revolutionary worm seemed to turn. Notable victories had been scored by the Red Army over the Whites. The intervention of the Western powers had slackened. For nearly two years, Russia had been cut off from the rest of the world; this period seemed now to be ending. Most encouraging of all, Pilsudski's march into the Ukraine had been turned back. While the congress was meeting, the Red Army under Marshal Tukhachevsky was speeding, largely without opposition, across Poland toward Warsaw. A Red Poland seemed imminent. And then—a Red Germany and a Red France and a Red Italy?

Gathered together at the Second Congress were over two hundred representatives from thirty-five countries who had come to hear the message of revolution and to spread it to the corners of the globe. As news of victories in Poland came in, great enthusiasm engulfed the congress. The outbreak of the revolution in the

West, the delegates were convinced, was only weeks away. Yet Lenin spoke of retreat, of achieving progress through joining trade unions and working for election to parliaments—not of the immediate seizure of power. Why, at a moment when success seemed imminent, did Lenin persist in a conservative line? Because Lenin thought he perceived two things: that the revolutionary situation of 1918 and early 1919 had passed; and that, as a result of war, civil war, and foreign intervention, Soviet Russia was weak. It could not squander its meager resources and endanger its own survival by seeking to spark an international revolution whose timbers had become water-logged.

Yet Lenin still hoped for revolution. And when, in the summer of 1920, the Red Army had Pilsudski on the run and there was hope that the Red Army might become the chief vehicle for revolutionary contagion, Lenin sent his forces across Poland. But before long, as the army ran out of gas and the workers in the West failed to revolt, Lenin realized that his earlier judgment, set forth in " 'Left-Wing' Communism," was correct. Although many at the congress did not agree, Lenin's views dominated the congress. By the time it closed, on August 7, he had succeeded in getting it to accept " 'Left-Wing' Communism." But Lenin had not gone unchallenged. On several occasions he felt obliged to make concessions, particularly to representatives of the colonial world whom he wished to cultivate. One such concession was made to Roy, who had impressed Lenin as he had Borodin. Roy's thesis—that in underdeveloped countries the national liberation forces should not trust the national bourgeoisie to help free their land from colonial rule—was allowed to coexist with Lenin's call for class cooperation. Subsequently Roy's position was obscured in the official ideology. But Roy did not forget. Years later, in a situation of immense consequence for Borodin, he emphasized that the Second Congress of the CI had accepted his position.

Upon the conclusion of the Second Congress, just as at the First, Borodin was set to work carrying out the purposes of the congress. He worked tirelessly, traveling, delivering instructions, attending meetings. Fishers of souls were no longer so urgently required, but evangelism had become second nature and his services were still required for recruitment, indoctrination, and supervision. His travels carried him chiefly to Germany. He was in Berlin so often that a contemporary saw him as "commuting" between there and Moscow. But at least once he traveled to Madrid in November to help extend the CI network in Spain and supervise developments since his earlier visit—and to represent the Soviet government at the International Postal Congress. Soviet Russia had not yet reintroduced postage stamps, and it was not until after Borodin's presence at the congress in late 1920 that Russian stamps reappeared.

Berlin had become the center of greatly expanded underground operations. During 1919 and early 1920 there had been such activity in Berlin, but it had focused chiefly on getting foreign delegates and a few Russian couriers in and out of Russia. Now there was the need to augment the operation, as regular contacts with an increasing network of parties throughout Europe were established. There were a number of substations on the Red underground railway but, outside of Russia, Berlin was the headquarters. Borodin played a key role in setting up the greatly expanded apparatus required for providing visas, papers, and identity cards for those who traveled the railway. Sometimes, as Borodin shuttled back and forth to Berlin (now a much safer journey than it had been a few months earlier), he was alone; sometimes he escorted other CI members being dispatched abroad, evaluating and indoctrinating them as they traveled. On a trip from Moscow in early October 1920, Borodin brought out both Fraina and Gomez, his old friend from Mexico City. A Latin American bureau for the CI was planned, and Fraina and the Japanese communist, Sen Katayama, assisted by Gomez, were assigned to take charge.

Fraina, whom Borodin had met in Amsterdam and Amersfoort and whose travel he had supervised two thirds of the way into Russia, was part of Borodin's "string," someone for whom, in a sense, Borodin was responsible. Fraina gave Borodin endless problems. First, an earlier charge that Fraina was a spy, based on the fact that his trip to Soviet Russia had been expedited by foreign intelligence agencies, continued to persist. Although Fraina had been cleared by both the Central Executive Committee of his own Communist Party of America and by the Soviet Bureau in New York, the charges preceded him to Moscow, circulated by Santori Nuorteva, a delegate to the Second Congress. Again, a committee was appointed to investigate the charges. Finally in September Fraina, who by now had become far more important to the Comintern because their "other" American, John Reed, had just died of cholera, was again cleared.

It was not just Fraina "the spy" who complicated things for Borodin. It was also Fraina "the lover." Fraina was in Moscow for only a few months, and he would never return, but he left Russia with a permanent memento of his sojourn—a wife. At the time she spoke no English and he no Russian, but they had the revolution in common—she was a secretary in the CI pool—and he had courted her by whistling "Beautiful Ohio" and "Till We Meet Again," tunes she apparently loved. The marriage, which followed a three-week courtship, took place without Borodin's knowledge. When he heard about it, he called Fraina a fool and thereafter rarely left him alone. When Fraina left Russia for the West—he was, among other things, to order the warring American communist parties to unite—he had to leave his wife behind. The separation was a painful one for the romantic Fraina, and he wrote to Esther: "I am not interested in anything. My main feeling is longing for you."

Borodin was able to get Fraina off to America through Italy. But when Fraina arrived in his native Italy, he became ill and had to return to Berlin. There he asked Lenin to permit his wife to join him. Lenin, perhaps thinking that Fraina was about to die on his hands as Reed had done, personally telephoned his consent. When Esther arrived at Fraina's pension, she found him in bed, with Borodin nearby examining an assortment of bottles to determine which medicine Fraina needed next. Once his wife was on the scene, however, Fraina's recovery was "miraculous." According to Mrs. Fraina, the illness had not been feigned; it was a case of genuine lovesickness. Borodin told Fraina when he had recovered, "You were not sick, you were lovesick, you poor fish." Both Frainas were so intrigued with the term that they began calling each other "fish." The disgusted Borodin thereafter referred to them as the "happy aquarium." "Fish" became one of Fraina's pseudonyms. In the end, Fraina, who later took the name Corey, proved to be hardly worth the effort. In 1922, he, with his wife and newborn daughter, left their CI assignment in Mexico without permission and returned to New York, where both husband and wife worked in a sweatshop until Fraina could get back into publishing, where he had professional competence. Later he became advertising manager of *Physical Culture* before going to teach at Antioch College.

Borodin's Berlin activities in the aftermath of the Second CI Congress included involvement in German politics. In preparing for the long haul, Lenin had directed the CI to take over working-class, trade-union, and youth organizations wherever it could. In Germany the Comintern tried to split the largest left party, the mass United Socialist Party of Germany (USPD) and amalgamate its more radical sector with the German Communist Party (KPD). But uncertain of success and seeking to hedge its bets, it gave Borodin the task of negotiating with the smaller Communist Workers' Party of Germany (KAPD), keeping it on the hook in case the merger failed. For over a month Borodin lived in rooms on Berlin's Kurfürstendamm, near KAPD headquarters, posing as a Russian immigrant and keeping in close contact with the KAPD. When the absorption of the USPD's left had been completed and the new party formed, it was no longer necessary to maintain KAPD contacts, and Borodin was ordered to drop them.

Later Borodin was involved in CI efforts to capture the German-based Communist Youth International, which, in spite of its name, was not a creation of the Comintern but an outgrowth of the pre-World War I Socialist Youth International. Headed by the indefatigable Willi Münzenberg, the CYI was a radical organization, prepared to accept the CI program. It was "revisionist" only in one respect: it insisted upon maintaining its independence. The struggle between Münzenberg's organization and Moscow centered on the symbolic issue of where the next CYI congress would be held: in Berlin or in Moscow. Borodin was ordered by the Executive Committee of the CI to attend the next meeting of the CYI executive and to make Moscow's position clear. At the meeting, Münzenberg pleaded with the executive to hold the next congress in the West, arguing that the political situation demanded it. To send delegates to Moscow now, when revolutionary potential was thriving, would be to remove them from the struggle for over a month at a most critical time.

One by one, all members of the CYI executive identified with Münzenberg's remarks—except Borodin and a confederate. Borodin then accused the executive of a serious breach of discipline in insisting on a Berlin meeting. The decision to meet in Moscow, he said, was not debatable; it had already been made. He warned them of the consequences of failing to acquiesce. In the end, the executive voted to send three delegates to Russia to tell Comintern headquarters that Moscow had been right all the time. The congress was held in Russia.

Borodin was busy in Berlin in late 1920 and early 1921. But Berlin was only one end of the route he regularly traveled. At the other end, in Moscow, he was also busy. There his activities revolved chiefly around M. N. Roy. Borodin's meeting with Roy in Mexico had been, perhaps, his luckiest political break. It came after he had failed to transmit funds to the Soviet Bureau in New York. His mission to the New World had seemed a failure. Then he met Roy, who gave him money to tide the bureau over, brought him into contact with the Mexican government, helped him establish a foothold for CI activities in Latin America, and became Borodin's chief convert to communism and the cause of the International. Intellectually acute and with good revolutionary credentials, Roy seemed an ideal candidate to spread Bolshevism to Asia. And Borodin had found him, nurtured him, won and delivered him. In Moscow's eyes this was no small jewel in Borodin's crown and helped to overshadow the loss of those other jewels.

But Roy had now become somewhat reluctant to accept the role that Moscow envisaged for him—that of leading the Indian revolution. India was too small. Even all of Asia was not acceptable because it was too remote from the international revolution he thought would soon break out in Europe. Shortly after the end of the Second CI Congress, when instructed to head the Congress of the Peoples of the East (designed to win Asian nationalists to Moscow's banner) he refused even to attend. When appointed to the Central Asian bureau of the CI, with headquarters in Tashkent, he excused himself on grounds that the Soviet ambassadorship to Afghanistan, a job he suddenly fancied, was still unsettled. Repeatedly, Borodin had to remind Roy that "discipline was the highest Bolshevik virtue."

While Borodin tried to keep an eye on Roy, there was no

dearth of new candidates for supervision—and conversion. Only now Borodin needn't scour the world for them. They had come to Moscow on their own. One of the most picturesque was Enver Pasha, the "Ludendorff" of World War I Turkey. Following the defeat of his country, his fortunes declined. A pretentious man, he never appeared in public except in full-dress military uniform, replete with large black tarboosh, built up to conceal his short stature. But Moscow recognized his continued support in the Turkish army and among the upper class and the clergy. He dreamed of reconstructing Tamerlane's empire in Central Asia and, culminating in a march into India, striking at the heart of the British empire.

But taking advantage of Enver Pasha's troublemaking potential was complicated by Moscow's commitment to Kemal Pasha. Naturally Kemal wanted no competition. Enver's mere presence in Russia was an embarrassment to Moscow. Enver could be used only if he could be won over to the international revolution, weaned away from his Turkish preoccupation. Borodin and Roy were given the job of directing his thinking and activities accordingly. They spoke with him repeatedly on the grounds of the Sugar Palace (named for its builders, the Kharistonenko family, who had made its fortune in sugar), the prerevolutionary capitalist manse where the three, as well as other CI and foreign commissariat personnel and their guests, lived. Enver was told the advantages of concentrating on the international revolution. It alone represented the future and the sure source of Middle Eastern liberation. But Enver, more of a "White" than a "Red," would not be diverted from Turkey or cast his lot with Kemal, as Borodin and Roy suggested. Sizing up the sterility of his hopes of Soviet aid, Enver left Moscow and assumed leadership of the right-wing anti-Soviet Bokharan nationalist movement, the Bashmachi. Two years later he died, in a skirmish against a Red detachment near the Afghan frontier. It has been alleged again and again that Borodin was heavily involved during this period in Turkish-Soviet affairs and that he was with Kemal in Anatolia. The chief basis for such an allegation would seem to be that there was a superficial similarity between the situations in Turkey and China, where Borodin was to go later, and the tactics employed in both by the Bolsheviks. But there is no proof that

Borodin was ever in Turkey. He could not have been there in 1920 because he was engaged elsewhere. In early 1921 he might have been there, since there are some months when his precise whereabouts are unknown. But the trip from Moscow to Ankara was a long and hazardous one, taking four to eight weeks, and Borodin did not disappear long enough to have permitted the journey, let alone remain on the scene. There is no indication that, other than in his talks with Enver Pasha, Borodin had any involvement in Turkish affairs. Moreover, there is no evidence that Kemal ever had Russian political advisers, though he did have military ones.

But though Borodin failed with Enver Pasha, there were other assignments and attempts to make converts, including a fascinating experience with the legendary Clare Sheridan. Sheridan was a vivacious, free-spirited sculptor and part-time journalist, a post–World War I emancipated daughter of the English aristocracy and a cousin of Winston Churchill (whom Lenin often cited as Russia's greatest enemy). Top Bolshevik leader Lev Kamenev met her in London and brought her back to Moscow in 1920, ostensibly to make busts of Lenin and Trotsky but hoping, not without some encouragement from her, to enlist her in the cause. According to Sheridan, Kamenev attempted to install her in his Kremlin apartment, but Madame Kamenev, Trotsky's sister, would have none of this *menage à trois*. Sheridan ended up in the Sugar Palace, where Borodin was asked to "guide" her. He took her on long walks, engaged her in philosophical discussions, captivated her with his "world historical" understanding, and gradually unfurled communism to her as, locked arm in arm, they paced for hours in his cathedral-like room.

Sheridan was not unappreciative of Borodin and his efforts. She devoted much of a book on her Moscow trip to him, years before he became a world figure. And while working on her famous bust of Lenin, she suggested to Lenin that he appoint Borodin ambassador to Great Britain. But she was not prepared to join the Bolsheviks. After she left for London, in a gold-appointed private railroad car, she indicated her continuing affinity for the West by writing a series of articles on her Russian venture for the *Times* (London) and the *New York Times* and following them up with magazine pieces and a book.

Besides Enver Pasha and Clare Sheridan, other Sugar Palace sojourners were entrusted to Borodin, the master proselytizer and cicerone. For example, there was Isadora Duncan, the *première danseuse* of the Western world, whom Borodin just "happened" upon while she and her foster daughter Irma were traipsing in their standard diaphanous garb around Moscow's Sparrow Hills. But with none of these did Borodin have the success that he enjoyed with Roy. Still he kept trying, among his other activities, during the fall and winter following the Second Congress of the Comintern when many, in spite of what Lenin had said and written, were convinced that the moment for the revolution to break out in Western Europe was finally at hand.

8

Assignment in England

The expectation, held by many Comintern members after the Second Congress, that revolution could occur momentarily in Europe was hardly realistic. Intellectually, many of the CI operatives had recognized for some time that the prospects for revolution were dim. But emotionally there was still hope that the revolution was imminent; and for many, the hope was strong enough to cloud reality. In March 1921 a series of events injected a harsh note of realism into the picture.

First, riots broke out in the Mansfield mines in Prussian Saxony, an area with strong communist sympathies. The German Reichswehr moved against the rioters, occupying the area and disarming the workers. When the workers answered with acts of violence, many in CI headquarters in Moscow concluded that the German proletariat was at last ready to move. Responding to Moscow directives, not sent out without heated opposition, the Central Committee of the German party called the workers to arms and proclaimed open insurrection against the government. But the fighting language of the Central Committee was not equaled by the revolutionary will of the masses. The ensuing defeat of the revolutionary cause in Germany in March 1921 approached the proportions of a major disaster. More than half of the party's membership abandoned its ranks almost at once. For those in the CI who had, against strong opposition, insisted that Germany was ripe for revolution, the continuation of a policy based on the hypothesis that revolution in the West was at hand and was now palpably untenable.

The need to face reality was further carried to the CI by a domestic disaster that simultaneously threatened the Russian part.

During the first week in March, the Soviet regime was faced by an uprising of sailors and soldiers stationed at the Kronstadt fortress in the Neva estuary near Petrograd. During the revolution and the civil war, the Kronstadt garrison had been counted among the Bolsheviks' most loyal troops. Their demands reflected the disillusion, frustration, and anger of the workers and particularly the peasants, who were heavily represented in the garrison personnel. Starvation stalked Russia's countryside. Much of the food produced on the farms was seized at gunpoint by Red Army detachments. Even so, there was little in the cities to eat and the workers bridled under a rigid military discipline which seemed more oppressive, many felt, than that of the tsarist regime. The Kronstadt detachment, reflecting the discontent of town and country, began calling for another revolution and for "soviets without Bolsheviks." Kronstadt looked upon itself increasingly as representative of the entire country against Lenin and his government.

Sensing that his regime was in mortal danger and determined to crush the opposition, Lenin put Trotsky and Tukhachevsky in charge of the military operations. For ten days the Kronstadt garrison held out against the Red Army units sent against them. Attempts were made by Kronstadt to arouse support beyond the base. But the rest of the country did not respond, in part because it did not know what was happening at Kronstadt. On March 18, during a snowstorm, a desperate attack was launched by Tukhachevsky across the ice; it was successful and the resistance was stilled.

The regime had been saved, but the meaning of Kronstadt was clear. The Bolsheviks, as Lenin had known even before, lacked popular support. The Kremlin was in danger of losing control. Accordingly, it was necessary to retreat, to ease up, to weaken the thrust of the revolution. The implications of Kronstadt permeated the Moscow atmosphere and, together with the failure in Germany, severely dampened revolutionary optimism. When, at the same time, treaties were signed by the Soviet state with Persia, Afghanistan, Turkey, Poland, and the imperialist giant Britain, treaties signifying a policy of conciliation and stability, the hands of those who wanted revolution *now*, and who sought to exploit every possible revolutionary situation, were further tied. Lenin decided that for the time being the security of the Soviet state depended upon its acceptance by its neighbors and the Great Powers. To continue pushing revolution where prospects for success were dim was to minimize the possibility of such acceptance and to undermine the safety of Soviet Russia. In revolutionary as in domestic policy, the late spring and summer of 1921 heralded a backing away from militance—and a turning toward consolidation until more favorable days should come.

On February 10, 1921, Borodin crossed back into Russia from Berlin, traveling via Stettin, Tallinn, and Riga. He would not travel abroad for another year. Partly this was because of the more limited Comintern vision. But events also conspired against Borodin personally.

More than a year earlier a decision had been made to emphasize "organization" in CI. Now as the potential for revolution shrank, that decision received increased attention. The CI decided to strengthen its own apparatus. One of those brought into the CI at this time to bring its international and often independent-minded personnel under control was Osip Pyatnitsky, a party professional since 1903. After the revolution, he had organized the Moscow railroad region and had brought its workers under party control. Now he was given the job of doing the same for the CI.

Specifically, Pyatnitsky was controller of Comintern funds. He was presented with a budget, and he insisted on strict principles of cost accountability. For example, he began to examine the records of past CI expenditures. In the rush to foment an international revolution, no one had paid close attention to the outlay of funds. Now Pyatnitsky noted that huge and unaccounted sums had been disbursed on several occasions, including the jewels Borodin was to smuggle into America. There was no record of their delivery; no acknowledgment, no chits. Pyatnitsky ordered an investigation. Borodin was in Moscow at the time and, although not particularly apprehensive, he was aware that trouble could come. A huge number of rubles was involved. He was more exasperated than alarmed—exasperated that the incident had occurred, that he had let the jewels out of his sight, that they had disappeared, that after all his services he was suspected, that he was still not the eminent figure he aspired to be, that others could still harass him for what, in the total revolutionary picture, seemed such a small matter. More than once Borodin confessed to being a misanthrope. He could upon occasion be bitter, and this was one of those times.

The transformation of the Comintern and his own situation forced upon Borodin, as it did others during this period, an opportunity to reflect. No longer was there a headlong rush to get things done. The comrades of all races, sexes, habits, and preferences who peopled the CI headquarters followed a more leisurely pattern. At the Lux Hotel where many of them lived, there were nightly soirées, often interrupted near midnight when the participants rushed out to get to the special shop for the party-privileged before it closed. There they would pick up a few bottles of vodka and continue "deliberating" into the early hours of the morning. Roy complained that, though occupied at night, he had to look for things to do during the day. He wanted "active revolutionary work." The reduced pace made comrades available for odd jobs. Once when Lenin wanted to know about third parties in American politics, especially the Farmer-Labor Party and its activities in North Dakota, Borodin was happy for work to do. He promised a report in five days.

For three years Borodin had been so involved in the work of the revolution that only infrequently and fleetingly had he pondered his future. For better or for worse, it was with the world revolution or, that revolution being postponed, its apparat. He could not return to being a schoolteacher in Chicago, even if so disposed. His activities as a Comintern agent, known to intelligence services in the West, precluded that, particularly while the "red scare" continued in full swing in the United States. He made his commitment to the Bolshevik way and, whatever his doubts, his future was there. But what had all his risks and frenzied activity brought him? He still took orders. He was given small jobs like riding herd on an impetuous ballerina and doing research on sideshow political parties in midwestern America. Would he ever have an opportunity to play the large role on the world historical scene he had so often unfolded to his listeners? Given the diminished state of the international revolution and his own prospects, it did not seem likely. In the midst of revolutionary and personal doldrums, he must have wondered: Was it right to leave Chicago? How were things with his family? It was a long time since he had taken the eastbound express to Moscow.

Borodin would never get back to Chicago, but he would soon see Fanya, Fred, and Norman. As the investigation into the disappearance of the jewels developed, witness after witness was called to testify. Borodin was officially cleared but he remained under a cloud. Then one day shortly afterward, Borodin received a coded message from Fanya. The jewels had arrived; what should she do? Borodin cabled her to come at once. Sometime later Fanya arrived in Moscow with the jewels and the boys. Now there would be another problem, a family. But Borodin had not previously permitted it to interfere with his revolutionary career; nor would it do so now. In any case, he was happy to have his family with him and relieved to be able to hand the jewels back. Now Borodin was fully restored to grace. There were still those who resented his name dropping, his air of knowing more than he was telling, and his comprehensive expositions of this and that. Stories about what he had been and done—his earlier Menshevism in Chicago—persisted. But he was not without supporters in high party circles.

In the second quarter of 1921, Karl Radek, one of the top CI leaders, sought assistance in dealing with what many saw as a potentially revolutionary situation in England; Borodin was his man. The winter of 1920–21 had been an economic disaster for England. Between December 1920 and March 1921 unemployment doubled. In coal, engineering, and cotton towns, over 50 percent of the labor force was out of work. On March 31, the government, seeking to minimize its involvement in a rapidly worsening situation, turned the wartime nationalized coalmines back to their owners. The owners, to avert near bankruptcy, began paying miners at marginal pits lower rates than in high-quality mines. The miners demanded a national pool to equalize wages; the owners refused. On April 1, with a large surplus of coal on hand and all the trump cards in hand, the owners began a lockout.

At this point the miners, who had the best-organized union in Britain, issued a general-strike call, but their erstwhile allies in the railroad and transport unions—the so-called Triple Alliance—urged caution. With surpluses on hand and the owners willing to close down, this was no time for a general strike. But the miners, the most radical of the unionists, persisted; some argued that British capitalism was strong and could afford the wage pool; others insisted it was weak and could be shoved over the edge into socialism. Although the other unions wanted the strike call rescinded, the miner leadership refused by a single vote to do so. On what would come to be known as Black Friday, just a few hours before the strike was to begin, the railroad and transport unions announced their nonparticipation, and the radical miners were left to go it alone. They did; they went out and stayed out until July 1. But in the end they had to accept terms worse than what they could have obtained in April.

The bitterness engendered by the "Black Friday betrayal" lent itself to exploitation by the British Communist Party (CPGB). But the CPGB was a loosely organized, fragmented group of unusually idiosyncratic radicals, unable to seize the hour. Its essentially non-English membership—it was made up largely of Irish, Welsh, and Russians—militated against achieving a mass following. Its intellectuals were mostly English, but they were unwilling to accept the centralized control the Comintern demanded. Moreover, as popular support for Russian Bolshevism increased in the United Kingdom, the British government took alarm and cracked down on the infant CPGB, establishing effective surveillance over its activities.

From Moscow's vantage point, however, England seemed ripe for communist advances. Borodin was put on the case. He still had other responsibilities, such as keeping the restless, trouble-prone Roy out of mischief, but increasingly Britain became Borodin's full-time assignment. Radek gave Borodin the job of preparing a report on the April-July miners' strike for the Executive Committee of the Comintern. Later Radek would praise the report in an address on the English question during the Third Comintern Congress. In that speech Radek said that, since the CPGB had been doing little in mining areas that were obviously ripe for organization, he had assigned "our friend Borodin" the job of "circulating an inquiry" among the delegates from Britain at the Third Congress. The results indicated, said Radek, that while the CPGB had called some organizational meetings among miners, these had been run haphazardly. To the question, "What do you tell the masses?" one respondent replied: "When I ascend the rostrum at a meeting, I know as little about what I am going to say as the man in the moon; but being a Communist, I find my way along as I speak."[1]

Radek was incensed at such insouciance. It was evident, he said, that the CPGB had no line. In many places, the party remained disguised as "workers' committees," so that credit for effective action and propaganda could not possibly go to the CPGB. The British party should direct a mass movement, but now it was not doing "even the simplest and most important things that are to be done in this sphere."[2] More and more, Borodin was given the job of telling the British comrades precisely what Moscow thought needed to be done. Radek and Lenin, who had optimistically assessed the revolutionary potential of the British miners, were both pleased with Borodin's performance. After Fanya's arrival with the jewels, eliminating that nagging problem, developing English communism increasingly became his major responsibility. In the autumn and winter of 1921, after the Third CI Congress, two successive issues of *Kommunisticheskii internatsional,*[3] the official CI journal, carried articles by Borodin criticizing the CPGB and giving it marching orders.

As Borodin became familiar with the English scene, he became convinced that Britain, in the spring of 1921, had represented a revolutionary situation but that the leaders of the workers' movement had betrayed the masses to the capitalists. His research indicated, Borodin said, that the masses were now receptive to fresh communist leadership—and that such leadership might soon lead the masses into battle. Borodin incorporated these conclusions in a monograph, "The History of the Great Betrayal," the longest of his published writings.[4]

In the style of Lenin, "The History of the Great Betrayal" cited abundant newspaper sources (*Daily Herald, Labor Leader, Times, Manchester Guardian*), quoted interviews, and provided tables as it sought to marshal "scientific" evidence. Borodin indicated in considerable detail the extent of the postwar disaster that had hit the British coal industry and argued that British capitalism was determined to use the crisis to destroy the unions. For their part, the workers were itching for confrontation, he said. Their spirit had not been dampened by unemployment or the fear of it. The "ghost of unemployment, depriving the worker of his will," was not present in Britain in the spring of 1921. Borodin listed town after town—Manchester, Lancaster, Cardiff, Liverpool, Norwich, Peterboro, Hamilton—where the workers were prepared to support the general strike. Dockers, sailors, stokers, tramway men, railroad and electrical workers were all ready to go out. But the call never came because the leaders were afraid; the specter of revolution had frightened them. In various ways they had been seduced by capitalism, including fraudulent appeals to patriotism. The interests of the nation, not of their class, came first with them.

And so the workers' cause failed. But, according to Borodin, it need not have happened. The government was frightened; it was on the run. Had the Triple Alliance held fast, there would have been no electricity, no train service, no newspapers. The capitalists quaked at the prospect, but it was the union leaders who surrendered. When it was all over, the workers were furious. "Once again we have been betrayed," they complained. Some refused to credit the capitulation and continued preparing for the strike. In other places they demanded the resignation of "treacherous" leaders. As many as 10,000 workers attended a single protest meeting. For nine pages, Borodin recorded the anger of the workers. Various excuses were given for the capitulation, including that the workers were apathetic and exhausted by the war. But where was that apathy, asked Borodin? The coalminers, although forced to act alone, had carried out a three-month strike involving a million workers. The workers were ready, but it is the leaders who failed.

"The History of the Great Betrayal" was Borodin's testimony on England's revolutionary potential. It rang with a conviction typical of CI journalism. But although Borodin wrote as if the English revolution was at hand, this didn't mean that he (or the CI leadership) believed it meant tomorrow. However, manifesting a proper revolutionary attitude—even though actual expectations might be more conservative—helped Borodin toward his next assignment: on-the-scene reorganization of the British communist movement. Borodin's mission to Britain would importantly affect his future, although he may not have foreseen this when the assignment was made. He knew the opportunity for revolution in Britain had at least temporarily passed. But there was an opportunity to prove himself after the jewel crisis. And he was gratified at being put to work again, particularly when so many Comintern hands were idle.

In early 1922, when Borodin arrived in Britain, the British Communist Party, despite Black Friday, was in disarray. It had no funds, it was losing members, and it was plagued by poor organization. Its difficulties facilitated Borodin's task of reorganization, of imposing Leninist democratic centralism and CI domination. Though some elements of the party, accustomed to the local autonomy characteristic of British socialism, strongly opposed central controls, others, particularly those who had been to Moscow, were convinced of its necessity. In February 1922 a three-man British delegation consisting of Harry Pollitt, Arthur McMannus, and Nat Watkins, all of whom favored democratic centralism, were summoned to Moscow to consult with the ECCI on strategies for reorganizing the CPGB. When they returned to London, Borodin went along as CI representative. They got there in time for a special policy conference (later renamed the Fourth Congress) of the CPGB, which met in St. Pancras Townhall on March 18 to fight over the future of British communism.

The party executive violently opposed the reorganization Moscow sought, and characteristically attempted to handle Moscow's "suggestions" by endorsing them and then ignoring them. But at this point, by prearrangement William Gallacher, a staunch supporter of the Moscow line, proposed the establishment of a commission to "examine the organizational matter" and to prepare plans for implementing CI instructions at the next party meeting. It was further stipulated that none of the members of the new commission should be drawn from the existing party executive, ensuring that those most strongly opposed to reorganization would not be on the commission. Gallacher's proposal was overwhelmingly supported from the floor. Thus within days after Borodin's arrival in England, the task was well begun.

The Gallacher strategy had been planned in Moscow. Even the membership of the three-man reorganization commission had been agreed upon there. Beginning on March 29, and for several months afterward, the commission met regularly, usually with Borodin present. Working in his accustomed style of depicting the grand scene and bringing his own influence and the authority of the revolution to bear upon the chairman of the commission (the half-Indian Marxist ideologist Ranjani Palme Dutt), the Leninist norms of organizations were placed in the British context. The eighty-page report, which reshaped the history of the CPGB, has been described by impartial observers as brilliant, and credit for this generally is given to Dutt, who took two firsts at Oxford. But behind him was the heavy hand of Moscow, administered by the fine hand of Borodin, who had learned from his experience with Roy how to handle Brahmins.

While Borodin's chief focus in England was to oversee the reorganization of the CPGB, his activities were not limited to that. A year earlier Lenin had been excited by information conveyed by Thomas Bell, then in Moscow for the Third CI Congress, that the South Wales Miners' Federation had decided to affiliate with the CI. "Perhaps it is the beginning of the real proletarian mass movement in Great Britain," Lenin wrote.[5] He wanted Borodin to learn more about the miners of South Wales as well as those in Fifeshire, who were rather consistent supporters of Bolshevik positions. In the late spring and early summer of 1922, after the work of the reorganization commission was well underway, Borodin visited both South Wales and Fifeshire, as well as other places. He traveled from union local to local to increase his knowledge of the British situation, to encourage membership in the CI's international trade-union apparatus, the Profintern— "Prof" is an abbreviation for "Profsoyuz," the Russian word for trade union—and to gauge rank-and-file sentiment should another crisis arise.

In his explorations of the coal country, Borodin's guide and companion was J. T. Murphy, whom he had known two years earlier in Amsterdam and Amersfoort and had then escorted partway to Moscow for the Second CI Congress. Borodin and Murphy ranged widely and, where possible, participated in union, leftist, and party activities. Together they attended the meeting of the British bureau of the Profintern, held in London in July. At the meeting of the miners' conference in Blackpool,

Borodin was influential in forming the Minority Movement, which would attain historic significance in British labor history.

Borodin, then, acted energetically and effectively in England. The CPGB was put on the road to reorganization as Moscow wished. He had familiarized himself with British labor and politics, became acquainted with much of the leadership on the left, and began to establish his own authority, over and beyond that of the revolution. But, increasingly, he wondered if he would have time to complete his mission. In 1922, in addition to its other woes, CPGB faced increased police pressure. The British authorities, uneasy about the possibility of revolution, strengthened their surveillance of the left. Informers were planted in party ranks, a process facilitated by the ordinarily open operations of the CPGB. Its meetings were monitored. On one occasion police agents were discovered underneath the stage of a theater where a meeting was taking place, and the party called in other police to arrest them. An intensive search was being made for those who had entered the country illegally and for resident aliens who had joined the party and were therefore subject to deportation.

For several months, Borodin apparently escaped detection. Not until July 7 was his presence in England confirmed by Scotland Yard. From then on he was watched closely, the Special Branch regarding him as a "most dangerous person." Scotland Yard knew of his presence at the London meeting of the British bureau of the Profintern and of his role at the conference of the Miners' Federation at Blackpool.[6] It could arrest him at any time. The moment came in late August in Scotland, where Borodin had gone while visiting local branches. Why the police stepped in at this point is unclear. Did they fear his continuing efforts to gather support? Or did they conclude that no more information would be gathered by allowing him continued freedom? Or did they fear that he was traveling north prior to fleeing the country?

In any case, information reached Scotland Yard that Borodin would arrive in Glasgow on the afternoon of August 22. On that day a telephone call and a confirming telegram were sent to Glasgow advising that George Brown, the name Borodin was using in England, would contact a local "anarchist and communist," Freda Cohen. A watch was put on Cohen. At 6:50 that evening she left her house and went to the Scottish Labor College. Fifteen minutes after she entered, fifty-three detectives swooped down on the college and found nineteen men and women in one of the meeting rooms. Seventeen were seated around a table; two were seated on chairs at the back of the room. One of these was Borodin, the other Murphy. Borodin, notes in hand, was preparing to speak to the group at the moment he was seized. He had been in Glasgow two and a half hours. "I knew from his [Borodin's] appearance," wrote the chief constable in his official report, "that he was a foreigner or a person of foreign extraction, and I asked him his name. He told me that his name was George Brown. I said to him, 'You are a foreigner,' and he replied, 'Yes.' "[7] Then Borodin was asked for his passport. He slapped his trouser pocket and said that "this—meaning money—had been his passport." The interrogation had begun.

Borodin had long ago decided in case of apprehension to deny his Soviet affiliation. To admit that he was a Soviet subject would endanger recently improved British-Russian relations, which were deemed important in Moscow. Acknowledgment would prove that the Soviets, while seeking friendly relations with the British government, were at the same time dispatching agents to help overthrow the British government. Accordingly, Borodin never admitted to Soviet citizenship; nor did the Soviet government recognize him as a Soviet subject during his imprisonment. When questioned, he variously described himself as a Yugoslav, Czech, or Austrian subject of "Slavonic" extraction. Confronted with evidence of his Russian connections, he admitted that he had been in Russia two years previously, but he steadfastly denied he was Russian. Scotland Yard contacted Prague and Belgrade regarding Borodin's citizenship, but in both cases fruitlessly. Later when Borodin needed a national identity, because a deportee needed a passport to travel, Borodin told the chief constable not to worry about a passport—"a few days" before he was to be released, one would be forthcoming.[8] But at about the same time, Borodin recommended to the British police that an attempt be made to secure a German passport for him.

A month later, Borodin's solicitor wrote that Borodin was a Czech, but since there was "some difficulty" in securing a Czech passport, he was contacting the Russian trade delegation in an effort to secure a passport for his client. The Russian trade delegation would not accept Borodin as theirs, but since his deportation was at hand, they proposed that the British government issue Borodin a document in lieu of a passport, which could be done for stateless persons and which the Soviet government would then visa. This method was followed to effect Borodin's departure from England. Thus, although the British knew Borodin was a Russian agent, and the Russians knew the British knew, the fiction was maintained throughout that Borodin was of some other nationality.

Almost equally obfuscated was the matter of Borodin's name. Borodin began by stating that his name was George Brown, but apparently faced with undeniable evidence that he was indeed "Borodin," he said that his real name was Georg Braun, which had been anglicized to George Brown when he arrived in England, but that in Russia he had been known as Borodin. At this point Scotland Yard ordered a compilation of Borodin's aliases. In it, the Yard listed sixteen different adaptations of Gruzenberg, Berg, Brown, and Borodin,[9] but these are only a few of the aliases Borodin utilized during his career. Just when Borodin began using that name is difficult to say. The 1922 Scotland Yard list is definitely not the first time that he had used this alias, by which he has been known to history, in the past. Where the name came from, as is the case with many revolutionary aliases, is difficult to determine. One possibility is that he had at times used the identity of Professor N. Borodin, an agricultural specialist, who had been a member of Ambassador Bakhmetiev's staff and had accompanied him on the visit to Chicago in August 1918. (Lenin apparently called Borodin by his real name, Gruzenberg, until mid-1921.)

When arrested on August 22, Borodin was charged on three counts: being an alien unable to produce a passport, certificate of registration, or identity book; refusing to answer questions reasonably put to him by the registration officer; and giving false information. There was no difficulty in proving Borodin's guilt and, in the speedy processes of British justice, within a week of his arrest he was convicted and sentenced to six months in prison to be followed by expulsion from Britain. On September 2, he was taken from Duke Street Prison, where he had been since his arrest, and remitted to Barlinnie Prison in Glasgow, where he would remain until deportation.

The occasion of Borodin's arrest and his imprisonment at Barlinnie provides the only written physical profile available of him. In later years, observers would repeatedly refer to Borodin's physically dominating presence, giving the impression that he was a great bear of a man. Yet in fact he was only five-foot-ten, taller than most of Stalin's entourage but scarcely imposing. His complexion was described as "fresh," his hair dark brown, his eyes gray. He had scars on the left side of his face and on both sides of his body, perhaps from his days as a barge worker on the Dvina. In the prison photo of Borodin, he wears a worker's cap, a striped suit, and a four-in-hand tie. Since he had moved among the British working class, he was outfitted as a trade-union leader. He had not yet assumed the Stalin moustache that marks his 1926–27 photographs and that he would keep thereafter. The prison photo shows a glowering Borodin, close-cropped and clean-shaven, looking remarkably like the actor Eli Wallach. (Unfortunately, the photograph is not available for reproduction.)

Borodin's arrest and incarceration produced two other important documents: the cover autobiography that Borodin gave to Chief Constable Even M. Gaskill on September 1 and 5, 1922,[10] and Scotland Yard's "secret" report on Borodin, issued on January 3, 1923.[11] It is not clear why Borodin gave such an extensive interview to Constable Gaskill. He had already been convicted. Gaskill probably hadn't threatened Borodin with physical abuse. Perhaps Borodin was following the classic spy precept that a story, any story, is the best way to get an interrogator off your back. Perhaps he was reinforcing his denial of Russian citizenship or seeking to confuse Scotland Yard or simply trying to relieve the boredom of prison life, though the latter seems unlikely.

Borodin's account was probably almost entirely fictitious as far as his antecedents, relatives, birth place, citizenship, and early life were concerned. But from 1906, when Borodin was in

England and his path was traceable in general outlines, Borodin told a straight story. He didn't tell everything, and sometimes he told less than all the truth, but there seems not to have been the kind of pure fabrication with which he described the first two decades of his life. The secret Scotland Yard report is important because it was made when Borodin's trail was still fresh, before it had become confused beneath the notoriety of his later experiences. Although the report is incomplete and uneven, it is particularly valuable for helping to pinpoint some of Borodin's Western European activities from 1918 through 1922, providing data that are confirmed by U.S. files opened in the late 1970s.

Borodin's stay in Barlinnie was wearing; he thrived on activity and he still had unfinished business in England. He had no opportunity such as Radek had been afforded in Germany in 1919 to hold court in his prison cell for the local left. After his arrest, Borodin had no contact with anyone, except his solicitor, the court, and his jailors. If we know Borodin, time hung heavy and he pondered, as he had before and would many times again, the wisdom of having left Chicago and what lay ahead. Borodin had often felt caged, even when free, wanting to burst forth and fully use the talents he felt were his. The prison bars only magnified his frustration. He spent his time fuming, worrying, mentally preparing the report on his mission he would give the Executive Committee of the CI on his return to Russia, reading what the prison library offered, and waiting for his release.

On February 20, 1923, the order for Borodin's deportation was signed. The following day Borodin was taken to Blyth, Northumberland, and placed aboard the *S. S. Loos*. And the next day, February 22, 1923, at 5:15 in the afternoon, six months to the day after he had been apprehended in Glasgow, he left Blyth aboard the *Loos* for Petrograd. He would never again be in the West. As Borodin walked the decks of the *Loos*, bundled up against the frigid cold of the North Sea, wondering about the reception he would receive in Moscow, he had no way of knowing that for him the best was yet to come—and that it would be, of all places, in China.

9

To Canton

When Borodin arrived back in Moscow in March 1922 after his release from Barlinnie Prison, the plan for reorganizing the British Communist Party that he had worked out with the Dutt committee had already been adopted by the British party congress "without dissent." Though the mission had terminated in his arrest, Borodin had been effective in Britain, and he certainly had more up-to-date firsthand information on the British situation than anyone else in Russia. Borodin assumed that he would continue to work on British affairs, or at least be involved in Comintern activities in the West.[1] And for the first months after his return, Britain continued to occupy his time. But while Borodin had been away, developments were deflecting both foreign policy and CI attention away from Europe and toward the underdeveloped sectors of the globe, most specifically the "East" and, in the East, China.

The Moscow revolutionaries had not been unaware of China's prospects. They knew that were ample reasons for Chinese ferment. For the better part of a century, it had been the victim of pernicious domestic and foreign exploitation. Ever mindful of a glorious past, China was dismayed by its humiliated present. It had grown increasingly indignant over its supine position among the nations of the world, the weakness of the government, the plunder of its people and resources by landlords, warlords, and imperialists.

Shortly after November 7, 1917, the Bolshevik regime had begun addressing itself to the Chinese people, declaring eternal enmity against all imperialists, calling for national independence and renouncing former tsarist concessions in China. Beginning in 1920, the Bolsheviks sent emissaries to China to check out the land. G. N. Voitinsky, Hendricus Maring, and S. A. Dalin all were dispatched to China at various times between 1920 and 1922 to gain firsthand information, to identify revolutionary circles, and to turn them toward Moscow. But these were very limited efforts. Moscow was only peripherally interested in China. Attention was primarily riveted on the West. Whether it was revolution or the recognition of its regime by foreign governments, the Kremlin sought these first in the West. Only as frustration set in did it give more than passing attention to the "peoples of the East"; even then, its interest was secondary. Revolution and recognition by China would not have the same impact as their realization in Britain or Germany or France. But turning to the East represented an alternative strategy when the main lines of advance were blocked.

Thus in late 1922 the experienced Soviet diplomat, A. A. Ioffe, whose activities had previously been in the West, came to China. His primary purpose was to secure recognition from the Waichiao Pu, the foreign office of the weak, warlord-dominated Chinese government in Peking. But as month followed fruitless month (it became increasingly clear that the Waichiao Pu was afraid to act because of pressure from the Great Powers, particularly Britain), Ioffe began to consider other lines of action. It was in these circumstances that Ioffe met Sun Yat-sen.

Sun had spent his life in the service of reuniting and revivifying China. For more than a quarter century, ever since 1896 when he had been rescued by Scotland Yard from the Chinese legation in London where he had been held by agents of the Manchu government, Sun had been the symbol, sometimes the only symbol, of revolution in China. Again and again in the early twentieth century, Sun had attempted to oppose the Manchus and failed. Each time his solution to failure was fundraising, where he had his greatest expertise. In the board rooms of Chinese banks, in the back rooms of Chinese laundries, in the kitchens of Chinese restaurants across the United States and Canada, in Malaysia and England, wherever there were Chinese, he preached the need to drive out the Manchus and to modernize China. Although not a dynamic speaker, and certainly an inferior theoretician, he was extremely persuasive on his obsession: reviving China.

As he traveled the world, Sun epitomized change in China to

millions of Chinese, particularly those living overseas. And when the revolution finally succeeded in 1911 and Sun returned to China—he was in Denver, Colorado, when it broke out—he was enthusiastically received as a great hero. But Sun was quickly frozen out of the regime that followed the collapse of the empire. In the next years his reputation declined as he proved less able at politics and administration than at fundraising. By 1920, Sun was desperately trying to maintain a foothold in Canton in South China, where he headed a jerry-built local regime.

For Sun, the role of chief enemy, formerly played by the Manchus, was now held by the militarists who had divided China into hundred of tiny fiefdoms, and kept it weak and decentralized. If Sun was to move against them, he needed a base and an army. But the only army available to him, since he could not raise his own, were those same militarist forces he saw destroying China. It was thus that Sun, the enemy of militarism, threw in his lot with the militarists, only to become their victim. As the militarists, immune to his reformist pleas, tired of him or were driven out by other militarists, Sun had to flee. More than once he escaped from his native Canton via motorboat to his refuge in the French Concession in Shanghai.

Now in his mid-fifties, Sun knew time was running out. If his dreamed-of Northern Expedition was to reunite China, it had to be soon. In his cave of despair he found hope in the concept of a new Lafayette. Just as the French marquis had helped George Washington save the United States, so a foreigner must be found to help him save China. Whenever he could, Sun now tried to interest the Great Powers in providing such a figure. But the Western nations were satisfied with the status quo and had no interest in resurrecting China. Time and again they turned down his pleas for aid, but still he continued to hope—a measure of his naiveté.

In his frustration, Sun's interest was piqued by Bolshevik visitors who came to see him in the early 1920s. He probed deeply: How had the Russians achieved their revolution? How had they driven out the invaders?[2] Sun's interest was mostly intellectual, however. He wanted contacts with the Bolsheviks, but the alliance the CI representatives intimated was another matter. Nevertheless, as one CI emissary followed another to Sun's camp, and as his desperation deepened, the prospect of an agreement with the Russians became more tempting. He considered it reluctantly, half-ashamed, secretly. In addition to his bourgeois predilections against the Bolsheviks, he realized that any agreement with Moscow would involve the acceptance of the fledgling Communist Party of China (CCP) within his own political party, the Kuomintang (KMT). Even more than many of his middle-class supporters, he recognized this as a direct threat to his control of the KMT. But no one else in the West was talking to him about establishing a military academy in Canton, as the Russians were doing.[3] No one else was discussing the dispatch of arms and advisers. After Sun was again forced out of Canton in mid-1922, he came face to face with the imperatives of moving toward reliance upon Soviet Russia. Given his goals, this seemed the only way.

Russian intelligence increasingly led them to regard him as their standard bearer in China. They had no illusions about Sun, who made no effort to hide those utopian and reactionary ideals of which Lenin had once accused him.[4] Even while Comintern delegate Dalin was in Canton, Sun had hired a new Western adviser, negotiated with the most reactionary elements in China, and had suppressed Cantonese even on the moderate left. But if they were to foster revolution in China, the Russians had almost as few options as Sun. The militarist generals, although some of them would occasionally bow to the left, were even less progressive than Sun. The CCP was too weak to act alone. Its leadership was inexperienced; it had little organizational know-how, little understanding of Marx, little revolutionary technique. It was more a talking society than a revolutionary unit. Sun's KMT, weak as it was, was the only quasi revolutionary party in China. Moreover, this was the period when Moscow urged a united front with almost anyone arrayed against the forces of national reaction. So the Kremlin decided to cultivate Sun, even if it didn't fully trust him. It wasn't sure it wanted to do anything in the East; it wasn't comfortable supporting any bourgeoisie; and it had doubts about *this* bourgeois in particular. Now and throughout their involvement in China, the Russians would look for other baskets for their eggs.

But in spite of their mutual suspicions, Sun and Moscow slowly drew closer together. In the wake of decisions set in

motion at the fourth CI Congress, a meeting was arranged between Sun and Soviet diplomat Ioffe in Shanghai in January
1923. Sun told Ioffe of his aspirations for China. He described
his dream of the Northern Expedition, lamented the lack of resources to embark upon it, and asked for financial aid and advisers.[5] Ioffe led Sun to believe that his requests would be met.
Out of these conversations, and Ioffe's failure to reach an accommodation with the government in Peking, came the Sun–Ioffe
agreement of January 1923, which stated that "the chief and immediate aim of China is the achievement of national unity and
national independence" and offered that "in solution of this
great problem, China would find the warmest sympathy of the
Russian people and could depend on the aid of Russia."

Despite the clear promise of aid in the agreement and the
assurances given by Ioffe, the Politburo and the Comintern
spent months discussing whether and to what degree assistance
should be given. There can be no doubt that the PB and the CI
knew their man well. Both Maring and Dalin had sent back devastating reports on Sun, his party, and his ideology. Sun had
made no secret of his opposition to communism and had insisted
that the opening paragraph of the agreement with Ioffe include
the statement that "the conditions for the successful establishment of either communism or soviets" did not then exist in
China. Moscow knew that Sun's party was woefully lacking in
organization and discipline. On the other hand, the KMT at
least had a following, which could scarcely be said of the minuscule and even more disorganized Chinese Communist Party.
And in Sun they had a time-tested leader, who was fiercely anti-
imperialist, at least in theory, who desperately wanted revolution and was eager to enter the fray.

At length the decision was made at the highest levels in Moscow (it was too important to be left to the CI) to send support, if
Sun, who was out of power at the time of the meetings with
Ioffe, succeeded in reestablishing a regime in Canton. Once Sun
was again installed in Canton, Moscow wired him, in May 1923,
that it was prepared to send the aid requested from Ioffe.[6]

A̲fter several months in Moscow, Borodin was aware that an
Eastern expedition of some sort was in the offing and that his old

acquaintance L. M. Karakhan, the deputy foreign minister he had known from Sugar Palace days, would lead it. Karakhan was a good choice because, in Chinese eyes, he was credited with the manifesto of July 25, 1919, in which Soviet Russia had appeared to surrender all claims to tsarist concessions in China. But Borodin apparently did not know that Karakhan's chief assignment would be to obtain recognition from the Peking government, or that it was planned to send a delegation of advisers to Sun Yat-sen in South China, which he, Borodin, was being considered to lead.

As Borodin told his son Norman years later, he was greatly surprised when, summoned before the Central Committee of the Russian party, he was told that he was being assigned as adviser to Sun Yat-sen, who had requested aid for revolutionary activities in China. The appointment was "completely unexpected,"[7] and one of Borodin's first reactions after recovering from the shock was to send an assistant out to collect material on contemporary China, a subject on which Borodin confessed to all but total ignorance. In many respects, Borodin was a logical choice. Other CI men might have been selected, including some who had been to China. But Borodin was a tested agent with an established reputation for effectively representing Moscow in often dangerous circumstances, such as those that would presumably face a Bolshevik agent in China. Borodin had just succeeded in carrying out a delicate and hazardous assignment in Great Britain, where he had competently exercised independent authority and displayed organizational skill in dealing with non-Russians. Those were the same qualities that South China now required.

Borodin had several other things to recommend him: he knew English and therefore could communicate directly with the English-speaking Sun. It is also barely possible that Borodin had known Sun previously. According to an *Ogonek* correspondent to whom Borodin gave an interview in 1927,[8] Borodin had met Sun in the United States and Borodin's son also believed his father had known Sun in Chicago,[9] though Sun, who would likely have commented on this if it were true, never mentioned it. Borodin, moreover, had demonstrated skill as a proselytizer, and the Russians yearned to convert Sun Yat-sen to communism.

Other than surprise, Borodin's reactions to the appointment can only be surmised. How important were China and the assignment to him? Not very, perhaps. For many young Soviet advisers, the sovetniki, who would go to China in the years ahead, the assignment would be a tremendous adventure. For recent graduates of military academies and technical schools, for language students learning Chinese during summer vacation, it would provide excitement and travel. But Borodin was no college boy. He was now thirty-nine years old. His oldest son was already fifteen. He had traveled too much to be exhilarated by such a venture. And he had had encounters with the police for two decades. Yet he knew that this might be his most dangerous assignment to date.[10]

True, Borodin was ambitious for the revolution and for fame and power. He was gratified that this mission was to be directly under the aegis of top party authority. But what were the prospects for success? For himself? A realist would have to be skeptical—and Borodin was ever the realist. Given the high risks and poor prospects, Borodin viewed it as less than an unmixed blessing. Not that he considered turning the assignment down. A Bolshevik didn't do that. As one who frequently lectured others about the necessity for discipline, he had no choice. But it seems unlikely that Borodin, in the spring and summer of 1923, saw China for what it was to become to him—the chance of a lifetime and his own passport to fame.

Whatever Borodin's doubts about the China mission, he threw himself at once into the work of preparing for it. He had to become informed on previous Bolshevik policy toward the Far East, on the files of earlier missions, on the current economic and political situation in China, and on his role vis-à-vis Sun Yat-sen. Borodin was a virtual *tabula rasa* on these topics. His bailiwick had been Europe, the United States, Latin America, even India—but not China. However, in Karakhan, who had been in charge of the East for the Commissariat of Foreign Affairs since 1919, he had an experienced and knowledgeable instructor. In Moscow, with the Comintern apparat, and later in Peking, Borodin studied, discussed, and ruminated, learning what was expected of him in South China: to reorganize Sun's KMT, to turn it into an active revolutionary force; and to provide it with its own military arm.

Since Karakhan's mission to the Peking regime was an undisguised effort to secure diplomatic recognition for Soviet Russia, and Borodin's purpose was a secret effort to organize a subversive movement against Peking, it was inadvisable for them to arrive in China together. Karakhan left Moscow first and arrived in Peking in early September 1923, where, somewhat surprisingly, he promptly sent a telegram to Sun Yat-sen, addressing him as an "old friend of New Russia" and telling him that "I count on your help in the business of realizing the great task of establishing the closest relations between our two peoples."[11] Sun Yat-sen replied in mid-September, assuring Karakhan of his support and goodwill. He further advised Karakhan that if difficulties arose in gaining recognition by the Waichiao Pu in Peking, he should come to Canton. Sun was certain they could work something out, such as recognition by Sun's government.[12] In the same communication Sun, warning Karakhan that the information was *"rigidly confidential,"* disclosed that he had already dispatched his "chief of staff and confidential agent"—Chiang Kai-shek by name—to Moscow "to discuss ways and means whereby our friends there can assist me in my work in this country."[13] On September 23, Karakhan wrote that he was sending his "personal representative," M. M. Borodin, south to join Sun. (Of course, Borodin was not Karakhan's personal representative: he was the agent of the Politburo of the Central Committee of the Russian party.)

Borodin followed Karakhan on one of the next trains out of Moscow. Traveling by wagon-lit along the Trans-Siberian as far as Lake Baikal, he then passed through Harbin, Changchen, and Mukden before finally arriving in Peking after more than a week on board train. In the Chinese capital Borodin was further briefed on China, especially South China. (It was soon to become clear that no one he met knew very much about the real situation there.) He discussed tactics again with Karakhan, received final instructions, and in late September left for Shanghai, where he boarded a vessel for Canton. The usual course for ships bound for Canton was to stop first at Hong Kong, then to proceed up the Pearl River to Canton. But Borodin feared that, if he landed in Hong Kong, he would be arrested by the British. He knew that, as recently as May,[14] British immigration officers at ports around the world had been warned to be on the alert for him. Accordingly he took the only available transportation on the direct Shanghai–Canton run, a small cattleboat.

Accompanied by V. Polyak, one of the first Soviet military *sovetniki* in China, and several hundred sheep, Borodin sailed south, encountering a major typhoon that forced the ship to take shelter along the Formosa Coast. As Borodin described it later, if the captain had not found a protected place, "the writer of these lines might have shared the fate of 200 sheep we had on board, all of which perished."[15] On October 6, the storm-exhausted Borodin and Polyak arrived in Canton and were greeted immediately by Sun. As Borodin described the meeting: "Sun Yat-sen welcomed me very warmly, made me sit with him and looked at me fixedly for several seconds."[16] He was basking in the presence of his Lafayette, come 8000 miles to help save China. It was a moment of fulfillment for Sun, maybe the beginning of the realization of his dreams.

Yet even as Sun rejoiced, his doubts persisted. This Lafayette was attired in the ideology, if not the uniform, of a Moscow commissar. His confidants had warned him that the Russians would soon seize control and install communism in China—in spite of Ioffe's assurances to the contrary—and replace the KMT with the CCP. Borodin had his own doubts. Nothing he had learned in Moscow or Peking minimized the magnitude of the job in Canton. This appraisal would shortly be confirmed.

Borodin and Sun had frank and thorough discussions of the task ahead and their respective roles. Sun stressed the importance of his long-cherished Northern Expedition. He acknowledged that, for the present, he needed to strengthen his hold on Canton and build up his forces there. For this he needed supplies, and he told Borodin that he placed great hopes in negotiations then being conducted by Chiang Kai-shek in Moscow. But, he stressed, his ultimate and overriding goal was the Northern Expedition to unite all of China. Sun's emphasis on the expedition troubled Borodin. It was not that Borodin and his superiors were opposed, but a great deal had to be done before Sun could launch his reunification forces toward Shanghai and Peking. The KMT must be rebuilt; an independent, non-warlord controlled military force must be established, an officer-training school created; and, from Moscow's point of view, by no means least, steps must be taken to "involve the masses": a program of social and economic reform had to be undertaken. Even if Sun agreed with all of this, the task would take longer than the impatient Sun would want. But Sun was not in agreement, and his longtime backers were even less so. Borodin's first job was to win over Sun.

Following the meeting with Sun on the day of his arrival, Borodin next saw the Chinese leader a few days later at an official reception arranged to introduce Borodin to the members of Sun's government. At the reception Sun spoke first. Borodin then told the audience, though his remarks were primarily for Sun, that Soviet Russia stood on three principles: democracy, nationalism, and socialism. Interestingly, Borodin said, he had just learned that the first two of these were precisely the same as *min-chuan*, people's rights, and *min-tsu*, people's nation, in Sun Yat-sen's Three People's Principles, the honored *San-min chu-i*. But, whereas in China these principles represented the hope for the future, in Russia they had already been realized. Our task, Borodin emphasized, is to help you bring them to your country as well.

While Borodin sought to establish ideological rapport with Sun, he did not avoid the issue that separated the Russians from Sun and would become sand in the craw of Russian-Chinese relations: differences over the third principle of the *San-min chu-i*. Then and in the years ahead, Borodin and others would try to bring Sun's third principle, *min-sheng* (people's livelihood), into line with Borodin's third Soviet principle, *socialism*. But the socialism that Sun was prepared to seek was not what the Russians had in mind. Above all, Sun's socialism did not involve the redistribution of land. As a bourgeois, he was not prepared to consent to the seizure of property. As a practical politician, he was not prepared to alienate most of his long-time supporters. Borodin would never win Sun and his cohorts over to his "interpretation." But he was ready to try.

On October 9, at the above-mentioned reception, on October 15 at a meeting of KMT members in a private garden, on the evening of the fifteenth at a dinner with the governor of Kwangtung province (of which Canton was the capital), on October 16 at a dinner with the foreign minister, and in numerous private conferences and conversations during his first weeks in Canton, Borodin assured his listeners that China could be free. But the struggle would require reorganization of the KMT and its conversion into a united, national-liberation party, which would revolutionize the masses. Borodin's message was, at best, politely received. The warlord officers, bureaucrats, and businessmen who made up Sun's retinue saw Soviet Russia, communism, and Borodin more as threats than partners. Those who wanted to see China unified and strengthened did not want it at the expense of their personal wealth and position.

In the initial weeks in Canton, Borodin faced resistance not only from Sun's entourage but from the left as well. The Chinese Communist Party, from the first, opposed Moscow's cooperation with Sun. The Chinese communists regarded Sun as a dedicated but ineffective bourgeois, who not only cooperated with but cultivated reactionaries. Why should Moscow support a pseudo-revolutionary when authentic communist revolutionaries were available? But Moscow had decided that the CCP had no chance to lead a Chinese revolution in the foreseeable future and therefore opted for Sun and his KMT. Outrageously, to the CCP, it had even ordered the CCP membership to join the KMT, and on Sun's condition that they come in not as units but as individuals. Moscow was not only selling out the Chinese communist organization, but was ordering its members to submit to Sun, on his terms. Resentment was inevitable and feelings ran deeply.

In Canton some CCP members such as Ch'ü Ch'iu-pai and Chang T'ai-lei, who knew Russian, were Moscow-oriented, and had been designated to work closely with Borodin, accepted Moscow's orders. But most were hostile to the Kremlin's demands. Borodin met with them, told them of his talks with Sun, outlined their role and responsibilities, and described the prospects for the KMT, the revolution, and the CCP. Borodin told local CCP members that, having surveyed the scene, he now knew that progress was possible in Canton and China. He tried to win the recalcitrants over by confiding that when he spoke to the press of building up the *KMT*, they should read *CCP*, for they would ultimately benefit. "While working for the stabilisation of the Kuomintang it must never be forgotten that in reality the work is done for the stabilisation of the Communist party."[17] Borodin pushed hard, but the local CCP members, like Sun's men, were unpersuaded.

The weakness of Borodin's position in Canton was monumental. He was thousands of miles from home, hundreds of miles from advice and support except for a handful of youthful sovetniki in Canton. He was alone in a foreign country, knowing little of its institutions and customs, ignorant of its language. Fortunately he knew English, as did many who surrounded Sun; it was one of Borodin's few assets that he could converse with the Canton leadership directly. But other than this, the "authority of the revolution," and promises of Soviet aid, he was perilously alone. No one on the Chinese side knew him or had reason to trust him personally. Some were uncertain about his intentions; many wished him gone. In sum, Borodin began with little more than his wits. But a situation was developing that was propitious for his work and would soon enable his talents to demonstrate their power.

Shortly after arriving in Canton, Borodin discovered that Sun Yat-sen's position was extremely precarious. Driven out the preceding year by his old nemesis, the militarist Ch'en Ch'iung-ming, Sun had returned to Canton only at the sufferance of other warlords. They in turn drove Ch'en out and placed Sun as nominal head of their new regime, turning to him because he was respected in some circles and was a useful front for their corrupt rule. Most of the militarists were from outside Canton. They had taken over the city in order to get rich, planning to return home as quickly as possible. The march northward and national unification interested them hardly at all. Even before Sun had returned to Canton, those who invited him had taken over and expanded the drug traffic, gambling, and prostitution. The city was their plum, to be governed and exploited as they saw fit. But there was no unity among them. Each general had his own fiefdom; he would ensure that the fruits of plunder were his alone. Clashes between one military detachment and another were frequent as the commanders tried to increase the size of the lucrative areas under their dominion.

From the moment of his arrival in the south, as he had done

before, Sun had to fight forces hostile to him as well as the abuses and anarchy of those nominally allied with him. Although the number of warlord troops in Canton fluctuated during 1923, it probably rarely fell below 40,000. At the same time, Sun had only 150 to 200 troops—his personal bodyguard—who were reliably under his control. Not only did Sun have to survive the various commanders and their detachments, but he had to provide for them. According to one report, this cost $26,000 a day. To meet his dire financial needs, he attempted to "unify" Canton's finances by placing all taxation under his administration. But the generals would not cooperate, and Sun's government had to resort to numerous and ingenious tax innovations to keep the regime solvent. In addition to the usual taxes "in advance," war bonds, and "voluntary" contributions, Sun sold public land, licensed automobiles (there were few, and foreign owners refused to comply), auctioned off temples, held for ransom the families of wealthy citizens who had fled Canton to avoid the new taxes, and placed new tariffs on mutton, fish, and a host of other items. Still his government fell deeper and deeper into debt.

In addition to Sun's other problems, pirates patrolled the rivers around Canton. No traffic moved without permission and tribute. Canton under Sun was besieged from within and without. It was characterized by paralysis, corruption, and fear. The situation deteriorated still further in August 1923, when the forces of Ch'en Ch'iung-ming, urged on by local Canton elements fed up with Sun and his militarists, tried to retake the city. In September, Sun's military headquarters near the Canton-Kowloon Railroad was destroyed. In October, when Borodin arrived, another showdown for Sun was fast approaching. In early November it came.

During his first months in Canton, Borodin sent Karakhan in Peking voluminous almost-daily reports of what was happening in the south. On November 12, he wrote Karakhan that Canton was experiencing a catastrophe;[18] the fall of the city and the collapse of the Sun government were to be expected at any moment. Up to this point Borodin had moved cautiously, kept a low profile and spoke softly as he sought to convince Sun and his adherents to follow the course he advocated.[19] But now with

Sun's defeat and explusion from Canton imminent, Borodin, with nothing to lose, began to provide the leadership others had failed to exercise. At the November 12 meeting of the Provincial Central Executive Committee (CEC) of the KMT, Sun's board of directors, collapse seemed so near that some members of the CEC asked if they should be meeting at all. Shouldn't they be at the front, or preparing for flight? As the spirit of defeatism spread, Borodin urged continued resistance. He assured them all was not lost, that the forces of Ch'en Ch'iung-ming were overestimated, that with a spirit of revolution they could still prevail. Won over by Borodin, the members of the CEC drove to their own neighborhoods to urge the local generals to hold fast and to help organize the defense.

The military stiffened its resistance, and the situation stabilized between the 12th and the 13th. On the 13th the CEC reconvened. Again Borodin spoke. Encouraged by the reaction to his leadership of the preceding day, he now abandoned all pretense of the soft sell. He "exploded," telling the CEC that if Moscow's plans for a reorganized KMT had been applied, their regime would not have faced this crisis. In one night they could have alerted and dispatched tens of thousands of people—the masses—to the front; the reactionaries would have been suppressed easily.[20] But Borodin continued that he had come not to criticize the past but to bring the experience that enabled Soviet Russia to overcome its foes under similar conditions.[21] He then proceeded to tell the CEC how it must appeal to the masses. Peasants must be given land taken from the large landholders;[22] the workers should receive an eight-hour day, a minimum wage, and one day off per week. His bourgeois listeners should not feel threatened by such measures because the more money the worker had, the more he would be able to purchase. With the KMT and the CEC advocating such measures, Borodin continued, they would unite the workers and peasants behind them. Any reactionary general about to fall on Canton would hesitate, knowing that he would now be attacking a society eager to defend itself.

Then Borodin turned to the task at hand: defense against the enemy at the door. He called for the immediate establishment of volunteer detachments under KMT personnel to go to the front and defend the city; he explained how this could be done. He promised that, spurred by promises of reform, the peasants and workers of Kwangtung would flock to the KMT colors and Ch'en Ch'iung-ming would be driven back. The city and government would yet be saved. Borodin's remarks evoked considerable enthusiasm. Here was the assurance of victory where yesterday defeat seemed certain. The members of the CEC, impressed by Borodin's advice, captivated by his confidence, put aside their doubts about land and labor reforms and adopted his proposals in toto.

But Sun was not at these meetings on the 12th and 13th. When he heard that the CEC had endorsed Borodin's proposals, including land and labor reforms, he was more than troubled. On November 14 Borodin appeared at KMT headquarters with decrees to implement economic proposals which had been adopted the preceding day: land was to be redistributed, wages raised, workdays shortened. All that was needed to make the decrees official was the signature of Sun Yat-sen. But Sun was nowhere to be found. Borodin looked in vain for him and for his San Francisco-born follower, Liao Chung-k'ai. Sun was at the front, or aboard a ship, or near Dunshan where the enemy was expected to attack. Sun was avoiding Borodin—and Borodin knew it. With Sun's signature unavailable, Borodin, stressing the need for immediate action, called upon the members of the CEC who were at Canton KMT headquarters to sign the decrees. But they refused, having reconsidered their hasty action of the 13th. Borodin was stymied; he was certain that mass appeal was essential to victory.

Borodin nevertheless continued organizing the defenses of the city, using the instruments he had: the CCP, the Socialist Youth League, and those KMT members who would cooperate with him. Activists were dispatched around Canton to seek volunteers, build morale, and prepare for the area's defense. At Borodin's instruction, CCP members arose at neighborhood meetings of the KMT to urge that each local organization take a military detachment under its wing, that the organization provide the detachment with materials and supplies—and courage. Such *sheftstvo* (stewardship) by active party elements for the military had proved successful in Russia, Borodin and his military assistants told the Chinese. It would work here too.

By the 15th, 540 volunteers had been recruited and sent to the front. Early the same day, the forces of Ch'en resumed their advance. Again Borodin urged Sun by letter to take the steps Borodin asserted were absolutely essential if the enemy was to be stopped: authorize economic reform. Again Sun refused to see him. Later that morning another meeting of the CEC was scheduled; again Sun was absent. Borodin sent still another note to Sun who, he was now informed, had returned from the front. The note emphasized the extreme gravity of the situation and the necessity for Sun's immediate presence at the CEC meeting. Thirty minutes later not Sun, but his aide Liao Chung-k'ai appeared, bringing a letter from Sun. Borodin was informed that there was widespread opposition to his proposals for land and labor reforms. Some of his supporters warned him, wrote Sun, that Borodin was calling for the sovietization of Kwangtung; if that was what Borodin wanted, he could not consent. Sun's letter reflected his indecision. He wanted to convert defeat into victory, but at the price of sovietization? By alienating his supporters of two decades and more? While the message didn't clearly commit Sun, it apparently freed his supporters to act as they wished.

After the letter had been read by Liao, he paused a moment and then spoke for himself. Up until now, he said, the KMT had professed principles, but it had never put a single one into practice. Now was the time to act. Personally, he declared, he favored Borodin's decrees and he urged the others to join him.[23] It was a fateful decision for Liao. In the years of Sun's wanderings, Liao had rarely played a leading role in KMT affairs. He had always stood in the shadow of others. But in late 1922 and the first part of 1923, almost alone among Sun's advisers he had encouraged Sun's exploration of the possibility of Soviet assistance. Now, in the midst of the November crisis, he threw his weight to the left. From now on, he would be the KMT leader closest to Borodin.

Freed by Sun and pressured by Liao and by Borodin, who pleaded that his proposals were not remotely sovietization, the KMT was told that the labor and land decrees would help the KMT accomplish its historic goals of uniting and freeing China. The CEC again went on record as approving the decrees, but Sun's signature was still needed and he still delayed. On the

16th, again boycotting the CEC session to avoid pressure and confrontation, Sun wrote that his support for the decrees would offend both his overseas and his domestic supporters; for them, the issue of sovietization was very real. However, he continued, he was prepared to accept some of the Borodin decrees, those affecting the urban workers. As for land reform, he wanted to consult the peasants themselves before he acted.

As soon as Sun's letter was read, Liao proposed that a special committee be established to discuss the land question. Whereupon another CEC member, who opposed all of Borodin's decrees, substituted, and successfully carried, a motion that special committees be established to discuss *all* of Borodin's proposals. With his entire program in jeopardy, Borodin insisted that Sun come to the CEC meetings and use his influence. Otherwise right-wing positions would prevail and any possibilities of reform and victory would be lost. But in spite of reports of continuing military deterioration, Sun refused to come.

Finally, on the afternoon of the 18th, Sun agreed to see Borodin, but only to discuss his escape. Disaster seemed but hours away and Sun was preparing to leave for Japan. The English, he concluded, would probably not let him stay in Hong Kong or Shanghai, where he had a home. But he would like to visit Moscow and Berlin. Could Borodin arrange for him to land in Vladivostok and to travel from there to Moscow? Borodin told Sun that this could, of course, be arranged. But he should not give up hope. Though Sun's refusal to sign the decrees had not helped, the situation was not yet lost. Borodin's tactics were beginning to pay off. The soldiers were beginning to be inspired by the "support of the masses." The defenses were beginning to hold.

Sun remained dubious and continued his preparations for flight. But events were soon to prove Borodin right. During the evening of the 18th, the forces of Ch'en Ch'iung-ming, unprepared to face an even moderately resolute defense, began to retreat. Canton and the Sun government were saved. Only a few hours before, Sun had been in despair, contemplating exile; now he was ecstatic. He announced that his beloved Northern Expedition would soon begin. It is impossible to know to what extent the sudden reversal of Sun's fortunes was due to Borodin's organizational efforts. The change was certainly due in no small part to the realization by the generals of their self-interest in a victory that would preserve their prospects for continued power and affluence. But Borodin, through KMT agents, had helped the generals reach that conclusion. Whether or not Borodin's efforts were crucial in stopping Ch'en, Sun thought they were. Sun believed he had been rescued by Borodin's intercession. It was Borodin who told him to hold on; it was Borodin who had organized the defense of the city; it was Borodin who had staved off imminent catastrophe. In Sun's eyes, his Lafayette had indeed, materialized.

Out of the events of November 18, the Sun-Borodin relationship ripened and Borodin's authority in China grew. Sun's newfound faith in Borodin was observable at once. For weeks Borodin had urged Sun's attendance at the meetings of the CEC. Sun had procrastinated and worried. Borodin's plans for mass mobilization were not Sun's way of doing things; they threatened his value system and his power. But on November 19, the day after the unexpected retreat of Ch'en's army, Sun summoned Borodin. He congratulated him on the previous day's success and assured Borodin that his plan for reorganizing the KMT was sound. As a matter of fact, said Sun, it was precisely his own plan, based on principles worked out by himself long before and fought for over the years. Borodin, who displayed great sensitivity in dealing with Sun, readily agreed that his ideas and Sun's were indistinguishable. He was prepared to do what he could to help Sun put them into effect. But he advised that, if those ideas were to be carried out, Sun must assert his leadership. Without Sun, said Borodin, many mistakes had been and would be made. Only if Sun would involve himself personally in the reorganization, could errors be avoided and success assured.

Thus Sun acquiesced to part of Borodin's program, though he still did not commit himself to economic and social reform. Borodin would incorporate "Sun's ideas" into a proposal, which Sun pledged to support actively in private and public. And Sun delivered. After November 18, rapid agreement was reached on the outline for an all-China Kuomintang congress, on the establishment of permanent KMT volunteer detachments, and on other matters that had previously been stymied. Sun spoke before neighborhood committees in Kwangtung and in private sessions to influential Cantonese, advising them of his decision to carry out his long-standing principles.

The events of November 18 moved Sun to a different level of cooperation with Borodin and Soviet Russia. Until then Sun had hoped for Russian help, and, even though he was wary of them, he was reluctantly prepared to get what he could. But now he knew they could and would help him. This did not wholly dispel his objections and doubts about working with them; it only weakened their restraining influence. It became evident, soon after the crisis had passed, that while Sun's ideas and Borodin's were broadly similar in some respects, they did not see eye to eye on the crucial question of mass mobilization. As preparations for the KMT congress picked up intensity, Sun indicated the limits of his commitment, and his ambivalence. His weathy Chinese patrons abjured him not to play the Bolsheviks' game. They deluged him with telegrams from inside China and from abroad, urging him to back away; some warned that, if he didn't, he could expect no further support. A group of Americans, seeking to turn Sun's mind against Borodin—and revealing their own antisemitism—asked Sun: "Do you know that 'Borodin' is a pseudonym? Do you know his real name?" "I know," answered Sun, "Lafayette."[24] On one occasion, when particularly hard-pressed, he warned his KMT cohorts: "If you do not cooperate with the communists, if the members of the KMT come out against such cooperation, then I will renounce the KMT and enter the communist party myself."[25] Still, Sun encouraged Borodin to tone down his language, to deemphasize class war so as not to antagonize Sun's old supporters. He urged his followers to pursue the "Russian method of struggle," to "rid themselves of preconceived opinions." Yet he often failed to heed his own advice. He was uncomfortable in league with Moscow. Sun could not completely give up hope that somehow, some way, the *real* West would come to his rescue.

In January 1924 Sun's discomfort would become particularly acute. It was time for the First Kuomintang Congress, and Sun knew that he could no longer avoid making clear—before delegates from eighteen provinces of China, and from such other places as Malaysia, Australia, and New York—that he had cast his lot, at least for a time, with Soviet Russia. Up to now, he could evade, could say that others had lied or that he had been misquoted; but at the congress he would have to turn to his supporters and tell them, face to face, in public, that he had indeed opted for Soviet support.

Borodin was also determined that Sun should control the congress. Borodin recognized that Sun was his greatest, almost only, strength. He had to maximize Sun's utility. Accordingly, following Borodin's suggestion, every province and "special" city of China was allotted six delegates to the congress—three to be selected locally and three to be selected by Sun. Borodin took pains that the "right" three be selected by Sun in each instance. Sometimes Sun insisted on naming old friends, both in China and from abroad, regardless of their political complexion. But Borodin did what he could to guarantee a favorable majority for Sun—and himself—at the congress. The difficulties were formidable. He faced constant, insistent, and multifaceted opposition, not only from the KMT but from his fellow communists as well.

Borodin arranged for CCP representation at the KMT congress. Although the CCP was in no position to lead a revolution, it had capable men who could learn by participating in one. And he needed their support. He secured communist representation at the congress by having Sun include communists among the delegates he personally chose. But unhappily, some communists were so opposed to accommodation with Sun that they refused even to attend the meeting. The events of November 18, however, had almost as much effect on some CCP members as upon Sun. In Canton, party members were aware of the desperate position Sun had been in, that his fortunes had dramatically improved, that Borodin was being given credit, and that Sun and Borodin had drawn close together. They were impressed by Borodin's real, or apparent, feats and by the position he now occupied. At the Central Committee CCP plenum in Canton at the end of November, Borodin was able to impose his authority upon the local cadre. From then on, the CCP in Kwangtung would, with growing confidence and even enthusiasm, follow his lead. But this was not true in the north, particularly in Shanghai.

By late December, in Shanghai both the CCP and the KMT were resisting cooperation. Neither approved of the new

Sun–Borodin relationship. At that juncture Borodin and Liao Chung-k'ai, Sun's increasingly pro-Soviet aide, went to Shanghai to meet the double challenge head on. On the scene, Liao worked to bring the KMT into line and Borodin tried to make the CCP understand the necessity of cooperating with the KMT. He told the Shanghai party organization that a legally constituted party plenum, as well as prior party decisions, had approved the entry of the CCP into the KMT. He reassured the Shanghai cadre that the position of the CCP vis-à-vis the KMT would not weaken the former but would increase the *aktivnost* (involvement) of the party, because it would participate in a mass movement for the unification of all China.

Liao, sometimes with Borodin present, always invoking the authority of Sun, similarly tried to reassure the KMT members, telling them that Sun was not succumbing to sovietization, that he stood as ever for the unification and regeneration of China, that the time to achieve that objective was at hand and that all Chinese should cooperate toward that goal. Neither Borodin nor Liao succeeded in silencing the opposition, but they were able to get Shanghai delegates selected so that this vital constituency would be represented at the congress.

Borodin spent New Year's Day, 1924, in the north. He spoke at the joint meeting of the CCP and its Socialist Youth League in Shanghai in early January and then, together with Liao, returned to Canton to complete final arrangements for the approaching congress. Now and in the years immediately ahead, Borodin was involved in every significant decision in the Canton administration. In part this was because of the responsibility and pressures that he felt as a representative of the Soviet party and government. In part it was because he found only a few Chinese upon whom he could rely—in addition to his small contingent of Soviet advisers. In part it was because of who he was, a man determined to succeed, to leave as little as possible to chance. Accordingly, every facet of the forthcoming KMT congress was his province. Not only did he formulate the organization of the congress and supervise the selection of its personnel, but he also prepared the documents to be submitted to it.

Before it concluded its deliberations on January 19, the provisional Central Executive Committee of the KMT, which had responsibility for the congress, had met twenty times and made over four hundred decisions. But it was too large a group to write definitive position papers. That job had been assigned to Sun's leading followers, Wang Ching-wei, Hu Han-min, and Liao Chung-k'ai, to the right KMT leader Tai Chi-t'ao, and to Borodin. The major burden was assumed by Borodin, who drew up statements for the others to consider.

Borodin presented the first draft of the major manifesto of the congress—the basic document governing the reorganization of the KMT, the KMT-CCP relationship, and, in effect, the terms of Moscow-Canton cooperation—at a joint KMT-CCP meeting in Shanghai. It led to what Borodin conceded were many heated controversies.[26] The CCP was unhappy because the manifesto was too tame, reflecting pressures from the right, and because it subordinated the CCP to the KMT. And the KMT was unhappy because communists were allowed in the KMT at all, and because of the document's specific and veiled intimations of class struggle. The document gave special attention to peasants and workers: they were to become the backbone of the anti-militarist, anti-imperialist national revolutionary movement.

Wang Ching-wei, who was Sun's voice on the editing committee and in charge of the final draft, toned down Borodin's language. Wherever Borodin spoke of "worker and peasant masses," Wang dropped "worker and peasant" or substituted "the people" for the entire phrase. When Borodin called for reforms to attract the "masses," Wang urged that reform pledges be postponed until after the revolution had succeeded, when the toilers would be given their reward.[27] Wang warned that Borodin's reforms were "undemocratic" and would turn the Great Powers away from China. Borodin, in turn, accused Wang—and by indirection all who shared his feelings—of knowing only the illusion of Western democracy and of continuing the will-o'-the-wisp search for foreign allies. "Who are these foreign allies? With which nations and governments do you wish to go hand in hand? And, if you turn to one country—for example, England—what do you find there? Lord Curzon, Lloyd George, Ramsay MacDonald, the communists . . . which of them epitomizes real democracy?"[28] The imperialists are the enemy, continued Borodin, and it is time to recognize it.

The infighting over the manifesto was intense. Sun would yield, grudgingly, only after Borodin pressed hard. Borodin continued to be discreet; he could not offend "the old man." But the peasants and workers must be drawn into the struggle for China's unification and liberation, or the revolution would fail. Borodin repeated this endlessly, sometimes hinting that, unless the masses were involved, he could not continue his role as Lafayette. The debate went on for weeks. The opening of the congress even had to be delayed five days as the battle continued. Finally a compromise was arranged, which provided a document that Borodin characterized as less than satisfactory but, at least, he said, the old empty phraseology had been reduced by 50 percent.[29] The battle still was not over.

Now Borodin had to win the CCP's support for the manifesto. While the final touches were being applied, the members of the CCP delegation had been invited to Borodin's house almost daily for "discussion." The communists asked how the CCP, operating under democratic centralism, could function within the KMT, which was also, according to the manifesto, to practice democratic centralism. How could two independent centers lead simultaneously? Did not one center have to dominate? And, if it was not the CCP, would it not be destroyed? Borodin admitted their logic. He granted the validity of CCP objections that the manifesto was loaded against them; but, he asserted, if the revolultion was to come, it must be led by the KMT. And to get the KMT in harness, the organization proposed in the manifesto had to be formed. It was the Kuomintang's day in history, Borodin argued.[30] He summoned all his authority to persuade the CCP members to accept the document and emphasized that the Executive Committee of the Comintern had only a few weeks earlier specifically instructed the CCP to work within the KMT to strengthen that organization. It was, as Borodin put it, the decision of Moscow that "the KMT, as the expression of the national revolutionary movement in China, must come to power."[31] After prolonged and fervent debate, the manifesto was largely approved by the CCP delegation—but not unanimously, and not before at least one communist delegate bolted rather than participate in the seeming emasculation of Marxist ideals and communist interests.

On January 20, 1924, the First National Congress of the KMT opened with three bows to the KMT flag and one to Sun Yat-sen, followed by the playing of the Kuomintang hymn. Present were 165 delegates, somewhat less than 15 percent of whom were communists. By gaining CCP acceptance of the manifesto in advance, no matter how grudging their acceptance, Borodin effectively stilled the opposition of the left at the congress. Karakhan later commented on the "good behavior" of the CCP.[32] He wrote on February 9: "At the congress the communists conducted themselves exemplarily, with discipline, and the general work was interrupted by no left-communist outbursts." But the right was there in force, under no such discipline as had been imposed upon the left. It was determined to change the direction of the KMT. On the right were found most of Sun's oldest friends and strongest supporters. How could he embrace this pro-Russia policy? They knew Sun from the old days: he was no communist.

The right could not accept Sun's cooperation with the Soviet Union and his apparent acceptance of the CCP into the KMT. Nor could Sun himself fully accept it. He was still uncertain—and his friends who had stood with him for three decades gathered in Canton from all over China and beyond, aided by telegrams arriving from abroad daily urging Sun not to allow the KMT to fall into Bolshevik hands, were able to cultivate that uncertainty. Sun was shaken by the intensity of the opposition. Even though he had privately acquiesced to the manifesto, he now delayed committing himself publicly. He argued, procrastinated, absented himself from the hall where the congress was meeting, avoided Borodin.

On the fourth day of the congress, Sun called Borodin to him. Must all of the manifesto be adopted? Perhaps the long statement of principles calling for the activation and organization of the workers and peasants as the main driving force of the revolution could be dropped. Surely it would be enough to have a "program" to direct the future? After all, it was action that was needed. Sun said that the "principles" of the manifesto would only antagonize large numbers of his supporters both in China and abroad, and needlessly. Borodin maintained that all of the manifesto was essential, the principles as well as the program.

There had to be an ideological foundation to this "leading and decisive document of the movement." Sun could not make up his mind and the discussion was halted.

But the issue could not be avoided. When the two men returned to it, Sun repeated his earlier argument that the manifesto would incur the wrath of the Great Powers. Borodin, writing to Karakhan, set down his response. "Again and again I put the question to Sun Yat-sen. How long would he entertain the illusion that the Chinese people would receive help from the U.S.A., England or Japan?" Borodin insisted that Sun must endorse the manifesto—publicly for all to see. One hundred and fifty million Soviet people, the working class of Germany, the multitudes of Turkey, Persia, India, and others throughout Asia stood behind him. Sun must decide now: Would he join with them, with the oppressed of the world, or with imperialism?[33] Given his goal of uniting China, seeing no alternative to accepting the manifesto, recognizing that Borodin would not retreat, Sun finally yielded to Borodin's logic, coaxing, and inspiration. Jumping up, Sun grasped Borodin's hand and shook it with visible emotion. He would do as Borodin urged, and he would inform the congress in person that he supported the manifesto.

Sun's statement on the floor of the congress on behalf of the manifesto broke the back of the opposition. Some of its members would continue to hold out and attempt parliamentary maneuvers to block it even after the entire document had been passed; but Sun's commitment silenced all but the most intransigent. Some of them were in effect silenced because they walked out of the congress, even as part of the left had previously done. Sun had now committed himself publicly, unmistakably. When on the sixth day of the congress, January 25, the news arrived in Canton that Lenin had died in Moscow on the preceding day, Sun, comparing his mission to Lenin's, delivered a statement that was more an affirmation than a eulogy:

> You, Lenin, are exceptional. You not only speak and teach, you convert your works into reality. You have founded a new country; you have shown us the path for the common struggle; you met on your way thousands of obstacles, which I have also met. I wish to proceed along the path pointed out by you, and although my enemies are against this, my people will hail me for it. You are dead . . .

but in the memory of oppressed peoples you will live forever, great man.[34]

Borodin and several others also praised Lenin on the 25th. With the conclusion of the memorials, the congress adjourned for the traditional three days of mourning.

The right used the period to regroup. When the sessions resumed on the 28th, even though Sun had indicated that those who opposed the manifesto were his enemies, resistance from the right arose again. The issue this time: the role of the CCP in the KMT. Once again Sun, who had no taste for the give and take of parliamentary debate and who saw himself as being above it, absented himself. Borodin was not personally present at the sessions, but Liao Chung-k'ai and others led him to believe that the opposition was even more adamant on this issue than on the "principles." Without Sun's presence, Borodin feared, the decision might still, in a flurry of emotionalism, go against him. He found Sun again and importuned him. The congress was about to make an explicit decision on the relationship between the CCP and the KMT. It was essential that Sun be on the floor to guarantee that the decision went the right way. Again Borodin prevailed, and Sun, reluctantly paying the price required by his dreams, appeared in the congress hall.

The opposition was near the end of its road. One of its leaders had told Sun on the opening day of the congress: "If the communists accept our program, they must abandon their own party."[35] Now his argument was put in the form of a resolution. To join the KMT, communists must abandon their CCP membership. Li Ta-chao, perhaps the best-liked and most conciliatory of the CCP leaders, was selected to fend off this attack. China is in trouble, he said. We all want to help. We want to realize the principles of Sun Yat-sen. We want to fight together with you against the militarists—and to prove our intentions and determination we are prepared to accept the rules and discipline of the KMT. But don't ask us to abandon our principles.[36] Liao Chung-k'ai, representing Sun, also implored the delegates to support the program for the future of China. Although the opposition counterattacked vigorously, the words of Li and Liao, together with the presence of Sun, were sufficient to carry the day. It was agreed that communists might join the KMT as individuals, still maintaining their CCP membership. The debate over communist membership in the KMT was the last real issue at the congress. That issue, decided on the 28th, marked a major triumph for Sun—and for Borodin, the Soviet Union, and the CCP, although all communists certainly did not see it as such. Sun, before the entire congress, signaled the road he would follow and the congress had endorsed his decision.

At the conclusion of the congress, a permanent Central Executive Committee (CEC) of the Kuomintang was set up, its membership largely determined by Sun and Borodin. The CEC consisted of twenty-four full members and seventeen candidate members. Of the twenty-four full members, three were communists; of the seventeen candidate members, six were communists. Thus between 20 and 25 percent of the top KMT officials were CCP members, a percentage out of keeping with the CCP's numbers in the congress and vastly disproportionate to its national membership. The CCP was even more favorably situated in committee chairmanships. Of the nine "departments," two—Organizing and Peasant Affairs—were under CCP leadership and the CCP was also strong in the Labor and Youth departments. From the communist point of view, the Organizing Department, with its responsibility for recruitment, job assignments, and supervision, was crucial. It was the counterpart of the secretariat in communist party organization. Along with its other assignments, the CCP had virtual carte blanche in dealing with its natural constituents—the peasants, workers, and young people. Borodin had done very well by the CCP.

At the end of the KMT congress, the military academy was also authorized. This was an integral part of Sun's plans for the Northern Expedition and Borodin had used it as a sweetener to attract Sun's support during the congress. Chiang Kai-shek, whom Sun had sent to Moscow when Borodin was dispatched to Canton, was made the military commandant of the new Whampoa Academy. Liao Chung-k'ai was given the primary civilian responsibility.

The Kuomintang congress was of great importance to Borodin. It gave legal sanction to the changes that Borodin had sought in Canton; it reorganized the KMT; it officially brought the CCP into the KMT; it placed CCP leaders in vital KMT positions; it recognized the KMT-Soviet association. It provided legitimacy for Borodin's entire enterprise in the south of China. The congress thus was a capstone to Borodin's four months in Canton. During those months he had not only become the major adviser to Sun but gained his confidence. He had discovered that, whatever Sun's vanity or his irresolution, control of Sun was the path to success in Canton. He had learned how to manipulate Sun. He had moved him off dead center, obtained verbal commitments to the left, and implemented some of them. He had developed plans for KMT reorganization and played a strong role in their adoption. He had engineered the involvement of the CCP in leading KMT organs and enormously increased its potential. He had made strides toward establishing an officer corps for a national army. In brief, in four months' time, Borodin had laid the groundwork for the revolutionizing and unification of China. Granted that he did not accomplish all this alone, granting even that revolution and national unity were ideas whose time may have come in South China, it was nevertheless an amazing performance.

10

Setting the Stage

Despite the dramatic successes in Canton in January 1924, the battle to convert the Kuomintang into a formidable revolutionary instrument was only just beginning. Obstacles abounded; even Sun Yat-sen was uneasy about the path he had chosen. Sun's old friends on the right continued their efforts to turn his course. Now and for the rest of his life, Sun vacillated, hoping to find an alternative to Russian dependence. But in the crunch Sun usually followed Borodin's lead, even if reluctantly, always with an eye to keeping his options open—and never when it came to land reform.

Borodin sized up the Kuomintang in his dispatches to Karakhan. The KMT, he wrote, was no political party, politically, organizationally, or theoretically. It had no program, no structure, no dues, no membership cards. It was a one-man operation, but not even that one man, Sun, knew how many "members" were in the KMT or who they were.[1] Not only was the KMT disorganized, it was bourgeois, wholly lacking worker or peasant membership. Its adherents thus far were drawn exclusively from the petty and national bourgeoisie, from the landowning class, and from the military. They were an improbable revolutionary instrument. In the end, the class orientation of the KMT would determine both the success and failures of the Chinese revolution of 1924–1927. For although the organizational insights, strategies, and aid of the Bolsheviks were capable of bringing victory to the KMT, there were fundamental suspicions and differences between the Russians and most of the KMT.

But these did not preclude hope and action. With the conclusion of the KMT congress in January, agents were dispatched to the major population centers of China to establish KMT bureaus. In March 1924 Borodin went to Shanghai to supervise the KMT reorganization there and in other cities outside the south. The organizational structure imposed was precisely that of the Russian communist party, and the most effective organizers were communists.

During 1924 and 1925, the size of the KMT at least doubled; according to one account it multiplied tenfold. Although its organization in practice remained loose, by communist standards, it was far more responsive to manipulation from the center than before. It became, under the pressure of events, a superficially formidable and, in later years, an increasingly feared political instrument. Sun submitted to party reorganization partially as the price for Russian cooperation, partially because he was convinced that KMT reorganization was necessary. But far closer to Sun's heart than political reorganization was the establishment of a military academy from which would spring his own army. Sun urgently felt the need for such an army, loyal only to him. It would lead his Northern Expedition.

Borodin, as indicated, first came to Canton at about the same time that a military delegation representing Sun Yat-sen arrived in Moscow. Sun's delegation consisted of four men—two communists, two noncommunists. It was headed by his chief of staff, Chiang Kai-shek. Loyal to Sun, Chiang was the scion of an upwardly mobile Chekiang family that had known adversity following the father's death. At that time, a military career attracted poor, ambitious Chinese. Chiang had struggled to receive a military education, first in China, than in Japan. He became an officer and pursued a military career for over a decade. But Chiang was no fighting man; he was primarily a military politician rather than a strategist. Nor was he a "warlord."

In Moscow, Chiang was wined, dined, interrogated, and advised by the headquarters staff of the Comintern. His most important sessions, however, were with representatives of the Russian party and government; they would ultimately decide how far the USSR would become involved in China. Chiang and his three colleagues found themselves in long discussions with Trotsky, Kamenev, the Revolutionary Military Council, and particularly the latter's deputy chairman, E. M. Sklyansky.[2]

By November the council had apparently settled on its recommendations. It told Chiang that although it sympathized with Sun's ambitions for the Northern Expedition, it was necessary to move slowly. It cautioned that "for all its desire" to help, the Soviet Union did not have a "large cadre of people who knew China and its language." Thus there was no possibility of sending significant numbers of military advisers to South China. It advised Chiang first to build an army and organize and propagandize the masses; only then, when there was broad popular support, should a military attack be launched on a large scale. "The moment for military operations will be possible when internal conditions will be favorable for them."[3] To undertake at this time (1923) the military action that Sun proposed would be "adventurous, leading to easy failure."[4] Kuomintang and Russian historiography have, though for different reasons, tried to represent Chiang as seeing the Kremlin through wide-open eyes; that, whatever impression he gave the Russians, he actually opposed them from the beginning. But there is evidence to the contrary: Chiang believed that the Russians could, if they would, help—and he was, then as later, more than willing to accept that aid.

Chiang remained in Moscow until after a special meeting of the Executive Committee of the Comintern on the national-liberation question and the Kuomintang. That conclave concluded on November 28 with a statement favorable to Moscow-KMT cooperation, and Chiang left the Soviet capital for home on the following day. Arriving in Shanghai, to which he had become increasingly attached after 1911 and where he had many friends in high places, Chiang was in no particular hurry to reach Canton. He arrived there finally in mid-January, in time for the First Kuomintang Congress. However, he was not a delegate to the congress, which was probably an affront to his ego. When he became a member of the Military Council established by the congress, and was appointed head of the seven-man commission designated to set up a military academy for the KMT, he was somewhat mollified. But the longer Chiang remained in Canton, the more apparent it became that he was not in Sun's inner circle. Wang Ching-wei, Hu Han-min, Liao Chung-k'ai, and a number of generals superseded him. His financial requests for the new academy, he felt, were inadequately heeded. Unhappy, he returned to Shanghai to sulk. (A number of explanations in addition to the one presented here have been given for Chiang's return to Shanghai in February 1924, including that he was upset because Sun would not except his negative evaluation of the Russians.)

Chiang's absence from Canton did not interfere with the development of the military academy, which was in the forefront of both Sun's and Borodin's immediate objectives. On February 23, Lio Chung-k'ai, who had proved unusually capable and responsible and was trusted by both Sun and Borodin, was made acting head of the preparatory committee. He would play the chief role in getting the academy started. In spite of his prima-donna tendencies, Chiang was recognized as having credentials much needed at that time by the KMT: he had military training and experience but was not a warlord; he had no army of his own; he was close to Sun and accepted his leadership. In the Kuomintang, such credentials were unique. Thus it was that Sun, Liao, Hu Han-min, and others asked Chiang to return to Canton, to become the commandant of the Whampoa Military Academy. He consented.

The academy, situated on Ch'ang-chow Island, called Whampoa at the time, was on the Pearl River, ten miles (thirty minutes by motorboat) south of the Canton docks. Its fort and provincial military and naval schools dated back to the 1870s. Still standing were the original wooden buildings, with lines of columns on all four sides to support covered passages offering protection from the torrential downpours common to South China. Some of the original personnel sent to Whampoa a half century earlier to man the fort still held the same jobs or had passed them on to sons and grandsons. Whampoa was hardly an ideal site for the new academy, but when resources were as sparse as Sun's, its facilities were welcomed.

The academy, with Chiang as its commandant, began functioning in May. The inauguration ceremonies in June were celebrated in grand style. Sun came down from Canton, accompanied by Borodin, Wang Ching-wei, and Hu Han-min. All four, plus Chiang Kai-shek and several others, sat on the platform as Chinese dignitaries made the first of what were to be many official speeches during the next two years to the students of the Whampoa Academy. Whampoa was at the very center of Russian and Chinese aspirations in Canton. Its graduates would drive the warlords out of Kwangtung, solidify the KMT's power foundations, and make possible the drive north. The opening of Whampoa, therefore, was a most significant milestone in the emancipation of China—as those on the platform that muggy June day recognized. But while Whampoa was indispensable for Borodin's plans and inextricable from his successes, it carried within it from the start the divisive virus of class interest.

The first students began arriving at Whampoa in the early spring of 1924. Although most of them came from Kwangtung and from Hunan, the neighboring nationalist and revolution-oriented province to the north, most of the eastern provinces of China were also represented. But wherever they hailed from, the cadets had one thing in common: they were, almost without exception, middle-class, the sons of landowners, merchants, professional men. This was guaranteed by the entrance requirements: one had to be a middle school or college graduate to enroll in Whampoa. Otherwise how could the recruits be quickly trained for the task at hand? No sons of the working class or the peasantry had such credentials. If they had, their orientation would have ceased to be working-class or peasant. Later on, when the full consequences of the class bias of the student body were recognized, a remedial program was inaugurated so that the sons of the poor might also become part of the officer corps of China's future, but the effort was half-hearted and late.

The Whampoa recruits wanted an independent China. They were devoted to the cause of Sun Yat-sen. They were nationalists. But, as bourgeois, they were not social radicals. They were not against private property and capital. Yet from the beginning of their Whampoa experience they were exposed to a message that was anathema to middle-class interests. The curriculum of the military academy at Whampoa was designed by Borodin's Russians on the basis of their own experience. One of the basic ingredients of a Soviet military education was political indoctrination. The idea that troops fought better if they knew why they fought was not a uniquely Soviet notion, but its emphasis was distinctly Russian, and it was certainly unique in twentieth-century China. Traditionally, soldiers fought for rice and silver, not for ideology.

While Chiang was in Moscow, the Russians had preached the importance of political training for troops. Sun, too, had heard it advocated over and again as one of the chief sources of Russian victory. Both were undoubtedly persuaded. But the critical questions were the content of the political instruction and who would provide it. In Kwangtung, there were no experienced propagandists the Russians thought qualified to carry out political indoctrination, nor were many Chinese interested in the job. It was a new, untraditional task, and what were the rewards? Accordingly, there were few applicants for the openings in political propaganda—and few complaints when Borodin appropriated the positions for special cadres largely selected from the Chinese Communist Party and the most radical elements of the Chinese trade-union movement. Under the direction of Russian specialists, who provided ideas, materials, advice, and supervision, such leftists as the future CCP leader Chou En-lai were given control of the political section at Whampoa.

The propaganda machinery at Whampoa was seen by CCP members and sympathizers as a matchless opportunity for the left, one that the CCP and Borodin sought to exploit to the full. The numbers assigned to propaganda work multiplied as Whampoa became the training ground for Chinese political commissars and propagandists, who would staff an expanding nationalist army. It served the same purpose for agitation specialists of other nationalities—such as Ho Chi Minh, the future Vietnamese leader—soon to be dispatched throughout Southeast Asia. But as this communist foothold grew, and as the purveyors of the message sympathized with radical worker and peasant goals and advocated the extinction of capitalists and landlords, the middle-class cadets reacted.

From the beginning, class tensions threatened the Kuomintang-CCP-Russian alliance. Still, all sides rejoiced when in October 1924 the first class of cadets, only part way through its training, joined in the victorious defense of Sun's government against another militarist attack. The cadets were seen as the first representatives of the new army, and, although the defeat of the opposition had many reasons behind it, the victory aroused great enthusiasm for Whampoa. The dream of an independent Chinese force, controlled not by warlords but by men dedicated to ridding China of foreign exploitation, was already being realized. As one Russian adviser wrote, the political influence of the school had already (October 1924) extended "beyond the limits of the island and had become a powerful factor in all political events in Canton . . . Gradually, the political activeness of the school had widened . . . it was at the head of the social-political movement in Canton."[5] But the greater the influence, the greater the stakes. Whampoa, the foundation of national strength, increasingly became the center of ideological dispute.

By the summer of 1924, the Russian enterprise in Kwangtung province was well under way. The reorganization of the KMT was completed; Whampoa had been founded. Neither development was free of opposition, and much more lay ahead. But in spite of controversy on many issues, progress was being made. Borodin, who had introduced these innovations and was supervising their execution, was becoming more secure.

The revolutionary tapestry that was being woven in Canton had been commissioned in Moscow. Suggestions for its effective execution came from many sources, but its actual design, the collection of the often delicate and scarce materials, and the strenuous and meticulous effort of weaving the fabric were the province of Borodin. His chief Chinese resource was Sun Yat-sen. Borodin never lost sight of the fact that Sun's support and cooperation were critically important. Whatever could be accomplished must be done through Sun. It was in Borodin's interest to build Sun up both because he was susceptible to flattery and because the more important Sun became, the more Borodin could do. It was in this vein that Borodin arranged for Sun to be elected *tsung-li,* leader, for life at the Kuomintang congress.

Sun, despite his continuing doubts about the Russians, was an excellent front man. He was pliable. Within limits, Borodin could bend Sun to his wishes, especially in the crucial ideological realm. Sun was, at best, an indifferent ideologist. Though he could be stubborn, he had a propensity for adopting whatever ideological formulation he last heard—and he heard from Borodin frequently. When it suited Borodin's purposes, he would speak to Sun hour after hour, day after day, about 1905, 1917, the civil war, Lenin, organization, the need for mass support, strategy and tactics. During these long hours, Borodin provided Sun with the new material and insights that he hoped to see reflected in Sun's public expressions. His efforts were often rewarded because when Sun spoke from the platform he tended to reproduce the most recent ideas he had heard, usually from Borodin.

Borodin cultivated and catered to Sun because he needed him. Similarly, Sun needed Russian expertise and armaments. That each was using the other did not preclude a successful association, since both had similar short-run objectives. Almost from the beginning of his sojourn in Canton, Borodin had proved that the Russians could deliver. As a result, Sun had come to trust Borodin, more than he did the Bolsheviks in general. Although he would continue to remain suspicious of the Russians, he had few doubts about his Lafayette. He came to regard Mikhail Markovich as his friend, upon whose advice he could rely and who could get him what he wanted. At every juncture Sun attempted to promote Borodin. Constantly at political gatherings and mass meetings, Sun presented Borodin as his friend and advocate, thus enhancing Borodin's stature. He involved Borodin in every area of KMT affairs, whether an organizational or a policy matter, whether domestic or foreign. Borodin was present at all important government and party meetings; participated in the most basic KMT decisions; had the crucial voice in the most fundamental questions.[6]

Sometimes Borodin overstepped his authority and incurred Sun's displeasure. Usually this was when he was frustrated in carrying out day-to-day tasks of organization. As Borodin attempted to introduce more efficient practices, he would inevitably create frictions. Most of those nearest to Sun for the past decades resented what Borodin was doing. They did not welcome his challenge to old authorities and ideas. Some of the more skillful bureaucrats thwarted Borodin when the right opportunity came. Occasionally Sun's cronies persuaded him to shorten Borodin's tether. But usually Sun supported Mikhail Markovich, who in turn handled Sun with deftness and sensitivity.

Though Sun was Borodin's trump card, it was not his only card. The KMT, whatever its shortcomings, still represented Chinese nationalism. As such, it attracted Chinese students in large numbers. As in most places and times, the students were the most susceptible to revolutionary fervor. Students had been involved in the outbreaks leading to the 1911 revolution, in the protests against the treatment of China after World War I, and in subsequent demonstrations against imperialism in China. Students were among the strongest supporters of Sun Yat-sen; students had lifted him on their shoulders and carried him into the city when he returned to Canton in 1923. In 1924, as the KMT reorganization began, many students became deeply involved.

In some Kwangtung schools, both native and missionary but especially the latter, the faculty discouraged student nationalist sympathies, declaiming against the so-called sovietization of Canton and threatening to dismiss those in their charge who participated in·revolutionary activity. But at Kwangtung University, as at many secondary schools, students held meetings in support of KMT renewal, helped to reshape the KMT, raised money for it, demanded that conservative professors be fired, and went on strike in behalf of their aims. It was from among these students that some of the most radical and fervent participants in the Chinese revolution were recruited. They were angry, impressionable, idealistic. Offended by the activities of the "imperialists," they wanted action.

Recognizing that it was from such youth that future revolutionaries would come, Moscow sought to have them properly trained, that is, by Moscow. In 1925, hoping to prepare Russian-speaking, Soviet-indoctrinated, and highly trained cadres to guarantee the revolutionary future of China, the Russian party established Sun Yat-sen University in Moscow, near the Kremlin. During the next two years well over a thousand middle school and university students, selected by the Control Committee of the CCP, attended at Moscow's expense. It was from their numbers that much of the future leadership of the CCP was drawn.

But in 1924 and 1925, these cadres were not yet trained, and Borodin badly needed reliable Chinese assistants. One of his more troublesome problems was finding Chinese who could understand him, for skilled Russian-Chinese translators were rare. The Russians, as well as most foreigners in China, communicated with the Chinese in English. It was a language that Sun knew, as did most of the upper echelon of KMT officials; it was also the language in which Central Executive Committee sessions of the KMT were conducted. But to establish Chinese-Russian communication at lower levels, Borodin needed other Chinese fluent in English. And this led him to the university-educated, Americanized Chinese living in Canton, who had returned home after being trained in the United States. Their numbers were not great, between two and three hundred, but Borodin needed them to staff his offices, communicate his ideas, operate his automobiles. He also needed them because they were the sons and daughters of important Canton families.

Returned Chinese students often felt out of place in their homeland. Abroad, the girls had learned to bob their hair, shorten their skirts, wear high heels; the boys learned to dress in white duck trousers, buck shoes, and to race autos and motorboats. They had developed a taste for jazz; now they listened to the victrola and danced the Charleston hour after hour. How could their parents tolerate such a backward China? Along with talk of movies and Gershwin and life in the West, they discussed republicanism and Chinese unity, no doubt intertwined with personal dreams of power.

Into this milieu Sun Yat-sen introduced Borodin. One teatime at a Cantonese salon frequented by returnees, Sun spoke to the young Chinese present. He asked for three minutes of silent "self-examination" and consideration of the doctrines of republicanism and self-determination. Then he introduced his friend Borodin, a man with a "genius for organization" who had come to help establish a republic in China.[7] Borodin bowed politely when introduced, but he did not speak on this occasion. However, he went to the salon on subsequent afternoons, becoming a regular visitor. He talked to the young Chinese of the need for high ideals, about Sun's aspirations for China and the means for accomplishing them. It was the kind of small-group situation in which Borodin flourished. He was pleasant, agreeable, respectful. In his discourses and conversation he was able to combine philosophical idealism, moral conviction, and practical prescription. He took the "long view" with the ex-students. His audience would sit enraptured as he described the new organizations that were to carry out Sun's designs and offered glimpses of their exploits. And, he told the returnees, there was a place for them in the new China; able men and women were needed.

The word spread not only among returned students in Canton, but elsewhere in China as well. Soon individuals, sometimes small groups, came south to Canton to enlist in the KMT, to learn the new techniques of propaganda and organization by day and to dance, visit cafes, and talk by night. These new recruits to the Chinese revolution were swept up in rounds of meetings, instructional sessions, and rallies; the early victories of the KMT strengthened their enthusiasm. Later, as it became apparent that not all Chinese revolutionaries had identical objectives and that to follow Borodin might cost them their inheritances, many began to drift away. But for a while they were important links in the development of the revolutionary apparatus, and some stayed on in spite of the feared consequences.

Among the bourgeoisie, there was still another group that Borodin sought to cultivate: the Chinese Communist Party. Although the CCP was middle-class, radical, weak in numbers and discipline, Borodin sorely needed its loyalty and abilities. But the CCP, by and large, had little sympathy with the pro-KMT strategy of Borodin and the Russians. The youthful CCP members chafed at organizing for the KMT instead of the CCP, and at the latter's subordinate role. For the most part, Borodin persuaded the Canton CCP to accept his direction. But as late as the spring of 1925 there were only about two hundred party members in Canton.

Elsewhere the CCP, particularly its Central Committee in Shanghai, resisted the Moscow-imposed line. In 1924 and early 1925, the differences grew between the Canton CCP members, under Borodin's guidance, and CCP members in the north. An analysis of the CCP journal *Guide Weekly,* January-May 1925 indicates the degree to which the Central Committee in Shanghai opposed continued cooperation with the KMT and berated the Canton party organization. The Kwangtung District Committee of the party was accused of doing Borodin's bidding at the expense of its own organization. Its members were branded as KMT "leftists."

In spite of these intramural disputes, however, the CCP in 1924–1925 did reorganize the KMT across China, in Peking, in Hupeh, in Hunan, and elsewhere. Where the work was done, it was done by the CCP. Under Borodin's aegis, the influence of the CCP in the KMT and the government in the south grew quickly. But its national membership remained infinitesimal. As late as January 1925, by its own reckoning, it had only one thousand members, and most of these were at loggerheads with one another. Gradually, however, as the KMT reorganization proceeded, as Whampoa's influence began to emerge, as Borodin's hand reached out, and the CCP suffered political defeats, conspicuous opposition to the KMT subsided among the party faithful. But it did not disappear.

Of all of Borodin's potential supporters, the workers and the peasants seemed, on the surface, the most promising. Certainly, the 700,000 workers in Canton had abundant reason for discontent. They worked up to twenty hours per day in exchange for a corner in which to sleep and some handfuls of rice. They had a seven-day week and received only three days of vacation per year. They were often whipped, branded, even burned with scalding water, at the employers' discretion. One could quit, but the competition for jobs in overpopulated Canton was intense. Foremen in the Canton factories regularly removed employees so their jobs could be given to relatives. The workers were constantly threatened with lower wages, because of high unemployment rates and because women and children, desperately in need of employment to supplement the family income, would work for less than the adult males who made up the regular urban working force.

On the other hand, the sting of the working-class situation in Canton was limited by the fact that 95 percent of the workforce was employed in small shops and businesses run on a family basis, with relationships tempered by everyday contact between employer and employee, who were usually related. Discipline was not, in practice, severe. Although in a retail shop one might sometimes work virtually around the clock, when activity was slack one could sleep on bags of rice stacked in the rear of the store. In time of need, the family would share its resources. And in the small Canton factory, the pace was far less rigorous than in Western-type factories.

In Canton, moreover, the guild system was in effect. Carpenters, brickmakers, jewelers, all had their own guilds, developed over hundreds of years, each with its own traditions, its own patron saints and temples and elan. Masters recruited and trained their apprentices, who in turn hoped one day to become masters themselves. It was often to the master's interest, having trained the apprentice, to hold him as long as possible, since he would thereby get experienced assistance at a minimum price. The journeyman might resent his predicament, but the desire to become a master usually kept him in line.

Canton, then, was a city with a large urban workforce, but it was still trapped in preindustrial relationships. Economic facts of life, as well as bonds of family and tradition, insulated it to a large degree from the call of trade-union organization. Though not equally true throughout China—Shanghai, a "new" city built on a mudflat in the nineteenth century for purposes of trade and later industry, was a noted exception—the Canton pattern predominated almost everywhere. Thus Chinese urban workers were not the rich breeding ground for radical causes they might have seemed to be. Their class consciousness was at an extremely primitive level. There was no sense of labor solidarity, the chief allegiance being to family and clan.

But, ideologically, the workers' movement had to be at the foundation of any Marxist movement; no Soviet representative could have been oblivious to this and still hope to justify his conduct in Moscow. Accordingly, Borodin pushed the trade-union movement, financing it liberally within his means. He engineered the assignment of CCP members of the KMT to the area of worker affairs. He imported Soviet statisticians, economists, and labor historians to investigate the Canton workforce, to evaluate it and determine the best approach in organizing it. And he assigned the trusted Liao Chung-k'ai, who wore a half dozen other hats, to be director of union activity. Liao set up an office, which functioned largely through a CCP secretary, flew the hammer and sickle over its door, and began generating new unions.

Though organizing efforts in Canton frequently met with apathy and conservative opposition, nevertheless 170,000 workers were brought together in the May Day 1924 demonstration, where Sun made a rambling address that went on so long that no one else had an opportunity to speak. The following month, the communist-run Conference of Transportation Workers of the Pacific brought agents of the Profintern—the trade-union arm of the Comintern—to Canton. These agents met with Borodin, Liao, and members of the existing trade unions, in particular the radical Seamen's Union. Out of their efforts came a flood of new unions—for rickshaw pullers, cart pushers, bricklayers, carpenters, and others. But most Cantonese workers remained outside the ranks of organized labor.

The trade-union movement probably would have continued to develop slowly but for an attempt on the life of the French governor-general of Indo-China, Martial Merlin. On June 19, 1924, while Merlin was on an official visit to Canton, he was fired upon by a Chinese The foreign colony demanded satisfaction; the response of Liao Chung-k'ai, the civilian governor, did not satisfy the resident colonials. The authorities in the foreign enclave of Shameen, which had been built by the British on a sandbar in the Pearl River, thereupon announced that all Chinese who crossed over to the island must have a pass with their photograph attached. This the Chinese denounced as an affront to their dignity. The several thousand Chinese who comprised the workforce of Shameen, doing everything from making beds to keeping books in the banks and order in the streets, walked off the job on July 15, creating the "Shameen strike."

The Shameen strike was based on national, not economic, issues. Accordingly, it had broad support throughout Canton. Under the nominal leadership of Liao Chung-k'ai, with Borodin and the CCP providing the bulk of the behind-the-scenes direction, a strike committee was organized; pickets controlled access to Shameen; antiforeign propaganda was issued in Canton and dispatched throughout China; a nation-wide campaign to raise strike funds was undertaken. Early in the strike the Chinese could and would have seized Shameen, but Borodin, fearing

British intervention, urged forbearance. After five weeks the strike collapsed, mostly because the workers needed food. But the Chinese of Canton had succeeded in largely paralyzing Shameen and had discovered that a nationalist cause and a local organization could bring effective mass action. Out of the Shameen strike of 1924 came a more highly sensitized Chinese population in Canton, prepared to be mobilized and ready, if not eager, for action.

Largely as a result of the Shameen strike, membership of Canton trade unions expanded substantially during the second half of 1924, followed by a similar upsurge in union activity elsewhere in China in early 1925. At the Second National Labor Congress, which convened in Canton on May Day 1925, one hundred sixty-six unions, claiming a membership of 540,000, were represented. Even assuming some inflation in numbers, this was a respectable showing.

On the same day that the Second National Labor Congress opened in Canton, another Borodin-backed congress was gathering in the same city: the First Kwangtung Provincial Congress of Peasants. Borodin was seeking to enlist the Chinese peasantry in the revolution, along with Chinese industrial workers. Certainly, the peasants, no less than the workers, had cause for discontent. In Kwangtung province, according to Borodin's staff, 70 percent of the peasants rented all or part of the land they tilled. Some 85 percent of the best land was held by absentee owners who rented it out at rates that varied from 50 to 70 percent of the crop. Stiff taxes—up to thirty different levies were imposed in some parts of Kwangtung—were extracted by the local authorities, mostly militarists. The latter were frequently replaced by other militarists, who promptly imposed their own taxes. Moreover, as the population increased, the need for additional land grew. Where were the impoverished tenants to get it? Taxes and famine often forced peasants to borrow money, usually at 3 to 5 percent interest a month, but sometimes as high as 50 percent. In spite of harvesting three or sometimes even four crops a year, the Kwangtung peasant was hopelessly mired in poverty.

In the past, the hard lot of the peasant had been expressed in the usually brief but fierce jacqueries that are characteristic of suffering peasantries throughout history. In the twentieth century, the secret organizations that had developed in China against the Manchus were also employed by residents of the Chinese countryside against the robber militarists and others who exploited them. To protect themselves, the members of these organizations would obtain arms and attempt to fight off the invaders. Successful in doing this, they would then begin to drive off all outsiders, particularly tax collectors. Sometimes they would turn against rich landowners and others who demanded usurious rates of interest. But sometimes more affluent landowners organized self-defense corps, to be used against the poor peasants as well as against outsiders. Thus, the "class" basis of such secret organizations as the Red Spears, which flourished in Hunan in the 1920s, was problematic.

Though to some observers, the Red Spears and similar organizations were the core of China's revolutionary potential, Borodin was wary about relying too heavily on the peasantry. The peasants were still engulfed in feudalism. Like the workers, their chief loyalties were familial. Their primary perspective was local, not national. If they could be a useful adjunct on a short-term basis, they lacked staying power. Nevertheless, with over 80 percent of the population involved in agriculture, Borodin was obliged to cultivate the peasants, minimally to neutralize them, maximally to draw them into the revolution. He recalled Roy's conviction that the peasants were the only dependable source of mass strength in a nonindustrial country.

So Borodin began to woo the peasants. He had long attempted to convince Sun Yat-sen that the peasants must be given incentives. At first, he had proposed that the land of rich absentee landowners be confiscated and handed over to the peasants. But Sun had refused even to consider this, unwilling to alienate the bourgeois support that had sustained him in the past. Borodin, working on CI instructions, then argued for at least "token" social reform in the countryside. Do something to involve the peasants. But the most Sun would accept, in spite of Borodin's pleas, was a 25 percent reduction in land rents. Even this, although approved by the KMT congress, was never put into effect.

Repeatedly rebuffed by Sun on land reform, Borodin nevertheless persevered in pursuing peasant support. In February 1924 the KMT government established, at Borodin's behest, a peasant section and in July it set up a Peasant Affairs Investigating Committee with Borodin as adviser. Organizers, for the most part CCP members, were sent into the countryside to propagandize the peasants. To train these organizers and propagandists, a Peasant Training Institute was opened with a faculty that was overwhelmingly CCP. Many of the future leaders of the CCP were involved with the Peasant Training Institute and its successors.

Although Sun consented to speak at the first graduation of the Peasant Training Institute in August 1924, and paid lip service to the idea of peasant participation in the revolution, he continued to have serious reservations. He counseled caution to the graduates of that initial class: "Speak only of the farmers' suffering, and teach them how to unite."[8] Emphasize peaceful solutions; avoid talk of confiscation. And when a peasant union became involved in a pitched battle with a landlord-organized "peasant brotherhood," Sun Yat-sen sent his personal bodyguard to support the landowners against the union. Out in the field, the peasant union organizers encountered mixed responses. In some areas, hired thugs of the peasant brotherhood beat and killed them. But in other places the organizers found a warm reception. In one village, 250 peasants attended the first organizational meeting. Elsewhere, a single emissary allegedly succeeded in organizing eleven districts in two weeks.

In general, peasant unions grew much more rapidly than the trade unions, if only because there were larger numbers from which to draw. In mid-1924, the peasant unions had 3000 members; by the time of the First Kwangtung Provincial Congress of Peasants on May 1, 1925, the number had grown to 21,000. By late September, more than 500,000 peasants in Kwangtung had been organized into unions. Shortly thereafter, Borodin told Lewis Gannett, a visiting American journalist and one of the few Western newsmen who thought the southern regime was worth attention, that "the peasants are eager to organize into unions."[9] But what were the implications of enrolling a thousand or a hundred thousand in a union? Could they become a disciplined force, capable of revolutionary fervor? Millions of poor peasants

Borodin in Chicago, around 1917. Photograph probably given to Fanya by Vincent Sheean.

Fanya and Borodin. From the Paris files of the *New York Times,* National Archives.

Borodin's 1919 visa, issued in Santo Domingo. Some of the information is obviously a cover. From U.S. State Department files opened in the 1970s, National Archives.

(Form. No 228)
(Established July, 1917)

CONSULAR No. 060

Declaration Of Alien About To Depart For The United States.

(Declaración de un extrangero próximo a salir para los Estados Unidos.)

Michael M. Gruzenberg
Title of office Place Date
Título de la oficina Lugar Fecha

I, *Michael M. Gruzenberg, Businessman* a Citizen or Subject of
Yo Name of declarant Occupation Ciudadano o súbdito de
Nombre del declarante Ocupación

Armenia, Russia, bearer of passport No. *6201* dated *April 12, 1919.*
Name of country Portador del pasaporte No. Fechado
Nombre del País

issued by, *Mexican Consulate* am about to go to the United States, accompanied by
Expedido por Name of office disponiéndome a salir para los EE. UU. acompañado por
Nombre de oficina

Wife _____, born at _____
Esposa Full name nacida en
nombre entero

Sons under 16 years of age as follows:
Hijos menores de 16 años como sigue:

_____, born at _____,
Name Nacido en Date
Nombre Fecha

_____, born at _____
Nacido en

And daughters under 21 years of age as follows:
E hijas menores de 21 como sigue:

_____, born at _____,
Name Nacida en Date
Nombre Fecha

_____, born at _____
Nacida en

1. I was born at *Vitebsk, Russia* on *June 9 1884*;
1. Yo nací en Place en Date
   Lugar Fecha

2. My father was a citizen or subject of *Russia* of the *Hebrew*
2. Mi padre era un ciudadano o súbdito de de la raza

race; my mother was born a citizen or subject of *Russia* of the
Mi madre nació una ciudadana o súbdita de de la

Armenian race;
race;

3. a) I last resided at *Scheveningen Kurhaus* on *June 14, July 24*
3. a Tenía mi residencia Address Fecha
   últimamente en Lugar Dirección

b) I have resided in or visited the following countries within the past five years: *Norway, Se*
b He residido en o he visitado los países siguientes en los 5 años pasados: Places, address and d.
Lugares, direcciones y fec.

Russia, Germany, Switzerland, Holland

4. I have _____ previously resided in the United States as follows:
4. he residido en los EE. UU. en la fecha, del puerto, y en el vapor como sigue:
Chicago, 2058 W. Division Str. My home is there
Dates Place and address Object of residence
Fechas Lugar y dirección Objeto de residencia
my wife and two children born there

5. I intend to depart for the United States on the date, from the port, and on the steamship as follows:
5. A mi intención de salir para los EE. UU. en la fecha, del puerto, y en el vapor como sigue:
August 23, 1919, Santo Domingo city, Huron
Date Port Steamship
Fecha Puerto Vapor

6. I name the following, with addresses, as references:
6. Nombro las personas siguientes, con direcciones, como referencias:
a *Will Irwin, 10 Jackson Pla Str. Washington D.C.*
In the country from which declarant starts
En el país del cual el declarante
b *Jane Adams, Hull House, Chicago.*
In the United States
En los Estados Unidos

7. I expect to go to the United States for *transit to Mexico.*
7. Es mi intención de ir a los Estados Unidos para

Object of visit
Objeto de la visita

as shown by *Passport # 6/201.*
como se demuestra por

Documents or other proofs of object
Documentos u otra prueba del objeto

to reside at *Temporarily at Mexico City* for a period of *two or more weeks.*
a residir en

City, street and number
Ciudad, calle y número

Por un período de

8. I have informed myself of the provisions of Section 3, Immigration Act of February 5, 1917, and
8. Yo me he informado sobre las disposiciones de la Sección 3, Ley de Inmigración de Febrero 5, 1917, y estoy convencido de

am convinced that I am elegible for admission into the United States thereunder;
que soy elegible para admisión en los Estados Unidos

9. a) I realize that, if I am one of a class prohibited by law from admission into the United States,
9. a Yo comprendo que, si soy de una clase prohibida por la ley de admisión en los Estados Unidos, seré deportado o detenido

I will be deported or detained in confinement in the United States, and (b) I am prepared to assume
bajo restricción en los Estados Unidos, y (b) soy preparado a asumir el riesgo de deportación y de un regreso compulsivo en caso de

the risk of deportation and of a compulsory return trip in case of my rejection at an American port.
mi rechazamiento a un puerto Americano.

M. M. Gruzeoberg.

Signature of declarant
Firma del declarante

Subscribed and sworn to before me this ___ AUG 23 1918 ___ day of _____,
Firmado y jurado ante mí este

día de

Month and year
Mes y año

Ga. A. Makinson

Official signature
Firma oficial

Remarks by official taking declaration:
Observaciones del oficial que tome la declaración:

Seeing off Chiang Kai-shek and staff from Canton on the Northern Expedition, 1926. Left to right: Borodin; Fanya; Mme. Liao Chung-kai; Chiang's new bride; General Blyukher; Chiang and his young son (his successor on Taiwan); seated in front, Chang Chiang-chiang (Chiang's "elder brother"). Probably taken by John McCook Roots.

Borodin at luncheon, Wuhan, 1927; Fanya in the background. Probably taken by Vincent Sheean.

Fanya and the new women of China, Canton, 1925. Probably taken by Anna Louise Strong.

Borodin in Canton, 1925; Wang Ching-wei, head of the Canton government, stands in front. Probably taken by Lewis S. Gannett.

Borodin, his arm in a cast from a horseback accident, Wuhan, 1927. Probably taken by A. Krarup-Nielsen. From the Paris files of the *New York Times*, National Archives.

Borodin shooting grouse in the Gobi Desert, 1927. Taken by Percy Chen, son of the foreign minister in the Wuhan government. From Chen's *China Called Me: My Life Inside the Chinese Revolution*, copyright 1979 by Percy Chen; by permission of Little, Brown and Company.

Main hall and reception room of the Sugar Palace, Comintern headquarters in Moscow. Taken by a member of the Kharistonenko family in 1916. When seen by the author in 1970, the furniture was virtually unchanged.

Borodin, thin and drawn, soon after his return to Moscow, 1927. From *Ot-chizna,* 1971.

and workers, each of them with his own tale of starvation, igno-
miny, and frustration, were prepared to turn on their oppressors.
The peasants and workers were collectively powerful, but they
were also uneducated, inflammable, sometimes fanatic, sometimes pushing beyond their leaders, sometimes unwilling to
move at all. They were, in brief, undependable. Borodin knew
this. An André Malraux, who was in Canton in the early 1920s,
had Garine (Borodin?) say in the novel *The Conquerors:* "All these
men whom I control, whose souls I have helped to create, how do
I know what they will do tomorrow?"[10]

This was Borodin's dilemma, not only with the workers and
peasants, but with almost all of those from whom he hoped to
forge a movement in China: What would they do tomorrow?
The class interests of educated personnel, civilian and military,
might lead them later to abandon him. Even the loyalty of the
CCP was in doubt. And the masses were amorphous, excitable,
unpredictable, organizable only in the most fragile sense. Out of
such a menagerie, one could make a jacquerie, but could one
make a revolution? In the hard light of Marxist ideology, of
logic, of revolutionary history and his own experience, Borodin
knew how slight were his chances for success. But the Leninist
attitude was like Napoleon's: *On s'agit et puis on voit.* Maybe something good will happen. Maybe new alignments will develop.
Borodin had his assignment, orders, ambitions, and a newly acquired sense of power—not to mention his series of successes that
sometimes obscured the larger prospects of failure.

We have seen that Borodin had few people upon whom he
could depend. There was his personal translator, Cheng T'ai-lei,
alternate member of the Central Committee of the CCP and
Borodin's representative to the Shanghai party organization;
there was Liao Chung-k'ai, the American-born confidant of Sun;
there was Fanya, who late in 1923 followed him to China with
their two children, and upon whom, others failing, he became
increasingly dependent; and there were the sovetniki.

From the beginning, Moscow conceded that it had few advisers to send. It never did send many, contrary to later reports
by hysterical observers in the north. The total number of Soviet

military and civilian personnel throughout China from 1923 to 1927 was only, at the most, a few thousand. Nor were all of these attached to Sun's regime. Throughout the period, Moscow continued to keep its options open by dispatching advisers to almost any headquarters in China that would accept them. This meant the presence of sovetniki in places like Kalgan and Kaifeng, as well as in Canton. Borodin never had more than 400 advisers, military and civilian. In Canton, in late 1923, he had 5 military advisers. By June 1924 the number of Russians had grown to 25 military and civilian advisers and support personnel. In January 1926 the number stood at 47 and in the spring of that year there were 58, some of whom had come south after the failure of missions in the north. In late 1926 and early 1927, the number of Russian advisers with Borodin increased somewhat, but not greatly.

The Soviet advisers who came to help make revolution were men and women of varied background and skills. A few had had wide underground and revolutionary experience, were veteran agents of the party and the Comintern. Most of the military personnel had distinguished themselves in the civil war and then had taken advanced work at a Soviet military institute. Among the civilian personnel were economists, sociologists, lawyers, historians, some already prominent, others destined to future leadership in their disciplines. China in 1924–1927 provided field experience for almost the entire school of budding Russian China specialists.

Many sovetniki kept diaries of their stay in China. Some of these were published in the late 1920s and early 1930s; others did not appear until the 1960s when they surfaced, for the most part, as source materials for memoirs by participants in the events of 1923–1927. But whether describing events then or four decades later, those who experienced China in the twenties saw the times as filled with excitement, drama, and revolutionary atmosphere. For many, their days in China were the highlight of their career.

The sovetniki lived a harrowing life. There were constant threats, especially when traveling: from bandits; from the Japanese; from the Whites—refugee Russians who had fought against the Bolsheviks and, losing, had fled to China. The military units to which the sovetniki were assigned frequently resented their presence. Chinese officers feared losing face if they accepted orders or even advice from Russian "underlings." The sovetniki worked in areas where there was a high incidence of typhus, dysentery, malaria, and cholera—and little medical care. In Canton, Borodin contracted malaria and dysentery (which proved to be chronic). Most Russians who remained in China for an extended period acquired ailments that plagued them the rest of their lives.

But in spite of the dangers and tensions that confronted them in China, many of the Russians reveled in the opportunities that China offered. They explored the local sights. In Peking they visited the Summer Palace; they climbed to the top of the Gates of Heavenly Peace. In Kaifeng, the Jews among the sovetniki became involved with the remnants of a Jewish community that had existed in that city for almost a thousand years. In Canton, they toured streets so narrow that one could touch the walls on both sides by stretching out one's arms. They walked through the sections noted for the artists who worked in bronze, marble, silver, gold, silk, wood, and lacquer. They visited the flower markets, fruit markets, flea markets, and a fish market that was a rare "ichthyological museum." They saw American movies starring Mary Pickford and Charlie Chaplin. They patronized the Chinese opera. They sampled a wide variety of Chinese restaurants; some became connoisseurs of Peking duck with doilies and thousand-year-old eggs. Some men ordered custom-made suits, an experience not to be repeated for decades. The Russian women had their own modiste, Madame Antoinette, a black woman who spoke only French and Chinese and made them wonderfully frilly things.

The sovetniki of the 1920s were not hampered by Stalin's Victorian norms that would follow a few years later. To be sure, there had to be second thoughts about riding in a rickshaw or being on horseback while infantrymen walked. But generally the sovetniki followed local patterns of behavior. Thousands of miles from home, mail reaching them irregularly, if at all, unable to speak the local tongue, regarded with suspicion and distaste by many, they naturally sought to enjoy the pleasures and adventures at hand. The sovetniki as a group were able and enthusiastic. As the groundwork laid in Kwangtung began to bear fruit, their enthusiasm grew. Although few in number, their service to Borodin and to the revolution in China was great.

Care must be taken not to overstate the role of Borodin in China, as sometimes is done. The Chinese people were distressed by the humiliation of their once-proud country, angered by the exploitation, foreign and domestic, from which they suffered and the second-class position that they, its citizens, endured in their own land. But such grievances, though leading to unrest, were not enough to create a revolution with lasting revolutionary consequences. The conditions for revolution in China had to be molded and forged. This is what Borodin tried to do. In some respects he would fail, but, in others, he met with extraordinary success.

Step by step, Borodin built his revolution. He knew that it was fragile and might at any moment fall apart. But he importuned, coaxed, patched, manipulated, and somehow held the disparate parts of his coalition together. Though jerry-built and wobbly, it nonetheless stood. When Borodin had first come to Canton, his apprehensions were great, and well founded. He wrote Karakhan in Peking almost daily, seemingly to protect himself by describing how perilous Sun's position was. But during 1924 Borodin reported less frequently. He was less concerned with Karakhan's reactions to his every step. Sometimes he bypassed Peking entirely, communicating directly with Moscow. And, in Moscow, his contact was with an old acquaintance of 1905, none other than Stalin, now emerging victorious in the power struggle following Lenin's death. Although much of the world was oblivious to Borodin's role in Canton, Moscow was not and Stalin was not.

11

First Steps

Moscow's plan for a Canton-led revolution required a period of relative tranquility before the revolution could be launched. But Sun, who was impatient to begin his Northern Expedition, would not wait—nor would events. Heroic though he may have appeared to some, because of his long struggle against the Manchus and his continuing fight for national regeneration, Sun was far from being universally revered among the Canton bourgeoisie. In middle-class circles, he was often identified with the warlords, who had brought him to power and who prospered by their arbitrary and mushrooming taxes on the bourgeoisie. But still Sun's treasury remained slim. The warlords, each of whom controlled and profited from his own area, were in business for themselves.

Faced with the burgeoning demands of his expanding political and military organization, Sun needed money. Beginning in February 1924, his government placed duties on the import of ammonium sulfate (used for fertilizer), rubber, and wood alcohol. Later in the month, every merchant was called upon to "lend" the government from $5 to $500, depending upon the size of his enterprise. The following month, a 10 percent surcharge was levied on restaurant meals. In April, banks were ordered to use stamped paper for business transactions, and soft drinks were taxed. In May, new taxes were levied on patent medicines, cosmetics, weddings, funerals, religious celebrations, and rickshaws.

But these new levies did little to increase Sun's revenues. In Kwangtung, taxes were paid not because they were levied but because the militarists sent their soldiers into the shops to demand them. Neither Sun nor Borodin was prepared to do this. But the new taxes did increase animosity toward Sun in the business community and, together with Sun's newfound Bolshevik friends, alarmed the Canton bourgeoisie. Some banks and businesses closed. In other cases, wealthy men continued to do business, but took their fortunes and their families to Hong Kong or Shanghai. More ominously, certain middle-class organizations began to arm.

In nineteenth-century China, as the control of the emperor had weakened and warlord depredations multiplied, individuals and groups had formed security forces to protect themselves. In early 1923 there was near anarchy in Kwangtung as the warlords became more brazen. Local merchants activated self-defense detachments, known as the Merchants' Volunteer Corps (MVC). At the head of the Corps was Ch'an Len-pak, former president of the Canton Chamber of Commerce, comprador of the powerful Hong Kong–Shanghai Bank, reputed owner of silk factories, ten banks, several pawnshops, three insurance companies, much land, and entire streets of houses. Under Ch'an's leadership, a professional staff was hired to organize and train the MVC. Every sizable Canton firm was assessed at least $150 toward the annual $300 maintenance cost of a volunteer. Some firms reportedly furnished funds to support as many as thirty volunteers. Although the figure was doubtless exaggerated, one journalist reported that in late 1923 the Corps had 50,000 men under arms.

At first, the MVC development was aimed at the mercenaries who had divided Kwangtung province among themselves and then proceeded to extort money from the people. But by the spring of 1924, the Corps had begun to shift its focus, away from the Kwangsi and Hunanese mercenaries and toward Sun Yatsen. The MVC's primary objective became to "save Canton from the Bolsheviks." At the end of May 1924, it was decided to strengthen Ch'an's organization and to order $1.5 million in arms from abroad.

During the early summer, merchant opposition to Sun continued to grow. Fears were heightened by the spectacle of workers paralyzing Canton's commerce during the Shameen strike. After the general strike had been canceled, the newly sensitized and unionized workers increasingly called wildcat strikes. First the opium workers, then the printers and compositors, then the match workers. The merchants were not pleased. In late July, news arrived in Canton that a shipment of used German military equipment ordered by Ch'an was about to be delivered by the Danish ship *Hav*. Although a permit to land was issued by the Sun government, when the *Hav* came into port it was seized by two KMT gunboats and escorted to Whampoa where its cargo was unloaded.

The MVC protested, claiming that Sun's government had acted treacherously by first permitting the guns to be unloaded and then seizing them. The Sun forces declared that the MVC was not a legal institution and demanded that the United Canton Merchants' Guild, the parent organization of the Corps, affirm its loyalty and cooperate with the KMT regime. The Guild responded with counter-demands upon the KMT. Sun, unwilling to further antagonize the middle class, seeking reconciliation rather than civil war, proposed to compromise. But the Merchants' Guild wanted the guns, and its members began withholding rice, causing prices to rise and further embarrassing the Sun government.

On August 23, the MVC headquarters threatened that unless the guns from the *Hav* were turned over immediately, a general strike would be proclaimed. Sun did not yield and, on August 25, the strike began. Borodin and his sovetniki had stage-managed the response to the MVC thus far. Now Borodin urged Sun to deal with the general strike by declaring martial law, warning that all shops not open would be liable to seizure, and forbidding the export of valuables from the city. At the same time, Borodin urged that the worker and peasant forces, which were beginning to emerge throughout Kwangtung, be called out against the MVC.

But neither side wanted a military confrontation. Both groups appealed for help from all quarters: the League of Nations, the British, the Japanese, the militarists. At the same time, each verbally assailed the other. Sun, among other things, threatened to bombard MVC headquarters; the British consul-general replied that, if Sun's forces fired upon the MVC, British naval forces would retaliate. Although dust was raised all over Canton by marching feet and threats were the order of the day, outright hostilities were avoided.

Elsewhere in China, war threatened to break out between Wu P'ei-fu and Chang Tso-lin, the two warlords who dominated the central and northern parts of China, respectively. Sun was allied with Chang Tso-lin. With military action impending, Sun announced his intention of becoming involved, hoping that victory with Chang would produce a united China led by him. Borodin protested vociferously. Like his military advisers, like the CCP and many of Sun's closest collaborators, he argued that military action now, when the reorganization of Kwangtung and the development of an army had only begun, would prevent the south from becoming a strong base and would be disastrous for Sun's entire enterprise. They pointed out the danger of leaving Canton when tensions with the MVC threatened to explode. But Sun shrugged off the possibility of serious trouble with the MVC. He was adamant about marching north. His alliance with Chang must be honored, he felt, particularly when it involved his Northern Expedition. On September 18, Sun, already in the field with 24,000 men, almost all of whom belonged to the militarists "allied" with him, again declared his support of Chang Tso-lin and the launching of the Northern Expedition.

In the midst of this bedlam, with civil strife looming in Kwangtung and Sun leaving the city with his dubious mercenary troops to wage war in the north, the first Soviet shipment of arms to Canton arrived aboard the ship *Vorovsky*. Soviet sources describe in detail the great joy among the sovetniki and their allies that greeted the arrival of the *Vorovsky*. That description accurately portrayed the feelings of Borodin and his associates. Surrounded by hostile forces, threatened by British gunboats, suspecting abandonment by Sun—now bent upon his Northern Expedition—and with little material evidence of Soviet concern, Borodin was deeply in trouble. Then suddenly, at a criticial moment, a ship arrived from the Soviet Union with large numbers of rifles, machine guns, and even artillery.

At this point, the record of events becomes confused, largely because many participants later sought to rewrite the record in order to justify and adorn their own actions. The following account seems closest to truth. When Sun heard that the *Vorovsky* was in Canton waters, he ordered Chiang Kai-shek to ship the Russian guns to his front the moment they were unloaded. But Chiang, convinced by the sovetniki that Sun had blundered in going north, defied instructions. Two days later, when Sun ordered him to leave Whampoa and join him at the front with his men, he again failed to act. In the meantime, Sun, seeking to pacify the MVC and obtain badly needed funds, made a deal with the MVC. Half of the *Hav*'s guns and ammunition were to be turned over to the MVC in exchange for $200,000. On October 9, the same day Sun had ordered Chiang to the front, he also ordered him to release the promised guns and ammunition. But Chiang continued to delay, offering to release guns but not ammunition. He employed other dodges to prevent delivery to the Merchants' Volunteer Corps, at least until government forces could be armed from the *Vorovsky,* the artillery placed in position, and the defenses of the city organized.

On the 10th, Sun Yat-sen once again ordered Chiang to the front. This time Chiang specifically refused, or so his records state, declaring that Whampoa must be defended to the death and Canton built up as a strong base for future operations. Further, Chiang implored Sun to return at once to Canton because the situation with the MVC was worsening. On the same day, fighting broke out in Canton. In mid-afternoon, a detachment of the Labor Corps, the Student Corps, and Whampoa cadets paraded along the broad bund paralleling the waterfront, carrying banners and shouting revolutionary slogans. Whether the group was merely on a holiday march to celebrate "10-10" day (the thirteenth anniversary of the 1911 revolution) or had been dispatched as a provocation is unclear. It is also uncertain if the paraders were armed. In any event, when the demonstrators reached the spot where guns from the *Hav* were being unloaded from junks, the leaders demanded that the guns be removed so that they could continue their march. MVC people unloading the guns refused. Suddenly a gunblast was heard and the MVC began firing into the crowd. The marchers fled in all directions with the MVC in pursuit. A dozen paraders were killed and others were wounded. Many of the demonstrators threw up their hands in surrender. Clearly the MVC had won a skirmish.

But this was only the opening scene. The MVC leadership

called a general strike, urged the overthrow of Sun's regime, and tried to get General Ch'en Chiung-ming, who had been expelled the preceding year, to return. On the 11th, a revolutionary committee was established by Sun, at Borodin's urging. It consisted of Sun, Wang Ching-wei, Chiang Kai-shek, Liao Chung-k'ai, the Cantonese militarist General Hsü Ch'ung-chih, the communist T'an P'ing-shan, and Eugene Chen, Sun's fiery, English-educated foreign-policy specialist. But on the same date that the committee was established, Sun again ordered Chiang Kai-shek to his front. Sun assured Chiang that victory for the Northern Expedition was certain and vowed that he would not return to Canton.

Within the next few hours, Sun changed his mind and returned to Canton. Perhaps it was because of the importuning of Borodin; perhaps it was to prod Chiang and his forces toward the north; more likely it was because of information that one of his allies in the north had fled to Japan and that prospects for the Northern Expedition were expiring. In any case, Sun returned to Canton on October 13 with several of his more reliable military units. Shortly thereafter, other pro-Sun forces were ordered into the city.

On the 14th of October, with Sun's assent, the revolutionary committee decided to act, since its position was now as strong as it might ever be. It had the weapons, including artillery from the *Vorovsky,* at its disposal. It had some of the guns and ammunition from the *Hav.* At a meeting on the 14th, a standing committee, consisting of Chiang, Liao, and Borodin, was established to guide the attack against the MVC, which was set for that same night at 10 P.M. Specific assignments were taken by each member of the committee and others were given to Wang Ching-wei, Chou En-lai, who had temporarily discontinued his propaganda work at Whampoa, and his fellow communist, T'an P'ing-shan. Chiang Kai-shek was placed in charge of the Whampoa units. His total forces consisted of 800 Whampoa cadets, 320 members of the Workers' Militia and Peasants' Corps, 220 cadets from the Hunan military school, 500 cadets from the Yunnan military school, 250 troops from two armored trains, 2000 policemen, and all the available military sovetniki. Although Borodin was reluctant to use the recently recruited and inadequately trained Whampoa cadets, they were the only troops he could trust.

The standing committee knew the risks were great. Consequently government funds were taken to the *Vorovsky*, and provisions were made for the speedy evacuation of Sun and his retinue, Borodin, and the sovetniki. But this was not necessary. Sun's forces, orchestrated by the sovetniki, were quickly victorious. By nightfall on the 15th, a day the MVC would later refer to as Bloody Wednesday, the battle was over.

The victory appreciably strengthened Sun Yat-sen, his government, Borodin, and the Russian presence. Again Borodin and the sovetniki had shown their mettle. Just in time, Russian arms had come to the rescue. And once more, Borodin had astutely appraised a complex situation and organized victory. Though Sun was distressed over the failure of Chiang Kai-shek to respond to his earlier orders, he was not one to argue with success. After the victory had been solidified, Sun ordered a triumphal arch to be erected on the street in front of the *Vorovsky*. Accompanied by Borodin—both dressed in white suits and sporting pith helmets against the autumn sun—Sun went to the *Vorovsky* to congratulate the crew and to indicate his pleasure with Soviet aid.

The October 15 success was pivotal, but it was still only one step forward if Borodin's and Sun's objectives were to be realized. The revolutionary forces remained isolated and surrounded by enemies. Though the Canton bourgeoisie had sustained a major setback, they still had to be reckoned with. Sun had no desire to confiscate their wealth or further alienate them; nor did Borodin dare counsel such action. But after this defeat, middle-class hostility ran deeper. And there were still the warlords, including those who had stood with the KMT against the MVC, who controlled most of the economic life of Kwangtung province, and who might at any moment turn on the Sun government. Beyond them stood the British and Japanese and Americans, with their ubiquitous fleets, unlikely to passively permit their major investments in China to perish. Though prospects in Canton were perhaps improving, they were scarcely bright.

By the autumn of 1924, it was clear that revolutionary success in China depended on the development of the army. The major goals of Sun and Borodin—the establishment of a base in Kwangtung, the solution of the economic problem, the march north—required a strong, nonmercenary military force, loyal to the Sun regime and prepared to fight for it. In late October, hard on the heels of the victory over the MVC, a military sovetnik arrived in Canton whose name would eventually become inseparable from the successes the Canton army would win in the years ahead: Vasily Konstantinovich Blyukher, known in China as "Galin."[1]

In his own sphere, Blyukher would be as influential as Borodin. To many Chinese, who could not accept Borodin because of his "Bolshevism," this brave soldier became a hero whose Russian connections could be overlooked because of his military exploits. Colonial Shanghai, learning of repeated victories by the southern armies, would attribute these to Blyukher; surely no Soviet could achieve such results. Blyukher, it was asserted, was really a Frenchman or an Austrian general of noble birth captured during World War I, converted to communism during the revolution. Actually he was a Russian peasant who had joined the Bolsheviks in 1916. For his services during the civil war, he was four times awarded the Order of the Red Banner, the highest Soviet military decoration, and came out of the civil war regarded as one of the Red Army's future leaders.

But even as Blyukher was arriving in Canton, Sun, who had invited him, Borodin, and the sovetniki to that city, was preparing to leave. While the remnants of the MVC were being mopped up in Canton, in Peking, fourteen hundred miles away, another transfer of power was occurring. Feng Yü-hsiang, the so-called Christian general, who once baptized his troops en masse with a firehose, and whom the Russians had sometimes considered a possible alternative to Sun, had taken over the city. Soon after, Feng, considered a liberal, called for a national reunification conference; among the broad assortment of Chinese leaders invited was Sun. Sun was amenable. The meeting sounded important. He was, moreover, tired of Canton, not being used to remaining in one place for long. And if it is true that Sun (a physician by training) suspected that he was fatally ill, as he was, he wanted this "last chance" to unify China.

Borodin, like others, doubted the advisability of the trip. Without his troops, Sun might be captured and held hostage. But these objections did not weigh heavily to Sun, and on No-

vember 1 he said he would accept Feng's invitation. Certainly
Sun's behavior, as he prepared to go north, indicated that he
was aware of his illness and was preparing to take final leave of
his government. During that period, with Borodin constantly at
his elbow, he labored incessantly to put that government in
order. The controversy over the MVC had cost him many remaining supporters. There were few able men upon whom to
draw, and the trusted Liao Chung-k'ai was given still heavier responsibilities. As a conciliatory gesture after the MVC clash,
Sun made Hu Han-min, who had numerous bourgeois contacts,
his chief of staff. Wang Chung-wei was given nominal charge of
the government, but the actual authority was Liao's. General
Hsu Ch'ung-chih was appointed head of the army, but Chiang
Kai-shek was given a position of almost equal standing. Liao,
appointed as "party representative" to the army, was to keep an
eye on both of them. Sun publicly reiterated his unswerving
support for the principles of the *San-min chu-i* and expressed his
faith in China's future. Repeatedly he referred to his gratitude
to Russia and his appreciation for the achievements of the October Revolution.

On the evening of November 12, his fifty-eighth birthday, Sun
began to bid farewell to his followers as 20,000 men passed
before him in a lantern-lit demonstration. On the following
morning, he called in the principal military men and government officials and an old friend or two, to say a few parting
words to each, one at a time. Then he went to Whampoa to
make his farewells to Chiang, the officer corps, and the cadets.
From Whampoa, aboard the *Yung-feng* that had carried him to
and from Canton so many times in the past, he took his last
leave of his native province and headed for Hong Kong. Aboard
the *Yung-feng* with Sun were more than a dozen traveling companions, including Wang Ching-wei, Eugene Chen, and Sun's
charming young wife, Ching-ling, the second daughter of the
wealthy Soong family and a graduate of Wesleyan College in
Macon, Georgia. Also aboard was Borodin.

After a year in Canton, Borodin needed to consult in person
with Karakhan and others in the north on his future course. It
was also thought desirable to keep an eye on Sun, to guard
against any deals he might make with the Japanese or the mili-

tarists while in Shanghai and Peking. But chiefly Borodin was there because Sun was still Borodin's passport to legitimacy and power in China. If Sun was about to die, Borodin needed to be at his side, to prove his loyalty, and to make certain that a dying Sun would not be turned against Russia in his last days. At 6 A.M. on November 14, the party boarded the Japanese ship *Shinyo Maru* on their way north.

Arriving in Shanghai, Sun spent several days at his house on the Rue Molière, where he was visited by many old KMT acquaintances. But some of his former allies found it hard to forgive the treatment accorded the MVC. As one disaffected follower put it, having massacred Kwangtung, Sun now had decided to leave it.[2] In Shanghai, Sun emphasized the importance of maintaining good relations with the Russians. He never spoke more eloquently against imperialism or for the Soviet Union. But on November 22, leaving most of his entourage (including Borodin) behind, Sun took a steamer for Japan. Sun went there to seek medical care, to make one last visit to a country he admired, and to line up support for the forthcoming unification conference. To further that goal he made some glowing pro-Japanese speeches. But just as Sun was embarking on his Japanese campaign, he became very ill, and by December 4 he was back in China, in a hostile Tientsin, where he was regarded as a Bolshevik. Rather quickly he departed for Peking.

Soon after Sun had left for Japan, Borodin, who could not accompany him for diplomatic reasons, went to Peking to consult with Karakhan. With considerable skill and after long and tedious negotiations, Karakhan had won recognition of the USSR by the Peking regime. More than that, he had become accepted by the Chinese as doyen of the diplomatic corps, and he had turned the Soviet mission into the center of nationalist and radical activity in Peking. Borodin was at the Soviet legation and received word of Sun's collapse. When Sun got off the train in Peking, Borodin was at the station to meet him.

By this time Sun's condition was desperate. Arriving in the city, he was taken to the Rockefeller-financed Peking Union Medical College Hospital. On January 26, he was operated on by a team of Western surgeons, who learned that Sun had an advanced case of liver cancer. His case was hopeless. A few days later he was taken to the home of V. K. Wellington Koo, later to become Chiang Kai-shek's ambassador to the United States.

With Sun on his deathbed, a Central Political Council was set up to represent his administration in Peking. The only politically important figure by Sun's side in the north was Wang Ching-wei, and he, faced with the imminent death of his leader, and anticipating his role as successor, played the traditional role of modest disciple. Other than Wang, the council was made up of lower-echelon men. At first this made little difference, since the council had nothing to do. But when it became necessary to act—as in deciding whether to participate in the reunification conference, where the cards were now stacked against Sun's government—there was no real leadership within the group. Borodin stepped into the breach. Chang Kuo-t'ao, who was a CCP member on the Central Political Council, indicates how Borodin took over:

> Cautiously keeping himself from becoming embroiled in the dispute which arose there, he seldom spoke. For the few important proposals he did introduce, he first obtained the endorsement of Sun Yat-sen and made sure that the Council would carry them before bringing them up in any detail. Consequently the Council generally adopted his proposals unanimously, and the Council members gradually came to believe that if an important issue were to stand a chance of being settled, it was best to have Advisor Borodin introduce it.[3]

By early February, it was apparent that Sun's days were numbered. In the struggle to determine their future, all elements in the KMT sought influence. The discussions, according to Borodin, were "conducted with great vehemence and frenzy."[4] Those who had opposed the KMT-CCP-Soviet alliance from the beginning thought the opportunity had come to smash it for good. Even among those committed to cooperation with the Soviet Union (and, necessarily, the CCP), there was the issue of maintaining the alliance. Above all, there was the burning question of who should be the new *tsung-li*.

For the Soviet Union, no less than for others, momentous decisions must be made. The first was to think about the selection of Sun's successor. In Moscow, where the principle of hagiographizing was well understood, China seemed an ideal place for its application. By employing his words and reputation selectively, the Russians could use Sun's image to sanctify Soviet goals more consistently after he died; in life he had never been the most constant of allies. Thus it was important for Borodin to be with Sun to the end, to ensure that others did not seize or distort the legacy. A commitment to the symbol of the dead Sun did not mean that the Soviet Union would maintain his policies. The Russians now asked: Should they continue to cooperate with the KMT? Without Sun, could Russia's position and representatives survive in the military and political quagmire that was Canton? Should they seek out some new Sun Yat-sen? In an area more conducive to revolutionary initiative than Canton? Might General Feng Yü-hsiang, now in Peking and a friendly figure with whom Moscow had contacts, be a viable successor to Sun?

In late 1924 and early 1925, Feng Yü-hsiang and his Kuominchun, the National People's Army, looked more and more promising to Moscow. Feng was attracted to a broad assortment of "liberal" ideals, though, as the Soviet Union had seen, he talked a more liberal line than he followed. But they had been looking for a progressive warlord whom they could support and work with. Feng might be that man. In October 1924 in Peking, Feng had released a number of communist prisoners, had permitted the KMT and CCP to operate openly, hold meetings, publish and circulate brochures and newspapers. Karakhan's and Moscow's interest in Feng began to mount.

On his part, Feng gave evidence of interest in a foreign ally to balance the support the Japanese gave rival warlord Chang Tso-lin, particularly since Feng's relations with Chang had soured. Feng was definitely interested in the arms, although not particularly in the advisers he knew were Moscow's price for cooperation. As it became clear that Sun was dying, Feng fancied himself assuming Sun's mantle, carrying forward the effort to reunify China. Early in 1925, Borodin went to Kalgan in Manchuria, where Feng's headquarters were located. There he and Feng had what one CCP member characterized as a "long and fairly successful talk,"[5] after which Borodin became "especially enthusiastic" about an alliance between the Kuomintang and the Kuominchun. This would also provide an alternative if

Borodin and the Russians were driven out of Canton or decided to leave. Still, Borodin was not certain of Feng's reliability and, in any event, he could not make this decision alone.

As Sun lay dying, Borodin and others in China addressed Moscow: Should further attempts be made to placate the right in Canton, as Sun had done? Or should the right be written off, and the remnants of the KMT captured by the CCP? Should they turn to Feng? It should be kept in mind that, in spite of the Kremlin's stake, China was of secondary significance to Moscow, both to those straining to succeed Lenin and to those devoted to international revolution. As Karakhan remarked to Paul Blanshard later in 1925, China was decidedly a "rearguard engagement" in the workers' struggle.[6] The men in Moscow competing for the succession were too preoccupied with that issue to be greatly concerned about China. They were also faced with a disconcertingly complicated situation and were uncertain what to advise. Not until much later did those at Moscow's summit become involved. By then, circumstances and the men on the scene had already set their course.

During February, Sun grew worse. Western medicine having failed, Chinese physicians were summoned. But they had no greater success. By late February, Sun's doctors warned that the end was near. On the 22nd, those nearest him told him that they needed to know his plans for the future. On the 24th he said that he was ready to talk for posterity. There is considerable agreement on what is contained in the testaments (the "will" and "message to the Soviet Union") that Sun left. But there is little agreement on what they meant or on who wrote them. It is uncertain who composed the warm message of friendship to the Soviet Union in which Sun declared:

> Dear Comrades! As I leave you, I wish to express to you my fiery hope—hope that soon the dawn will come. The time will arrive when the Soviet Union as the best friend and ally will greet a powerful and free China, when in the great battle for the liberation of the oppressed nations of the world both countries hand in hand will go forward and achieve victories.[7]

For fifty years politicians and scholars have presented conflicting versions of the authorship of the Russian testament. Was it written by Borodin alone and attributed to the dying Sun? Or by Borodin and Wang Ching-wei? Or by the publicist Eugene Chen? Or was it dictated by Sun to a number of close colleagues including Borodin? It is uncertain, then, whether Borodin was close to Sun at the end. Russian sources place Borodin in constant attendance; a noncommunist source says Borodin failed to see Sun Yat-sen even once during his final illness, from January 26 on.[8]

The epistle to the Russians was not inconsistent with what the dying leader might have composed—or at least assented to. It was, as one Sun scholar has observed, in his style.[9] But whether Sun wrote or dictated the letter, whether it was a leftist fabrication composed after his death or whatever its source, it received the widest circulation and was then accepted as being his own.

Once the testaments had been written, Sun delayed signing them, saying that he did not want to bring anxiety to his young wife. But on March 11, when it seemed that he only had a few hours left, the documents were brought to him and he signed them. On the following day, March 12, at ten minutes after nine, he died, reportedly breathing the words, "Peace . . . battle . . . save China."[10] Once Sun was gone, Soviet representatives on the scene activated their campaign to capitalize on his memory. Karakhan immediately ordered the Red flag to be flown at half mast at the Soviet embassy and at all Russian installations throughout China. (No other foreign power did so until the following day.) Karakhan also ordered a special coffin from the Soviet Union, one like Lenin's, in which Sun's remains would lie in state. Two days after Sun's death, Borodin addressed a memorial meeting in Peking and recalled that, on the day of his death, Sun had repeated again and again: "If only Russia will help. If only Russia will help." And, added Borodin, he asked to be buried like his friend Lenin.[11] That wish was thwarted when Sun's family insisted on a Christian funeral. Even so, in the funeral procession on March 19 Karakhan occupied the place of the chief mourner following behind the surpliced choir.

But when Sun's body was being carried to its resting place, Borodin was not among the mourners. He had already left for Canton. On March 13, an auspicious development occurred in the south. Whampoa forces had taken the offensive against the armies of warlord Ch'en Chiung-ming, and the Whampoa units had won. The triumph of the Whampoaites, organized, supplied, and led by the Russians, removed all doubt that the Russians *could* remain in Canton. Moreover, with the coming of age of the military, it seemed likely that the Russians would want to remain on the scene. There were opportunities to be seized. Karakhan could nourish and exploit Sun's image in Peking and guide the KMT succession there. Borodin's job was to oversee developments in the south. And so, without waiting for Sun's final rites, Borodin went to Canton.

While Borodin had been away, Blyukher was the chief sovetnik in Canton. He had arrived in Canton too late to participate in the battle against the Merchants' Volunteer Corps. But almost immediately afterward he began directing the Whampoa forces, seeking to consolidate Kwangtung under the KMT. He planned first to move against Ch'en Chiung-ming in what came to be known as the First Eastern Campaign. A precise and methodical man, Blyukher drew up plans in detail, assigning each unit its specific task. For the first time, the propaganda facilities of Whampoa were to be widely utilized: hundreds of thousands of proclamations were prepared for distribution to the soldiers and to the peasant population encountered during the campaign. More than 50,000 copies of revolutionary songs were printed; instructions were given for holding meetings of workers and peasants in captured towns and for organizing them. As the work proceeded, it became more and more apparent to Blyukher that, if the campaign against Ch'en was to succeed, the brunt of the fighting would have to be done by the highly motivated but sparse and still inexperienced Whampoa forces. (The militarist generals with whom the KMT was still allied were not interested in attacking their old friend Ch'en.) But this did not deter Blyukher; in February 1925 he believed that all of China could be swept by three to four well-trained divisions. "Quality, not quantity, must play the chief role."[12]

On February 8, Blyukher, General Hsü (who was nominally in command of the KMT forces), members of the Canton government, and, according to one usually reliable source, Borodin[13] met on a train in Kwangtung to make final plans for the attack. During the next weeks, the two regiments of Whampoa men, sometimes assisted by the Cantonese forces of Hsü (who personally hated Ch'en), fought the enemy under the most forbidding conditions. There were no roads, no transport, no physicians. But with Blyukher and the sovetniki always nearby and sometimes leading the battle, the KMT armies repeatedly routed forces seven or eight times their size.

The successes against Ch'en in the First Eastern Campaign confirmed Blyukher's faith in what a few well-disciplined and supported, nationalistically inspired troops could accomplish in China. Canton, he declared, could not only be held, but Kwangtung could be consolidated. There had been triumphs in Canton before, but this was the first in which aggressive action was initiated by the Whampoa forces—and they had defeated experienced warlord troops. Prior to the news of Blyukher's successes in the south, the struggle to succeed Sun revolved around little more than who was chief heir to an image and a reputation. Now the victory against warlord forces suddenly seemed to offer much more: control of an organization, in power, in Kwangtung, with its own victorious army and with prospects for still more victories. That was a prize worth fighting for. The victory of the Blyukher-directed force occurred at a most fortuitous moment to help determine Russia's course.

During the months ahead in Canton and Kwangtung, Borodin would be enmeshed in an infinitely convoluted series of evolving "situations," usually closely related to one another but each with its own complexities. In general, the major situations that Borodin encountered on returning to Canton in the early spring of 1925 were the struggle for power inside the KMT, the battle to consolidate control in Kwangtung, and the development of the national revolutionary movement. Each of these contained its own momentum; though each complemented the others, each often seemed to compete with the others for attention. Now one, now the other, situation required priority. All were part of the evolving design for Chinese independence; yet the complexities were such that even Borodin sometimes lost sight of what that design was.

12

Victory Without Success

The death of Sun left no clear heir apparent. Sun had been asked to name his successor, but he had not done so. Now there was no one whose reputation, character, or style unmistakably qualifed him as the new *tsung-li*.

The Cantonese right had no viable candidate. In the center, the able but lackluster and indecisive Sun Fo, Sun Yat-sen's son by his first marriage, received scattered support as a compromise candidate. Mostly this came from those in and outside China who knew little of what happened in Canton. (Those who supported Sun Fo were sometimes referred to as the Crown Prince Faction.) Others advocated the leading role for the Harvard-educated T. V. Soong, younger brother of Sun's second wife (his supporters were referred to as the Uncle Faction), but he was never really in the running. Those with the strongest claim to be the new *tsung-li* belonged to the Elder Statesmen Faction. These were Hu Han-min, Wang Ching-wei, and Liao Chung-k'ai, all of whom were Sun's closest followers. Of the three, Liao was farthest to the left.

From Borodin's point of view, Hu Han-min was the least desirable of the three. At the time of the Merchants' Volunteer Corps crisis he had shown himself less than dedicated to the KMT strategy. The son and grandson of imperial bureaucrats, he was by the 1920s not favorably disposed toward radical change. Although no dedicated right-winger, he had serious doubts concerning accommodation with the CCP. He never belonged to the group that clustered around Borodin. But in Kwangtung, he was known as one of Sun's closest allies, and he had a support base. In this he differed from Wang Ching-wei, who had no group to whom he could effectively turn for support. Regarding himself as Sun's "closest disciple" and the executor of his testament, Wang wanted to walk in Sun's footsteps. But he lacked Sun's personal magnetism. He was respected for his role before 1911 and for his loyalty to Sun, but he was not an effective political leader. Like Sun-Fo, he was indecisive. Yet, for all his shortcomings, only Wang had prestige comparable to Hu's. As it happened, each despised the other.

As for Liao Chung-k'ai, he had surpassed Sun in cooperating with the Russians. Born and raised in America until he was seventeen, he reacted favorably to Borodin's contention that what he was trying to introduce into Canton was not communism but American standards of governmental competence. Although Liao had been with Sun since 1905 and was regarded as the Kuomintang's fiscal expert, he had never developed the stature of Hu or Wang. He was an energetic worker for Sun, and later for Borodin. His loyalty and administrative effectiveness could be relied on. He was not, as Borodin had found so many of Sun's colleagues and allies to be, hobbled by considerations of saving face. A circle of followers had recently begun to form around him. But it is doubtful that he saw himself, or that many others saw him, as the new *tsung-li*. Borodin preferred him, however.

In addition to these candidates for power, two others in Canton had claims that could not be ignored: General Hsü Ch'ung-chih, militarist, long-time supporter of Sun Yat-sen, an opium addict; and the young Whampoa commandant, commander of the new army, Chiang Kai-shek. About Hsü, it suffices to say that his time had passed; Canton required someone who seemed more contemporary. As for Chiang, his time had not yet come. His status and power were growing, but his forces were small and their exploits few. In the period immediately after Sun's death, moreover, both Hsü and Chiang had their hands full with Ch'en Chiung-ming. Whatever their ambitions, they could not join the struggle for power.

There were, then, three plausible successors to Sun. Of the three, two—Liao and Hu—were in Canton; Wang was in Peking. With Sun's death, Borodin hurried to Canton because holding on to what had been achieved there required a firm hand and considerable political skill. But Wang Ching-wei had his own vision of the future. His immediate aim was to reunify China, not merely to gain control of the KMT, and the place for accomplishing that objective, he felt, was Peking. He remained in the north and prepared for a KMT plenum scheduled to meet in the capital in mid-May of 1925. But ten days before the plenum was to convene, Wang received an urgent telegram from Liao, Hsü, and Chiang, appealing to him to come south immediately for an emergency meeting on the KMT leadership. The trigger for the telegram was Hu Han-min's announcement that he was moving from "acting" chief of staff in Sun's stead to chief of staff. He had taken over. There was no legal basis for his power, but there also had been none for Sun's appointment of Hu as his stand-in. There was no legal method to remove him because when Sun acted, anything was legal, because he had done it. But without Sun, the system was stalled. The system demanded a new *tsung-li,* and Hu had hurried to answer the call. But what of the ambitions and futures of the others—Wang, Liao, Chiang, Hsü, who loathed Hu? And what of the role of the CCP and the Russians, who were deeply suspicious of Hu?

Liao, who did nothing without consulting Borodin and usually acted on Borodin's initiative, organized the meeting. It was to take place near the coastal city of Swatow, Ch'en Chiung-ming's capital, then under attack by Hsü and Chiang. Recognizing the threat from Hu's assumption of power, Wang headed south. There, during the second week in May, he, Liao, Hsü, Chiang, and the Yunnanese general Chu P'ei-te met and made "plans to put an end to individualistic actions," that is, to stop Hu. Combining ambition, military power, and political respectability, they were not about to let Canton fall to Hu by default. At Swatow, plans were laid, after which Wang and Liao went to Canton. Hsü and Chiang completed the capture of Swatow and then turned their troops back toward Canton.

But when Liao and Wang arrived in Canton, they found that they could not reach KMT headquarters in the city's center because, in the absence of loyal troops, Canton had come under the control of two of the many warlords who had been part of Sun's "revolutionary alliance," Yang Hse-min and Liu Chen-huan. With Chiang's and Hsü's units engaged elsewhere, they had struck out on their own. The government, Borodin included, had been forced to flee once again from Canton to Whampoa. The coalition formed at Swatow now had two tasks before it: to liberate Canton from Yang and Liu—and to remove Hu Han-min from power, in that order. During the six weeks following the Swatow meetings, these tasks would dominate the Kwangtung scene, even though events of tremendous consequence for all of China would simultaneously unfold in the north.

On June 13, the forces of Chiang and Hsü, assisted by several warlords and advised by Blyukher, moved against Yang and Liu, who were outclassed and outmanned. In less than forty-eight hours 17,000 prisoners and 16,000 guns were taken. On the 14th, mop-up operations were completed by Cantonese soldiers and workers, who had come to detest the "foreign" invaders Yang and Liu. On the 15th, a plenum of the Central Executive Committee of the KMT was called. Borodin, whose prestige profited from the victory over Yang and Liu, knew what he wanted from the plenum, and its business was speedily concluded. It stated that there would ·be no successor to Sun as *tsung-li,* thus undercutting Hu Han-min. Further, it legalized the Political Committee that had been established in Peking when Sun had been ill and had not included Hu. Then it declared the Political Committee to be the supreme political body, although the Central Executive Committee was declared to be the highest KMT organ. The relationship between the CEC and the PC was precisely that between the Central Committee of the Russian party and the Politburo, where the legal authority was vested in the Central Committee but power belonged to the Politburo. The plenum further decided that there would be a new "national" government.

By the end of the month, the Swatow coalition had replaced the old revolutionary government, which Hu Han-min had headed, with the National Government of which Wang Ching-wei was both president and chairman of the Political Committee. But the real power was in the hands of the Liao Chung-k'ai, who, if not Borodin's voice, was his closest confederate and took counsel from him. As for Hu, surprised and bewildered by the turn of events, he was reduced to the honorific position of foreign minister.

Within months after Sun's death, Borodin had become the chief power in Canton. Carefully wrapping himself in the words and memory of Sun, he had unobtrusively assumed his mantle. While decisions formally were made by a few KMT leaders, Borodin's voice usually was decisive. And when decisions were made, Borodin insured faithful consequences by acting through the loyal and able communist T'an P'ing-shan, whom he had had appointed director of the important organizational department of the KMT. As far as the CCP in Canton was concerned, Borodin completely dominated it. Its local headquarters, the Kwangtung District Committee, unfailingly followed his instructions, which were often at variance with those received from party Central Committee headquarters in Shanghai. As one observer noted: "Not only did he fail to consult it [the Kwangtung District Committee] before something happened, but after the event he would not tell the committee the full story."[1]

Borodin was now in charge, but he was not without critics. Some communists, as well as noncommunists, called him the "dictator of Canton." On the other hand, he was criticized because his success was limited. While his achievements were recognized in the highest places in Moscow, it was sometimes pointed out that he had not yet succeeded even in revolutionizing even Canton. In mid-1925, that antique metropolis remained

> a curious city on whose backward and chaotic foundations a tinge of revolutionary color was being overlaid. Opium dens and gambling houses abounded along the Bund. They were the source of revenue for the Yunnanese and Kwangsi armies. There were only a few private automobiles, most of which were owned by militarists. They often sped along the roads, with two or four armed soldiers riding on the outside and military passengers and their families inside. The books and magazines published in the city retained the character of "old" literature, and "yellow" reading materials made up the majority of the publications. Such a backward atmosphere was rare even in the northern cities.[2]

By the time the forces of Yang and Liu had been subdued, Hu Han-min had been reduced to a shadow, and Borodin had taken over in Canton, an event had occurred hundreds of miles to the north that would soon turn Canton into a cauldron of open revolutionary activity.

Shanghai was, and is, China's industrial capital. It was also, in the 1920s, the center of the imperialist spirit in China. In the latter part of 1924 and early 1925, a depression hit Shanghai. Some of the twenty-seven Japanese factories in the city were closed; others offered only part-time work at reduced wages. But simultaneously with the economic crisis, trade-union development began to accelerate. By February 1925 a number of the Japanese factories had been struck. The strikes were not altogether successful but, given the economic climate, they exasperated the Japanese owners and emboldened the workers. On May 15, Chinese employees struck the Japanese-owned Number Seven Nogai Cotton Mill, located in Shanghai's International Settlement. A lockout followed. The workers went to the factory to demand that it be reopened. In the course of the negotiations, members of the Japanese staff fired on the Chinese workers, killing one of them. The Settlement police responded, as usual arresting some of the Nogai workers and trying to hush up the incident. Gradually, however, news of the killing leaked out. By the end of the month, the irate Shanghai workers were close to the flashpoint.

For almost a year, communists Li Li-san and Ch'en Tu-hsiu had been organizing a group of radical youth at Shanghai University. Nominally the group—the Shanghai Student Federation—was pro-KMT, but actually it was CCP-dominated. After the Nogai incident, the Student Federation unlimbered a propaganda campaign to protest both the slaying and its source, imperialism. On May 30, several hundred students marched the streets of Shanghai, making speeches, carrying placards, handing out statements against imperialism and its Shanghai incarnation, the International Settlement. Shortly after 3 P.M. a non-Chinese member of the Settlement constabulary arrested two students and moved to take them to the Laocha police station. A crowd of about two hundred students swelled to ten times that size as they neared the station. Sikh police, under British command, were drawn up in a line to protect the station. The Sikhs fired on the mob, killing eleven and wounding more than forty.

By evening, a decision had been reached in leftist circles to establish a broadbased anti-imperialist committee and call for an immediate general strike. On June 1, the strike was begun. By June 2, over 155,000 workers had walked off their jobs. Before long, over half a million Shanghai workers *and* bourgeoisie struck to protest the Laocha incident.

Throughout China there was angry reaction to the "massacre" at Laocha station. The fire that had long smoldered within the Chinese people had now burst out. Rickshaw haulers hung signs on their vehicles stating: "We do not carry foreigners." Messenger boys and janitors left their jobs in Western offices. Students in Shanghai wrote to friends all over China informing them of what had happened and urging them to join the protest. In the chief cities of northern and central China there were demonstrations in which bourgeoisie and working class alike participated. Even in placid Peking, crowds sang the *Marseillaise* and students used their own blood to pen slogans against the imperialists. In Kalgan, Chinese merchants refused to take Western currency.

Only in Canton among the major cities of China was there no overt reaction to Laocha. It was not that Canton did not know what had happened in the north or did not care, but at the moment a local crisis, the occupation of Canton's center by Yang and Liu, had more immediacy. Borodin won agreement from strike sympathizers that reaction should await the settling of the local crisis. But once the city had been freed by the forces of the Swatow alliance, the south could demonstrate its feelings too.

On June 21, announcements painted on red paper were posted throughout Canton, particularly where Westerners lived, urging all workers employed by imperialists to strike. On the 21st and 22nd, there were meetings among the Chinese in the city and practice demonstrations, in which the Whampoa cadets participated. A major protest against the Shanghai shootings was clearly being readied. Rumors spread throughout the foreign colony that the Chinese were getting ready to attack Shameen, that sandbar in the Pearl River where most foreigners lived. Peering out from behind their barbed-wire entanglements on Shameen, seeing and hearing the agitation going on in the city, the Great Power troops and colonials were edgy.

On the following morning, June 23, three meetings took place simultaneously in Canton's huge Dunsyaochan Square. In the center, strikers who had come from Hong Kong to participate in the demonstrations, Canton workers, and a few peasants congregated; to the right, Whampoa cadets, soldiers, and the local constabulary; on the left, students and merchants. From the platforms, each of the groups was harangued by recitations of the great wrongs done to the Chinese at Shanghai and elsewhere, of the need to seek redress and to stand up for the rights of all Chinese. Then the "estates" formed a line of march: strikers, workers, and peasants, followed by students and Boy Scouts in uniform, followed by tradesmen, with cadets and soldiers bringing up the rear. The demonstrators turned on to the street lining the river and marched along it toward Shameen, shouting anti-imperialist and anti-British slogans. Suddenly, as the student delegation was passing the Victoria Hotel—the incarnation of imperial British presence on Shameen—a shot rang out. (Who fired it has never been clear, although each side sought to blame the other.) Shooting went on from both sides for twenty to thirty minutes. Before it was over, there were over 150 casualties, mostly among the marchers, including a considerable number of Whampoa cadets. Thus occurred what came to be known as the Shakee Massacre of 1925 (Shakee was the name of the street where the shootings occurred). A sudden summer downpour would quickly wash away the bloody evidence of battle, but its aftermath would prove of such value to the revolutionary cause that Borodin was accused of having planned it all. To which Borodin replied: "We did not make May 30. It was made for us."[3]

And indeed it had been, for together with the events at the Laocha station, the Shakee Massacre provided the KMT with a burning nationalist cause around which to rally mass support, bourgeois and proletarian alike. In Canton, as elsewhere, Chinese of all classes were outraged. They demanded action. Some wanted Chiang's, Hsü's, and other forces in Canton to retaliate against the resident imperialists. An attempt to overrun Shameen seemed imminent. But Borodin, fearing as before retaliation by the British, and aware of how unprepared his forces were for extended confrontation, urged moderation. Radicals argued that while a British counterattack would come, it would not occur for a month or two; by that time, the revolution would have spread to all China. Such appeals were intoxicating to young Chinese and to some Russians as well. But Borodin held off the firebrands and proposed instead a blockade of British-owned Hong Kong, to be effected by declaring that no vessels that stopped at Hong Kong could dock at Canton. Hong Kong was primarily a way station into and out of China. The blockade, if successful, would cripple Hong Kong's vital trade role. Borodin was right: once the blockade was set up, the bustling Hong Kong port, which in 1924 handled more freight than New York, was nearly paralyzed. Hong Kong businessmen lost $20 million a month. Rents decreased by 40 to 50 percent. Banks and shipping companies fell into bankruptcy.

The chief responsibility for enforcing the Hong Kong blockade in Canton went to the "Hong Kong strikers." In Canton, there were only about 55,000 workers engaged in modern industry and commerce from whom a tough union might be formed. But in Hong Kong there were hundreds of thousands of seamen, dockers, and public-service employees, many with trade-union experience, who were prepared to strike. By the end of June, ten days after the strike began, over 50,000 Hong Kong workers had arrived in Canton to reinforce the Canton strikers. By mid-July, the number had risen to 80,000. Before the strike was over, more than 137,000 workers made the thirty-mile trip up the Pearl River from Hong Kong to Canton in support of the strike.

Once they arrived, they were organized into sections under the Hong Kong–Canton strike committee, largely led by the radical Seamen's Union. The strikers were provided with uniforms: blue trousers and shirts with a red bandanna tied around the arm. They were housed in office buildings evacuated by foreigners, all of whom had left Canton except for the Russians and a German (whose hatband was marked in Chinese "I am a German"—presumably because his country had lost its empire in World War I, he hoped he would not be considered an imperialist). At night the strikers slept on straw mats. During the day the mats were rolled up and the offices were used for union purposes. Cooking was done in the halls over fire pots.

The strikers were deployed in picket units charged with examining all arriving and departing goods and persons. They had their own courts, levied their own fines and prison sentences, ran their own jails, newspapers, and schools. The latter offered courses in "What Is Imperialism?" "The History of the Imperialist Invasion of China," "The Labor Movement in China," and the "World Labor Movement." At the height of its power the strike committee employed a dozen gunboats to enforce the blockade. In some circles the Hong Kong–Canton strike committee was referred to as government Number 2.[4] Obviously the Hong Kong strike committee was being groomed, or was grooming itself, to seize all power in Canton. Some Russians also anticipated that role, but Borodin was not among them.

Borodin was aware of the contribution the strikers were making toward the revolutionary movement in China. Everything that was accomplished in Kwangtung, he said later, "became possible thanks to the strike." "If the Hong Kong and Shameen (Canton) strikes had not occurred, I do not think . . . our enterprises would have been so successful."[5] From the ranks of the strikers were molded cadres of trade-union members and leaders, agitation and propaganda workers and organizers, and KMT and CCP enrollees. But though some of the strikers made good revolutionary recruits, many of them came to Canton for free lodging and board. They often spent their time gambling and smoking opium rather than carrying out revolutionary tasks. They supplemented their incomes by armed robbery and muggings and by accepting bribes to allow unauthorized persons or shipments to enter or leave Canton. The strikers often performed their picket duties so poorly that Whampoa cadets had to be dispatched to oversee them. From time to time "purges" became necessary to eliminate opportunistic comrades. Borodin saw the strikers as riffraff, not the stuff of which revolutions are made.

But not everyone in Canton, not to mention Shanghai, Peking, and Moscow, agreed with Borodin's view of the strikers. Some were convinced that the Hong Kong–Canton events proved that the time had come to turn the KMT into a working-class party, to end the kowtowing to the middle class and to follow a clearly communist line. But Borodin could tell that working-class support for the strikers and their radical strike committee was already flagging. As the strike dragged on, huge crowds still turned out to protest imperialism, but increasingly the working class and the middle class came to fear the strikers. Borodin tried to keep the strikers under control. Again and again he counseled moderation and discipline. Disorder and violence were beginning to polarize the population and intensify fears of radical action. The middle class, previously apathetic or even mildly pro-KMT, were now alarmed by the stridency and anarchy of the strikers. Their Canton, they feared, was about to disappear. Local warlords, too, feared for their future.

Insistent rumors of plots to overthrow the Canton regime began to reach Borodin and the Political Committee. In Hong Kong, the bourgeois press accused Liao Chung-k'ai and other members of the Political Committee of being communists. Some articles openly called for their assassination, and there was talk of killing Borodin as well. Such threats were sufficiently believable that the Political Committee recruited a small staff of body-guards to protect its members. But such efforts were insufficient. On the morning of August 20, as Liao Chung-k'ai arrived at KMT headquarters in Canton, he was fired on by five or six gunmen hiding in the columns that surrounded the building. Borodin, Wang Chang-wei, and Chiang Kai-shek, among others, rushed down the stairs from the KMT offices to see what had happened and found Liao mortally wounded. He was rushed to the hospital, and his colleagues returned to headquarters to decide how to cope with the latest crisis.

Borodin proposed that an extraordinary committee—a cheka—be set up, consisting of Wang, Chiang, Hsü, and himelf, with all power in Canton—political, police, and military—concentrated in its hands. Borodin's proposal was adopted, and the cheka faced the twofold danger of other attacks on government leaders and a coup. To handle the first, Borodin proposed to surround KMT headquarters with reliable troops. For the second, he urged that warlord generals Liang Hung-kai and Ch'eng Jun-chi, whom he believed had instigated the attack on Liao, be expelled from Canton. But the cheka resisted the latter proposal. General Hsü, himself a warlord, balked at acting against his fellow militarists. As he put it: "I see that Liang Hung-kai plays a counterrevolutionary role, that he is untrustworthy; but he is my old friend, and it is impossible to move against him."[6] Eventually, however, Hsü yielded and the cheka moved against Hsü's old colleagues and against the ousted Hu Han-min, regarded as "the ideological leader" of the assassination, whether or not he knew of the specific plot in advance. On August 23, Hu was taken into custody. Two days later, in standard Chinese fashion, generals Liang and Ch'eng were arrested at a banquet, and their troops surrounded and disarmed. Orders were given to seize a number of other militarists, but most had been forewarned and had escaped to Hong Kong.

Liao Chung-k'ai had died while being taken to the hospital. It was a serious blow for Borodin. Liao had supported and followed him from the first; he had not only been an excellent front man, but was an energetic and versatile lieutenant who could be fully trusted. Borodin's job would now become much more difficult. At this critical point, Borodin also lacked the services of Blyukher. His old war wounds had acted up in the heat and humidity of Kwangtung, forcing him to go north. (It is sometimes suggested that Blyukher had departed because of friction between him and Borodin.) Blyukher was replaced as chief military sovetnik by V. P. Rogachev who, new to the situation and generally lacking Blyukher's leadership and military talents, was of little help to Borodin. He had had little enough top-level assistance from the beginning. Now, with Sun gone, Liao gone, Hu ousted, Wang Ching-wei ineffectual, and Chiang Kai-shek inexperienced and largely untested, Borodin concluded that the revolutionary enterprise in Canton demanded his direct and undisguised control. The situation was too grave for any other choice.

Borodin resolved to move against other potential threats. The events of late August had made it clear that Hsü could not be trusted. Either Hsü or his staff were apparently negotiating with General Ch'en Chung-ming, who still had forces in Kwangtung, and with the British to overthrow the Canton regime. On the night of September 19, Chiang's Whampoa cadets surrounded Hsü's forces, and Hsü was deported to Hong Kong. Three days later, Hu Han-min, who had been under house arrest, was appointed ambassador to the Soviet Union and left Canton the same day, accompanied by other members of the KMT old guard. The departure of these old Canton hands only served to increase tensions in Canton. However, the capture and subsequent disposal of Hsü's troops had unsuspected long-range effects. With Hsü ousted, his officers and men were incorporated into the KMT army. This enlarged the army—but with warlord troops whose motivation and political attitudes differed sharply from those of the Whampoa units.

Whampoa, it will be recalled, was founded so that the Canton government would have an army of its own, not led by mercenary officers but by Chinese patriots, dedicated to the cause of national independence. During 1924 and 1925, rapid progress was being made toward that goal. But the introduction of large numbers of traditional commanders and troops from Hsü's forces set a pattern that, to Borodin's distress, would be repeated again and again. Borodin knew there were not enough Russians or ideologically correct Chinese to indoctrinate or discipline what, on August 26, 1925, became the National Revolutionary Army (NRA). Idealism would become a declining force in the NRA, as warlords carried their traditional standards with them into the army. Still in September 1925 the wholesale incorporation of new forces was seen by many as an optimistic development. The enemy could be subdued more quickly; Kwangtung could be consolidated sooner. In October, the Second Eastern Expedition attacked the remnants of Ch'en Chung-ming's army. On November 2, Swatow, which Ch'en had reoccupied, was retaken by Whampoa detachments. By mid-November, Ch'en was in full retreat to Fukien province; many of his troops, like those of Hsü, were now incorporated into the NRA.

N. I. Konchits, later a Soviet general, described what life was like with the warlord forces in the NRA. Many of the soldiers and officers were opium addicts. Reconnaisance was almost nonexistent. When the Russians insisted on reconnaisance missions regarded as dangerous, the scouts ran away. Officers had to be bribed to follow orders, and many enlisted men as well. As the Russians learned, military success could be won easier with cash than with troops. But the natural desire to enlarge the army, plus the danger that these troops might otherwise be turned against them, dictated their continued absorption into the NRA. By the beginning of 1926, the military opposition in Kwangtung, except for stragglers, had either been driven from Kwangtung or incorporated into the NRA.

With the warlords largely dispatched, Borodin's financial position improved. Finances were centralized under the control of the government; a new coinage was being accepted; a central bank was in full operation. During November and December 1925 more taxes were collected by the Canton administration than in all of 1924. By the end of 1925, then, about two years after reaching Canton, Borodin had molded the KMT and its army into viable organizations. Kwangtung had been pacified. Though Wang Ching-wei and Chang Kai-shek shared his power in Canton, Borodin's voice was the decisive one. Both Wang and Chiang knew they needed him. A more determined Wang, less prone to see himself as a "disciple," perhaps might have successfully gone it alone. He was a figure of importance in KMT circles and had been so for decades. Chiang, on the other hand, was much less known. He had played litle other than a military role in the KMT until the summer of 1925. Chiang owed his rising fortunes to Borodin and to Russia. He still lacked a major following and suffered occasionally from fits of depression and lack of confidence. He did not, however, lack ambition.

On December 11, 1925, at a victory banquet in Swatow, Chiang acknowledged his debt to the Russians and specifically to Borodin. He declared that the KMT should accept Russian direction of the Chinese revolution and compared the Sino-Soviet relationship to that among the Allied powers during World War I. As commander in chief, Chiang said, Marshal Foch's position was comparable to Borodin's. He reminded his audience more than once that Sun Yat-sen had said that Borodin's views were his views. The implication was clear: to follow Borodin was to follow Sun.[7] Borodin's power and prestige had reached a new high. His authority was virtually unquestioned in Canton. On all sides, including Moscow, the vast improvement in revolutionary prospects was ascribed to his policies. Since Blyukher and Karakhan had returned to Russia, all eyes were on him.

Despite Borodin's remarkable success and status, some of those close to him in late 1925 found him depressed. Perhaps this was partly due to physical problems. Like most of the sovetniki, he had acquired chronic dysentery and malaria as well. Partly, perhaps, he was concerned about his sons, now sixteen and ten, who had been with him in China for over two years and who were now neither American, Russian, nor Chinese. Their formal education was being neglected, and their future was cloudy. But Borodin had other problems too. His successes only seemed to multiply his headaches. He had become a prime assassination target. And he was the target for other kinds of attacks as well. Some of the sovetniki protested his "interference" in military matters and disapproved his methods.[8] Such complaints reached his detractors in Russia, including Karl Radek, who had become a China specialist while rector of Sun Yat-sen University in Moscow, and his chief deputy, Pavel Mif. In certain Moscow quarters the Hong Kong-Canton strike was thought to have produced the first worker-peasant government in China. With this tangible evidence of the popular mood, why did Borodin not move faster toward the national revolution? Were his interference and dubious methods delaying the revolution in China?

Then again, Borodin was criticized for going too fast. He was attacked in the north, especially by the Central Committee of the CCP, for acting too drastically against the Canton right. Perhaps his action was justified by the situation in Canton, it said, but the left was not so strong elsewhere. It required continued cooperation with other groups to achieve its goals. He had erred, therefore, in disposing of Sun's old allies, Hu Han-min and General Hsü. These criticisms, however, disturbed Borodin less than the dawning realization that almost every success he achieved in Canton violated the basic concept of the United Front. The First KMT Congress, the reorganization of the KMT, the defeats of the Merchants' Volunteer Corps, of Ch'en Chung-ming, of the other warlords, of Hu Han-min, the Hong Kong–Canton strike, and the organization of the workers and peasants—all were victories but all had led to greater hostility among the bourgeois elements of the KMT. From Janury 1924 on, each Borodin triumph caused more bourgeois to leave Canton. Many of these favored a united and strengthened China, but not in alliance with Bolshevism. From the moment of his arrival in China, Borodin had repeatedly stated that China was not ready for communism and would not be for decades. But the regime's successive rebuffs to old-line members of the KMT and their allies fueled the accusation that the Kwangtung leadership of the KMT viewed all capitalists as enemies.

The growing hostility of the middle class was reflected in the so-called Sun Yat-sen movement among the Whampoa cadets. In February 1925 a few students at Whampoa established the Society for the Study of Sun Yat-senism. It seemed an innocuous expression of loyalty to the dying *tsung-li*. But within weeks, the society became a hotbed of anti-CCP sentiment. The communists and their sympathizers at Whampoa countered by establishing the Union of Military Youth, which by and large only reproduced the CCP cadre among the cadets. It attracted few additional adherents, but the Society for the Study of Sun Yat-senism grew rapidly and moved to the right, as the power of the left in Canton increased during 1925. By the end of the summer the society had absorbed a considerable portion of the Whampoa student body. Almost a year after its inception, Borodin tried to change its direction by holding an official "inauguration" for it. Perhaps he hoped to coax it to reveal its total membership, including its secret activities, at the inaugural parade. Perhaps by signaling his acceptance of its legitimacy he would weaken it. In any case, he did not succeed. As its members left Whampoa for the field, their anti-Russian and anticommunist sentiments went with them. Members of the society were scattered throughout the army and even among the student body at Sun Yat-sen University in Moscow. Borodin did not underestimate the threat.

The growth of the Society for the Study of Sun Yat-senism was not the only sign that more conservative KMT elements were working to establish their credentials as the true heirs of the *tsung-li*. When in late 1925 the Central Executive Committee of the KMT decided to summon a Second KMT Congress to meet in Canton early in 1926, conservatives in the north decided to call their own meeting. On November 23, the self-styled Kwangtung Central Executive Committee of the KMT opened its sessions in the Western Hills outside of Peking where the royal hunting lodge, the dowager empress' sumptuous marble ship, and hundreds of hotels and summerhouses were located. Between November 23 and December 5, KMT conservatives from Canton and elsewhere in China debated how to save the KMT from the left. Decisions were made: all communists must be ousted from the KMT; the Political Council must be abolished; the headquarters of the CEC must be moved from Canton to Shanghai; Borodin's "contract" was to be canceled. The assemblage also decided to move against Wang Ching-wei and Chiang Kai-shek. Wang was censured and ousted from the KMT for six months. But, at the last moment, Chiang, advertised by his friends as a practical and reasonable man, was spared formal censure. Shortly thereafter the "Western Hills clique" adopted the slogan: "Alliance with Chiang to overthrow Wang."

Borodin responded to the Western Hills clique at the Second KMT Congress. On the surface, the congress was another victory for him. It seemingly put the final touches on Borodin's work over the previous two years. But it also underscored the dilemmas his triumphs had produced. The congress, which began on January 4 and continued through the 19th, was inaugurated amid great pomp and ceremony. There were impressive military and civilian demonstrations. Hundreds of thousands of persons raised their voices in revolutionary shouts and songs. Planes flown from Moscow, across the Urals, Lake Baikal and the Gobi to Peking and then south, soared in formation above the city. Everywhere were seen huge portraits of Sun—and the hammer and sickle.

Wang Ching-wei presided at the congress, and Chiang Kai-shek was present. Both seemed to lean heavily on Borodin. Chiang had had little experience working in such public assemblys. And although he received the applause of the delegates, and his self-assurance had risen considerably during the past year, he acknowledged he had much to learn and paid tribute to his mentor, Borodin. As for Wang, he was a capable presiding officer and an excellent orator. But fearful of making a misstep, he cleared everything with Borodin. For Wang, Borodin now played the master's role that formerly had been Sun's.

With both Wang and Chiang deferring to him, Borodin managed the entire congress, apparently with only the most minimal interference, even from Moscow. The majority of the delegates to the congress, no less than the leaders, were in Borodin's pocket. Of the 278 attending, 168 belonged to the left including the CCP, 65 to the center, and 45 to the right. This left-dominated Second KMT Congress made Sun *tsung-li* forever, retired the title, accepted his testaments, adopted his writings as the fundamental documents of the party, and established the proper forms for showing respect to his memory. It sanctioned Sun's moves, following the First KMT Congress, to increase cooperation with the Soviet Union, gratefully acknowledged Soviet contributions, and voted overwhelmingly to continue the collaboration. In the new Central Executive Committee elected by the congress, 7 of the 36 members belonged to the CCP and 14 others to the left. Almost all the critical departments in the government were placed in the hands of the left or the CCP, positions going to such future stalwarts of Chinese communism as Mao Tse-tung, Chou En-lai, Madame Chou, and Madame Liao Chung-k'ai.

Had he wished it, Borodin could have arranged even stronger majorities. But a united-front policy was still being pursued; again and again Wang called for the spirit of unity. It was necessary, moreover, to dissipate the fears of communist takeover stimulated by the Western Hills clique. Even Tai Chi-tao, the spiritual father of both that clique and the Society for the Study of Sun Yat-senism, was reelected to the CEC. Further, a rule was passed limiting the CCP members on any KMT committee or council to one third of its total membership.

Still, Borodin could not get everything he wanted from the congress. Even the moderate agricultural reform enacted at the First KMT Congress was set aside, although there is no evidence that Borodin made more than a token effort to get it passed. A series of incidents during the congress indicated that the issue of right versus left was far from resolved even in Canton and Kwangtung, let alone in the rest of China. Though only ten of the delegates were aggressively rightist, it was obvious that many others were sympathetic. Significantly, the exiled Hu Han-min received more votes than any other candidate for the Central Executive Committee.

By early 1926, Borodin had done almost all he had told Sun he would try for. He had reorganized the KMT; created an armed force, albeit not so free of warlords as might have been hoped; brought all of Kwangtung under the KMT colors. But in so doing he had progressively aroused those whose cooperation, or at least apathy, he required to achieve victory: the middle class. Each victory, strengthening his own hand, drove more and more of the bourgeoisie away. He was, in a sense, repeating the history of the Russian revolution in which support for the Bolshevik regime had grown narrower and narrower even as its military successes had increased. But China was not Russia. Borodin was not Lenin and, even if he had been, he lacked Lenin's organizations and resources. Moreover, in the background there lurked as a constant threat, should his forces appear too great a danger to their interests, the imperialist navies and armies of Britain, Japan, and the United States, perhaps not anxious to intervene but prepared to do so and being pushed in that direction by their nationals resident in China.

How strong was Borodin—and the revolution—in 1926? The bourgeoisie was not behind him, having become ever more suspicious of his intentions. The CCP had maybe 10,000 members, most of them recent recruits. Even had the CCP been a united and disciplined unit, which it was not, it was far too small to lead a revolution in populous China. Borodin acknowledged that the trade-union movement had made remarkable strides, but it remained immature, inexperienced, and undependable. As for the peasants, although their potential power was enormous, they were even more unreliable.

Lacking effective mass support, he also lacked capable and trustworthy colleagues. Sun was gone. Liao had been murdered. Hu and others could not be counted on. Wang was willing to serve Borodin in most matters, but he was not a strong figure. Chiang was gaining strength but, neither an intellectual nor an idealist, he was not receptive to the philosophical appeals Borodin made so well. He was also being actively courted by the right. And so, with all his triumphs, Borodin and his *sovetniki* stood more alone, more exposed, than ever. In a sense, Borodin even stood alone vis-à-vis Moscow, for he had been making more and more decisions on his own. Obviously the Kremlin trusted him, but he lacked the security that more detailed Soviet instructions would provide.

Borodin had serious doubts about his and China's future, but for the time being he was in command of the situation in

Kwangtung. With his South China objectives achieved, Moscow would choose the next road. Accordingly, a delegation of high-level Moscow officials was designated to travel to Peking. There they would meet with Borodin, with Karakhan, who had returned from Moscow, and with selected sovetniki to map the future. When Borodin sailed from Canton in February aboard the *Pamyat Lenina,* he planned to go first to the Peking meeting and then to Moscow for further consultations and a much-needed vacation.

He got to Peking but not to Moscow. In his absence, Canton blew sky high, and Borodin was needed to pick up the pieces.

13

Holding On in Canton

When Borodin went north on February 4, 1926, few of his contemporaries knew he was going to Peking to consider the future course of Russian policy in China with a secret investigative commission from Moscow. So secret were the deliberations of the commission that even some of those scheduled to testify were unaware of its existence until shortly before they were called to appear. Since the commission was appraising the prospects for revolution against a supposedly friendly power, such secrecy was not remarkable.

The commission was headed by the prestigious A. S. Bubnov, a party member since 1903 and, since 1924, chief of the political arm of the Red Army. Its other members were N. A. Kubyak, secretary of the Far Eastern bureau of the Central Committee of the Russian party; I. I. Lepse, a high-ranking apparatchik of the trade-union international, the Profintern; and R. V. Longva, a Red Army commander, hero of the storming of Brest-Litovsk against Pilsudski. All were members of the Central Committee, which included the top hundred political leaders of the USSR.

To meet with the commission, Karakhan, who had been instrumental in bringing Borodin into China and who had been in Peking from 1923 until August 1925, returned from Moscow, where he had been acting minister of foreign affairs. G. N. Voitinsky, who had been involved in China even earlier than Borodin, was also there, as were most of the more experienced sovetniki.

Borodin spent much of his time aboard the *Pamyat Lenina* preparing his report to the commission. When he arrived in Peking, the Moscow delegation had already begun its hearings. It had been presented with a resume of events in China since September 1923, and it had learned, if it did not already know, that there was sharp disagreement among the sovetniki on future strategy and tactics.[1] One group argued that the 30,000 to 40,000 KMT troops already under arms in Kwangtung could defeat the militarists of central China in two to three months and then roll on to Peking. The other side insisted that a march north was premature. It was necessary, they maintained, to continue political work in Kwangtung and to undertake it in other provinces as well. More armed forces, trained like those at Whampoa, must be developed and supplies must be accumulated. In a year or two, perhaps, a "Northern Expedition" might be feasible. Even then, the advance northward should be slow, with the political situation in each occupied area stabilized before another advance was made.

On February 14, A. I. Cherepanov, who had served in Canton under Borodin since 1924, was leaving the building where the commission met, after giving testimony, when he heard a young boy calling to him. Coming toward him he recognized Norman, Borodin's ten-year-old son. Then he saw Fanya Borodin with Fred, the Borodin's older boy.[2] Fanya, dressed in customary Chinese fashion, greeted Cherepanov warmly and invited him to have tea with her and her husband. (Only subsequently did Cherepanov realize that Fanya and the boys had been waiting for him.) Mikhail Markovich was soon to testify before the commission, and he wanted Cherepanov's sense of the commission's sentiments. What kind of reception had Cherepanov received? What seemed to be the attitude of the commission? After their discussion, Borodin showed the future Red Army general a copy of the report he planned to submit. Forty years later, recalling the impact of the document on him, General Cherepanov related how exciting it was to read Borodin's interpretation of what had happened in Canton over the past two years. Borodin, wrote Cherepanov, gave "historical significance" to what he and others had seen only partially.[3] He saw how developments came together in a broad and purposeful mosaic where others saw only a meaningless jumble of events. The celebrated Borodin style was still impressing his hearers.

Borodin knew that he was not merely plotting future Russian

involvement in China, but defending his record in Canton. Increasingly, after the death of Sun, he had operated on his own. Information from him in Canton had recently been infrequent and sparse. Why was there so little information in Moscow about South China developments, Bubnov wanted to know? One of the sovetniki replied that there had been so much to do that the Russians in Canton could not spare the time to report or risk having communications fall into enemy hands. But even if this explanation satisfied the commission, it did not erase the necessity for Borodin's reporting on what he had done. Some of Borodin's detractors had argued that the CCP, the working class, and the peasants were being prevented from realizing their full revolutionary potential; the rotten and corrupt KMT was being nurtured at the expense of the CCP.

Bearing in mind his critics' charges that he was moving too slowly, Borodin carefully developed his defense. The CCP, he testified, had played a vital role, much greater than its numbers might indicate. And the contribution of the working class had been great. But the commission must recognize what Canton was like. It is a "kind of Tower of Babel in which it is possible to get lost completely."[4] It was hard, continued Borodin, to find two men in Canton who could agree on anything. And in Kwangtung the power of the old order remained great, its principal strength being in agricultural relationships. Then, beginning to respond to some of his critics, he said agrarian reform was absolutely imperative. "Otherwise nothing will come."[5] Borodin related how, from the beginning of his association with Sun Yat-sen, he had pushed for agricultural reform. On one occasion he thought he had succeeded, only to realize that all he had was an empty document for his archives. Again and again he had been frustrated in his attempts to achieve even limited reform. But he was forced to conclude, he told the delegation from the Central Committee, that if it insisted on agricultural reform, the KMT would disintegrate. And the KMT, with its strong bourgeois involvement, was indispensable to the revolution.

Since nothing could be accomplished in China without agricultural reform, and agricultural reform would destroy the possibility of revolutionary success, what then did Borodin recommend? He told the commission that the revolution could not remain in Canton, since it would sooner or later "rust out." "To remain longer in Kwangtung is not possible."[6] The Northern Expedition is the only way out. When the revolutionary forces fanned out from Canton, Borodin suggested, they could take with them plans for political and economic reforms. Peasants and workers would be swept up by the liberation forces. As the revolutionary winds picked up velocity, the bourgeoisie could no longer stifle change, as they had in Canton. In this way, agricultural reform could be brought about and the success of the revolution assured. Borodin listed a number of steps necessary for the Northern Expedition: the development of a political and economic program; the strengthening of the left wing of the KMT; increased agitation among peasants and workers; the further Bolshevization of the CCP; the augmenting of leftist sentiments in the army—all measures to mollify the left, who suspected Borodin's Bolshevik orthodoxy.

Borodin said he was not unaware of ideological problems in the army, particularly among forces most recently incorporated into the Canton armies. But so far, the old warlord detachments had behaved well. Though their revolutionary commitment was weak, they could be brought to appreciate the national revolution and all it entailed. There were greater problems, he said, than the new generals and their men. Specifically, "of the six corps commanders, four can be counted on as trustworthy. With them there can scarcely be any doubt ... with these commanders it will be possible to do great work."[7]

At this time, then, Borodin expected, or said he expected, no trouble with the generals. Whether his conclusion reflected his best judgment or was conjured up because he needed some way out of the Canton dilemma remains open to question. Given the political climate in Moscow, where the battle for succession was being fought out and ideological reliability was under constant fire, Borodin could not justify major Russian support for China, if the likely result was to be either early defeat or the strengthening of the bourgeoisie. And certainly Borodin could not recommend a pullout when, on the surface, the situation now seemed more favorable than at any time in the past two years. With the clearing of warlord opposition from the province, Bolshevik influence in Kwangtung appeared to be at its zenith. If Borodin had said there was no further work to do in China, he would have seemed a quitter, a man of little faith. Such a decision would have been unacceptable to all factions in Moscow as well as disastrous to Borodin's fortunes, not only because his conduct would seem to indicate a lack of revolutionary commitment but because he might have seemed to be saying that the Soviet Union should never have come to China because it was a no-win situation. This was a position that everyone in Moscow involved in the China situation would have found impossible to accept. Borodin needed a way out of the dilemma, and he found it in advocating the Northern Expedition and asserting the political reliability of the Canton forces.

Borodin's voice carried much weight with the delegation. He was regarded by the sovetniki as the "great" man, and they did not hide this estimate from the commission. Moreover, Borodin was in personal communication with Stalin, which the delegation undoubtedly knew, since Bubnov and probably the others were Stalin's men. To them, Borodin was the model of what a sovetnik should be. One of the decisions of the commission was to look for other Borodins, particularly a man to be sent to General Feng Yü-hsiang in the hope that that vacillating but not unsympathetic militarists might yet be won over to the revolution. But the most important indication of Borodin's standing was the delegation's endorsement not only of his evaluation of the Chinese situation, but of his recommendations in general and of the Northern Expedition in particular. The commission would not have reached such a conclusion without prior authorization from Moscow, if the hearings suggested that course. But it was Borodin who persuaded the commission that it was the proper course, and perhaps the only way to avert disaster.

The Bubnov commission completed its work during the first ten days in March 1926. Then with great enthusiasm, the commissioners proceeded to Canton to make an on-the-spot investigation of the revolutionary base, to give advice, and to observe firsthand what was needed for the Northern Expedition. Although reports differ on the reason, Borodin apparently remained a while longer in the north, delaying his departure for Moscow. He was there when the incredible news reached him that on March 20 Chiang Kai-shek had unleashed a coup in Canton, had arrested the communists at Whampoa and in the army, as well as the newly arrived Bubnov delegation, and had placed the sovetniki under protective custody.

What had gone wrong? When Borodin had left in February the situation was seemingly stable. Why had the one general upon whom Borodin was depending to the greatest extent, the one whose immediate prospects were most bound up with the left, turned his world upside down? The root causes of the coup cannot be discerned clearly from the myriad accounts of this momentous event. All those involved had their own axes to grind. It seems likely that sooner or later Canton would have erupted against the communists and the Russians. That it happened sooner was probably due to Borodin's departure north.

Chiang Kai-shek was an ambitious and complex man, a nationalist, a pragmatist, but more comfortable with a traditional than a radical China. Whatever Chiang had earlier thought of his prospects as Sun's successor, a year later, with both Liao Chung-k'ai and Hu Han-min out of the picture and Borodin gone, Chiang saw only Wang Ching-wei as his immediate competitor. Wang, in spite of his indecisiveness, was a formidable rival. He was regarded as a revolutionary hero and as an early and leading follower of Sun.

As long as he was in Canton, Borodin had been able to contain the jealousies and rivalries among the revolutionary elements. He had always been sensitive to considerations of face, both personal and national. But when he left in February, he had no one of equal or near equal authority and skill to leave behind. (Blyukher had left Canton in November.) Placed in charge were two military men, N. V. Kuibyshev and V. P. Rogachev, and a political adviser, I. Ya. Razgon. Kuibyshev, the brother of the powerful Moscow political figure V. V. Kuibyshev, was the dominant personality in Borodin's absence. But Kuibyshev—known as Kisanko in China—displayed none of Borodin's concern for Chinese "habits, customs and etiquette,"[8] nor apparently did he have much appreciation for the United Front strategy that Borodin had so carefully nourished. On more than one occasion, Kuibyshev openly expressed his disdain for Chiang and for Chinese officers in general. He distributed Soviet aid directly to Yunnanese and Kiangsi militarists, by-passing Chiang. He preferred Wang Ching-wei's company to Chiang's. And when he urged Chiang to send troops north to help the faltering legions of Feng Yü-hsiang, Chiang concluded that Kuibyshev also favored Feng's interests over his.

Moreover, Kuibyshev was attracted to radical programs, the CCP, the sovetniki and to young Chinese firebrands, newly home from Russia. And Chiang was alarmed by the resolutions of the recent KMT congress and by increased communist influence at Whampoa. Chiang knew he needed the Russians and their arms; he had tried, therefore, to prove his revolutionary zeal. In February, as before, Chiang repeatedly made public utterances attesting to his commitment to the revolution. Whatever he may have later written, it is not clear that such assertions were pure subterfuge. But no matter how revolutionary he sounded, he thought Russian support for his rivals was rising.

While Chiang was feeling threatened from the left, conservative forces in Canton and beyond were pushing him to the right. They warned that accommodating the Russians could only end with a communist China, that the forces of the left were becoming a major menace and that it was time to move against them. Such sentiments were represented in Canton by the Society for the Study of Sun Yat-senism. Additionally, they were presented personally to Chiang by, among others, his "elder" brother, the deformed and wealthy banker and dealer in artworks (and bean curd), Chang Ching-chiang. Chang came south in January, probably at the behest of the Western Hills clique, to attempt to swerve Chiang to the right. Thus in March 1926 Chiang was an ambitious but insecure man being wooed by the right and spurned by the left. As he repeatedly told Blyukher later, he feared being frozen out.[9]

Soviet sources claim that the top officers of the First NRA army, including Chiang, met secretly as early as March 9 and decided on a coup in cooperation with the Fourth, Fifth, and Sixth armies.[10] But the commanders of the other armies held back. What happened next has been the subject of heavy debate for over half a century. Many of the facts have been clarified, but the immediate trigger of events remains uncertain. During the night of March 18, the commander of the gunboat *Chang-*

shan, who was a CCP member, received a telephone call ordering him to move the *Changshan* from Canton to Whampoa, which he promptly prepared to do. The appearance of the *Changshan* at Whampoa was interpreted by Chiang as an attempted coup from the left. But where did the order originate? Did it come from Kuibyshev? Did it originate with a radical CCP member determined to push Canton to the left? Did it come from the right, anticipating that the *Changshan's* move would provoke Chiang to attack the left? Or was Chiang himself seeking an excuse for crushing the CCP and its confederates? All of these explanations have been argued by participants and by others. Although some seem more plausible than others, there is no hard evidence that would cause any of them to be totally ruled out.

But, if the course and motivation of the phone call to the captain of the *Changshan* are uncertain, the response is not. At 3 A.M. on March 20, the *Changshan* appeared at Whampoa. Chiang immediately ordered its captain seized, the city of Canton placed under martial law, the headquarters of the Hong Kong–Canton strike committee surrounded, the pickets disarmed, the sovetniki, Bubnov, and the other members of his delegation placed under protective custody, and all CCP members at Whampoa or in the First Army arrested.

The sovetniki considered resistance, but there were fewer than forty of them in Canton at the time. Wang Ching-wei, informed by telephone of what had gone on, was enraged but, characteristically, did nothing. The city of Canton was safely in Chiang's hands. The Soviets at the embassy in Peking were shocked and furious. They berated themselves. They should have mistrusted Chiang Kai-shek all along, they told themselves. They should have realized that they were only being used by him and the KMT. Borodin used to say, "The KMT, like all bourgeois parties, is a toilet, which, as often as you flush it, still stinks!"[11] But now was not the time for self-flagellation. The immediate question was: Is anything salvageable in Canton? Or, as Karakhan put it to Cherepanov on March 21: "Do you think Chiang has broken off with the communists and with us completely?"[12] Only twenty-four hours after Chiang had struck, Karakhan and Borodin had agreed that reasonable possibilities for cooperation with Chiang still existed, and Borodin prepared to return to Canton immediately.

It soon became apparent that Borodin and Karakhan, if they had not judged Chiang correctly, had correctly assessed the immediate situation: Chiang, in spite of his actions on the twentieth, did not want to sever relationships with the Russians; indeed, he was eager to resume those ties. For Chiang's position was far from strong. If he had expected other generals to join him once the coup succeeded, events proved him wrong. The majority of NRA generals opposed him. They did not favor the left, but they did not see Chiang as Sun's successor. And although Chiang may have preferred the right, it could not or would not provide him with the trained armies and weapons he needed to maintain power. At least for now, the required support could come only from the Russians and the left.

Whether Chiang had considered this before he acted on March 20 depends on whether he had moved precipitously or after careful deliberation. In any event, his concern for the Russian reaction manifested itself within hours of the coup. The Moscow commissioners and sovetniki (who had been under house arrest) were released before the day was over. That evening Chiang, meeting with Bubnov and his Central Committee colleagues, told them that their arrest and that of the sovetniki had been a great mistake, done against his will; he promised to go to the sovetniki and beg their pardon.[13] On March 22, the counselor at the Soviet embassy was told by Chiang that the latter's actions had had nothing to do with the Soviet Union, but were purely personal. Chiang indicated, as the counselor saw it, that if the offending Kuibyshev, Rogachev, and Razgon were shipped to Russia and Borodin and Blyukher returned to Canton, all would be well.[14] In early April, Chiang issued a manifesto declaring that the alliance between the Soviet Union and China was as strong as ever. On April 16, at Whampoa, he proclaimed that the Chinese revolution was "organically" related to the world revolution and indicated that the KMT was still prepared to accept Comintern direction. Increasingly, Chiang took the position that March 20 was wholly the result of a series of misunderstandings and that those against whom it had ostensibly been directed were not really involved at all. The CCP was exonerated and the commander of the *Changshan*, previously regarded as the chief villain, was released from custody. Chiang even apologized to the picketers he had arrested.

To resume relations with the Russians and, to a lesser degree, to secure support of the left, Chiang was prepared to make a strenuous effort to redeem himself. Attempting to reassure the left by moving against the right, he criticized the Western Hills clique. He ousted such leading right-wingers as the Canton chief of police and the commissioner of the provincial government, and he abolished the Society for the Study of Sun Yat-senism. But at the same time, Chiang made it clear that the status quo ante was not to be restored. The pickets of the Hong Kong-Canton strike committee remained disarmed, even though they had Chiang's apology. Not only was the Society for the Study of Sun Yat-senism outlawed, but so was its left counterpart, the Young Soldiers' Association. All political work in the NRA was ordered suspended. In time it would become apparent that Chiang's moves were directed not so much at the right or the left as at any source of opposition to himself. Thus Wang Ching-wei was not rehabilitated and eventually had to leave the south. In April and May, the forces of the right increased in Chiang's ranks, but they were rightists beholden to him. Once Chiang had purged the Society for the Study of Sun Yat-senism of those elements he considered dangerous to himself, he fostered its growth as a source of personal support.

Whatever the origin of March 20, Chiang was now on top. His position was shaky but his opposition was leaderless. As the weeks passed, Chiang's confidence grew. Like Sun and Borodin, he wanted the Northern Expedition too. He would need the Russians for that. As soon as they recovered from the initial shock, Karakhan and Borodin had decided that Chiang could be handled. Borodin had headed for Canton on the 21st, but the militarist Chang Tso-lin's occupation of the northeast blocked his speedy return. Chang and his Japanese supporters would have liked nothing better than to lay their hands on Borodin. In order to by-pass the areas held by Chiang, Borodin had to travel northwest out of Peking to Outer Mongolia and from there by train to Vladivostok, where he could board one of the Soviet steamers commuting regularly to Canton. Using this route, it took nearly six weeks for him to reach Kwangtung. In the meantime, the dust would have settled in Canton; reports from those on the scene on March 20 would have been read and digested by

Moscow. Alternative strategies would have been considered to deal with the new circumstances in the south.

The first recorded analysis of March 20, by one who was present at the events, was Bubnov's. On March 24, addressing the dismayed and bewildered sovetniki, Bubnov set forth what became the accepted Soviet explanation: the coup had not weakened the case for continued cooperation with the KMT, leading to the Northern Expedition, but had enhanced it. The revolution was still going, and it was necessary to prepare for its extension. This could be done, Bubnov continued, only by strengthening the Kuomintang. "Needless to say ... this will demand especially great persistence from the Chinese Communist Party, which will have to adopt flexible, very quiet, and very controlled tactics."[15] Bubnov's remarks indicate that while March 20 resulted from several factors, the excessive zeal of the CCP, coupled with its inexperience, was viewed as the central one. This theme gained increasing favor in the weeks and months ahead, until the missteps of the infantile CCP came to be seen in Stalinist circles as the chief, if not the only, cause for Chiang's action.

Following Bubnov's line, V. A. Stepanov, a ranking sovetnik who remained in Canton, reported late in March or early April that the revolution would continue, with Chiang Kai-shek at its head. Stepanov evaluated Chiang, listing his strengths and weaknesses, and concluded that, given Chiang's ambitions, he would sooner or later turn on the Russians. But as for now, continued Stepanov, the Russians were too strong for him and he could be used.[16] In another report shortly thereafter, Stepanov was more pessimistic about the immediate future of the Russia-Chiang relationship. He was confused, he wrote, by Chiang's friendliness with the Russians concomitant with his close relations with militarists and other conservatives. Had Chiang learned his lesson—that he needed the Russians—or was treachery ahead? It made no difference, wrote Stepanov: whatever the case, there was no alternative to cooperation with Chiang.[17] Some sovetniki in Canton questioned this. And some CCP members were highly critical of the Chiang-KMT axis. But their voices had long since been discounted by Moscow's agents in China. The reports that Borodin and Karakhan heeded confirmed their earlier judgment: Chiang was salvageable; the fundamentals of the Northern Expedition strategy adopted in February were still sound. Yet, even if cooperation with Chiang was to continue, Borodin suspected it would not last for long. Other alternatives must soon be found. This was nothing new, however. From the outset of their involvement, the Russians had sought for options to Sun and the KMT. After March 20, the search assumed greater immediacy.

One of the Bubnov commission's conclusions had been that the Soviets should continue large-scale aid to General Feng Yü-hsiang, who had recently met reverses. Moscow had early sought to recruit Feng as an alternative to Sun. When Sun died, Feng was viewed as a possible successor, but events in Canton had caused this option to be temporarily set aside. In the meantime, Feng had been driven out of Peking and announced his intention to retire to the Soviet Union for seven years of "instruction and contemplation." He wanted to become a simple toiler and a good example for China. Obviously this was only a ploy to gain Soviet support. The Russians knew that Feng was an opportunist who had cooperated with imperialists as readily as he did with them. He consistently promised more liberalism than he delivered. But in the past he had served as a foil against Chang Tso-lin and the Japanese in the north, and he probably could be used in that capacity again. Moscow, which had few cards in that part of China, decided to play along with him.

During the early months of 1926, Feng was moving by slow stages across the Gobi to the USSR. In early April in Urga (now Ulan Bator), he was brought together with Borodin, who had just arrived from Peking by way of Kalgan, en route to Vladivostok and Canton. For the Borodin group, which consisted of Fanya, Norman, Cherepanov, V. M. Primakov (Feng's chief sovetnik, who had been at the Peking conference), long-time CCP member T'an P'ing-shan, and seven or eight other Chinese, the auto trip from Kalgan had been a difficult one. The desert sands had blown incessantly, stinging their hands and faces and carving drifts that stalled the high-wheeled touring cars. At night the travelers slept in abandoned huts or in primitive lean-tos made of sod. Their food was only what they had brought along, plus an occasional partridge felled by a sharpshooter.

When Borodin met Feng, he tried to convince him to return to China—even as Borodin was returning—and take charge of his armies. Those armies were staggering, but still intact. Borodin urged Feng to take the revolutionary path, to root out the imperialist toadies from his ranks, to organize a provisional government, cultivate mass support, and ally himself with Canton.[18] Borodin and Feng talked at length on April 5 and again on the 6th. But Feng was adamant. He seemed determined to continue his Moscow pilgrimage. On April 7, Borodin resumed his trip to Canton.

From Urga, the Borodin party traveled toward Verkhneudinsk (now Ulan Ude). The journey was hazardous and laborious as the frozen rivers and streams began to melt. Sometimes the ice would hold them; at other times they had to wade through freezing waters. Once they had to wait on the banks of a river until a camel caravan came along. The drivers demanded 300 rubles, an extortionary sum, to ferry the party across on camelback. Finally the travelers arrived at Verkhneudinsk, just across Lake Baikal from Irkutsk and a stop on the Trans-Siberian Railway. There a special railroad car awaited Borodin on the siding. It was coupled to the next train going east. In Vladivostok the party paused a few days while Borodin recruited a retinue of stenographers, drivers, and guards to accompany him south. Waiting for Borodin was Blyukher, who was also returning to Canton at Chiang Kai-shek's request. Whatever differences may have existed between Borodin and Blyukher were submerged as they discussed the delicate situation that awaited them in Canton. To avoid the possible loss of both men should their ship be seized, which seemed a not unlikely possibility, they decided to travel separately. Borodin left first, arriving in Canton on April 29.

Immediately upon landing, Borodin went to Whampoa to meet with Chiang. He anticipated that Chiang would be tractable, but Borodin knew he was also unpredictable. Chiang might go left, he might go right; during the past six weeks he had gone in both directions. According to those who saw Borodin on the 29th, he was in a very agitated state. Not until he had seen Chiang, talked with him, and ascertained if a deal could be made would Borodin know where he stood.

It soon became apparent that an accommodation was possible, because by May 2 Borodin had calmed down. During the next two weeks, Borodin, Chiang, and Chang Ching-chiang, (Chiang's "elder brother") met constantly—always at the crippled Chang's quarters—and the terms of a compromise were worked out. The KMT organization was to be "readjusted," with communists and Chiang's enemies removed or clearly subordinated. There was to be no CCP criticism of the *San-min chu-i*—meaning no criticism of anything Chiang did. No communist could be the chief of a KMT or government department. No member of the Kuomintang could join the CCP. All orders to the CCP had to be filtered through a committee made up of CCP and KMT members and Comintern representatives. Chiang thus gave the Russians full responsibililty for members of the CCP. If they gave trouble, the Soviets would bear the blame. Finally, a list of all CCP members in the KMT was to be handed over to the standing committee of the CEC, which meant to Chiang. Clearly, this was far from the status quo ante in Canton. Whether or not Chiang needed Soviet Russia, or Borodin, Chiang gave the contrary impression. He told Borodin that Hu Han-min, who had returned to Canton from Moscow only shortly before, had urged him to detain Borodin—just as Chiang had detained Kuibyshev. Borodin knew that Chiang could do it.[19]

Borodin accepted this "compromise" agreement with Chiang because he was under orders from Moscow to regain a footing on the Canton scene at almost any cost. The reason was to save Russia's and Stalin's prestige. In the Kremlin, the struggle for Lenin's place was reaching a climax. For the Soviet Union to be ignominiously kicked out of China at that point would have seriously damaged the Bolshevik image and embarrassed Stalin as well, since he had specifically endorsed the United Front strategy. Once the USSR–KMT alliance was reestablished, however tenuously, and the Northern Expedition begun, something might happen to favorably alter the situation. But for that to occur, it was necessary to be in on the Northern Expedition. So Borodin was prepared to pay whatever price Chiang demanded, including the further sacrifice of the Chinese Communist Party.

Not until a large shipload of arms for the Northern Expedition had arrived from Russia during the second week in May, and the CCP, under heavy pressure, had apparently acquiesced to being bound and gagged, did Borodin rest easier. Some CCP members in Canton had urged him to turn at least some of the newly acquired weapons over to them, in preparation for the inevitable split with the KMT. But Borodin refused. His orders were to get back in; now that he was in, he would not risk the consequences of such a move. But Borodin was no longer at the center. The arrangement with Chiang had severely clipped his wings. Since Sun's death in the spring of 1925, most of the potential Chinese leaders in Kwangtung had been eliminated. Now in early May, Chiang got rid of two more: Wang Ching-wei and, once again, Hu Han-min. Wang, who had been in Canton on March 20 as the nominal leader of the government, had done little to challenge Chiang's new position. He continued to hope that something would return him to power, but when Borodin told him he could do nothing for him, the latter left for the north, with Hu Han-min. Hu, recently returned to Canton from Russia, where he had been sent after the murder of Liao Chung-k'ai, had hoped, minimally, to replace Wang in the reorganized KMT government. But Chiang saw no need to share the stage. Hu's followers had melted away; he could add little to Chiang's support. And so Hu also left Canton.

Borodin sought to do what he could with his stripped-down toolchest. He made it clear to Chiang that he had the full authority of Moscow behind him. To this end, Borodin made Chiang aware of messages from Moscow verifying the former's position. There is no doubt that, vis-à-vis Moscow, Borodin was stronger than ever. Chinese affairs were less and less influenced by the Comintern, where there were mixed feelings about supporting the KMT. Stalin, recognizing that failure in China could adversely affect him, was taking a direct interest in events there. And he had opted for the United Front, for supporting Chiang Kai-shek, and for Borodin, his old acquaintance of the local committee days of 1905–06.

Borodin's sharply reduced power did not preclude a vigorous political life in Canton. His large, gloomy house was a beehive of activity, growing ever busier as planning for the Northern Expedition went forward. On the first floor, translators rendered Chinese documents and newspapers into English and Russian, and orders written in English and Russian into Chinese. There was the constant rumble of presses running off multiple copies of political leaflets, research reports by the economic sovetniki, and other materials in support of the forthcoming military effort. In his living quarters upstairs, usually with Fanya doing secretarial work, taking notes, bringing in tea, Borodin received a steady stream of visitors of every political persuasion. However shrunken his power, Borodin remained an intellectually commanding figure. And he continued to devour all the information he could find. He consulted with his economic and political specialists. He read every available and relevant report. And he made decisions. But the decisions pertained to the left, to the CCP and the workers' and peasants' movement. After March 20 no Russian, not even Borodin, was permitted to do organizational work in other sections. Borodin had long ago concluded that the workers and peasants would not soon be the backbone of the revolution in China. But both were prime areas of Bolshevik ideological concern, and Borodin had been accused of neglecting them. Now he had the time—as well as Moscow orders—to cultivate them. Yet he well knew that the land reform necessary to bring the Chinese peasantry into the revolution would not be taken. Sun had not permitted it, and Chiang was even less inclined to do so.

Even where Borodin was permitted to function, however, Chiang kept his activities restricted. On May 1, 1926, immediately after Borodin's return to Canton, the Third National Congress of Labor and the Second Kwangtung Provincial Peasants' Congress opened in Canton. Chiang gave a banquet for the delegates to the labor congress and spoke in tones as revolutionary as ever. But after the congresses ended, Chiang formed a new catchall Alliance of Workers, Merchants, Intellectuals, and Peasants of Kwangtung. Without actually suppressing the CCP-dominated organizations that covered those groups, he sought to hobble them by creating his own overlapping organization.

Borodin was hardly content with his new position. In private, he speculated about a new leader or leaders who might serve as a counterforce to Chiang. But he did nothing to threaten the United Front and tried to restrain others who might do so. The adverse turn of events in China, plus Borodin's recurring malaria and dysentery (which worsened in the summer heat), necessarily affected his spirits. Although careful to preserve a correct appearance to the outside world, among confidants he displayed a growing cynicism, a characteristic more evident as his power waned. To a member of the CCP he described China as "no man's land," ripe for whatever foreigner had the capacity and daring to seize it. So it had been throughout history. Why shouldn't it be the Russians' turn now?[20]

Whereas Borodin was increasingly kept from the center of KMT activities after March 20, Blyukher, who had returned to Canton in mid-May, was kept nearer the hub. Chiang considered Blyukher's cooperation absolutely vital for the success of the Northern Expedition. Chiang consulted with him frequently on matters of strategy and tactics. On innumerable occasions during the next year Chiang would countersign Blyukher's orders without even reading them. But he rarely asked Blyukher's advice on personnel,[21] reserving that area for himself. Moreover, he kept Blyukher isolated from other Chinese. As time went on, the quarantine, not only of Blyukher but of all the military sovetniki, became stricter. They complained that there was no longer even a Chinese communist around with whom to converse.

Once the constricting arrangement between Borodin and Chiang had been made, the latter hastened to have it ratified by the KMT. On May 15, the Second Plenum of the CEC of the KMT opened in Canton. Before it would end its sessions May 22, it would make official the Chiang-Borodin agreement or, as it was officially known, the Party Affairs Readjustment Plan. The CEC plenum also gave its approval to the Northern Expedition. During the next six weeks, Chiang, Blyukher, Borodin and the Russians, and the CCP would bend every effort toward getting the expedition under way. All wanted to leave Canton as soon as possible and to make the Northern Expedition a success—though for quite different reasons.

The Russian presence in China had, from the first, been predicated on the Northern Expedition. Sun Yat-sen had accepted the Soviets only to bring it to reality. Whether the Russians were sold on it or had countenanced it only to appease Sun, they now considered it indispensable for their own purposes. As early as March 1925, soon after the capture of Swatow, Blyukher had discussed his plan for the Northeren Expedition with the victorious Chinese generals, and in late 1925, while on his way back to the Soviet Union, he put "The Great Kuomintang Military Plan" to paper.[22] In the plan, Blyukher called for part of the NRA to remain behind, to hold Kwangtung and protect it against possible attack. Meanwhile the bulk of the NRA "will move together, like a fist, through one of the provinces, Kiangsi of Hunan, and finishing with one of these will quickly move to clean up the other . . . Possessing Hunan and Kiangsi, and having in the course of operations formed the new temporary units needed to defend the occupied positions, not losing time, the whole mass of the active forces will [next advance to] capture Hankow, Hanyang, and Wuchang"[23]—the three cities on the Yangtze that formed Wuhan. Blyukher's plan called for a single offensive, but Chiang envisaged a two-pronged attack that would assault the forces of two warlords, Sun Chuan-fang and Wu Pei-fu, at the same time. It took Blyukher more than a month to convince Chiang that the NRA was not strong enough to fight both generals simultaneously and that all efforts should be directed against General Wu. On June 23, shortly before the campaign was to begin, Chiang adopted Blyukher's proposal. But, as events would prove, only for the time being.

Both before and after the beginning of the Northern Expedition, Chiang Kai-shek made diplomatic efforts to ally with various warlords. Blyukher was in sympathy with this course, having included it in his "Great Plan." Borodin, not being able to object effectively but hoping that some other militarists might threaten Chiang, agreed. As Borodin now put it, any militarist prepared to fight imperialists was a "good" militarist.[24]

Early in 1926, the Kwangsi armies, having joined six established Cantonese armies, were collectively designated the Seventh Army of the NRA. Now in June, the forces of T'ang Sheng-chih, the Hunanese militarist, came over to the NRA and became its Eighth Army. By the time the NRA was ready to roll in July, it had more than 70,000 men in its ranks. As preparations for the Northern Expedition proceeded, Chiang continued to consolidate his own position. On June 5, he named himself commander in chief. During the rest of June, he worked to make both the National Government and KMT headquarters subsidiaries of his office. On July 5, he had himself appointed director of the military department of the KMT, and on the following day he was elected by a Central Executive Committee plenum to be the chairman of the standing committee of the CEC. On the day after that, the table of organization for the office of the commander in chief was issued, and it crossed the t's and dotted the i's of Chiang's power; all military and civilian lines of command ran directly to the commander in chief. He was legally, as well as factually, the center.

On the same day, July 7, 1926, Borodin was awarded the rank of "Higher Adviser to the CEC KMT." The appointment led foreign observers who were paying attention to what was happening in Canton to believe that Borodin was advancing from strength to strength. But those near the center knew that Chiang was directing the orchestra and Borodin was bowing a weak second fiddle. Unmistakably, the baton in the Chinese revolution was now being wielded by Chiang Kai-shek.

14

The Northern Expedition

On the eve of the Northern Expedition, feelings ran high in Canton. Some Cantonese were elated just to be rid of the KMT, the army, Chiang, and they hoped, the Bolsheviks; others welcomed the national and personal opportunities that the expedition seemed to offer. Even the marginal nationalists were exhilarated by the great adventure that was about to get underway to unite China.

Once in the field, the advance of the National Revolutionary Army was phenomenal. Wherever the brown-uniformed forces of the NRA marched, they met with success. Such resistance as they encountered was either brought off or easily overcome. Despite the absence of major armed engagements, word spread from Canton north that the NRA forces were irresistible.

Along with the troops came hundreds of propagandists. While the propaganda was mostly prepared by the CCP, its content was nationalist, not communist—and it was disseminated in the name of the KMT. The main themes were the future of China, the yoke of imperialism, the increasing power of the NRA, dissension within the imperialist camp, and the desire to fulfill the KMT slogans.[1] The slogans rarely attacked the bourgeoisie. They were anticapital, but the capitalist enemy was foreign, not domestic. The message was simple, designed for a mass audience and spread by tens of thousands of poorly printed posters produced by hectograph. As Borodin probably overstated it: "We paid as much attention to posters as to rifles."[2]

Sometimes the agitprop people preceded the military, encouraging potential resisters to lay down their arms; usually they marched in with the troops. As soon as a town or village was entered, posters were put up and a meeting was called. At the meeting, the agitators told the townspeople that they had come not as conquerors but as liberators. The members of the NRA were, of course, soldiers, they said, but the people need not fear this new type of Chinese soldier. Whatever they needed they would pay for, not confiscate, as warlord soldiers had done. Oppressive local leaders would be replaced with men representing the people's interests. To arouse and perpetuate popular support behind the new regime, the agitators created a variety of new organizations. Branches of the KMT were opened; trade and peasant unions were formed, if none previously existed; youth, students, and women were provided with their own groups. In many towns and villages of Hupeh and Hunan, the workers' and peasants' unions became indistinguishable from the new government; spurred on by the agitprop people, they conducted revolutionary campaigns, aimed at identifying and extirpating counterrevolutionary elements.

But these new "administrations" were pasteboard. They would last only as long as they had military support. Radicalism was now popular among KMT generals, many of whom were outright opportunists. But that was not true of all generals, some of whom harassed revolutionary regimes as soon as they appeared. In most instances, when the troops moved on, the agitprop workers went too, leaving the newly invested leadership to fend for itself. Sometimes guns and ammunition were left behind for defense purposes, sometimes not. "Rear area" men were supposed to follow the propaganda workers, but often they did not appear or, lacking military backing, were ineffective. Despite the NRA's arrival, most areas were unchanged; the same people held power.

Numerous assertions to the contrary, particularly by communist sources, the successes of the NRA were only slightly attributable to the agitprop forces. Victories came rather from large, comparatively well-trained, well-financed, and well-equipped military forces, expertly led. No doubt propaganda work strengthened the fighting morale, but the effort to engage the masses, though temporarily helpful, was too brief, shallow, and unsupported to create a lasting revolutionary atmosphere. There was still no effective plan for organizing the masses into a disciplined and resolute force capable of seizing and maintaining control in China.

As Sun and Borodin had foreseen, the NRA was the revolution's greatest strength, even though that strength primarily sprang from the weakness of its adversaries. Like other Chinese armies, it mostly operated without maps, advance information, or meteorological data. Reconnaissance was almost unknown. Commanders might obey or disregard their instructions as the spirit moved them. They would often refuse to aid another unit if they disliked its commander. But the troops did not live off the country, as other Chinese armies did. They had better morale and a greater sense of purpose than other forces. They received able advice from the sovetniki, who fought in the ranks when the going got rough. They were, overall, the best troops in China south of the Yangtze. Whether they were the best troops in all China is open to dispute. Certainly as they moved north, lost many of their original members, and replaced them with recruits from warlord units, their claim to uniqueness was vitiated.

But in the early months of the Northern Expedition, nothing stopped the NRA, not even a serious epidemic of cholera. By September the NRA had reached the Yangtze, well over 500 miles north of Canton. It had grown from eight to fourteen armies. It numbered 150,000 men, compared to the 70,000 who had left Canton. The victories, however, sharpened the latent frictions within the KMT. From May to July these frictions had been submerged by the common desire to be on the move. But once they were out of Kwangtung and easy victories had been scored, the opposing ideological forces sought to exploit those victories for their own ends. Success widened the breach between Chiang and the left.

Chiang Kai-shek had originally wanted to advance north in a two-pronged attack. He had apparently allowed Blyukher to dissuade him; but in September, as the NRA approached the triple cities, Chiang decided to follow his original inclination. He feared being swallowed up in Wuhan. Unlike Canton, Wuhan was a semi-Westernized metropolis, having a fairly modernized 170,000 person workforce with trade-union and strike experience. Wuhan was a railway hub and, even though it was seven hundred miles from Shanghai and the ocean, it was one of the chief ports of China. It had many cloth, tobacco, tea, and cement factories, foreign-owned and therefore disliked. Much of the left's hopes for the Northern Expedition centered on capturing Wuhan and using its working class as the chief support for its authority and for revolution. Because Chiang feared the left might do this, he preferred to bypass Wuhan.

So while part of the NRA, under general T'ang Sheng-chih, the Hunanese militarist recently converted to the KMT, drove toward Wuhan, Chiang turned his other forces, including most of the Whampoa-trained armies, eastward toward the coast. On August 18, without informing Blyukher, Chiang sent his troops into Kiangsi. All went well at first, thanks in part to widespread bribing of enemy officers. But when the eastern column of the NRA reached Nanchang, in northern Kiangsi, resistance stiffened. On September 30, in response to Chiang's call, Blyukher arrived on the scene and urged Chiang not to attack. But Chiang, afraid that Blyukher secretly favored the leftist Wuhan strategy, ordered his men to attack. Lacking adequate offensive weapons, reserves, and planning, Chiang was repeatedly repulsed with heavy losses. His position soon became perilous.

Although Blyukher disapproved sharply of Chiang's course, he could not, as one of the chief architects of the NRA, see it destroyed. In early October, Blyukher traveled west to seek help from the victorious NRA armies that, after hard fighting, had taken Wuhan. Blyukher told Borodin that, whatever the victories of the NRA elsewhere, failure at Nanchang would doom the Northern Expedition. Blyukher received Borodin's approval for a number of dependable units to proceed to Nangchang from Wuhan. With their aid, some new equipment, a few Soviet planes, and more silver with which to cross militarist palms, Nanchang was taken during the first week in November.

The victories of the NRA, however attained, startled Chinese and, especially, foreign observers, who had heretofore largely ignored developments in Canton. But these successes were costly. The forces that left Canton had suffered 50 percent casualties by the time they reached the Yangtze. At Nanchang alone more than 15,000 men had been killed or wounded. Still, the NRA had tripled its original size to 220,000 men. But the new armies were made up of mercenaries—the defeated or bought-off troops of the militarist opposition that always gravitated to the victor. They had no sense of mission; there was little opportunity to indoctrinate them; they fought for their rice bowl—and as infrequently as possible. Significantly, fifty-one of the fifty-six KMT generals were large landowners, hardly devoted to radical causes.

Nanchang told Chiang that he still needed Russian arms and leadership. And the Russians had no Chinese leader at their disposal who could compare with Chiang either in stature—news of the victorious NRA had spread throughout China—or in military strength. But their mutual need did not draw them together. And so in central China in late 1926, there came to be two NRA headquarters and two "capitals," one at Wuhan, the other at Nanchang: neither was prepared to break with the other, but neither dared turn its back on the other.

During the march north from Canton, the headquarters of the KMT government (and of Borodin) had remained in the south. At first glance, it would appear that Borodin's power and position in Canton improved once the expedition was under way and Chiang was gone. A Joint Council was established to replace the Political Council that Chiang had bypassed. Its purpose was to recapture power Chiang had seized. Borodin was one of the seven members of the Joint Council, nominally a nonpartisan body; Borodin and his allies soon moved it to the left. On October 19, at Borodin's direction, a conference of the CEC of the KMT was convened in Canton. Of the sixty delegates at the conference, the majority were on the left. Those assembled enlarged the cabinet to include ministries of war, transport, and justice, thus seeking to supersede Chiang's authority as head of the Military Committee, under which he had subsumed all governmental as well as military functions. In general, the platform adopted by the conference, at Borodin's urging and by his design, was more radical than that of the Second Kuomintang Congress. The new platform called for a 25 percent reduction in land rents, authorized the formation of peasant "self-defense" units, demanded as 54-hour work week, ordered compulsory arbitration, invited Wang Ching-wei to return, and sent greetings to Feng Yü-hsiang, now back from the Soviet Union and seen as a possible alternative to Chiang. By Bolshevik standards, it was a mild program—but it was well beyond what Sun Yat-sen would have sanctioned, and it was unblushingly anti-Chiang.

The left direction of the government in Canton was further indicated by its vigorous and lavish celebration of the ninth anniversary of Russia's October Revolution. November 7 was declared a public holiday, and all shops and factories were ordered closed. The entire city was decorated with Soviet flags and emblems, and with pictures of Lenin and Sun Yat-sen. Speaking platforms were set up on hundreds of street corners, with each trade and peasant union and social organization having its own center. Orators stressed the accomplishments of the revolution in Russia and the value and durability of Soviet-Chinese unity. That evening Borodin addressed a huge banquet, emphasizing the same themes. All of this was well reported by the local (and Soviet) press. Anyone reading them, as well as other press reports from Kwangtung in October and November, would not have doubted that Canton was communist.

The truth, however, was much different. Despite appearances, in Canton it was not the revolution but the counterrevolution that was advancing. When the NRA set out on the Northern Expedition, it took most of Canton's revolutionary strength: the Whampoa-trained fighting forces of the NRA, plus the youngest, most active, and committed members of the civilian left. Remaining behind were mostly older men, bureaucrats, opportunists, and a few militarist detachments in addition to some picket remnants of the Hong Kong–Canton strike. The latter, with their government subsidies, their own administrative and judicial units, and paramilitary forces, offered a leftist threat to Chiang's rear guard.

Along with the other concessions that Chiang had obtained from Borodin in May was an agreement, implicit or explicit, to terminate the year-long Hong Kong–Canton strike. On July 16, just prior to the Northern Expedition, Chiang outlawed all strikes at "socially important enterprises" (those necessary to supply the NRA) and placed such factories under the protection of the army. Entrepreneurs responded by declaring all enterprises to be socially important, thus precluding further strike activity in Kwangtung. And just before heading north, Chiang also placed the city under martial law. On August 6, instructions were given for all picketers to be disarmed. Although the order was not enforced, because the picketers were too strong, it was a clear indication of ultimate intentions. Lest there be any doubt, there were periodic reminders from the police and right-wing generals that strikes were counterrevolutionary, against the interests of the Northern Expedition, and would not be tolerated.

The only way Borodin could counter Chiang's rightward moves was by bureaucratic maneuvering and his personally controlled press. He had practically no military units, and the picket forces were weak. Still, the veterans of the Hong Kong–Canton strike did not respond passively to Chiang's repressive measures. Beginning in August, the Chinese press regularly carried accounts of battles between union and antiunion, Red and anti-Red forces. Labor confrontations involving mercenaries hired to oppose unionists were scarcely new in Canton, but they occurred now in increasing numbers, spurred on by Chiang's allies on the right. In December and January, the final crackdown came. Workers were specifically forbidden to picket, to organize demonstrations, or to withhold arms from the authorities. By then, the radical workers were so demoralized that the August order to disarm them could be carried out. The triumph of the right was all but complete. But by early 1927, when this happened, Borodin was no longer in Canton.

For months there had been discussion among Borodin and the left about moving the government from Canton to Wuhan. As Canton became less and less hospitable, an early departure became a necessity. The conference of the CEC of the KMT had specifically authorized the transfer to the north, so plans were now begun in earnest. Within days after news reached Canton of the fall of Nanchang, indicating the virtual end of resistance south of the Yangtze, Borodin and a core government cadre left the Kwangtung base for the north. This so-called First Group headed for Wuhan was made up of Borodin; Madame Sun; Sun's son, Sun Fo; the British-trained foreign minister Eugene Chen and his two daughters; the wealthy, Harvard-educated T. V. Soong; and various military and civilian sovetniki. In all, some thirty dignitaries accompanied by several hundred guards and others embarked on what would turn out to be a dangerous and fateful journey.

The trip began by train. But the entourage soon reached the end of the line and had to transfer to palanquins, each of which required four bearers. These not being readily available, the guards accompanying the party went to the nearest opium dens to round up the required personnel. Since the bearers escaped each night, the procedure had to be repeated daily. Finally, the company transferred to flat boats. Sometimes junks were used, occasionally ponies. But for more than half the trip, the chief means of locomotion was footpower.

S. A. Dalin, a Russian who took the trip, described the hazards of the road.[3] The journey was carried out under daily rainstorms that made the almost impassable "highway" even more difficult. At times, the only thoroughfare from one town to another was a narrow footpath one person wide between paddies or mountains. For the most part bridges did not exist, and streams and rivers had to be crossed either on steppingstones or, more often, by wading. Dalin said he now understood why the imperialists and their predecessors had only partially conquered the country and why foreign military intervention could occur only in places like Canton or Peking or along the Yangtze. The revolution could be safe as long as it kept away from such accessible centers. These observations were not unique to Dalin, but they are important to understanding later Maoist successes in China.

As the voyagers traveled northward, they could never be certain of the reception they would receive. Sometimes they were greeted sullenly, with the town almost closed down as the drawn-out line of exhausted travelers entered it. Borodin and his troop feared an attack momentarily. At other places, they were met by local officials who, waiting for the travelers at the outskirts of town, gave them calling cards as they approached. After the First Group had left Kwangtung province and had moved into Kiangsi, it was sometimes enthusiastically greeted by revolutionary-appearing Red Spears, native self-defense forces dressed in black uniforms decorated with mother-of-pearl buttons and armed with long spears from which hung red banners. In the larger towns they were at times received by local CCP and Young Communist cadres.

At such stops, the travelers saw encouraging revolutionary slogans: "The spirit of Lenin lives among us." "Imperialism is capitalism in this stage of development." "The right KMT is a weapon in the hands of foreign imperialism." They attended meetings at which the more revolutionary the statement, the louder the shouts of approval. The "International" and "Young Guards" were sung, sometimes to organ accompaniment, with great fervor. But as Borodin considered the implications of what he observed on his northward journey, he reached the conclusion that, in spite of appearances, nothing had changed fundamentally in China. Prostitution, gambling, opium smoking, all the old revolution-debilitating values, were as firmly ensconsed as ever. Particularly in the countryside, where the great majority of Chinese were to be found, the old order—landowners and merchants—still prevailed.

Just as their reception varied from town to town, so did their accommodations. Sometimes they slept in comfort, but more often in schools, police stations, or aboard boats where, in unhospitable communities, they felt more secure. Once, they arrived in a village after sundown and were told there was no place to stay except a temple. They spent the night there, only to discover at dawn that the building contained a century's accumulation of refuse, mold, and cobwebs. Borodin sarcastically remarked that, when the Chinese cheka got around to ridding China of counterrevolution, dirt, and cobwebs, it would make the Soviet cheka's work appear to be a child's plaything.[4]

As the trip continued, the pedestrians grew increasingly exhausted and testy. Borodin was irritated by affronts to himself and the sovetniki, who included some rather distinguished Soviet academicians. But to the many Chinese they met, the Westerners were merely traveling among important Chinese; the Russians, Borodin included, were often seen as servants, foreign ones at that—and treated accordingly. By the end of November, the weary travelers reached Tszianfu, proceeding from there to Nanchang where Chiang came out on a cutter to greet the junk carrying Borodin and his delegation.

The First Group did not have to pass through Chiang-held territory to get to Wuhan. They could have gone through Changsha to the west, which was controlled by ostensibly friendlier forces. But the "government" wanted to meet Chiang. Most of the Cantonese were far from dedicated leftists. They were uneasy about supping and sleeping with Bolsheviks, particularly when the latter's fortunes were sagging as Chiang's advanced. Chiang's authority had grown tremendously in recent months. He was now unquestionably the prime Chinese figure in the revolution. And though most of those approaching Nanchang disliked him politically or personally, they did not want to be on the losing side. Even KMT members with leftist inclinations argued that Chiang spoke like a revolutionary, promising reforms, lashing out against imperialist privileges and exploitation of China. They did not want to see the revolutionary forces split at this point. Nor did Borodin, if he could help it, though he doubted he could. But even if Borodin regarded a breach with Chiang as inevitable, he would not seek to deny the other members of the government the possibility of meeting with Chiang. It gave Borodin, moreover, an opportunity to size up the situation in Chiang's own territory.

Borodin readily understood why Chiang had selected Nanchang for his headquarters. It was a conservative, medieval, provincial town with only one industry, enamelware, and a small electric plant. It was a retirement community for wealthy landowners. In times of stress, rich landowners went there to find safety behind its walls. There was no unruly proletariat in Nanchang for Chiang to worry about. In this it differed from heavily industrialized Wuhan, where Borodin and the others from Canton now asked Chiang to move. Chiang had heard of the mounting leftism in Wuhan. But it was not only the left that Chiang feared. The city was already occupied by other NRA troops, chiefly those of the Hunnanese warlord T'ang Sheng-chih, whom Chiang regarded as his rival. Going to Wuhan opened the possibility of a contest under unfavorable conditions with the forces already there. Moreover, marching west to Wuhan would move Chiang further from Shanghai, where he had reason to expect support.

Nevertheless, Chiang told Borodin and his companions during their meetings, which were held from December 5 to 8 in the resort village of Kulin in the hills above Nanchang, that he would consider moving the capital to Wuhan, and that he had no objection to Wang Ching-wei's being invited to return from abroad. Experience told him that he had little to fear from Wang. The Kulin meetings resolved nothing. Just as the visitors were attempting to conciliate Chiang, so he was seeking to attract support from the First Group. Though he did not succeed at that time, the ground for later defections was cultivated.

Sensing that nothing was to be gained by further talks, Borodin and his entourage resumed the journey to Wuhan on a riverboat, arriving there within a few days. They were dog-tired but happy to have safely completed the hazardous and exhausting twenty-five day journey from Canton. Wuhan was adorned on all sides with slogans decrying imperialism, calling the Chinese revolution inseparable from the world revolution, and hailing Borodin as "the leader not only of the Chinese but also of the international revolution."[5] The city was seemingly in the throes of that revolution. Within forty-eight hours after Wuhan had fallen in October, more than sixty thousand workers had gone out on strike. By the end of the first week of occupation, fifty-two factories had been struck. And between then and Borodin's arrival, the pace of revolutionary activity had not slackened. Under the direction of Li Li-san, an able Moscow-trained member of the CCP, schools had been set up to teach strike techniques and trade-union organization, to offer leadership and military traini .g. Street meetings took place daily at the major intersections, usually followed by parades. Wuhan's thoroughfares were dominated by picketers wearing red star or hammer and sickle insignia, and greeting one another with the clenched-fist salute.

The day after Borodin arrived, 300,000 noisy partisans assembled to welcome him and his group. The crowd was so large that its members could not all be addressed by the same speaker at the same time. The leading members of the delegation moved from one group to another, until they had extended greetings to all. Overhead three NRA planes circled, emphasizing the power of the revolution. In the background firecrackers exploded. Above the din were heard voices praising Chinese-Soviet friendship, shouting "Down with imperialism!" "Long live the dictatorship of the proletariat!"—and "Ten thousand years to adviser Borodin!"[6] In the weeks immediately ahead there would be even larger and more enthusiastic meetings.

Borodin was immensely pleased with what he was seeing. Not only by the revolutionary fervor, but by his immediately cordial relations with the occupying general, T'ang Sheng-chih; by news that the majority of the NRA generals were dissatisfied with Chiang; by the reports that Feng Yü-hsiang was about to break out of the west, where he had been reorganizing after his return from Moscow; by the evidence of a growing peasant movement in the country back of Wuhan. But Borodin remained aware of the undependability of the undisciplined worker and peasant masses. He knew that the Wuhan strikes, while gratifying to the revolutionary spirit, were paralyzing its factories, whose output was needed to supply the NRA. Borodin realized that no matter how many radical slogans T'ang shouted, he was still a warlord, guided by self-interest rather than revolutionary ideals; that the other generals were no more radical than T'ang; and that Feng Yü-hsiang was unlikely to come to their aid.

The verities of the situation were confirmed for Borodin by the first moments of his arrival in Wuhan. As he came to shore aboard a small motorboat decorated with paper flags and bunting that bore greetings to the KMT, the advisers, and to Borodin in particular, the British cruiser *Cockleshell*, one of the foreign warships stationed at Wuhan, turned toward his vessel and side-swiped it. Borodin made it safely to shore. But the incident underscored the fact that in Wuhan, in addition to other difficulties, he would be operating under the constant threat of foreign intervention.

In spite of certain forebodings, Borodin embarked upon the Wuhan experience with enthusiasm. His reputation had never been greater. He was greeted by Wuhan's masses as more than a Lafayette, more than a Foch, almost as a Caesar. As he told one of his former Canton collaborators he now met again in Wuhan: "We shall begin a new life—write a new book."[7]

15

The Wuhan Experience

The Wuhan at which Borodin arrived in December 1926 was an ancient city with a modern facade. Its westernized section had a green swathe along the Yangtze planted with rows of palm trees. Parallel to and beyond the green was a broad asphalt-paved avenue, two hundred feet wide, the bund. And lining the bund were substantial six- and seven-story office buildings, apartments, and mansions inhabited by Wuhan's international contingent. One of the correspondents who traveled up the Yangtze to visit the new revolutionary headquarters remarked that Wuhan along the bund reminded him of Euclid Avenue in the Cleveland of his youth. In normal times, Wuhan's triple cities made up a thriving industrial and commercial metropolis, the gateway to a large part of Central China. Wuhan, with its 2.5 million people, was the third city in China in exports and the fourth in imports.

But December 1926 was not a normal time in Wuhan. Its fall to the National Revolutionary Army on 10-10 Day, 1926, had ushered in a revolutionary period that now, two months later, had far from run its course. The daily life of the city overflowed with evidence of revolution. But despite appearances, the city's revolutionary forces were in growing disarray. The United Front that Borodin had so assiduously cultivated was disintegrating. In October and November, when the NRA first arrived, even rich merchants in Wuhan had shouted "Long live the world revolution!" But by December the alarmed bourgeoisie was shipping its gold and silver down river to Shanghai.

The liberation of the city had led to a rapid proliferation of trade unions. By December, there were over three hundred of them, with hundreds of thousands of members engaging in many major and hundreds of minor strikes each month. Strikes in foreign-operated plants, whose managers were required to maintain production, were usually settled quickly by granting concessions to the underpaid and overworked laborers. But the Chinese middle class was less flexible. By the end of 1926, its leaders were paying NRA generals to help suppress strikes. The lock-in became commonplace, with NRA soldiers, supposedly instruments of the revolution, blockading plants, forbidding workers to leave or food to enter. Armed clashes between workers and soldiers often resulted. On the day Borodin arrived, there was a serious skirmish in which several workers were killed.

Radicalism was rife in the city. Unemployed and striking workers paraded through the streets, shouting defiance and making threatening gestures. At any hour of the day, groups of twenty or thirty—or up to several hundred—might be seen coursing through the "Chinese city," one of the non-Western parts of Wuhan. Their grievances depended upon the vagaries of the moment. Almost any complaint would arouse indignation in the fevered atmosphere that prevailed.

Agitation and propaganda cadres sent out by the KMT (consisting largely of CCP members) tried to direct the mobs. Sometimes they succeeded, but only to a limited degree. It was easier to arouse the mobs than to control them. Moreover, the objectives of agitators and demonstrators were not always identical. The KMT sought to direct antagonism to certain foreigners and warlords. But the Wuhan street mobs were against *all* bosses, *all* authority. The situation in Wuhan had its own dynamic—and when Borodin arrived on the scene it had already swirled out of control.

Wuhan's economy was rapidly disintegrating. Middle-class Chinese, frightened by the frenzied strikers and their supporters, began closing their factories and businesses, throwing still more people into the streets. With production crippled, it was impossible to collect the revenues needed to support the regime. Ordinarily the government might have expected financial support from the countryside; but the emergence there too of radical elements led to further chaos. Above all, Wuhan suffered from the deterioration of its commerce. Wuhan lived by trade. By December, that had been cut to a trickle, either because merchants would not ship to Wuhan or because the channels were blocked by rebels or those who posed as rebels. Raw materials, fuel, and food grew increasingly scarce. In addition to radicalism, unemployment, cold, and hunger menaced the city. Thus, even though the atmosphere of Wuhan was far more revolutionary than Canton's, Borodin knew he had a prodigious job to do.

His recent visit with Chiang Kai-shek convinced Borodin that there was nothing to be gained by kowtowing to Chiang. Perhaps it was still possible to unite with Chiang, but that objective could be obtained only if Borodin had something to bargain with. There was, of course, the risk that obduracy in dealing with Chiang would widen the existing rift, but that could not be helped. The present situation could not be allowed to continue. Chiang must be brought in, or that such was not going to happen must be made clear. Borodin proceeded to force Chiang's hand. On December 14, a few days after arriving in Wuhan, Borodin and his colleagues established a United Commission of the Council of National Government to supersede all other governmental agencies, including those ceded to Chiang Kai-shek following the March 20 incident. This was done in the name of the Central Executive Committee of the KMT, nominally the ruling group in the KMT. Later in the month, Borodin summoned members and candidate members of the CEC to attend a plenum in Wuhan, to endorse these and other actions so that, as it was put, the *San-min chu-i* of Sun Yat-sen might be immediately carried out.

Not to be outdone, Chiang held his own session of the CEC. Making use of a "Second Group" of KMT officials and others (including Borodin's wife) who, bound from Canton to Wuhan, arrived at his headquarters at Nanchang on December 31, Chiang by persuasion and, where necessary, by force—they feared they would not be allowed to leave Nanchang—brought the Chinese members of the delegation into a rump session of what he called the "Politburo" of the Central Executive Committee of the KMT. From his Politburo he obtained a vote in favor of *his* continued independence. That was on January 3, 1927. For the moment, the Wuhan and Nanchang maneuvers did not significantly alter the situation. But something was developing in Wuhan almost at the same time that the Politburo in Nanchang was making its decision, which would, at least temporarily, seem to strengthen Borodin's hand.

During the weeks following Borodin's arrival, the spread of chaotic radicalism in Wuhan worried him. He feared that if mob actions continued, not only would the economy suffer but foreign intervention might occur. That, he believed, would mean not only an end to Bolshevik participation in the revolution but an end to the revolution itself. As Christmas approached, antiforeign resentment and indignation mounted, intensified by news that the KMT had been suppressed in the British concessions in Tientsin and Shanghai. In the former, seventeen Kuomintang members had been arrested and handed over to the northern warlord Chang Tso-lin, who had executed seven of them.

The news from Tientsin and Shanghai helped focus antiforeign agitation against the British. It reached a new peak of intensity during the first days of 1927, which marked the official celebration of the victories of the National Revolutionary Army and the moving of the Canton government to Wuhan. Revolutionary excitement ran high. Hundreds of thousands of people went into the streets to join in the festivities. Fireworks, firewater, and fiery rhetoric inflamed the throngs. At 3:00 P.M. on January 3, a crowd gathered in a square adjacent to the British concession, to hear anti-British diatribes and harass British marines guarding the compound of the Hong Kong and Shanghai Banking Corporation. Taunting the marines had become a favorite sport of street mobs during the preceding weeks.

It seems unlikely that agitators on the scene, assuming that they were under the control of the KMT Political Department, wanted to create an incident. Certainly Borodin didn't. In the past few weeks he had made a number of anti-British speeches, but his intent had not been to incite the street mobs to attack the British, but mostly to direct peaceful hostility against Great Britain so that the other Big Powers would not be inflamed. But Borodin feared that Britain, confronted by provocative actions, and prodded by other edgy foreign governments, would move if it felt its interests sufficiently threatened. Whatever Borodin's intent, the marines, exasperated by recent harassments, fired on their tormentors, inflicting a number of casualties. The crowd was stunned. Faced by British guns aimed directly at them, the people slowly drew back from the square.

But early next morning, an enraged throng stormed into the British concession. Howling as it ran through the streets, it smashed windows, automobiles, anything or anyone that came in its way. It beseiged the staff of the British consulate, shouting "Beat the foreigner!" "Kill the Englishmen!" and demanded that the English come out from behind their consulate walls. Other targets of Chinese enmity, such as the Jardin Estates and the headquarters of the British Volunteers, were also surrounded. But unlike the previous day when the marines fired on the crowd, this time the badly outnumbered English retreated to their boats—and left the British concession to Chinese conquerors. KMT leaders now came upon the scene, succeeded in calming the crowd, kept it from sacking the concession or moving on to other concessions, and arranged for the release of captured British subjects.

Four days later the British withdrew from another concession downstream at Kiukiang. They made no immediate attempt to regain their concessions and soon entered into negotiations with Eugene Chen of the Wuhan regime to legally relinquish both areas. Regardless of class, the populace of Wuhan rejoiced at these remarkable developments. No matter how they felt about the social and economic upheaval Wuhan was living through, most Chinese exulted at seeing the British "driven out."

Borodin was troubled because the radicals now argued that successful direct action by the masses, combined with their willingness, when ordered, to disperse without either destroying the British concession or moving against the concessions of other powers, indicated that a new and "better-organized" stage of the revolution was at hand. Now the masses could and must play the leading role. However, Borodin and others disagreed. They were grateful that no foreign lives had been lost, that property damage had been minimal, that the British had decided not to fight, and that the attack had been limited to one concession. Borodin warned against repeating the act against other powers. Particularly must they avoid confrontation with the Japanese: first, because Borodin wanted to use them as a counterforce against the British rather than driving them together;[1] second, because the Japanese had more ships and soldiers in the vicinity than the British and were less likely to brook such provocation.

Taking the British concession was not what Borodin wanted. But now that it had occurred without bloodshed, and the British lion was behaving more like a kitten, Borodin was not averse to taking advantage of the euphoria that the "rout" of the British produced. He used the occasion to announce the establishment of a new government. On January 6, Wuhan telegraphed Chiang in Nanchang: "The situation is strengthened, the masses believe us. The taking of the concession . . . demands the presence of the national government in Wuhan; the leaders must be at the head of the people at the time of the movement."[2] On the following day, Wuhan dispatched another telegram to Chiang and sent delegates demanding his immediate presence in Wuhan.

Chiang in turn wired Borodin, calling upon him to come to Nanchang. But Chiang's response was only a face-saving gesture. His generals were continuing to give him trouble and, in spite of the support coerced from the "Politburo" of the CEC, his government lacked legitimacy. The sucessful storming of the British concession, for which the Wuhan regime received credit, seemed to weaken his position still more. On the other hand, Chiang was aware that the Wuhan mob action had frightened some members of the Wuhan regime, as much as it had those in Nanchang. Certainly it had alarmed the Wuhan bourgeoisie, who might now be more amenable to Chiang's leadership. So despite the loss of face involved, Chiang agreed to go to Wuhan. In the second week of January, he arrived ostensibly for another effort at reconciliation.

On January 13, Chiang was officially welcomed by the Wuhan notables. And after a government-organized parade that ended at the Race Club, Chiang, Blyukher (who had accompanied him from Nanchang), Borodin, and most of the Wuhan leadership, surrounded by tens of thousands of shouting supporters, celebrated the reunion. In speech after speech they congratulated one another on regaining the British concessions in Wuhan and Kiukiang.

Although the proprieties were strictly observed, it soon became evident to Chiang that little had changed since he had met with Borodin a month before, except that Borodin was in a stronger position and less inclined to compromise. If a reconciliation was to be effected, it would have to be on Wuhan's terms. To be sure, Chiang saw placards proclaiming "Long live Chiang Kai-shek, chief of the National Army," but beside them were others that declared "Long live the National Government in Wuhan"[3] and still others hailing Wang Ching-wei. In a public address at the banquet that evening, Borodin told Chiang: "Comrade Chiang Kai-shek, we have come with you to the Yangtze. I hope we will also go further hand in hand."[4] But he quickly made it clear that, if they marched together, it would be based on a socialist version of the *San-min chu-i*.[5] And, Borodin added, "If someone doesn't want to listen to our advice, there are other oppressed peoples of the world, for whom our advice is necessary."[6]

Much of this was bluster on Borodin's part. The events of the past few days had undoubtedly raised his spirits and given him something to work with. But they had not obscured his limitations. Real revolution was not yet possible. On the issue of social change, therefore, he was prepared to compromise. But when it came to power, Borodin was not prepared to yield a scintilla more than necessary—as Chiang quickly learned. Chiang had hoped that his journey to Wuhan would help him recapture some of the power he had lost by the government reorganization in Wuhan. But his attempts failed to redress the voting balance in Wuhan's organizations by inserting his own men. His overtures to General T'ang, the landowner-militarist now in charge of Wuhan's armies, were also sterile. It was apparent to Chiang that he could not work out an acceptable compromise. But he did discern that many important people in Wuhan were dismayed by events in that city. Representatives of the Wuhan bourgeoisie, including some liberals, encouraged him to restore order in Wuhan and to bring those promoting disquiet under control.[7] But Chiang was in no position to act on this advice.

By having come to Wuhan at all, Chiang had lost face. Now, having achieved so little, the affront was felt even more keenly and he became angry. Like Borodin, he concluded that there was no longer anything to be gained from a conciliatory approach or from concealing his antileft feelings. Toward the end of his Wuhan sojourn, the meetings with Borodin and the Wuhan government deteriorated into shouting matches. Clearly T'ang and Borodin had become his foes: Borodin was the nerve center and catalyst of the left; T'ang provided Borodin with military strength. At one point, Chiang openly attacked Borodin and demanded that T'ang should go. And before he left Wuhan, Chiang "suggested" that Borodin also should return to Moscow—to provide the Kremlin with accurate information of the situation in China, he said. Borodin, however, was in a strong position within the Wuhan government. He had the backing of those who counted. A disappointed and disgruntled Chiang, leaving Blyukher behind, returned to Nanchang.

The weeks immediately following Chiang's departure produced various maneuvers by both Wuhan and Nanchang. Chiang spoke increasingly of the "intrigues of Borodin" and told one of the sovetniki that Borodin's departure from Wuhan was the price of any return to the fold.[8] More than the price of his return, it was the only possibility of his return. Chiang sensed that the KMT leadership in Wuhan consisted of political weaklings, except for Borodin. Chiang would not return unless he could dominate, and he could not dominate while Borodin was there. But still in need of Soviet military aid and advice, Chiang told the forementioned sovetnik that it was only Borodin he opposed. Another Soviet leader would be perfectly acceptable—he suggested Karakhan or Radek.

But the left was not then prepared to pay Chiang's price. There was much talk in Wuhan of "dictator" Chiang, much apprehension about what he would do if he took over. The Wuhan leaders recognized that with Chiang in power their future was dim. They were not enamored with the radical turn of events in Wuhan, and some of them saw Borodin as a liability. Though in practice he opposed radicalism, as the representative of the Soviet Union he symbolized it. But, like Chiang, the KMT officials in Wuhan also recognized that Borodin was the greatest source of their strength.

Frustrated at Wuhan, Chiang turned to building his strength elsewhere. During the balance of January and into February, a stream of emissaries moved in and out of Nanchang. Chiang was now in communication not only with his longtime supporters in Shanghai, but increasingly with militarists throughout the country and with foreign governments, particularly the Japanese. Some fundamental factors worked strongly for Chiang. Until the end of 1926, few in the north had taken the Canton regime seriously. But the military successes of the NRA, and reports of a radical social upheaval in its wake, kindled fears of a Red takeover in China among generals, landowners, bourgeoisie, and the residents of the international settlements. There was a bull market for anticommunism—which Chiang represented. At the same time, as the commander in chief of the NRA and a longtime confederate of Sun's, he could portray himself as an authentic revolutionary, carrying out the *tsung-li*'s dream of uniting China. Chiang then could simultaneously draw support both from anticommunists *and* revolutionaries. He could successfully claim to be antiradical and prorevolutionary, and he could appeal to those who held either or both of those positions.

By the end of February, Chiang had sealed, or was close to sealing, an anticommunist bargain with capitalist bankers on the coast and their backers among the Great Powers. From late February on, the tone of Chiang's utterances became increasingly anti-Red. In March, he repeatedly urged respect for foreign property and halted all anti-imperialist propaganda. Nevertheless, Chiang was far too good a politician to burn all his bridges behind him. He made it clear, from time to time, that his opposition was not to all communists, but only to Chinese and certain "bad" Russian communists, such as Borodin. "Good" Russians (that is, those Chiang thought he could use, like Blyukher) were welcome. In February, after Chiang had seen how badly he needed Blyukher, he requested that the latter, who had traveled with him to Wuhan in January and then remained behind, come back. True, the Russian general could constitute a fifth column in his headquarters. But Blyukher's strategy and leadership had proved decisive in the past and might be so in the future. Blyukher returned to Nanchang.

Why did Borodin agree to send Blyukher back? The answer is to be found not in China but in Moscow. Stalin, fearful of admitting the failure of his United Front strategy, continued to insist that the KMT-CCP-Soviet alliance he kept alive at all costs.

So if Chiang wanted Blyukher, he could have him. Moreover, it could be argued that there were potential advantages in having an important military adviser in Chiang's camp. The situation might change too. For Borodin, the chief enemy was still imperialism and warlordism, not Chiang. Since both Borodin and Chiang sought the reunification of China, that shared objective might hold the alliance together. The chances were slim but they must be taken.

In late January and February, Borodin knew only too well the weakness of the Wuhan position. He had said again and again that success in China depended on the army—and he could not count heavily on T'ang. With every passing hour, T'ang seemed to invoke the revolutionary idiom with greater enthusiasm, speaking of the world revolution, as one Russian put it, "not less than ninety-nine times a day."[9] But Borodin knew T'ang was a militarist, a capitalist with financial interests in ships, hotels, and real estate; his 50,000 Hunanese troops were largely untrained and undependable, no match for the northern armies they would soon face. The only reliable troops Borodin had were those of General Chang Fa-k'uei, and they were too few to constitute an effective force. Sometimes he allowed himself to think of a linkup with Feng Yü-hsiang, but Feng, though back from Moscow and again at the head of his troops, was staying in Shensi. Who knew when he would break loose?

If not the army, who else could Borodin call upon? The left KMT? The CCP? The workers' and peasants' movements? In theory, they might seem formidable, but in fact they were ropes of sand. The left KMT were few in numbers, largely bourgeois and fearful for their class interests as they beheld ominous radical action in Wuhan and in the Hunan and Hupei countrysides. Most of the KMT who remained with Borodin did so out of concern for personal political advantage, not because of leftist ideological conviction. As for the CCP, although gaining in experience, it continued to be small, disputatious, and doctrinaire rather than realistically pragmatic. During the Northern Expedition, the party had grown considerably, but the new members were untried and untrained. Nevertheless, in spite of his qualms about the readiness of the party for revolutionary leadership, Borodin continued to advance its members within the ranks of the Wuhan regime. But every time he did so, it added to bourgeois anxieties about the future. Borodin had reasons for keeping the CCP under wraps.

For similar reasons, Borodin had too much historical perspective to rely upon the workers' and peasants' movements. Currently, worker-peasant radicalism burned brightly enough, but it was a wild flame that would soon go out. One could use it, but not depend upon it. And to the extent that it was used, other elements more essential to that stage of the revolution would be alienated. Certainly the more Borodin utilized the workers' and peasants' movements, the more remote became the possibililty of maintaining the support of his military forces in Wuhan and of securing the support of General Feng.

Borodin sought to remedy his military weakness, taking the same initial step he had taken in Canton. The already existing Central Military and Political Academy was revamped to become almost exclusively a training academy (Whampoa-in-Wuhan) for Chang Fa-k'uei's Fourth Army, from which Borodin hoped to build a new NRA. But he faced the same stubborn problem as in Whampoa: officers needed education, and in China to be educated was to be middle-class. Of more immediate consequence, the trainees at the Central Academy were few and the hour was late. There was no time to build for the long run.

Borodin tried to conceal the weakness of his position. The propaganda pouring forth from the Wuhan presses reiterated endlessly that the worker-peasant forces were growing and the revolution spreading. One or two of the handful of airplanes that had been flown into China from the USSR were sent up daily to do aerial acrobatics over Wuhan, shadow boxing, as it were, with the steadily growing fleet of foreign men-of-war lining Wuhan's bund. While the exploits of the Russian pilots delighted the masses, they could not affect the power balance. The forces of Chiang and the imperialists were growing stronger—and Borodin's were very frail.

Later Borodin would be severely criticized by the radicals for having "done so little" in January and February. They thought he should have accelerated the organizing and arming of the workers in Wuhan and the rebellious peasantry in the countryside; backed the workers in their more radical demands; and urged the seizure of foreign concessions and property. Borodin was well aware that a sweeping radicalization of Wuhan was advocated by some communists in China and Moscow; he was also aware that other communists in both places believed he was moving too fast against Chiang and not doing enough to placate him. But Borodin felt that nothing could be gained by surrendering to Chiang except extinction; that the workers and peasants could not be relied upon; that even to appear to favor them threatened the United Front strategy Stalin demanded. There were occasions when those who differed with Borodin ranted and raved in his presence. But Borodin, at least publicly, remained unmoved. He and Stalin were in agreement on overall strategy. Borodin continued to have Stalin's ear, as from time to time both Russian and Chinese returnees from Moscow verified.

In retrospect, it can be argued that even if all-out support of the worker-peasant movement could not bring success, victory for Russia in China was impossible anyway. It would, therefore, have been more revolutionary to have backed a worker and peasant revolution, even in a losing cause. But this is arguing from the vantage of hindsight. In February-March 1927, Chiang Kai-shek's position did not seem impregnable. He had strong internal opposition. The British were backing down in Wuhan and Kiukiang, not only *de facto* but *de jure;* and there was still hope that Feng would yet ride out of the northwest to the rescue. It seemed premature to write off the United Front strategy. In any case, Stalin would not have permitted it.

Late in February, Chiang began to advance on Shanghai, home base of his banker friends, center of imperialism in China, and since May 1925 a hotbed of revolution. In the preceding October, Chiang had appeared ready to seize Shanghai, and the city's revolutionaries, not recognizing his turn to the right, were prepared to help him. But Chiang then concluded that the groundwork for success had not yet been sufficiently laid, and he held back. Now he began his move. Once more the revolutionary forces in Shanghai began to stir. Acting on Moscow's instructions, they still saw Chiang as *their* revolutionary. Thwarted in

October, they had spent the intervening months preparing for the "next time." On February 17, the NRA took Hangchow on the coastal approach to Shanghai. By the 18th, the army was less than fifty miles from Shanghai. To the radical General Trades Union, which provided revolutionary leadership inside the city, the time for action had come. On the 19th, over a hundred thousand workers responded to its call for a general strike. One of the warlord generals then controlling Shanghai sought to curb the strike by having his headsman chauffeured from one sector of the city to another. Stopping from time to time, the executioner would lop off the head of a striker picked at random, decapitating a score of victims throughout the city. But the terror seemed only to enflame the workers. By the 22nd, over 350,000 strikers were in the streets.

By that time, the revolutionary leadership in Shanghai, convinced that the NRA would enter the city at any moment, decided to turn the general strike into an armed uprising. On the 23rd, the workers and their allies marched on two sectors of Shanghai. Police headquarters were successfully attacked and weapons were seized. But once again the advancing NRA troops were halted by Chiang, in spite of impassioned entreaties by his Russian advisers that he continue toward the city. Once Chiang halted, the northern armies that still held Shanghai turned on the strikers, executing more than a hundred of them. The severed heads of victims were placed on poles or platters or in baskets, and displayed through the city. Such tactics, however, did not stifle the appetite for revolution. Preparations for the "next time" began almost immediately.

While the revolution in Shanghai was thus encountering a series of false starts, in Wuhan it was continuing to deteriorate. Polarization increased; the economic situation further disintegrated. More demands were made by workers; more factories were closed; more unemployed were thrown into the streets; more middle-class Chinese were alienated; and more middle-class and wealthy Chinese and foreigners left for the coast. At the same time, week by week, more foreign gunboats and larger war vessels were pulling to anchor along the bund. The Borodin-led regime was increasingly menaced.

As the danger to the regime grew, some urged reconciliation

with Chiang at almost any price. Although Borodin was opposed to such a course, he could not flatly rule it out, if only because Moscow continued to portray Chiang as a great revolutionary leader. But Borodin had observed Chiang at close
quarters for three years. He had dealt with him in the difficult
period after March 20, and he knew that Chiang was like when
he had the upper hand. Chiang knew the uses of power and did
not carelessly squander his political opportunities. Borodin
maintained, and Blyukher, who was at Chiang's side, concurred,
that Chiang would yield only to credible political or military
pressure. Borodin had little of either, but he could not stand still.
He called a plenum of the Kuomintang to meet in Wuhan on
March 10, thinking to use it against Chiang. Before that convo-
cation could assemble, however, an episode occurred that
touched him personally and had potent political implications.

In mid-February, Borodin's wife Fanya, who had been in
China since late 1923 and had become increasingly involved in
his work, traveled downstream from Wuhan to Shanghai to put
their younger son Norman, now eleven, on board a steamer for
the Soviet Union. It was too dangerous, both she and her husband felt, for Norman to remain either in Shanghai, where he
had been in school, or in Wuhan. Fred, now eighteen, had already returned to Moscow to embark upon a military career.

In Shanghai, Fanya Borodin put her son aboard ship for Vladivostok and then boarded the *Pamyat Lenina* to return to her
husband in Wuhan. She had been on the ship before, when it
traveled the Vladivostok-Canton route, but now, with the transfer of bases, it was Vladivostok-Wuhan. On the second day out,
going up the Yangtze, as the *Pamyat Lenina* approached Nanking,
it was stopped and boarded by a local "admiral," a vassal of the
northern warlord Chang Tso-lin. Fanya realized that, if detected, she might be used as a hostage. Given the recent execution of revolutionaries in Shanghai, she might, as Borodin's wife,
even be in danger of her life.

To her dismay, Fanya soon found that concealing her identity
would be virtually impossible. The "admiral" had stopped the
Pamyat Lenina because he had learned that she was aboard. But
nevertheless she tried to dissemble. When asked if she was Borodin's wife, Fanya replied that her name was Grossberg (not too

far from Gruzenberg), the same as that of the captain of the *Pamyat Lenina* and the name she had signed on the ship's register. She insisted on that identity, until her calling cards printed in both Chinese and English were discovered in her cabin. However, lest she be accused of falsely signing the register—a crime that could give legal justification for her being held—Fanya continued to maintain that her maiden name was Grossberg (it was Orluk) and that Soviet practice permitted her to use it after marriage.

Her captors knew what a prize they had; before long Chang Tso-lin was to claim her for himself. While in custody, Fanya was treated well. Her militarist jailers kept in mind that Borodin might yet win, or at least be useful, and they wished to be remembered favorably. There were many occasions when a "guest" of Fanya's stature could be useful. They invited Fanya to banquets. Some of them sent wines; others ordered American food for her from the local YMCA. But Fanya could hardly be at ease. She was aware of the Chinese custom of executing enemies after they had unsuspectingly eaten their fill at banquets, and she was afraid that the next banquet might be her last. As week after week of detainment passed, she became increasingly depressed, in spite of efforts to keep her spirits up through exercise, "positive thinking," and concern for her fellow prisoners.

In Wuhan, Borodin was of course greatly agitated by the news that his wife had been seized. He was not sure where Fanya was, or even if she was still alive. At night, he walked up and down the bund, hoping against hope that a boat with her aboard would materialize out of the darkness.[10] Her transfers from one jail to another were shrouded in secrecy. There were repeated rumors that she had already been executed. The fate of a number of Chinese communists, who were garrotted at the orders of Chang Tso-lin and other commanders, only heightened his concern. In an effort to protect her, at least one Soviet consul issued a statement implying that Fanya was an American citizen, with no connection whatsoever to the Soviet government.

By late March, Borodin seemed almost reconciled to whatever might happen to Fanya. Penning a public thank-you note to all who had expressed concern for his wife, he wrote: "A child is born through great pain and suffering. How much more so is the birth of free nations and a free world . . . the loss of a comrade is keenly felt by all revolutionists. We are, however, always ready to bear with a stout heart our losses and the pains they cause us."[11]

The quality of the relationship between Fanya and Mikhail Markovich is open to question. There are suggestions that it was not close. He had left her in 1918 to join the revolution. Considering Fanya's appearance—big, square, with an axlike face—one might wonder if he had wanted to run away. But he had brought her to China. There she was by many accounts his close coworker and confidante, and, as both his responsibilities and his isolation had grown, they had come closer together. While the holding of Fanya as a hostage to influence her husband's behavior had no major impact on his conduct of the affairs of the Wuhan regime, it must have brought him pain and heightened the impression of impending catastrophe that was gathering about him.

The news of the seizure of the *Pamyat Lenina* reached Wuhan on March 24, as the delegates to the Third Plenum of the KMT were gathering in that city. The plenum, whose thirty-three members were dominated by delegates favorable to Wuhan, came together in an atmosphere of rising tensions throughout China, not only between revolutionary and antirevolutionary forces but between the revolutionary right and the revolutionary left. In early March, accounts of the arrest and execution of workers by KMT generals in the provinces were becoming more and more frequent, as were reports of new revolutionary worker and youth organizations being founded by Chiang in areas he dominated. These new organizations were, of course, meant to outflank and ultimately replace the old revolutionary leftist ones. Wuhan responded to these challenges with a fierce "Down with Chiang Kai-shek!" campaign. On March 11, to show his defiance of what he suspected the Third Plenum had in store for him, Chiang for the first time permitted, or ordered, the execution of a CCP member.

The Third Plenum, with Borodin firmly in command, met from March 10 through the 17th and proceeded to undermine Chiang's official status. All chairmanships including his were abolished and the collegiate principle instituted to "settle the Party versus Persons issue."[12] Even so, Chiang was not flatly removed from his offices, but was given the opportunity to resign because of the "pressure of duties" at the front.[13] And he was kept in the government. Obviously, there were those in the Wuhan regime, Borodin included, who were still not prepared to sever the last tie with Chiang.

The Third KMT Plenum was conducted with a semblance of unity. It specifically denied that its decisions were directed against Chiang. The party, it was stated, was above personalities, any personalities.[14] But the fact was that Borodin, General T'ang, the noncommunist left, and the CCP agreed significantly only in that they opposed Chiang. Beyond that, they had different and sometimes contradictory goals. The plenum was marked by numerous resolutions of high purpose and revolutionary ardor. But other than pass resolutions, Wuhan could do little to limit Chiang's turn to the right or his growing power.

Even while the plenum was in session, and at least partially as an expression of contempt for it, Chiang moved his armies again on two fronts, one aimed at Nanking, the old southern capital, the other at Shanghai. As soon as Blyukher returned from Wuhan, Chiang had put him and his aides to work planning the offensives in detail, overseeing the training of his forces, and arranging material support for the operation. But when Chiang left for the battlefield on the evening of March 15, Blyukher was not with him. On the previous day, an angry Blyukher had left for Wuhan.

Whether he left on his own or was ordered back by Borodin or was fired by Chiang is in doubt—but not the reason for the split. Blyukher had based his plans for the capture of Shanghai on coordinated attacks from inside and outside the city. He wanted to use the Shanghai revolutionaries, who had been awaiting the NRA for months. But by mid-March it was becoming apparent to Blyukher that Chiang had been stringing him along, that he had no intention of sharing victory and power in Shanghai with communist-led radicals over whom he had no control. In the past, Chiang had refused to march on Shanghai when the forces inside the city had risen up because he said he wasn't ready. But now that he was prepared, he still would not join hands with them. Blyukher, who had sovetniki inside Shanghai and had been advising them on how to direct the attack within the city, felt betrayed.

Blyukher had placed one of his men, A. A. Khmelev, in charge of the uprising inside Shanghai, so that previous "mistakes" would not be repeated. There would be careful organization, effective direction, and steps to coordinate action with the forces of the NRA now less than twenty miles outside the city. A troika was appointed to guide the preparations; below the troika was an executive committee of thirty-one. Specific plans were made for each of the seven districts into which the city was divided. Tasks were assigned in connection with the seizure of key points and the involvement of the masses. There was a shortage of weapons—only 150 revolvers plus an assortment of clubs, axes, and knives were available—but a police headquarters, where a large number of rifles were known to be stored, was set as a primary objective. The army nearest to Shanghai was scheduled to arrive in the city between March 20 and 22. The uprising was scheduled for March 21. But shortly before it was to begin, Khmelev, the troika, and the executive committee were informed that the NRA was not coming. However, the machinery for the uprising had already been set in motion. Enthusiasm and expectations were high, particularly since the occupying warlord forces had mostly withdrawn in anticipation of Chiang's advance. The decision was made that, with or without Chiang, the effort to seize the city from within was going forward.

On the 21st, at noon, a general strike began, followed an hour later by an armed uprising. Perhaps as many as 800,000 responded to the strike call. By that evening, six of the seven sections of the city had been taken. By early the next day, the last major point of opposition had been successfully stormed, its defenders fleeing into the adjoining international settlement. In nineteen hours it was all over. Shanghai, one of the great cities in the world, with a population of 3,250,000, had fallen to Chinese workers, led for the most part by the CCP and its sympathizers.

The world, however, did not learn that the capture of Shanghai was a triumph for the internal forces. On the 23rd, a day after all resistance had ceased, the NRA entered Shanghai and claimed credit for its capture. And because there was widespread anticipation that Chiang's forces would take the city, Chiang (with Moscow's aid) was able to make this claim stick. In the Soviet Union and wherever communists were under Moscow's control, the fall of Shanghai was celebrated as a great victory, not of communist-led worker revolutionaries but of the NRA under the leadership of General Chiang Kai-shek. It was presented as a prime example of Stalin's wisdom in continuing to support Chiang.

In the Soviet capital, headlines saluted the triumph. The great poet Mayakovsky composed a hymn of praise in its honor. Parades and demonstrations and meetings were organized, the largest of which terminated outside Comintern headquarters, where thousands listened to impassioned speeches praising what had been accomplished in China and forecasting a still greater revolutionary future. The fall of Shanghai was treated as one of the greatest revolutionary successes in history, as it was. But its authorship was denied.

Not only had Chiang Kai-shek not participated in the fall of Shanghai, but when the attack came, he was not even in the vicinity. He had gone to the Nanking front where his forces were marching on the old river port. On the 23rd, when the NRA moved into Shanghai, his forces reached the heights above Nanking. On the 24th, they occupied the city. But by the 26th, Chiang was in Shanghai. Disembarking from the gunboat that had brought him from Nanking, he expressed respect and appreciation for the accomplishments of the revolutionary forces inside the city. But Chiang did not mean this. The leftists who had captured the city and the provisional government they founded represented a major threat to him. They were radicals with their own goals and organization. They might cooperate with him for the moment, but this would not last. They were seen as a threat not only by Chiang, but by the wealthy Chinese in Shanghai, who were bankrolling Chiang, and by the Great Powers, who had decided that the bolshevization of China had gone far enough.

During the next weeks after his arrival in Shanghai, Chiang would be very busy. Though he headed a victorious army, his position remained far from secure. Much, if not most, of his support came from circles that regarded him with less than enthusiasm. He lacked strong popular support. He had few distinguished or trusted lieutenants to serve him. Ever the astute politician, Chiang tried to form a coalition that would survive this turbulent period. He courted the Chinese bourgeoisie. He contacted leading independent warlords, offering some of the money his Shanghai contacts had made available to him. He tried to bring back esteemed KMT figures like Hu Han-min and Wang Ching-wei. And he renewed contacts with members of the Wuhan regime, who might be more amenable to persuasion now than they had been earlier.

But Chiang was busy on another front as well. As he was attempting to build relationships in one direction, he was preparing to destroy them in another. Even before his arrival in Shanghai, Chiang had plotted the destruction of the revolutionary forces in the city. He ordered that all irregular military units, meaning all those not controlled by him, be disbanded. Unauthorized persons were forbidden to own or carry arms. Strategic sites held by workers were to be surrendered. On April 25, all troops among his own forces suspected of being sympathetic to the left were ordered out of Shanghai. At the same time, Chiang founded the General Confederation of Workers of Shanghai and the China Union of General Progress to replace existing radical-controlled unions in Shanghai. He established his own commissioner of police to make sure potential enemies were arrested and his own chief magistrate to make certain they were put away. On April 8, he formally established his own government, replacing the provisional government set up at the time of the workers' takeover, and began arresting Wuhan supporters in Shanghai. On April 9, he invoked martial law, outlawing all meetings, demonstrations, and strikes. Clearly, the destruction of the leftist revolution was already underway. And not only in Shanghai, and not only by Chiang.

In early April, throughout China the hard-pressed left was being squeezed still harder. Strikes, some of which had gone on for months, were suppressed. Trade-union headquarters, usually the local centers of leftist activity, were smashed. Union officials were arrested and shot. And in Peking, the Great Powers approved and supervised the invasion of the Soviet embassy, which, along with Canton and Wuhan, was a center of Russian revolutionary involvement in China.

That the Soviet embassy had collaborated with Moscow's revolutionary involvement in China was no secret on Peking's embassy row. For years, sovetniki, CCP members, and other leftists had been observed going in and out of the compound. But there had been reluctance to move against the embassy. If the powers ordered their own troops into the Soviet legation, this would have precipitated an international incident; to have permitted the Chinese to march against the legation of a foreign power would have set an undesirable precedent. So nothing had been done. But now that the decision had been made to destroy communism in China, Chinese police and selected units of the warlord Chang Tso-lin were ordered onto embassy property.

On the morning of April 6, with members of the diplomatic corps looking on from a window in the nearby Dutch embassy, Chinese forces forced their way into the Soviet embassy compound. As soon as they realized what was happening, the Soviet diplomats, sovetniki, and Chinese communists who were in the compound began burning the embassy files that contained, among other things, copies of messages, orders, and bookkeeping accounts transmitted to and from such places as Canton, Wuhan, Kalgan, Vladivostok, and, not least, Moscow. But firemen of the Legation Quarter, who had been standing by, climbed quickly onto the roof of the building and, lowering a hose down the chimney, extinguished the fire, and saved most of the documents. By the time the operation was completed, eighty Russians and Chinese had been arrested and a huge assortment of Russian documents seized. Many of those arrested proved to be CCP members. Their allegiance and the discovery of a store of documents (whose contents would only be incompletely known for some time since many of them had to be dried out and all had to be translated into Chinese) provided Chiang with "legal" justification, if any was needed, to further develop his campaign against the "radicals." (Abetted by Moscow's heated denials of their authenticity, there long was doubt as to the reliability of the documents; it was alleged that they were pure fabrications or, at the least, had been tampered with. Though the latter remains a possibility, the content of many of the documents has been largely confirmed by Soviet publications of the 1960s and early 1970s, which indicate the utilization of what seem to be identical documents in various Soviet archives.)

In Wuhan, Borodin was not ignorant of what was going on

elsewhere in China. He knew that the ax was about to fall and, though he did not surrender to despair (there was still Feng), his pessimism grew. Some again urged him to patch up his differences with Chiang. But he had known, even before Shanghai, that there was no chance for Russia and the Chinese communists to remain in Chiang's revolution. To move to the left, as others urged, would alienate still more groups and would almost certainly frighten off Feng. And there was one more reason why Borodin, even if he had been so inclined, could not turn to the left: Stalin's orders remained to the contrary. Borodin had to hold on. Something might yet happen to save the situation.

And so he held on. On April 1, he had assembled the government's Central Executive Committee to issue more edicts limiting Chiang's powers. The CEC repudiated Chiang's authority over Wuhan in foreign affairs, fiscal matters, and communications. It so informed Chiang and warned him that any breach of these rules would be regarded as a counterrevolutionary act. On the following day, the CEC ordered Chiang to leave Shanghai and return to the front. And the Military Council of the CEC, which since March 10 had supposedly been the repository of all military authority, demonstrated its weakness by petulantly demanding that military officers obey only its orders and not those of other military leaders.

Such toothless statements, demands, and orders created scarcely a ripple in Shanghai and Nanking. There were opportunities for greater action in Wuhan. For example, on April 3, a drunken Japanese sailor, probably overcharged by a rickshaw driver, killed the driver. (The rickshaw men were a particularly truculent lot.) Angry Chinese marched on the Japanese concession, but Japanese marines responded with a fusillade in which several protesters were killed and more wounded. In other circumstances, such an occurrence would have resulted in violent protest and furious mob action. But now Borodin ordered the propaganda people to keep the lid on. Trade-union leaders were dispatched from one group and section of the city to another, with instructions to use all necessary measures to calm the crowds. Foreign intervention, Borodin argued, was increasingly likely as more and more foreign men-of-war showed up on the Yangtze; this could destroy any remaining possibilities of revolutionary success.

During the weeks following the NRA's takeover of Shanghai in late March, the Wuhan government kept hoping that things were not as bad as they seemed. But by early April, it was almost impossible not to read Chiang's mind. On the night of April 8, the Politburo of the CEC decided to send two loyal army corps to Nanking to "disarm" Chiang Kai-shek and then move the capital to that city.[15] But on the following day, the Politburo postponed the departure of the troops, voting to wait to hear what Wang Ching-wei, back from Europe and from visiting Chiang in Shanghai, had to say.

Wang had been invited back by the Wuhan government to serve as a foil to Chiang; an invitation had also come from Chiang. Wang had arrived in Shanghai only a few days after Chiang, who, though he disliked Wang, nevertheless rushed to see his "beloved friend and teacher." Chiang offered to "share power" with Wang. Wang, partly because he did not trust Chiang, partly because he wanted to be the great conciliator bringing all factions together, took Chiang's offer under advisement. On April 7, Wang boarded a steamer for Wuhan. Disembarking at the leftist capital on the 10th, he was greeted by government dignitaries, many of whom (particularly the old KMT hands) saw in Wang a last hope. As always, Wang was effusive with expressions of optimism and assurance. He had come as Sun's successor, he told them, and now that he was back, all would be well. Reconciliation with Chiang was possible, if only they would actively join Chiang in his quest for uniting China. After hearing Wang, the Politburo of the CEC decided to send its armies not against Chiang but against Peking, renewing Sun Yat-sen's Northern Expedition. Perhaps, by beating Chiang to the ancient capital, Wuhan would gain a strong bargaining position.

Meanwhile, Chiang was completing arrangements to crush Wuhan's allies in Shanghai and elsewhere. On April 11, removed from the scene of action to avoid personal identification with the planned bloodshed, Chiang gave the order to wipe out the Shanghai radicals. At 4 A.M. on the 12th, several thousand members of the Red and Green gangs, mostly city toughs and strongarm men recruited for the purpose, joined by some regular NRA units, attacked at twenty points around the city. There were three thousand armed picketers in Shanghai, mostly under

CCP control, but they had orders from Moscow not to resist Chiang at this time.[16] Only at the Commercial Press building in the workers' quarter of Chapei was there extended resistance. But when the group leader was killed and the attacking force brought up cannon, resistance there ceased as well. By noon of the 12th, the second armed battle for Shanghai was over.

Seemingly undaunted, the CCP-led General Trades Union ordered a strike for the next day. Demonstrations were launched in several areas of Shanghai. In spite of Chiang's repressive measures, which involved isolating different parts of the city from one another, as many as a hundred thousand in Chapei alone responded to the general-strike call. At this point, Chiang's forces opened fire, killing several hundred strikers. On April 12 and 13, and in subsequent executions of those arrested at that time, between 800 and 5000 of those whom Chiang regarded as enemies were shot. It was the end of the workers' movement in Shanghai and the end of its CCP leadership.

The events of the 12th constituted a clear proclamation by Chiang of his intent to destroy the CCP and its supporters throughout China. Open season was declared on communists, labor leaders, and all others who might be out of favor with the local militarists. In city after city, union headquarters—usually synonymous with CCP headquarters—were closed down and those in or near them shot. Within a few days, the radical movement had been virtually liquidated not only in Shanghai, but in such places as Ningpo, Amoy, Swatow, Nanking, Foochow, and even in Canton, where the revolution had begun. Only Hunan, Hupeh, and Kiangsi provinces escaped the purge—and then only partially and briefly. The end of revolution there, too, was in sight.

Up to April 12, it had been possible for those in the Wuhan government to delude themselves into believing that Chiang was not as strong as he seemed to be, nor so bent on the destruction of the left, and that their own position was less precarious than it was. April 12 made it almost impossible to deny the ascendancy of Chiang and the imminent disintegration of Wuhan. For all but willful dreamers, it was obvious that for Borodin and the Wuhan government their days in power were numbered. From April 12 on, it was every man for himself, to make the best deal he could before all hell broke loose.

16

The Hard Truth

The news of the destruction of the workers' movement in Shanghai on April 12 spread dismay, anger, and fear among the members of the Wuhan government. To Borodin and others alert to recent developments, it came as a shock but no surprise. In addition to all the other indications of Chiang's intentions, there had been the experience of the so-called Big Three, Earl Browder of the United States, Tom Mann of Great Britain, and Jacques Doriot of France. These stalwarts of the international movement, sent by Moscow to demonstrate worldwide support of the Chinese revolution, had on their way north from Canton to Wuhan in March encountered instance after instance of counterrevolutionary activity. When they passed through Nanchang, where they had expected to see Chiang, they were told he was too busy to see them; they were then escorted to a banquet where they were harangued with speeches explaining that the Chinese revolution was not part of the world revolution, that it was necessary to modify the present KMT program to meet reality, and that what was needed was a strong leader, Chiang Kai-shek.

Borodin's initial interpretation of April 12 was that the attack in Shanghai reflected the combined unhappiness of the Chinese bourgeoisie and the Western colonialists (who had called upon their governments for help). If a similar intervention in Wuhan was to be avoided, it would be necessary immediately to mollify these elements. On April 20, Borodin told his Wuhan associates: "To cope with such an adverse situation, we can only adopt the strategy of retreat for the time being . . . The imperialists may stop their attack on us because of the change of our strategy . . . If the strategy of retreat can correct the misinterpretation by some people in Hunan and Hupeh provinces, it should be carried out; if the strategy can assure the nationals of the imperialist countries of safe operation of their businesses under the National Government, it should also be implemented."[1] Borodin then presented a five-point program aimed at enforcing revolutionary discipline among the workers—that is, bringing them under control, creating a favorable climate for business in Wuhan, and generally reassuring the national and international bourgeoisie that they were welcome in Wuhan.

During March and early April, while Wuhan was trying to counter Chiang Kai-shek, it had taken on the appearance of a world-revolutionary capital. An international coterie of radicals had assembled in the city and, working with Chinese (usually communists) trained in Canton or Moscow, inundated the city with revolutionary slogans, posters, meetings, and demonstrations. The already extremist Wuhan proletariat was urged to make heavier demands: to ask for salaries paid two to three years in advance, for fifteen months of salary every twelve months, for four-week annual paid vacations plus two weeks off at the Chinese New Year, three days off at the Western New Year, and all revolutionary holidays off. If there was death or marriage in the family, a six-month bonus was to be paid. If a worker was fired without cause, he was to receive the equivalent of three years' salary. Rickshaw men became particularly demanding, swarming around the visitor who arrived at the bund, not permitting him to carry his own luggage, then charging him five dollars per bag and many times the normal rickshaw fare. Of course, workers used to receiving twenty-five to thirty cents for sixteen or more hours of work had a legitimate complaint. But that was not necessarily the way employers saw it. Many well-to-do Chinese and two thirds of the foreign population left Wuhan. Of those British, Japanese, and Americans who remained, most lived aboard ships on the Yangtze, unwilling to risk the city at night.

Borodin knew well that the Wuhan workers could not be easily disciplined and that there were dangers in even appearing to oppose them. They might turn on him and the KMT as well. But now he saw a far greater threat from the right. And in early April, even before the Shanghai suppression, he moved to merge the radical rickshaw and the more restrained police unions so that the latter might bring the former under control and prevent further incitement. But the events in Shanghai on April 12 and the subsequent closing of Japanese factories in Wuhan on the 13th, throwing seventy thousand more workers out of work, exacerbated an already bad economic situation and heightened worker-mob disposition to violence. At the same time, the line of foreign battleships anchored in the Yangtze had extended to over a mile and was lengthening daily. Any incident might bring the marines in and the government down.

On April 17, a lead article in the official Wuhan KMT press, which was at Borodin's disposal, quoted the minister of labor, a member of the CCP, as telling labor leaders to do everything in their power to assist the government, "particularly in the avoidance of any incidents in which labor might be involved."[2] This was being done, the article specifically stated, so that what had happened in Shanghai would not be repeated "here." Moreover, the government's intention to avoid labor incidents, the article continued, has been made particularly clear to the proper Japanese authorities—who owned most of the ships in the river, most of the investments in Wuhan, and had the shortest fuse. The article concluded: "If foreigners do not resume work in Wuhan, it cannot be charged against organized labor."

Later in the same week, the government announced the official protection of all foreign-owned buildings, declaring that they could not be confiscated without the owner's permission. A front-page headline of the *People's Tribune* on April 24 stated: "Labor imposes self-discipline as aid to government." Another article reported that the government and foreign companies were negotiating directly to settle disputes, that the unions had agreed to accept the agreements made, and that all who broke those agreements were counterrevolutionaries.[3] Two days later, it was announced that Foreign Minister Eugene Chen had arranged the reopening of the Japanese factories and the removal of troops and pickets from the Japanese concession. This was accompanied by a settlement of the bank workers' union strike, the reopening of the banks and of the English-language *Hankow Herald*, which had been shut down in late March because of its anti-regime statements. An allout effort was being made by Borodin and his associates in Wuhan to stave off economic collapse and prevent foreign intervention.

Although Borodin's policy was to allay the fears of the imperialists and the bourgeoisie, there was little inclination to mollify Chiang. Borodin had argued since December that it was futile to seek a reconciliation with Chiang; April 12 had seemed to verify his judgment. But channels to Chiang had been kept open. Moscow itself had not given up on a rapprochement; indeed, it had acted as if relations with Chiang were still good. But finally Moscow now decided to break with Chiang. It denounced Chiang as a traitor and "ally of imperialist bandits." For his part, Borodin threatened to "get" Chiang.[4]

But this was pure bluff. Borodin had no way of getting Chiang, and he knew it. When a Japanese newsman asked him if Wuhan was going to move against Chiang, Borodin replied: "This will hardly be necessary. The process of disintegration has already set in [in Chiang's camp] . . . Allow them a little time to run their course and they will be finished from within."[5] Borodin was whistling in the dark once more. About all that Borodin could do was to put on his best front and launch a massive propaganda assault against Chiang. Chiang was labeled a traitor and friend of imperialists. Slogans plastered about the city read: "Punish Chiang Kai-shek." The unemployed were organized in huge demonstrations to denounce him.

Not all who remained in Wuhan, however, shared this anti-Chiang sentiment. Before April 12, those who had opposed mob radicalism had mostly either left the city or kept silent. Now increasing numbers expressed open opposition to the regime. It was suggested to Borodin by some of his comrades on the left that he should handle these discordant elements in the "Moscow style."[6] While security arrests apparently were carried out in a few instances, Borodin knew that opposition reached high in the KMT and was widespread among the middle class. To strike at them would further endanger what was left of the United Front, which, in a sense, was his last protection. Moreover, though Moscow had broken with Chiang, it had still not repudiated the United Front.

The massacre in Shanghai and the sense of despair engendered in Wuhan provided the milieu for the Fifth CCP Con-

gress, which opened in Wuhan on April 27. While the meeting in
Wuhan was a congress of the Chinese Communist Party, attended by men like Mao Tse-tung and Chou En-lai, the two
principal actors were an Indian aristocrat, M. N. Roy, and an
Americanized Russian, Mikhail Borodin.

Roy had left Moscow for China late in 1926. He had been a
thorn in the side of the party ever since he had come to Moscow
in 1920 as Borodin's adherent. Brilliant but incorrigibly independent, he insisted now as he had at the Second Comintern
Congress in 1920 that the national bourgeoisie was not to be
trusted, that the basic premise of the United Front was wrong
and had been wrong from the beginning. In the underdeveloped
world, only a movement based on the peasants and workers
could be successful. No matter how promising a worker and
middle-class front might seem, Roy argued, in the end the latter
would always turn against revolution. In 1920 Lenin, not wanting to alienate someone with great leadership potential, allowed
Roy's and his own position to coexist, though in practice only
Lenin's prescriptions were followed. Now in late 1926, at the
Seventh Plenum of the Comintern, Stalin followed a similar
course. He permitted both his own position on the United Front,
as presented by his young house expert on China, Pavel Mif, and
Roy's position to be linked in the plenum's China statement.
The statement declared that the revolution was indeed to be
handed over to the peasant and worker masses, as Roy advocated but *only if the Kuomintang agreed,* which, Stalin realized, it
would never do.

At the plenum Roy had been elected to the Presidium of the
Comintern and to its China Commission. As soon as it was over,
Roy boarded the Moscow-Valdivostok express, accompanied by
T'ang P'ing-shan, a CCP leader who had also been at the meeting. Roy was anxious to go to China to implement his ideas,
which he was convinced the CI had endorsed. Roy and T'ang
went first to Canton and then to the new capital. By the time
they arrived in Wuhan on April 3, 1927, it was clear to Roy that
a move to the right was imminent in China. Like Browder,
Mann, and Doriot, he had seen much evidence of it along the
way north. Upon arriving in Wuhan, he began to argue his old
antibourgeoisie position. The events of April 12 only confirmed

Roy's confidence in the correctness of his views. Intense arguments developed between Borodin and Roy during the Fifth CCP Congress.

Not on the floor of the congress, however. Borodin and Roy did not want to appear to dominate a Chinese conclave. Moreover, Borodin suggested that, at such a critical juncture, dirty linen should not be washed in public. Accordingly, the decisive meetings of the Fifth Congress were held in Borodin's apartment, where the Politburo of the CCP gathered. Also present were other leading members of the CCP, such KMT leaders as Wang Ching-wei and Sun Fo, San Yat-sen's son, as well as Stalin's man, Mif, and one of Sun's earliest Soviet visitors, Voitinsky, who had been in Shanghai at the time of the April 12 catastrophe and had succeeded in escaping to Wuhan. Here, in Borodin's home, the fate of the fading Chinese revolution was heatedly discussed.

Roy argued from long-held principles: the peasants must be the backbone of the revolution; they must be won over by confiscation of the land; the Wuhan base (which, as seen by Roy, included the hinterlands of Hunan and Hupeh provinces) must be consolidated before any further military offensives could be undertaken. He supported his position with the undeniable fact that the peasantry in Hunan and Hupeh had already rebelled against the landowners and driven them out. Perhaps as many as fifteen million peasants had joined the newly established revolutionary peasants' unions. What was done in Hunan and Hupeh could be accomplished elsewhere, if only Wuhan would stop temporizing and unequivocally back the peasant revolution.

Borodin retorted that such a decision would mean the end of the United Front, which, in spite of the disintegration of the KMT, remained for him, as for Stalin, the only hope. To maintain the United Front, he said it was essential not to encourage the peasants and workers but to curb their excesses. But Borodin could not ignore the peasant revolution. The Comintern plenum statement and Pavel Mif, who had supervised if not written it, indicated that he must at least pay lip service to it. Accordingly he called for confiscation of all landlord-held plots *except* those belonging to officers of the NRA and the KMT, their relatives and friends, and the land of small landlords—which meant, in effect, that practically all land was exempt from confiscation. As for military action, in contradiction to Roy's advocacy of staying put, Borodin announced that he favored a resumption of the Northern Expedition. But at other times Borodin seemed to support a northwestern policy, which would bring the Wuhan government into closer contact with General Feng, and closer to the Soviet Union should escape become necessary.

With Roy and Borodin taking such different positions, the Chinese delegates to the congress arranged themselves at various points around, between, and occasionally beyond them. Clustered around Borodin were Ch'en Tu-hsiu, general secretary of the CCP, and Ch'ü Ch'iu-pai, one of the earliest Russian-speaking Chinese communists. Roy was supported by T'an P'ing-shan, his constant companion since he had left Moscow. But on individual issues, each man would receive backing from a variety of sources or be abandoned by erstwhile supporters as, in the free-for-all that the Fifth Congress became, the various participants felt impelled to present their versions of where the revolution had gone wrong and what was needed to be done to get it on track again.

Toward the end of the congress, Roy saw he was losing out and wired Moscow seeking confirmation of his position that the revolution should be "deepened," as opposed to the "widening" that Borodin advocated. Stalin, who had been shaken by the news of Chiang's coup in Shanghai and was more anxious than ever to protect himself, wired back with decisive indecisiveness in favor of both deepening and widening. And the final draft of the theses of the Fifth CCP Congress did call for both. But, in essence, Borodin won because his policies were later followed. His occasional advocacy of a "northwestern strategy" was rejected as defeatist, but otherwise the status quo was maintained and a resumption of the Northern Expedition was approved.

Clearly Borodin's authority at the congress had not been undisputed. He could not prevent Roy from talking—and Roy's stance was bound to win support. But among the shell-shocked and confused Chinese communists, many of whom had been present at the Shanghai disaster and who were receiving information daily about the spread of the counterrevolution, Borodin was a symbol of assurance. In spite of Roy's presence, Borodin in their sight was *the* representative of Moscow, the home of the revolution, to which they now more than ever had to look for help. In addition, the middle-class Chinese who made up the CCP's top leadership were not attracted to Roy and regarded him as an arrogant Johnny-come-lately. Besides, he was an Indian.

Borodin, then, carried the day at the Fifth Congress, but to what end? To keep the ship afloat a bit longer, desperately hoping that something or someone—General Feng?—would come to the rescue. Meanwhile, the Wuhan regime was weakening daily. The regime had been on shaky financial footing from its inception. The backbone of its commerce had been broken even before April 12. After the 12th, the blockade of the three cities by the combined imperialist fleet became stronger. Foreign-owned banks were closed. Shanghai banks refused to accept Wuhan currency or to honor checks made out to Wuhan accounts. By mid-May, when the CCP congress ended, Wuhan shipping was in dire straits. The situation became even more desperate when Ichon, the source for the opium trade, which constituted a significant share of Wuhan's income, was taken by forces allied to Chiang Kai-shek.

At the sme time that the economic squeeze was choking Wuhan, the regime's needs continued to mount. An income of $15 million to $17 million per month was required to support its soldiers, most of whom belonged to the militarist tradition and were primarily mercenaries. Now the government was planning a major military campaign, calling for greatly increased expenditures. And this was while more and more foreign-operated shops and plants in Wuhan were being closed down. Unemployment figures had reached at least 200,000.

Borodin and his sovetniki had made extraordinary efforts somehow to meet the financial crisis. Within three days after Borodin arrived in Wuhan in December, he had ordered the property of counterrevolutionaries seized and sold. But no one with gold and silver—much of which had already been shipped out or was in the process of being sent downstream—wanted to spend it to purchase land, buildings, artworks, and used cars from a government they expected might disappear at any moment. Taxes on commerce and on the wealthy yielded little; there was not much commerce, and the wealthy had fled. In classic fashion, the government next resorted to printing huge amounts of paper money to cover its expenditures. By May, Wuhan had both inflation and huge and growing unemployment. It also suffered from severe shortages of food and fuel and a rapidly spreading cholera epidemic from which thousands had already died.

Even more devastating was the near anarchy that gripped the city. After April 12, trade-union demands in Wuhan abated. There were fewer cries for higher wages, shorter hours, better working conditions. But the restraint of union leaders had little effect upon the picketers, strikers, and unemployed who continued to parade the streets of Wuhan shouting anti-everything slogans at the top of their voices. They seemed out of control. To further destabilize the situation, the military forces that helped keep the mobs in check were being asked to resume the Northern Expedition.

On every side evidence was seen of growing social and governmental chaos. The government issued orders, but fewer people listened. For Borodin, the strain of holding on and of waiting for Feng was almost unbearable. News then arrived that, on April 28, twenty members of the CCP, previously arrested in the raid on the Soviet embassy in Peking, had been strangled by the soldiers of Chang Tso-lin. Fanya was also held by Chang's men. Would she too be strangled, or had it already happened? Simultaneously, reports began to filter into Wuhan that Chiang's forces were marching on the city. Would Borodin's peril soon equal Fanya's?

Ironically, at the very moment that Borodin's universe was falling apart, his international reputation was at its zenith. In late April and May 1927, when the world thought the Red revolution was succeeding throughout China, Borodin was burning papers and preparing to get his sovetniki, their families, and himself out of China. That the revolution was so misinterpreted was due almost entirely to the international correspondents who, in the spring of 1927, ventured upstream to see what was happening in the "Red capital."

Until the success of the Northern Expedition, the correspondents, like the Great Powers, had paid small heed to the revolution in the south. They knew Sun and, though he had occasionally been good newspaper copy, he was hardly worth a trip to Canton. Even if a journalist did plan to visit Canton, Sun might be driven out again before he arrived. When the revolution reached the Yangtze, newspaper editors perked up. But in their offices in New York, London, and Zurich, as well as to many of their men in the field, all Chinese revolutionaries were essentially the same: Chiang Kai-shek was as Red as anyone in Wuhan. Why bother to go upriver when you could stay in comfortable, European-like Shanghai and cover the story from there? Only as lurid tales of rampant revolution in Wuhan began to circulate, mostly emanating from Shanghai bars, did editors seek on-the-scene reports from Wuhan. Particularly was this so after April 12, when it became clear that there were differences between Wuhan and Chiang, that all Chinese revolutionaries were not peas in a pod.

In Shanghai there was a rumor a day on developments in Wuhan. Many concerned the expropriation of property. Others revolved around the demise of the regime: its economic bankruptcy, political collapse, the momentarily expected flight of the Bolsheviks back to the Soviet Union. But the tales that provoked most interest in Shanghai and around the world were those that described the sexual mores introduced into Wuhan by the Bolsheviks. On the one hand, it was said, wives were treated abominably. Like property, they were held in common. Any women unclaimed by age sixteen, or "unused" for six months, were appropriated by the peasant unions for redistribution. But another genre of reports described emancipated Chinese women who went to bath houses and demanded that their husbands wash their backs. Above all were the repeated accounts of naked parades. According to an article in the *North China Standard,* one of these featured three hundred beautiful, eager nudes, "amazons" all. Marcher qualifications were determined by officers of the NRA, who personally inspected each applicant to see if she was "physically fit." Such rumors were so widely believed that the government was obliged officially to deny them. (They were wholly fatuous.) But such denials did not discourage the international correspondents who now flocked to Wuhan, attracted as much by fantasy as by fact.

In spite of Borodin's anger at the rumors that had brought

journalists to Wuhan, he was not displeased at their presence; often he sent a car to pick up a reporter who was landing. Sometimes he personally greeted the new arrival. The correspondents were important to Borodin because they brought news of the outside. As the world closed in on him, his channels of communication, already undependable, were breaking down. He was famished for information. What was happening in Nanking? In Shanghai? In Shensi province to the northwest? How quickly was the counterrevolution spreading? Were the imperialists more inclined to intervene directly? Where was Feng? Any news about Fanya?

If Borodin sought information, he also hoped to disseminate it. He wanted the Great Powers to know that there was no communism in Wuhan, that radicalism was being contained. He wanted to correct false impressions about the city, impressions that could lead to various disasters. Borodin also welcomed the reporters because, in a curious way, they gave him a measure of security. In chaotic Wuhan they represented a more stable world. To associate with them was to make contact with New York, Chicago, and Paris. They made him feel less isolated and trapped.

The correspondents who visited Borodin in Wuhan during the late winter and spring of 1927 included such journalistic stars as Henry Francis Misselwitz of the United Press, William Henry Chamberlain of the *Christian Science Monitor,* Vincent Sheean of the Newspaper Alliance of America, Arthur Ransome of the *Manchester Guardian,* Paul Blanshard of the *Nation,* Randall Gould of the *New York Times* (whom Borodin had met in Peking in 1926), and the redoubtable Anna Louise Strong, the American journalist-lecturer who was on excellent terms with Moscow and whom Borodin had known before. Borodin saw all of them, as well as reporters from Japanese, German, French, Swedish, and Swiss newspapers.

Borodin was good copy. Here was the mysterious man regarded by Shanghai colonials as the "Red beast" of the "Red capital." He had been given many titles, names, affiliations, and histories. Borodin did little to diminish the mystery built up around him. He rarely discussed his past. When questioned, he would give such answers as "I was born in the snow . . . and I live in the sun—yes? What good are facts?"[7] Reporters came to interview Borodin at his headquarters in the big gray building at the end of Han Chung Road in the former German concession. The first floor housed the KMT propaganda offices where the government's official paper, the English-language *People's Tribune*, its Chinese counterpart *Minkuo Jihpao*, and a number of other publications in Chinese, English, and occasionally other languages were printed. On the second floor were Borodin's offices and his staff, made up for the most part of the wives of sovetniki. Borodin lived on the third floor.

As often as not, Borodin received the reporters in bed. He was frequently ill in the spring of 1927 from the effects of the malaria he had contracted in Canton. He had also recently suffered a fractured left arm in a fall from a horse. But whether Borodin received them in his bedchamber or his office—where Lenin's picture was replaced by one of Sun Yat-sen—he intrigued and captivated reporters with his breadth, his grasp, and his celebrated "long view." The reporters in Wuhan in those days of headline journalism were looking for sensational material to spread the fame of their bylines. It was in their self-interest to build Borodin into a figure of Herculean proportions. In their columns, although Borodin was ill and seriously worried about the fate of his wife, the prisoner of cruel and murderous Chinese warlords, he never worked less than eighteen hours a day for the revolutionary cause. Still he found time to ride horseback, to read and play chess, at which he was "unbeatable." He was interested in art, literature, history. He read everything that came his way; for example, he was now into *Elmer Gantry*. He was capable, with "Lenin's detachment," of viewing every fact, every idea, every situation as part of the unfolding of destiny. A philosopher, a man of remarkable physique, with a booming voice and an iron will, he was a magnet toward whom all eyes were drawn. He dominated every gathering by his sheer presence, so the reporters wrote.

In Wuhan, Borodin led an international entourage of Chinese, Russians, Americans, English, Indians, and Indo-Chinese, who generally worshiped him. True, he had detractors and their numbers would grow. Blyukher, for example, had a different temperament, had clashed with Borodin, and got along with him only on a "professional" basis. As one observer put it, only the greatest tact on Borodin's part kept them from each other's throat.[8] Some ideologues, both Chinese and Russian, opposed his strategies. But in the heyday of "Borodinism," their caveats and carpings scarcely made a dent in the heroic image that was being created. At the head of Borodin's clique in Wuhan was Rayna de Costa Simons Raphaelson Prohme. Red-headed, of fiery temperament, she was described as the "Wildest Bolshevik in town."[9] Because of the role she played in Wuhan and shortly before her death in Moscow, she won a reputation as a classically tragic, revolutionary heroine—a reputation that survived for decades.

Rayna Prohme was born into a well-to-do Sephardic family in Chicago on January 23, 1894, and took a degree in botany from the University of Illinois in 1917. The following year she married a classmate, Samson Raphaelson, who was to become a distinguished playright. The marriage soon crumbled; the couple divorced, and Rayna began wandering the world. In the early 1920s she was in China, then returned to the United States where she married Bill Prohme, then an editorial writer and assistant managing editor for Hearst's *San Francisco Examiner*. Together they went back to China, where Bill worked as a newspaperman. Rayna contracted tuberculosis, but it did not slow her down. She became interested in newspaper work herself and found a job in 1926 with Eugene Chen, who was then publishing the *People's Tribune* in Peking. Under the influence of Chen, her work on the *People's Tribune,* and the success of the Northern Expedition, she became a fervent supporter of the revolutionary cause. When Chang Tso-lin took Peking and closed the *Tribune* in January 1927, Chen moved the paper to Wuhan. The Prohmes, both of whom were working for Chen by now, went along and soon became deeply involved not only in the work of the newspaper but in all that transpired in the Red capital.

Rayna worked long hours for the *Tribune.* She was to be seen all over Wuhan at meetings, demonstrations, and parades, her long red hair even more evident in a Chinese crowd than it would have been in the West. The Prohmes' apartment became a sanctuary for anyone in Wuhan who spoke English, whatever their ideology. On any given evening, one might expect to find there one or more of the younger sovetniki; possibly a CI agent or two; A. J. Todd, adviser to the Hupeh Dike Commission, with whom Borodin worked closely to stem the floods that threatened Wuhan in 1927; J. B. Grant of the Rockefeller foundation, in charge of sanitation in the area; Milly Billy Mitchell, a newspaper acquaintance of Rayna's from the West Coast, now working on the *People's Tribune;* Irma Duncan, fresh from Kropotkin Street in Moscow, who had come to China to dance for the revolution; Eugene Chen, the nonstop talker, editor, and foreign minister in the Wuhan regime.

At the Prohme salon, the activities were varied and cosmopolitan: in addition to drinking, they included discussions of current fashions in literature, such as the Broadway hit *The Jazz Singer,* soon to become the first talking picture. (The script, written by Samson Raphaelson, Rayna's first husband, had been sent her to read.) Sometimes the group would listen to classical records or join in singing revolutionary songs such as the IWW's "There'll Be Pie in the Sky when You Die." Years later, one reporter who had been in Wuhan in 1927 would declare that it had been "more like an excited lot of college freshmen than a real revolution complete with blood."[10] But that wasn't how it was seen in 1927. In April and May, there was revolution afoot; the masses were aroused; the danger was great; most of those who met nightly at the Prohmes' were young and they were having the time of their lives.

For this coterie, the hero of the day was Borodin. Although Rayna Prohme led the worshipers, she scarcely was alone. Russians, Chinese, Americans, all praised the stupendous abilities and magnificent figure of Borodin. In Rayna's eyes, there had never been anyone like him. Her excitable, high-strung husband shared her admiration. He described seeing Borodin standing "on a wagon, towering over all, encircled by universal adulation—strong, wise, truthful, a majestic man. Alongside of him all the Chinese officials and ministers seemed like, and were, docile puppets."[11] In 1927, Borodin was a figure of "massive authority" and "physical magnificence"[12]—it will be recalled that Borodin was five foot ten—"accustomed to look at each individual concrete question from the point of view of the broadest conception of the whole."[13]

It was into this atmosphere of boundless adulation that the international correspondents were introduced. Most Western journalists in China obtained their information on local conditions by interviewing other Westerners. That situation prevailed in Wuhan as well. The foreigners with whom the correspondents came in contact almost entirely belonged to the left; the others had gone. Often met at the landing by Borodin or Rayna Prohme, squired by the Prohmes by day, entertained by them at night, their view of Borodin was acquired through adoring eyes. Few reporters were not impressed. And when a reporter had a proclivity for radical causes or a tendency to hero worship, he was as likely to be as carried away as were the Prohmes. Thus young Vincent Sheean—proud grandson of a Fenian rebel—the equally young Randall Gould—who had brought his bride to Wuhan on a honeymoon—and the international reportorial gadfly Anna Louise Strong transcribed the "cult of Borodin" for posterity and provided the basis for his international idolization. (The play *Barrabas* of 1927 by the Norwegian writer Nordahl Grieg, in which Borodin is identified with the New Testament's "insurrectionist," is just one example.) Yet his cause moved inexorably and ever more rapidly toward collapse.

If some of those in Wuhan in 1927 saw Borodin as bigger than life, they were nonetheless dealing with a most extraordinary man. Without him the Wuhan government would have collapsed months before, if indeed it would ever have existed at all. This is why Chiang Kai-shek demanded Borodin's departure. Borodin gave strength, direction, and purpose to the motley crew of warlords, bourgeoisie, and intellectuals who made up the Wuhan regimse. In times of crisis, General T'ang, Wang Ching-wei, Eugene Chen, and the CCP looked to him for guidance. Throughout China, moreover, those who followed national affairs were aware of his achievements and his contribution to Chinese national pride. As the governor of Shantung, an enemy who temporarily had custody of Fanya, told her: "We greatly respect the genius of his organizing ability, his deep knowledge of China, his sharp psychological approach to our people. We recognize the strength of his influence, attracting to himself 200 million Chinese. We know that . . . he knows how to engage the hearts of the best people of halt of China."[14] But Borodin, no more than Canute, could halt the advancing counterrevolutionary tide that now flowed so strongly.

During the last ten days of April, 70,000 troops left Wuhan for the north. Each train's departure was accompanied by marching bands, speeches, and demonstrations by large crowds. Borodin and other luminaries of the Wuhan regime—Wang Ching-wei, Madame Sun Yat-sen, Sun Fo, Eugene Chen—came to the station to see the soldiers off. Impassioned addresses were delivered by such firebrands as Kuo Mo-jo, the CCP intellectual fresh from the disasters of Shanghai. When Kuo shouted "Down with Chiang Kai-shek!" "Down with northern militarists!" "Down with imperialism!" the crowd echoed and reechoed his words. Other government figures and representatives of worker and peasant organizations also sought to inspire the crowds and the troops. One departing general responded: "We won't come back—we won't come back until our mission is fulfilled!"[15] Then, as the general stepped onto the train, which was covered with graphic anti-Chiang and anti-imperialist slogans and cartoons, the agitprop people in the crowd led the rest in the renewed cries against Chiang, against imperialism, against counterrevolutionaries, and for the Northern Expedition. With bugles blaring above the din, the train pulled out of the station.

This renewal of the Northern Expedition was of the greatest importance to all those in the Wuhan government; their political, and perhaps physical, survival depended on its success. To maximize the chances of the expedition, it was considered essential to get as many men as possible—and their best troops—into the field. This meant that the defenses of the city were left to raw recruits, the worker-pickets, and detachments of Young Pioneers. In effect, Wuhan was defenseless.

Within a week after the armies had left, rumors of imminent attack appeared. Chiang Kai-shek or his generals were said to be on the way. On May 14 there were confirmed reports that troops under General Yang Shen were less than a hundred miles away. Then on May 17, news came that General Hsia Tao-yin, who had been allied with Wuhan and whose forces were located between Wuhan and Changsha to the south, had defected to Chiang Kai-shek. This report had an especially chilling effect.

The end of the line seemed near; for many, it was time to consider immediate escape or surrender. Borodin began burning his papers. News on the 18th that Hsia was less than twenty miles from Wuhan increased the sense of doom. On the 19th, all the anti-Chiang posters in town were torn down.

At this point M. N. Roy and others urged (or so they claimed later) that the workers be armed, that the guns being manufactured in Wuhan's Hanyang Arsenal be used by them in order to resist General Hsia, who had only a small attacking force. Borodin refused, as before, to arm the masses. As he saw it, arming the mobs might ultimately prevent the sovetniki and the Chinese who had dedicated themselves to Borodin from getting out of China alive.

Even at this juncture, the KMT leaders in Wuhan vigorously opposed arming the workers. But they were not opposed to military action against Chiang's man, Hsia. A small force—made up mostly of cadets from the Central Military Academy (now called the Military Political School), new recruits, and several hundred peasants from Mao Tse-tung's Peasant Movement Institute—was organized by Borodin and sent to the front under General Yeh T'ing.

Before that detachment could see action, however, news came on May 19 of a victory for Wuhan's forces in the north, at Chumatien. The report was handed to Tom Mann, the venerable British trade-union leader, as he was addressing a crowd of 30,000 gathered at the German football field to welcome the delegates to the Pan-Pacific Labor Conference scheduled to open the following day. Mann shouted the news of the victory to his audience and then, to enthusiastic applause, leaped across the stage in an imitation of the retreating enemy. The success in the north buoyed up the Wuhan regime and its forces, as did General Yeh's success in blocking the way to Hsia's army. Realizing that anticipated help from within Wuhan was not forthcoming, and having learned of Wuhan's success in the north, General Hsia decided to retreat toward Shensi province. The siege of the city was lifted.

But Wuhan's troubles were far from over. On May 22, news reached the city that Changsha, capital of the ultra revolutionary province of Hunan, had fallen to the counterrevolution.

Hunan had become the center of revolutionary activity in China in May 1927. More than five million workers and peasants had joined unions there and hundreds of thousands of new members were enrolling each week. In Hunan the movement advanced "with the strength of a hurricane,"[16] and Changsha was its eye.

When junketing communists Tom Mann and Earl Browder had visited Changsha early in May, they found it to have the "best organized" mass movement in China.[17] Although their train arrived at 4 A.M., ten hours late, 100,000 demonstrators were waiting in the rain to greet them. The revolution had taken over completely. Citizens' councils had replaced the traditional magistrates. Schools had been closed; the classics outlawed; the only body of knowledge permissible for study was Sun Yat-sen's *San-min chu-i*. Shop raids, confiscations of property, and arrests of the bourgeoisie were the order of the day. The slogans in Changsha were: "Anyone with land is a bully," "No member of the gentry is not evil," "In correcting a wrong, we must be excessive in upholding the right."[18] Prisoners were not permitted to defend themselves or to have counsel. Judges were union heads; juries were formed of those at hand.

Borodin had disapproved of the radicalism at Hunan, if only because most of T'ang's officers, who led Wuhan's chief force, came from that province. The confiscation of land and the insults and injuries to Hunan landlords could only undermine the loyalty of T'ang's officers toward the revolution. Even in most CCP circles in Wuhan, events in Changsha were referred to as "left infantilism." But whatever the reaction in Wuhan, the province was a stronghold of the revolution—one of the few remaining. News of the counterrevolution in Changsha, then, had a devastating effect on Wuhan morale. The spirit at Wuhan headquarters became "chaotic and unstable, and everyone was extremely gloomy as if they had lost their way and had doubts on every question."[19] It might be too late to escape. Preparations for a last-ditch defense of Wuhan were intensified.

Not everyone gave way to pessimism. Some who had been closely involved with the radical Changsha developments during April and May wanted to use the rebellious peasants in the Hunan countryside to counterattack. General Hsü K'o-hsiang, who had taken over Changsha, was said to have as few as 700 troops and no more than 2000. In the area surrounding Changsha, it was held, hundreds of armed picketers had escaped the massacre that followed Hsü's triumph. Joined by thousands of armed peasants and tens, if not hundreds, of thousands of militant members of peasant unions, they might be able to recapture Changsha if only the signal were given.

At first, Borodin agreed and gave the desired signal. But he quickly reconsidered. Wuhan's Northern Expedition was doing well. Feng Yü-hsiang had scored repeated victories, conspicuously reported in the *People's Tribune*. Now Feng was on the verge of a major triumph at Loyang. To arm and unleash the masses would prevent his making common cause with Wuhan. In spite of the desperate situation in Wuhan, Moscow and Borodin still sought a continued role in the revolution, not a glorious explosion that would mark the end of it all. Neither Stalin nor Borodin had faith in the wild masses of Hunan.

From May 19 on, all meetings of the Wuhan authorities took place in a beseiged-fortress atmosphere at Borodin's headquarters. Following the news of the Changsha counterrevolution, there were heated debates over the relative wisdom of a radical course or a United-Front strategy. Borodin still favored the latter after a momentary lapse immediately following the fall of Changsha. One sovetnik, coming to work on May 26, reported that the headquarters room was in complete disarray, as though a torrid battle had taken place.[20] As usual, Borodin won his point. The United Front was maintained; counterattack on Changsha was called off. However, not every Hunan radical knew of or followed Wuhan's decisions. On May 31, thousands of peasants marched on Changsha. But inadequately trained, equipped, and led, they were beaten back with heavy casualties.

Generals Hsia and Hsü were not the only defectors with whom Borodin had to deal. At the end of May, there was almost daily news of additional defections to Chiang. Wuhan was being deserted on all sides. And there was nothing Borodin could do about it. He and his government could only hope for victories by the Wuhan forces in the north and by General Feng. Borodin's CCP followers officially backed him up. Although they had no doubt that peasant agitation was understandable, they stated that as a matter of necessity it had to be checked and controlled.

But as the rings of defeat made narrower and narrower circles around Wuhan, Borodin's opposition grew increasingly bold. Unable to convince Borodin and the CCP of the need for mass revolutionary action, Roy decided to appeal again to Moscow. He sent a radiogram to Stalin. Although Stalin was steadily gaining strength in Moscow, his opposition was still consequential. It sought to blame the Shanghai debacle on the "completely false" thesis of Stalin; while not demanding the end of the United-Front policy per se, the opposition called for "mass soviets" in China as in the 1905 revolution in Russia.

On May 18, while the forces of General Hsia advanced on Wuhan, the Eighth Plenary Session of the Executive Committee of the Comintern opened in Moscow. The "China question" was not the only important problem facing the ECCI, but it had the greatest urgency. For Stalin, it appeared as a giant boulder blocking his consolidation of power. To the increasingly desperate opposition, led by Trotsky, it was a smaller stone which, properly aimed, might yet dispatch Goliath.

Stalin, confronted with a host of problems on both the domestic and international fronts, took extraordinary pains to ensure that the business of the plenum was conducted in camera. Instead of using Andreyev Hall, throne room of the tsars, where former CI plenums had met, a smaller room, usually reserved for meetings of the Presidium of the ECCI, was designated for the sessions. Thus there was insufficient room for nondelegates (particularly Russian nondelegates) to attend. Documents upon which discussions were based were delivered at the last moment so that they could not be studied. At the end of the plenum, all documentation, including the stenographic accounts of the delegates' own speeches, was collected. Anyone who did not turn in his papers, the delegates were bluntly told, would not be permitted to leave the country. For the first time, no record of the proceedings of a plenum was printed in the Soviet or CI press. For the year following, the only items published about the Eighth Plenum were the minimal resolutions and a few other materials that supported Stalin.

As Stalin had feared, the sessions of the plenum were stormy—and incriminating. Stalin had tried to wriggle out of the April 12 catastrophe in Shanghai by hiding behind previous ambiguous pronouncements of the Comintern. Events, he had declared, have "fully and entirely" proved the correctness of the CI line.[21] But in the privacy of the small Kremlin room, the matter could not be handled so simply. The opposition, although its interest in China was comparatively recent and its own position had been unclear, sought to capitalize on Stalin's vulnerability. Stalin had clung to the united-front policy after Chiang's March 20, 1926, coup in Canton. He clung to it now. Whatever the harsh realities might be, he could not concede his policy was wrong. The united front, not offending the Great Powers, and waiting for Feng—these offered the only hope to avoid catastrophe. But this path required cooperation with the bourgeoisie and militarists, and upon discouraging worker and peasant radicalism. How could a Bolshevik be against the masses and for the bourgeoisie and foreign imperialists? To counter this argument, Stalin's policy statement said that while the Wuhan regime was not now an organ of a "revolutionary dictatorship of the proletariat and peasantry," it had every chance of developing into one.[22] Encouraging peasant and worker movements and forming soviets was good revolutionary strategy, *but not now.* The concept was good, the timing bad.

But the opposition would not let Stalin off the hook so easily, particlarly when news of the fall of Changsha was accompanied by evidence that the Hunan peasantry was ready to take the offensive and regain the city. The situation was discussed at a meeting of the Chinese Subcomittee of the ECCI at which Politburo member Nikolai Bukharin, Palmiro Togliatti, later the head of the Communist Party of Italy, and Albert Treint of France were present. Bukharin held that the peasants must be curbed. Treint argued the contrary. Togliatti said little. At a critical moment, Bukharin, perhaps fearful that he was losing the argument, demanded that Stalin be heard. He telephoned Stalin, who came to the room and contended that Treint did not "take the real situation in China into consideration. To fail to take a position at the present time against the peasant revolts would be to set the left bourgeoisie against us . . . The left bourgeoisie is still powerful. Its armies will not disband in the twinkle of an eye, and we will then be defeated in civil war."[23] To emphasize his point, Stalin read several telegrams from Borodin, stressing that the leadership of the KMT had decided "to struggle against the agrarian revolution even at the cost of a split with the [Third] International." The question, said Stalin, is whether to fight, as Treint and others wanted, or whether to maneuver. To fight, he felt, would mean certain defeat. Maneuvering would gain time and the possibility of becoming stronger and fighting later in conditions where victory could be counted on. And, since Stalin said it, maneuver it would be.

On June 1, Borodin and Roy received a secret radio message from Stalin that, in effect, answered Roy's appeal for clarification. Stalin's instruction, dispatched on May 31—the Eighth Plenum of the ECCI had closed on the 30th—called for the confiscation of land, but not that owned by officers of the NRA or their relatives. It further ordered the stemming of the peasants; the destruction of unreliable generals; the arming of 20,000 CCP members; the creation of a new 50,000-man army from among the workers and peasants of Hunan and Hupeh; the coopting of workers (communists) and peasants into the CEC of the KMT; and the organizing of a revolutionary court, headed by a "well-known" member of the Kuomintang, to try reactionary officers.

If Stalin meant these instructions to be followed, he had lost contact with reality. But that was not their purpose. Stalin's instructions were not meant for Borodin, but to protect himself. Every criticism or potential criticism of Moscow's policies was provided for in the message. Obviously the "instructions" in the message could not be carried out. Given the nature of the situation, they diametrically contradicted one another. But no matter what happened, Stalin *could*—and would—point to his instructions of May 31 to prove that the CI line had been "correct" and that failure was due to improper execution in the field.

When the message from Stalin was read at the next meeting of the Politburo of the Central Committee of the CCP, no one knew whether to laugh or cry.[24] Borodin, CI agent Voitinsky, the head of the CCP, Ch'en Tu-hsiu, even Roy, agreed that this "fairy tale from overseas" could not be carried out.[25] After discussing the instructions further, the bewildered KMT Politburo, in the name of the CC, sent Stalin a noncommittal message: "Orders received. Shall obey as soon as we can do so."[26]

While the ambiguity of the May 31 message from Moscow afforded future protection for Stalin, it also offered support for virtually every policy under consideration in Wuhan. Certainly it strengthened the firebrands. For Borodin, it meant that he should continue as he had been. For Roy, it signified that Moscow had backed him up politically.[27] At last, Moscow had called for the deepening of the revolution, and he tried to convince Borodin of this. But Borodin, more attuned to Stalin, knew that that was not what it meant—and Borodin held the power. Later Roy lamented that Borodin "functioned as the dictator of the Communist Party. Being mostly his disciples, and ideologically akin to his way, the top leaders of the CP of China followed him, disregarding repeatedly the instructions of the International, and in defiance of its representative [Roy] on the spot."[28]

Roy was a brilliant ideologue and an ardent revolutionary, but time had not improved his judgment or made him more receptive to party discipline. Frustrated again, he tried to mobilize Blyukher against Borodin and sought other allies as well. He convinced himself that Wang Ching-wei was disposed toward following the mass revolutionary course or could be influenced that way. He recalled that Wang had passed through Moscow earlier in 1927 and that there had been a Wang-Moscow agreement on cooperation. But, as Roy now saw it, Wang felt that the Soviet Union had not delivered. He had been turned away by Borodin's reliance upon the generals rather than on the worker-peasant masses. And he had become alienated from the USSR. Stalin's telegram, Roy told himself, could be used to reassure Wang that he had not been abandoned by Moscow.[29] Moreover, Wang's support could be won by giving him the opportunity to lead the workers' and peasants' revolution.[30]

Whether for these reasons or because, as Roy also suggests, everything else had failed, or because the message was "obviously meant" for Wang, Roy decided to strike out on his own.[31] Without consulting anyone, he showed Wang Stalin's secret comunication calling for the confiscation of land, the arrest of generals, the establishment of a new workers' and peasants' army, and the taking over of the KMT Central Executive Committee by radical elements. Wang was, needless to say, "very astonished" by the telegram.[32] Far from reassuring him, it violated his most basic political premises. It seemed to provide clear evi-

dence that Moscow meant to break the United Front, to violate
the Sun-Ioffe agreement, and, worst of all, to usurp the KMT.
When Wang saw Borodin in the latter's office on either June 1 or
2, he exploded. Borodin, he shouted, had failed to take him into
his confidence, was working behind his back, was guilty of double cross. Borodin, ill and almost numb from the tensions of the
past months, was badly shaken by Roy's action. Borodin did
what he could to calm Wang. He promised him an absolute end
to all agrarian activities. There would be no attempt at land
confiscation, no mobilizing of the peasants, no reforming of the
KMT government. Borodin further requested that Moscow recall Roy immediately. Of course Roy had not upset Wang
nearly so much as Stalin's message had—and that could not be
recalled.

Roy had also shown the Stalin messsge to Madame Sun, Eugene Chen, and the other important KMT leaders in Wuhan,
much to their dismay and displeasure. The result was to make
Roy, in some circles, a whipping boy. He was accused of impet-
uosity, of rebelliousness, of having "messed everything up." Now
and later Roy would be blamed, by some, for having undermined the United Front and, worse, for the Soviet failure in
China. That, of course, was absurd; the United Front was
doomed long before Roy came along. By June 1, when Roy
handed Stalin's message to Wang, the United Front was staggering, and Wang, like most KMT leaders in Wuhan, was trying
to jump ship and join Chiang. Roy did not change the direction
of history, but he did push Wang and his KMT cohorts more
rapidly toward the right. If they had hesitated because they
hoped Borodin would yet save them, that hope now vanished. If
they held on through loyalty to Sun Yat-sen, they now were ab-
solved; it was not they who had broken the Sun-Ioffe agreement,
but Stalin. If they had procrastinated because of inertia, they
now knew that rapprochement with the right was the overriding
imperative.

17

Going Home

In the wake of the Stalin-Roy bombshell, the race to get off Wuhan's sinking ship was on. But the question remained, how to get off without drowning? Although the KMT in Wuhan now saw its interests diverging from those of the Russians and the Chinese communists, all of them looked to General Feng Yü-hsiang. Feng's recent advances had brought him into the center of the Chinese military scene. But, as always, Feng played a cozy game and followed an independent course.

The Wuhan forces had won the battle at Chumatien (the victory Tom Mann had so boisterously celebrated) but, as those back in Wuhan subsequently found out, only at a terrible cost. Of more than 70,000 troops that had gone north in April, at least 20,000 were lost in some of the bloodiest battles in recent Chinese history. By June 2, more than 9000 wounded had arrived in Wuhan; they continued to arrive at the rate of 500 a day. And only the less severely wounded reached the triple cities; the others died in the field or succumbed on the hard trip back from the front. To treat the wounded, emergency hospitals were set up all over Wuhan, in stores, cafes, and warehouses, wherever vacant space could be found. The government, lacking sufficient doctors and supplies, urgently requested medical assistance from elsewhere in China. To secure funds, a series of benefits was directed by Madame Sun, at which, among other things, the property and artworks that Wuhan had confiscated were auctioned off for whatever they would bring. Eugene Chen's daughters, Yolanda and Sylvia, danced the "Cat and the Canary" at benefits for the wounded.

By the last week in May, both the Wuhan forces and the opposition armies in the north were exhausted. Only then did Feng intervene. On May 26, he took Loyang in northern Hunan. Five days later he took Chengchow to the east, on the Wuhan-Peking rail line. There he linked up with Wuhan's armies. On June 1, with the northern forces in retreat, Wuhan troops under General Chang Fa-k'uei occupied Kaifeng, still further east. But they could advance only because Feng had opened the way for them. Their strength was severely sapped. In that part of China, Feng now held the trump cards. Feng was the man of the hour, sought after by Chiang, by Borodin, and by the Wuhan KMT alike. Chiang, whose earlier attempt to take Peking failed, was keenly aware that, if Feng allied with even a weakened Wuhan, he could be a formidable adversary. On Chiang's side, he could be invaluable.

The Russians in Moscow and Wuhan had earlier allowed themselves to become increasingly convinced that Feng would come their way. In the Soviet capital in the spring and early summer of 1926, Feng had been at his revolutionary best, pointing out his peasant background, extolling workers and peasants, and promising eternal fealty to the revolution. Moscow called him "great," "a new Kemal." By August 1926, Moscow's investment in Feng amounted to six million rubles in guns, cannon, airplanes, and ammunition, plus advisers. Subsequently, it advanced him millions more.

Moscow thought it had bought Feng in spite of considerable evidence to the contrary. All along there had been those who had doubted Feng's dependability. In the areas under his control, he had consistently suppressed strikes. He had never permitted the CCP to operate legally. In the spring of 1927, Feng's behavior suggested he was rethinking his relationship with the Russians. In March, a sovetnik attached to Feng wired that "Feng has not changed outwardly as regards 'leftwardness,' but he [now] is afraid of the commissaries [sic] and of the peasants' organizations."[1] On May 10, Feng ordered anti-Chiang posters removed from the areas under his control, and shortly thereafter he stopped all anti-Chiang agitation on the grounds that he and Chiang were fighting the same enemy, Chang Tso-lin. On May 30, he went further, declaring that Chiang's Nanking regime was not counterrevolutionary, as Wuhan held.

These and other steps taken by Feng in May, at least some of which were known to Borodin, dampened his hopes for Feng. Panegyrics for Feng, which had become *de rigueur* in the *People's Tribune,* were missing in the last few days of May and in early June. But Borodin's hopes for Feng were all he had left. The KMT leaders still in Wuhan also had to hope in Feng. They now tried to negotiate an alliance with him. A conference was set up in Chengchow for June 10. On June 7, most of the remaining important figures in the Wuhan regime, with the exception of Borodin and Eugene Chen, left on a special train for Chengchow. Borodin remained behind, he said, because he was too ill to travel, but he may have seen little point in going and feared capture outside Wuhan. Moreover, the KMT didn't want him in Chengchow, fearing that his presence would make a deal with Feng more difficult. Chen stayed because he had cast his lot with Borodin—he cut his hair and moustache like Borodin's and wore similar clothes—and someone had to mind the shop. But Wang Ching-wei, Sun Fo, and Madame Sun went to Chengchow. There they met General T'ang, commander of Wuhan's forces that had won a pyrrhic victory at Chumatien, as well as a number of Russian sovetniki, led by Blyukher. Anna Louise Strong and Rayna Prohme were also there from Wuhan to help keep Borodin informed and "cover the story for the press."

As the central figure, Feng was the last to arrive. He came on a freight train, to which he had transferred from a luxurious warlord's coach at the last stop before Chengchow. Feng always sought to give the appearance of modesty and simplicity. All the other personages of distinction came down to the station to greet him. As his train pulled in on June 9, the band struck up the KMT anthem, set to the tune of "Frère Jacques." Wang Ching-wei, along with the other Wuhanites, bowed in Feng's direction and shook hands, while Feng gestured to the crowd.

If, as seems unlikely, Feng was not aware of the diversity of opinion within the Wuhan government and the desperate situation of that city, he soon found out. In the conference and at special meetings, all positions were aired: Soviet, CCP, KMT for peace with Chiang Kai-shek, KMT against peace with Chiang. In these discussions, Feng learned just how precarious Wuhan's economic situation was, information that must have greatly interested and disappointed Feng, who badly needed money for his armies.

During his long career, Feng Yü-hsiang was praised by various observers for often contradictory reasons. In spite of his efforts to appear a simple peasant in mufti, Feng was much more complex. He had been attracted to a spectrum of ideologies and orientations. But one thing was constant: his determination to survive and succeed. He had allied himself with Moscow in 1925 and 1926, when the Kremlin was shopping for leaders in China and had much to offer Feng. Feng had verbally embraced the left and the revolution, though he had kept it at more than arm's length in the areas under his control. But now, in the late spring of 1927, it seemed to Feng that Moscow's power in China was ebbing fast. He drew the obvious conclusion.

But while Feng wanted no part of the Soviets or the communists in the Wuhan camp, the noncommunist Wuhanites were another matter. Personalities like Wang Ching-wei and Madame Sun still had value as a foil to Chiang. They still commanded some military forces; they came as suppliants; they were Feng's to command—and he did. In sessions that lasted eighteen hours a day, he was promised whatever he wanted: Honan, Shensi, and Kansu provinces; the CCP ousted from the Wuhan regime; Borodin sent back to Moscow. It was agreed that General T'ang would return southward to quell radical activities in Honan. To save face for Wang and his cohorts, Feng was not averse to acknowledging openly his loyalty to Sun Yat-sen, to the *San-min chu-i*, his willingness to carry out the orders of the CEC at Wuhan, and to move with Wuhan's General Chang Fa-K'uei against the northern forces of Chang Tso-lin. When Feng and Wang separated, most of the Wuhanites were convinced that Feng was now united with them, minus the CCP and Borodin, and against Chiang Kai-shek.

The decision of the Chengchow conference was announced publicly—except for the agreement to jettison the CCP and Borodin. Wang Ching-wei arrived back in Wuhan on June 13, greeted by a huge demonstration replete with fireworks, slogans, and cheers. Wang announced "that the results of the Chengchow conference were very good and that Feng Yü-hsiang supported Wuhan."[2] On the next day the headlines in the *People's*

Tribune screamed "Chengchow Conference Achieves United Front."[3] The truth was, of course, the opposite. Chengchow was actually the final step in the destruction of the United Front.

Borodin was advised privately of his expulsion and accepted the news calmly. He was not surprised. But because he feared that his departure from Wuhan would lead Chang Tso-lin to believe that he could dispose of Fanya as he wished—she was no longer valuable as a hostage—and presumably because Borodin lacked instructions from Moscow, he asked to be allowed to remain in Wuhan a little longer. Permission was given. Borodin knew this was virtually the end of the road in China. Ill, exhausted, deeply concerned about his wife, uncertain of his future, there was no more than a glimmer of hope that Feng might yet save the day for him, too.

While the dismissal of Borodin had been easy enough to accomplish, the ouster of the CCP was not so readily arranged. There were still KMT members who, in spite of Chengchow, wanted to maintain the old alliance. In the CEC of the KMT, Madame Sun and Eugene Chen argued stubbornly against tossing the CCP overboard, largely on grounds that it contravened Sun Yat-sen's testament. For ten days after the return from Chengchow, the notables of the dissolving Wuhan KMT met in the house of Wang Ching-wei to discuss the expulsion and how to "de-Borodinize" Wuhan.

General Feng made Kaifeng his headquarters. Through contacts that had been previously made with Nanking, a meeting between Feng and Chiang Kai-shek was set up for June 20 in Hsuchow. While at Chengchow, Feng had repeatedly confided to Wang Ching-wei, as he often had to others, his distaste for Chiang Kai-shek, reportedly describing him as a "wolf-hearted, dog-lunged, inhuman thing."[4] And Chiang had no more affection for Feng. Still they needed each other. Though Feng was in a strong military position, his army required large sums of money. He lacked resources of his own; living off an impoverished people was no longer feasible; and the Russians doubtless would help no more. After what he had seen and heard at Chengchow, Feng knew that Wuhan's army was weak, its leaders divided, its coffers bare. He also knew that Chiang had foreign support, which Feng believed indispensable, and plenty of money. Feng had also heard rumors that Chiang had entered into negotiations with General Chang Tso-lin; he might be frozen out if Chiang and Chang reached a territorial agreement on the control of China. Chiang Kai-shek, for his part, was interested in dealing with Feng because the latter had a strong army, controlled several provinces, and had an alliance with Wuhan—all of which could be turned to Chiang's advantage, particularly in negotiations with Chang Tso-lin.

When Feng and Chiang came together in Hsuchow on June 20 and 21, for what were reported as forty-two hours of continuous negotiations, the whole panoply of questions facing China was raised. Out of those talks came decisions to unite against Chang Tso-lin; for each to retain control over his own area; and for Wuhan immediately to make peace with Nanking. The latter was to be achieved by the immediate ouster of Borodin, and by eliminating the CCP and all Wuhan leaders unwilling to join the Nanking government. Failure to effect these decisions would bring military action against Wuhan. The military ultimatum was sent by a telegram dispatched over the name of General Feng. The telegram began "Our leader Sun Yat-sen is now in heaven, and from there he sees all we do." It ended: "It is my desire that you accept the above solution and reach a conclusion immediately."

The telegram from Feng, which included Chiang's position on Borodin, arrived in Wuhan a day or so after the Chiang-Feng meeting had concluded. Borodin had no reason to be surprised by its contents. After Chengchow he had outwardly entertained the hope that Feng would not demand the ouster of himself and the CCP. But whatever hopes might have been raised were dashed by Feng's telegram spelling the end for Borodin and the CCP, demanding a shotgun marriage for Wuhan with Chiang Kai-shek.

Still Borodin saw a tiny ray of hope. The Feng telegram had come not from Hsuchow but from Nanking, Chiang's capital. Perhaps, he said, it was a fake disseminated by Chiang to speed defections to his side. That ray soon went out. As three Western correspondents were leaving Hsuchow, Chiang showed them a copy of the ultimatum to Wuhan. They had then traveled aboard Chiang's train to Nanking, from which point two of them went to Shanghai to file their stories, and a third, the Swedish correspondent Aag Krarup-Nielsen, set out for Wuhan. Three days after the Hsuchow conference, Krarup-Nielsen arrived in Wuhan. The moment Borodin learned that a correspondent had arrived from Hsuchow, he had him brought to his headquarters. Obviously agitated, Borodin wanted to know exactly what had happened between Feng and Chiang at Hsuchow. Krarup-Nielsen gave him a stenographic report of the speeches made by Feng and Chiang at the banquet that had ended the meetings. He also handed him a copy of the Feng telegram, identical with the one Borodin had earlier received. Borodin went through the ultimatum "paragraph by paragraph and recognized that it was really a genuine document and that Feng had definitely taken sides against" him and against Wuhan.[5]

It was all over. The journey that had started in Canton in 1923 was all but completed. Borodin asked the journalist to leave and to return later. At 9:00 P.M., either on June 23 or 24, Krarup-Nielsen reappeared at Borodin's headquarters and was ushered into Borodin's apartment. Borodin thereupon gave Krarup-Nielsen the following interview. (Although Krarup-Nielsen has given varying versions of this meeting with Borodin, and it is necessary to place what he has written in the context of the sensationalist journalistic style of the 1920s, his accounts generally ring true.)

"That evening, as I sat in a deep English Chesterfield chair opposite Borodin in his study, another voice seemed to be speaking. Perhaps it was due to the shaded light and the stillness, but Borodin seemed a changed man. Here he appeared at peace, and in a calm, restrained voice that now and then responded to the intensity of his thoughts, he described the events that were perhaps going to draw the curtain on his activities in China." Even now, Borodin considered it unpolitic to admit there was no hope. The next few days would tell, he said. In the meantime he would remain in Wuhan "and wait for further developments."

When asked about Chiang and Feng, knowing that his personal safety and that of the other sovetniki depended on those men, Borodin spoke discreetly. Chiang "has been my friend ever since I first came to Canton." Of Feng he spoke "very warmly." Asked what he would do "if the men with whom you have been working should leave you in the lurch . . . would you then try to fight for a purely communist regime to the bitter end?" Borodin replied: "If the Chinese leaders who have been my friends and fellow workers for four long years believe that the moment has come when they can continue the fight without my help, then I shall submit, for I have played my part and given my advice. I have no intention of fighting for communism in China—the time is not yet ripe."

Then Krarup-Nielsen asked Borodin, "what brought you to China of all places, and what made you stay here in spite of the dangers and difficulties in which you lived, and in spite of the fact that your policy was often almost wrecked in the sea of hatred and bitterness that had risen up around you?" Borodin didn't answer for a long while. He sat "slowly stroking his little black moustache, but finally he said in a deep, muffled voice: 'I came to China to fight for an idea. The dream of accomplishing world revolution by freeing the people of the East brought me here. But China itself, with its age-old history, its countless millions, its great social problems, its infinite capacities, astounded and overwhelmed me, and my thoughts of world revolution gradually sank into the background. The revolution and the fight for freedom in China became an end in itself, and no longer a means to an end. My task was to grasp the situation, to start the great wheel moving, and as time has passed it has carried me along with it. I myself have become only a cog in the great machine.' "[6]

Perhaps such sentiments were part of a performance that Borodin put on for all foreign journalists. But there was a credible sincerity in much of what he told Krarup-Nielsen that night. Although he could never have been unmindful of developments in Moscow, China's struggle had become his struggle; he *had* come to think more and more about China and less and less about the world revolution, which meant the Soviet Union.

Now his part and Wuhan's part in the revolution was over. But before leaving China, he desperately needed to unburden himself to someone who would tell the world what had happened in China and how it had happened. The world should know, and it would never learn through Moscow. But the ill and worn Borodin had more pressing matters to care for. Most important, he was concerned for the safety of the sovetniki and his personal circle. Even before the confirmation by Krarup-Nielsen of the Hsuchow ultimatum, the sovetniki had been ordered by Borodin to make preparations to leave. Still earlier, Borodin had prepared for the worst by instructing one of his translators to teach Russian to Madame Sun in case that woman, once called by Borodin the "only man in the whole left wing of the Kuomintang,"[7] should be forced to leave for Moscow.

For the sovetniki, living out of knapsacks, packing was no great problem. Much more of a problem was the route to be taken out of China. There were three possibilities: down the Yangtze to Shanghai, then by boat to Vladivostok; by rail to Kalgan, then by truck into the USSR; or across the Gobi. Of the three, the first was the easiest, but would Chiang permit it? The second passed through Chang Tso-lin territory; the third was politically possible, but geographically difficult. For the sovetniki, the route via Shanghai seemed best, since Chiang Kai-shek was still drawing a distinction between Borodin and Moscow, still seemed interested in Soviet good will (though on his terms), and since the other generals, hedging their bets against another day, would probably let "technicians" through. Passage was booked down the Yangtze aboard British vessels, Borodin banking on British authority and principles for protection should any warlords try to arrest the sovetniki. In Shanghai the Russians were to transfer to the Soviet-chartered *Henley* for the trip to Vladivostok.

But before the sovetniki reached the end of their journey, they may have wondered if they had chosen the right route. Aboard British ships, they were constantly under the guns of White Russian mercenaries who stood on the bridge with carbines aimed directly at them. In Shanghai, where they had to await the arrival of other sovetniki before departing on the *Henley,* they saw grisly indicators of counterrevolutionary work. Throughout the city, the severed heads of revolutionaries were on display. Nanking had placed a price of $30,000 on Borodin's head, and hundreds of "wanted" posters with his picture were plastered all over Shanghai.

When all were finally and safely aboard the *Henley,* a detachment of municipal police accompanied by "Captain" Eugene

Pick, a Russian who had worked in Borodin's headquarters in Wuhan, but now wrote anti-Bolshevik exposés for appreciative colonials, came aboard with drawn Mausers to search the vessel. Several of the sovetniki, with their distraught wives looking on, as well as a number of CCP members, were led away. Subsequently, the CCP people were beheaded, and some of the Russians tortured. It was not until the sovetniki had begun a hunger strike on the sixth day of their imprisonment and Chiang Kai-shek, informed of their arrest, had intervened, that they were allowed to continue their northward trip to Vladivostok. But before that happened, at least one of the Russian wives aboard the *Henley* suffered a nervous breakdown.

For Borodin, the Shanghai and Kalgan routes out of China were too risky. In spite of malaria and exhaustion and his broken arm, which was still in a cast, he would have to take the arduous trip across the Gobi Desert. But it would take time to prepare for such an expedition. Besides, he did not want to leave China until Fanya's fate had been determined. Chang Tso-lin had decided to put her on trial for conspiracy against the northern government. Her trial began in Peking on June 13, but it had been adjourned and its resumption was repeatedly postponed.

Fortunately for Borodin, the remnants of the Wuhan regime were now less insistent on Borodin's immediate departure than they had been following their meeting with Feng in Chengchow. After the Chiang-Feng agreement, they realized that their eagerness to do Feng's will at Chengchow had gained nothing. Whether Borodin left tomorrow or next month made little immediate difference—unless Wuhan was being attacked. Borodin's personal authority in KMT circles in Wuhan remained high, and his old allies would not toss him to the wolves, particularly if the wolves were not in sight. Furthermore, they might all have to go to Russia.

In late June and early July, the Wuhan KMT continued to search for an alternative to abject surrender to Chiang Kai-shek. They knew, if they were to have any leverage with Chiang, they had to have a general and an army. These prospects being poor, their best candidate was Feng. It is true, wrote the *People's Tribune*, which by now was free of Borodin and CCP influence, that

Feng had been "forced" to make peace with Chiang, but that didn't mean that Feng was anti-Wuhan.[8] Feng would soon realize that Chiang was a "serpent" and turn against him.[9] It could happen any day.

But while Wang Ching-wei and Wuhan sought a general and an army, the economic paralysis worsened. A few troops friendly to Chiang Kai-shek walked into the city and took over sections of it. An attempt was made on Blyukher's life and, though he escaped, his aide was killed. On-the-spot executions by counter-revolutionary forces, and by radicals too, became commonplace. No official dared move about the city without his own body-guard. The CCP discussed heatedly and interminably what could yet be done to save the revolution, and, more to the point, what should be done if such steps failed. As for the thousands who had been swept up in the revolution in February and March, most had returned to more prosaic paths. By July, an observer noted, the girls who had bobbed their hair in the spring were letting it grow long again.[10]

In spite of ubiquitous indicators of the revolution's demise, revolutionary rhetoric could still be heard in Wuhan. Some believers were determined to go down in a blaze of revolutionary glory. From June 19 through 28, the Fourth Congress of the All-China Labor Federation met in Wuhan. It had been long scheduled, and in spite of the emergency—or because of it, since this might be the last open communist-dominated congress in China—it was decided to go ahead with it. Addressed by Lozovsky of the Profintern, whom Borodin had known in Stockholm in 1906, and by Roy, Wang Ching-wei, and Chinese communist leaders Li Li-san and Liu Shao-ch'i, the congress adopted an uncompromisingly radical program. There was no longer any reason to hold back. Demands were made to arm the peasants, to punish the reactionaries, counterrevolutionaries, rowdies, and local gentry. The congress warned the Wuhan government that it would withdraw its support if the latter did not act at once against these enemies. It was all play acting, and the Wuhan government, almost immediately after the congress closed, destroyed trade-union headquarters and disarmed the Workers' General Picket Corps. At this moment, the CCP Politburo fleetingly considered armed action. But Borodin, never an advocate of the futile gesture and thinking now of the return trip to Moscow, directed members of the Picket Corps and all others with weapons to lay them down.

As Wuhan floundered in early July, Chiang Kai-shek had his problems too. His troops had encountered reverses in Shantung. His capital was dispirited; few in Nanking seemed to have faith in him. Various go-betweens, largely at Feng's instigation, continued to work for a Nanking-Wuhan reconciliation. On July 12, T. V. Soong, who had earlier gone to Shanghai to represent Wuhan's "interest" there, and had subsequently made peace with Chiang, arrived in Wuhan and was immediately closeted with government officials until late that night. Soong told the Wuhan KMT that an agreement had been worked out for a unity plenum to be held in August, at which time Chiang Kai-shek "might" resign, giving Wuhan an opportunity to determine China's future leadership. But, said Soong, the deal could be arranged *only* if Borodin and the CCP were physically expelled from Wuhan at once.

Borodin had made it clear that he didn't want to leave while Fanya's fate was in the balance, especially since it had been announced in Peking that she was being tried on charges that could lead to life imprisonment or even death. But as fate would have it, on July 12, the day on which Soong arrived in Wuhan, Fanya was released. She had been held in various prisons in North China since February. Rumors of execution, actual or pending, constantly circulated. Indeed, it seems likely that Chang Tso-lin was planning to have her killed. He told United States Senator Hiram J. Bingham of Connecticut, who was then visiting in China, that he had had twenty communists strangled yesterday, and "tomorrow" would be Fanya's turn.[11]

But, on July 12, just before noon, the presiding judge at Fanya's trial appeared in court and announced that evidence against Fanya was inconclusive; she was to go free. Fanya gathered her few possessions, ran out of court with her Russian lawyer, A. K. Kantorovich, into a waiting car, and drove quickly away. Within five minutes she was at the Soviet embassy. Just as quickly, the judge, later rumored to have been paid $200,000 for his decision, left for Tokyo by way of Tientsin, leaving his wife, two children, and a brother behind to suffer the consequences of Chang Tso-lin's anger at Fanya's escape.

News of Fanya erased the last barrier to acceptance of the

terms Soong had brought. Both Borodin and the CCP knew it was high time to leave. The CCP, at last freed from its commitment to the United Front, published a declaration condemning the Wuhan government and accusing it of opposing "the interests of the great majority of the Chinese people as well as Sun Yat-sen's fundamental principles and policies." Its members fled the city.

The details of Borodin's trip still remained to be worked out. According to one report, Borodin was told by Soong that there was no reason why he should not follow the same route out of China as the sovetniki, down the Yangtze to Shanghai, then by boat to Vladivostok. Chiang Kai-shek would not interfere. But Borodin was aware of the $30,000 price on his head and the experiences of those who had followed the Shanghai route; moreover, Madame Sun, among others, warned him against trusting Chiang Kai-shek. He would have to get out via the long overland route across the Gobi.

It was best for all concerned if Borodin got out of town. The forces of warlord General Ho Chien were about to descend on the city, and the demands of the counterrevolution could no longer be held back. It was decided that Borodin should go to the resort city of Lushan, to await completion of plans for his departure. Soong, who knew Lushan well and felt obligated to protect Borodin, would accompany him there. Some KMT leaders appreciated what Borodin had done and continued to value him for it. Also in the entourage to Lushan was the Moscow-trained Ch'ü Ch'iu-pai, whom the Russians had designated head of the CCP as successor to Ch'en Tu-hsiu, as well as a small number of Russian and Chinese bodyguards.

Borodin and his traveling companions left Wuhan secretly sometime between July 13 and 16. Immediately afterward, General Ho Chien's men, advised that Borodin had gone, arrived at the now-deserted headquarters and opened fire. With that volley, the counterrevolution took over *de jure*. Martial law was declared. Organizations identified with the Wuhan regime were raided, and people who had not already fled were arrested, and many killed on the spot. The *People's Tribune*, which had been out of CCP hands for over a month, was seized. Even the last statement of the revered Madame Sun, published after she too had left the city, was suppressed. By July 18, Wuhan was plastered with antiradical, anti-CCP, and anti-Borodin slogans and posters.

Lushan, where Borodin now went, had been founded by the English in the nineteenth century. There the British and other foreigners retreated each summer to avoid the blazing heat of the Yangtze Valley. It was a three-hour trip up the mountain, in a palanquin carried by bearers over narrow mountain paths and across swaying bridges. Lushan offered Borodin an opportunity to rest and recuperate, and to prepare for the difficult journey ahead.

In Peking, there were rumors that Borodin and Rayna Prohme—who had already left for Shanghai—were carousing at nightly champagne parties. Actually, Borodin spent most of his time at Lushan in the company of Ch'ü Ch'iu-pai. Borodin, the *sovetniki*, and some CCP members were leaving China; Mikhail Markovich would be replaced by a Comintern operative, who was scheduled to arrive in Wuhan any day. But most of the Chinese comrades would remain in their own land. How would the CCP survive, given its new clearly defined enemy status? Ch'ü's presence with Borodin in Lushan was tantamount to a laying on of hands. He was the chosen one and his captains were to be Chang Kuo-t'ao, Li Li-san, Chou En-lai, Chang T'ai-lei, and Li Wei-han. In consultation with Borodin, and at Moscow's instruction, it was decided to blame the disaster in China on the former secretary-general of the CCP, Ch'en Tu-hsui; the Comintern and Moscow should, of course, be exonerated of any blame. Ch'ü agreed to take the lead in making Ch'en the scapegoat for all that had or would go wrong.

Borodin had been in Lushan less than a week when word came that all was in readiness for his return to Moscow; Feng had agreed for a price to provide Borodin with safe passage through his territory and had even consented to receive him. Borodin's entourage had been selected and outfitted. Five touring cars—four Dodges and a Buick (for Borodin, an eight-cylinder deluxe convertible with mahogany interior fittings)—and five trucks had been requisitioned. They were serviced, packed, and loaded on railroad flat cars to be transported to the end of the line at the edge of the Gobi.

Borodin returned to Wuhan early in the fourth week of July. The counterrevolution was in full swing. Executions in the streets were daily occurrences. In an effort to guarantee Borodin's security, his friends decided he should take up residence in T. V. Soong's house, it being hoped that no one would invade the premises of Chiang Kai-shek's brother-in-law. On July 23, Borodin's successor in China, a young Georgian, Besso Lominadze, arrived in Wuhan from Moscow, and Borodin was officially relieved. During the next few days, he received the traditional courtesy calls from many of his old associates who, according to custom, begged him not to leave. But though they continued to admire him, they wanted him to go, in the interests of their own security.

On July 27, Borodin and a company of thirty, protected by a detachment of still loyal troops and Borodin's personal bodyguard, arrived at the Wuhan station to board the special train waiting for them. Soong, Wang Ching-wei, and other officials of the Wuhan government were there to bid him goodbye. Wang, Soong, and Borodin sat at a table in one of the cars and drank tea and soda pop, and talked. Once again, according to the requirements of mandarin etiquette, Borodin was asked to remain. When he refused, Wang handed him a letter from the Central Executive Committee of the KMT, expressing "friendly sentiments." Borodin thanked Wang and his colleagues and said goodbye. The government delegation arose and left. In a few minutes the train started up, and Wuhan was soon out of sight. Some of the Chinese who remained behind on the platform cried. Others made snide remarks.[12]

For Borodin, it was all over now: Canton, Wuhan, China, revolution, his days in the sun. It was not only the end of Borodin's life in China; it was the end of his life. He would go on living, but only in the backstreets and alleys of history. At the end of the track from Wuhan, oblivion awaited him. Did he suspect as much, or worse? There can be no doubt that he did.

At this point in our story, it is appropriate to assess his and the USSR's role in the Chinese revolution. Whatever that assessment is, it will differ from that of many others. Virtually every chronicler of that period—Wuhan or Nanking KMTers, Stalin-ists, Trotskyites, Chinese communists, dissident Chinese commu-nists, liberal journalists, conservative journalists, and permuta-tions and hybrids of each—has made a summation. To some, Soviet policy was blameless; to others it was the incarnation of evil and perfidy. In some eyes, Borodin was the embodiment of charisma and dedication; to others, such as Mao Tse-tung, he was at best a blunderer.[13] Being objective about the Chinese rev-olution is extremely difficult if not impossible. Even half a cen-tury away and from a wholly different milieu, it is easy for the outside observer to become affected by the prejudices of the par-ticipants; or of one's own preconceptions; or hopelessly entan-gled in an endless skein of might-have-beens.

The Russians entered the Chinese revolution because the rev-olution failed to develop in the West. By 1920, Lenin had reached this conclusion and set in motion changes that would lead to Stalin's "socialism in one country," with its priority for Russian national security over the interests of the international revolution. But Marxism and many Marxists were committed to international revolution; nor was it easy to surrender such a fun-damental tenet of sacred doctrine. Accordingly, the tenet was retained. But its primacy was sharply weakened and the scenario for its realization altered. The international line now dictated that the revolution in the West would be speeded by undermin-ing the strength of the West in the underdeveloped countries.

It was in such circumstances that Borodin and the sovetniki came to China beginning in 1923. Moscow was hesitant to spend much of its limited resources on China. But when a small ex-penditure of men and resources seemed to yield startling re-sults—a possible revolution of historic dimensions in China—the implications were momentous. And in a Moscow beset with pri-vation, longing for victories, and involved in a struggle for power, the successes of the Chinese revolution became magni-fied, particularly their ideological components. The impression spread that the revolution that was succeeding in China was not only a national revolution but a social, a communist, one—which was never the case.

From the point of view of aiding national revolution in China, it is difficult to seriously fault Moscow's actions in South China during 1923–1925. But on March 20, 1926, with Chiang Kai-shek's coup in Canton, the exact nature of the Chinese revolution became clearer: the national bourgeoisie had seized control of the revolution and was determined to see it through as a national revolution for the reunification of China, but not as a social one. At that point, had Moscow been in a position to objectively evaluate what had happened in China, had it not been so concerned with the effect of failure or success in China on the struggle for power in the Kremlin, it could have discerned the existence of the various alternatives:

—get out of South China altogether;
—end the KMT-CCP alliance and support the CCP in social as well as national revolution in China;
—end support for the social revolution, but continue to support Chiang Kai-shek toward the aim of accomplishing the national revolution as speedily as possible, thus speeding the eventualization of the social revolution—which, according to Marxism, was bound to follow—and, at the same time, gaining the appreciation of the next Chinese government and masses for the Soviet Union and, by extension, for communism;
—get back into Chiang's good graces in any way possible with the avowed purpose of then moving the revolution out of Kwangtung toward the north, in the hope that something fortuitous would happen there to permit continued Russian involvement and to advance the social revolution.

Taking the "long view," it is arguable that from the interest of the Soviet Union, China, and communism, the third alternative, continuing to support Chiang and dropping the social revolution, offered the greatest advantage. But it was not an alternative that could be accepted by Moscow, any more than the two preceding ones. After the rave notices that the revolution in China had received in international working-class circles, to leave there after suffering no more than a small coup d'état was unthinkable. No self-respecting communist movement could abandon the front at so slight a cause. If the alternatives facing Moscow were only simple withdrawal or withdrawal as the result of a glorious, revolutionary failure, it is likely that the latter would have been chosen.

But these were not the only possibilities. Instability still ruled supreme in China. Anything could happen; but for the Russians to be involved, they had to be on the scene—and to be on the scene, at least at this point, they had to be in Chiang Kai-shek's good graces. Determined to remain in the revolution, Stalin was prepared to consent even to the suppression of the CCP.

These, then, became Stalin's and Borodin's goals in 1926: First, to remain in China in alliance with Chiang Kai-shek in the hope of a development or series of developments that would enable the Soviet Union to remain in China still longer or, should it have to withdraw, to do so under circumstances less dangerous to Stalin's Russian fortunes. Second, and a very remote second, to promote the CCP and the cause of the social revolution in China.

Borodin's involvement in China falls into two main periods, separated by the events of March 20, 1926. Before that date, his primary function was to develop a national, hopefully social, revolutionary movement in South China. Increasingly, he acquired authority to carry out that development along lines of his own design, although always within the limits of Soviet purposes and the somewhat looser bonds of Marxist doctrine and experience. After March 20, 1926, his objectives changed. His primary goal became the maintenance of the Soviet presence on the Chinese revolutionary scene. In that mission, too, he had great authority and was empowered to use considerable initiative in realizing its objective. He was usually listened to in Moscow, particuarly by Stalin. There can be no doubt that over the years Borodin developed more than just an outsider's interest in China. He was fascinated by it; by its people and the vastness of their numbers and their suffering. And he became involved in its problems and its struggles. But he acted always in the context of Stalin's priorities. Although he undoubtedly provided materials that aided Stalin in shaping those priorities, and there is no evidence that he disagreed with them, it must be realized that the final decision to remain in China, come what may, was Stalin's. But never was Stalin prepared to be identified with failure. Someone else would have to shoulder the responsibility for Moscow's not having achieved the victory it had led itself to expect, and the expectation of which it had maintained long past the day when it was possible.

On his way out of China, Borodin knew that he personally was being blamed in some Moscow circles for the disintegration of the revolution. Ch'en Tu-hsiu had already been tabbed as the official scapegoat, but there were bound to be others. As Borodin left, tired and sick, he was further burdened by the very real fear that he was jumping out of the Wuhan frying pan into the Kremlin fire.

18

Reality

By late July 1927, almost all of Moscow's emissaries to the Chinese revolution, except those like the recently arrived Lominadze, specifically assigned to see the revolution through its "next stage," had left for the Soviet Union. They were accompanied by Chinese allies and others who might find it too dangerous to remain in China. But it was dangerous to leave too, and few of those departing left without anxiety and discomfort. Though assurances had been given by Chiang that those without Comintern affiliations could leave freely, who knew when he might change his mind or where the search for those with such affiliations might lead? Chiang might regard every sovetnik as a colleague of Borodin, upon whose head there remained a substantial price.

While almost all of those departing China for the Soviet Union—Madame Sun, Rayna Prohme, Roy—encountered difficulties, none experienced greater dangers or hardships than Borodin. Not only in China but throughout the world, in Zurich, Paris, London, and Washington, he was seen as the mastermind of the Chinese revolution. Whether regarded as hero or villain, responsibility for what had happened in China was assigned to him. Whether Chiang really wanted to capture Borodin or not is arguable (he too may have respected Borodin's contributions to Chinese regeneration), but for the sake of Chiang's anticommunist posture and his relations with his Chinese and imperialist allies, he must appear to seek his arrest. Certainly the northern warlord Chang Tso-lin would have had few qualms about seizing Borodin. And after Fanya had escaped from Chang in Peking, she was scarcely less "wanted" than her husband.

When Chang Tso-lin heard that the court had ordered
Fanya's release, he was livid with rage. He ordered guards
placed around the Soviet embassy, where Fanya had fled, to arrest her the minute she stepped outside. When she did not appear, he ordered the embassy searched. Not finding her, he
scoured Peking and all North China looking for her, to no avail.
Ten days after her escape, a Japanese news agency dispatch
from Valdivostok reported Fanya's arrival there. On August 13,
a news report from Moscow said she was on her way there on the
Trans-Siberian Railroad and was expected to arrive shortly. A
few days later, the successful conclusion of her trip in Moscow
was announced and an interview with her was printed. In China
her escape was explained in various ways, among them that it
had been engineered by a Portuguese agent, with the help of his
Russian wife and his Chinese concubine (who was related to the
judge) and a Jewish confederate.

Actually Fanya had not left Peking. Shortly after arriving at
the Soviet embassy, she was spirited away to a no longer active
Confucian temple, which had been subdivided into a number of
apartments occupied by both Chinese and foreigners. It was evidently not considered noteworthy by passersby when one summer evening a car drew up to the temple and out climbed two
Westerners followed by a portly nun dressed in a huge, winged,
white headdress. Nor, again, was anything particularly surpris-
ing when several weeks later, in the company of the same
foreigners, "Sister" Fanya, attired as before, left the temple.

With Fanya supposedly in Moscow, the search for her ended.
It was decided at the embassy that the best bet for getting Fanya
safely out of China was to disguise her as an American woman
and to send her to Tientsin in the company of the American
correspondent Vincent Sheean, who had been in Wuhan with
Borodin but was free to travel on his U.S. passport. Sheean was
agreeable, but second thoughts suggested that the proposed
route—Peking-Tientsin-Shimonoseki, in Japan, where Fanya
would board a Soviet vessel—was too risky. Eventually she was
taken out through Mongolia, reaching Moscow in early October.

As for Borodin, his special train, plastered with pictures of
Sun Yat-sen and guarded by a small detachment of loyal troops,

headed north on the Peking line. Leaving Wuhan on July 27, Borodin arrived in Chengchow a few days later. There General Feng, who had promised protection, awaited him. But while Borodin was in Chengchow, news reached Feng of an uprising by Chinese communists against the Chiang Kai-shek forces at Nanchang on August 1. Although his position seemed secure, Feng did not want it said that he was protecting communists when communists were taking up arms against the NRA. When he received a telegram from Wuhan calling for Borodin's arrest or, according to Feng's own account, his execution, Feng decided Borodin must leave. On August 3, after a brief sojourn during which he suffered sorely from a bout of malaria, Borodin, joined by those sovetniki who had been attached to Feng's armies and by a detachment of Feng's soldiers reassigned to protect him, boarded his special train for the next stop on the way out of China.

One day and a hundred miles later, the train reached Shenchow, the end of the rail line. There the five cars and five trucks, which were to carry the party the rest of the way, were removed and filled with assorted suitcases, baskets, beds, water buckets, thermoses, teakettles, primus stoves, canned goods, spare tires, and twenty jugs, each filled with ten gallons of gas. When the cars were fully loaded, it was impossible for the driver, looking in his rear-view mirror, to see over the piles of equipment and supplies jammed in the back seats of the open cars. The thirty passengers, including Eugene Chen's two sons, Anna Louise Strong, Borodin's Chinese cook, and assorted sovetniki and Chinese comrades, had to squeeze in as best they could. They placed their coats under the seats; their revolvers for use in case Chiang came near were hung from windshield screws; they sat on top of heaps of clothing and blankets, stood on the running boards, or sat on fenders.

Thus prepared, Borodin's expedition set out from Shenchow at dawn on August 5. Three hours later it had gone nine miles. After five rain-drenched days it had traveled 130 miles. Roads, where they existed, were made almost impassable by downpours. Ruts and holes were so deep that, when a car fell in, it had to be pulled out. When the entourage reached a river or a bridge with a particularly high arch, the vehicles had to be unloaded and then loaded again. At such times, all of the travelers had to help, along with whatever labor could be recruited on the scene. When the unloading and reloading had been repeated a number of times, some of the baggage was abandoned.

After the first few days, the rains slackened and the speed increased. Sometimes they made fifty to sixty miles in a day, sometimes five or six miles. Melons, peaches, plums, and fried noodles (it wasn't rice country) were purchased at stands on the side of the road. If they stayed in a town over night, they dined at the local restaurant. Anna Louise Strong noted that in Kansu the food was excellent, especially the fried pork balls and the local pumpkin.[1] When they stopped at day's end or for repairs, they set up a machine gun for protection. Next they bathed in the Yellow River, which paralleled the road for some distance, or in a nearby stream. Then they would sit at the side of the road in the shade of the trucks and discuss the day's happenings and their future prospects. They slept wherever they could: a guest house, a museum, under the stars. In the morning, they washed in the river and set out again. Traveling thus, Borodin and company averaged a bit over thirty-five miles a day. They half-jested that they could have come as far as fast in peasant carts. On the evening of August 12, they reached Ningsia, the last major city before the Great Wall, on the other side of which lay the equally great Gobi Desert.

By the time Borodin arrived in Ningsia, the trip was taking its toll on his strength. The malaria hung on stubbornly, the arm was still in a cast, the weather was debilitating, the temperatures daily rose above 100 degrees. As the expedition approached the Gobi, the wind blowing in covered everything with dust. Every inch of exposed surface was caked with it. Borodin now had ample time to worry about Fanya and his sons. About his health, too. Would he ever make it to Moscow alive? And about his future, which appeared increasingly black as he thought about it.

The sarcasm that had surfaced in Borodin on other occasions of adversity now became pronounced. He was irascible much of the time. Only when he saw those with whom he still had an official role to play—Feng, the governor of Shensi province, local KMT representatives, or surviving members of the CCP—did Borodin resume the posture of statesmanship, talk of the revolution's future, hint that he might some day return to China. But for the most part his conversation was laced with bitterness. He was critical of almost everybody. Even with Feng he let the mask slip. Asked for the difference between Wuhan and Nanking, Borodin replied that "there is no difference. Once there was, but now there is none."[2] Then why do they still fight? "Rich chow. Rich chow." Like all warlords, they contend for the spoils.[3] It was during this period that Borodin described the KMT as "a toilet, which, as often as you flush it, still stinks."[4] Borodin was acidulous about Chinese generals. When the next Chinese general comes to Moscow and shouts, " 'Hail to the World Revolution!' better send at once for the GPU. All that any of them want is rifles." When one of the sovetniki took exception, saying that a particular general seemed sincere, Borodin shot back: "He's young; they are all good when they are young."[5]

Neither Chinese, British, nor even Russians were exempt from his barbs. Late in August, after the expedition had been on the road for almost three weeks, Borodin blasted Russian inefficiency in maintaining motor vehicles. He castigated the "never-mind" attitude of the Russian chief of transport, who paid attention to the cars only after they had completely broken down, "who never has appliances at hand or lights ready to function, or spare tires, available for blowouts, and who misplaces flashlights, screwdrivers and his own overcoat with equal facility and indifference."[6] Borodin told Anna Louise Strong: "When I get angry, it is not just at a few mechanics: it is at our Russian temperament. I say to them: 'Look at that American sedan. They have a flashlight and every one can find it. They have a certain order in their car and each of them knows it. They do not say, Yes, I put it in the car, but now, the devil!' This is no accident. It is a whole culture in action. When shall we Russians learn it?"[7]

This is one of the few times Borodin is ever quoted as referring to his American experience—and now only when he was agitated. But with all their efficiency, Borodin concluded, not even the Americans could cope with China. "China will break many American machines," he told Strong, "before they break her."[8] Burdened with illness, fatigue, worry, and frustration, Borodin's nerves were sorely frayed. Sometimes, however, he reminisced in a more mellow mood. Those who had lived through the days of the Northern Expedition and the Wuhan regime could never forget them, Borodin, least of all. Occasionally he would sit in the fields on a three-legged camp stool under the Shensi moon and talk about the revolution, what it had been, what it might have been—if only the bourgeoisie had not been bourgeois, the British had not been imperialists, and China had not been China.

Borodin and his caravan remained in Ningsia sixteen days, cleaning and resting and accumulating stores and stamina for the grueling trip across the Gobi. Even before they reached the environs of Ningsia, they had been covered with dust. But as they approached the city in the early evening, the road they traveled suddenly became a canal, used to carry off excess water from the fields that lined it. The company drove right down the middle of the canal and arrived in Ningsia with "feet and clothes and the insides and outsides of the cars covered with caked or liquid mud."[9] All of the trucks and cars needed overhauling; arrangements had to be made for gasoline and supplies; information had to be gathered on the route ahead. This last was one of the tasks that Borodin, even though tired and weak, could do. He spoke with anyone who knew anything about crossing the Gobi or about Mongol life—even with missionaries, who were probably the people in Ningsia with whom he had the most in common.

After a few days in Ningsia it became apparent that there would not be enough gasoline for all the vehicles. Three trucks and a car were abandoned; some of the baggage would have to go by camel. Accompanied by other camels to pull the vehicles from shifting sands, Borodin and his party departed Ningsia on September 5. Next stop: Ulan Bator (Urga until 1924), capital of the Mongolian People's Republic, more than a thousand miles away. On September 6, the caravan passed the Great Wall of China. It was now out of China and away from the last protection that Feng could provide. From Chengchow on, Feng's troops, or those of local allies, had provided an escort; now the refugees traveled alone.

They were able to travel fairly rapidly. The route they followed was an ancient camel trail across the Gobi, thousands of years old, often hard-packed. Sometimes they could go forty miles an hour, but if a car wandered off the track, even a few feet, it would sink into the sand, have to be unloaded, pulled out by the camels (when they came), and be loaded again. When sand hills loomed ahead, the passengers got out, helped push the vehicles up the incline, then jumped in to ride down the other side.

Leaving the camels behind, the caravan now traveled past the last trading outpost, surrounded by high walls and monasteries, nestled among the mountains of the Ala-Shan. The farther north the travelers went, the flatter the land and the sparser the vegetation became. For several days they passed through black sand covered with low green undergrowth. Then came the endless white and yellow sands of the Gobi—and immense silences. The contrast with the sights and sounds of Wuhan was striking. Only rarely was any life to be seen. Once the travelers saw a trader; again a few nomads; another time a group of twenty Chinese students returning to China from Sun Yat-sen University and from the Communist University for Toilers of the East— both in Moscow. On the cold evenings, when they stopped to rest, a French comrade, veteran of the Hamburg uprising and a radio specialist, set up an antenna that sometimes brought in faint messages from the outside world.

The trip across the Gobi was a brutal one. Later, Borodin would allude again and again to its rigors and to how sick he had been. As the expedition pushed on, through hot days and cold nights (for which its members were ill prepared), it had to cope with shifting sands, dying animals that must be hauled off the path so the cars could pass, automobile breakdowns and shortages of fuel and water. Accidents injured several and killed the French radioman. Still another car and truck had to be abandoned, which meant that all had to climb into the remaining two trucks, the Buick, and the two Dodges. After ten days in the desert, the by now thoroughly spent travelers crossed over a peak from which the track led steadily downhill. They followed the path for over a hundred rugged mountainous miles. At last, they saw some blades of grass and a few other signs of vegetation, enough to know that the Gobi was behind them. Borodin was so elated by his survival that when he spied a herd of wild goats, he ordered the driver to pursue them. Removing the revolver that had been hanging from the windshield screw on his Buick, he took potshots at them, unsuccessfully. Then, anxious to reach civilization—even that offered by Ulan Bator—Borodin stopped the chase and raced for the Mongolian capital. Soon he passed through a gap in the hills and saw lying before him the towers of the Gandon Monastery, the golden roofs of Sharsum, and the few hundred yurts—Mongolian tents—that made up 95 percent of Ulan Bator.

Borodin entered the city in a kind of mini-triumph, with an airplane flying overhead to greet him. He was ensconced in the best house in town, occupied by the Russian head of the Mongolian National Bank, who was also the Soviet viceroy in Outer Mongolia. He spent the next two weeks resting, receiving a constant stream of visitors (even in defeat, he was a hero), and catching up with political developments. Stalin's representatives greeted him and advised him how Moscow wanted the collapse in China handled. Borodin was offered a podium in Ulan Bator to indicate that he had received, understood, and was prepared to act in accord with Stalin's wishes. He was invited to address the ruling Revolutionary Mongol People's Party, assembled in Ulan Bator for its Sixth Congress.

Appearing in the People's House—a giant yurt with a green dome—Borodin delivered his message to the 162 brightly attired delegates, who were almost without exception from the Mongolian bourgeoisie. Borodiin began by telling the assembled cattle owners, princes, priests, and foreign guests about the sorry state into which Kwangtung and all of China had fallen by the early 1920s. Sun Yat-sen knew well, Borodin said, the causes of China's plight and "understood that for the achievement of victory it was necessary that the Koumintang be based on the workers, peasants, and petty-bourgeoisie and that its own revolutionary army be organized." This was done; the KMT took the correct revolutionary path, and great results were achieved.

But at the moment of triumph, "the forces of the revolution fell to pieces on the Yangtze as the result of inner contradictions." Bourgeoisie and landowners who had supported the nationalistic aspects of the revolution now began to fear for their future. The bourgeoisie decided that it did not want the imperialists, upon whose trade their prosperity rested, to be completely driven from China. The landowners adamantly resisted agricultural reform. The militarists concluded that their interests lay with the bourgeoisie and landowners. In the crunch, as bourgeoisie, landowners, and militarists defected from the revolution, the petty-bourgeoisie broke apart. In the final showdown, many of them also found that they were against socialism. In China, therefore, there was no revolutionary class except for the workers and peasants and the poverty-stricken elements of the petty-bourgeoisie. And so the KMT split: landowners, bourgeoisie, militarists on one side; workers, peasants, poor bourgeoisie on the other.

Borodin explained the KMT miscarriage without blaming anyone except the offending classes. The split was finally made official, he explained, by Chiang Kai-shek's perfidy in Shanghai on April 12. Once that had occurred, the Comintern recognized the necessity of deepening the agrarian revolution and the class struggle in the cities. But the leaders of the CCP did not completely master the instructions of the CI and continued to support the petty-bourgeoisie rather than the agricultural revolution and the class struggle in the cities.

This, then, was the explanation that Borodin gave for the "failure in China." Everything went according to plan until the United Front fell apart; then the CI gave the correct instructions but the CCP failed to follow them. Thus the CCP was to blame for all that followed. That is what Moscow wanted him to say to the Sixth Congress of the Revolutionary Mongol People's Party—and he said it. But he did so quickly, not dwelling on the errors of the CCP—which, if errors, were his own and Stalin's—and passed on to the future of the revolution in China and of the CCP, about which he was highly optimistic.[10]

Following Borodin's lengthy exposition, the meeting was thrown open for discussion and questions. There were more than thirty of the latter, originating from undetermined sources. What is clear is that the questions were considered too dangerous to be published. *Izvestiya Ulan-Bator-Khoto* noted twice the great interest in Borodin's address, which it printed, and mentioned the number of questions his remarks generated. But it did not see fit to deal with them, except in a statement, one day later, based on "remarks" made by "Comrade Bandalyan" at the congress. Titled "Mistakes of the Chinese Comparty," Bandalyan dwelt at length on what Borodin had glossed over—the errors of the CCP, particularly its failure to exploit the revolutionary potential of the workers and peasants.

In Ulan Bator, if not before, Borodin became fully aware that he would have to take instructions and make compromises in explaining what had happened in China. He did both in his address. But how could he blame the hapless Ch'en Tu-hsiu and the CCP for following policies that he had forced on them and that he had believed and still believed were correct? Borodin's self-image was still strong. He had been the central figure in China, the mover of armies and governments. His authority had been tremendous. How could he become a second-rate apparatchik, giving the lie to all that he saw himself as having been? By the time Borodin left Ulan Bator, he knew that more would be expected of him than he had presented in his remarks. Moscow, even in October, would likely be hotter than the Gobi desert at high noon.

Yet Borodin wanted to get back, if only to see Fanya—of whose escape from China he just learned—and his sons. At the end of September, accompanied only by Percy Chen, one of Eugene's sons, he flew to Verkhneudinsk (Ulan Ude), the first stop on the Trans-Siberian east of Lake Baikal. He arrived back on Soviet soil on September 28, 1927.

Borodin spent several days at Verkhneudinsk, the most provincial of provincial Russian towns, which nonetheless seemed like a jewel of civilization after Ulan Bator and the desolation of the Gobi. Still appearing as the great man, he visited with local officials, addressed a mass meeting called in his honor (there is no record available of what he said), and then he boarded the Trans-Siberian express for Moscow.

Back in western Russia, Borodin kept out of sight except for an address to the Society of Old Bolsheviks, on October 23. He received treatment for malaria and rested up from his exhausting journey. A picture of him at that time shows that he had lost weight: his face was thin, drawn, and creased, and his neck swam in his collar. He spent much time being "debriefed" and reeducated about what had happened in Russia since his departure. And he apparently received more specific information as to what was expected of him.

By the time Borodin spoke to the Society of Old Bolsheviks in late October, his friends from Wuhan who had opted for Moscow, rather than Nanking, had reached Russia; most were in the Soviet capital. Madame Sun Yat-sen, who had escaped from Shanghai by night, arrived in Moscow on September 9, via Vladivostok, accompanied by Eugene Chen, his two daughters, and Rayna Prohme. A special train had been placed at the disposal of Madame Sun and her entourage, and at station after station along the way from Siberia, crowds and bands assembled to honor the Chinese revolutionaries. Whenever the train stopped, Madame Sun, as always carrying her umbrella, and Chen would alight from the train, accept the proffered bouquets of flowers, and thank the assembled delegation for having come and the Soviet Union for its cooperation and support. And while Madame Sun and Chen thus talked and bowed their way across Russia, the Chen sisters, Sylvia and Yolanda, to the accompaniment of a victrola that they kept constantly blaring in the wagonlit, foxtrotted across the steppes to Moscow.

Following Madame Sun and Eugene Chen, an assortment of other Wuhan people arrived in Moscow. Among them were not only political figures like Fanya, who reached Moscow on October 6, and M. N. Roy, but also a newspaper contingent, including Anna Louise Strong, who wanted to join the Russian communist party. (It didn't want her.) Vincent Sheean, who had fallen in love with the flaming Rayna Prohme and had followed her to the Red capital, was also there.

The Wuhan "family," reassembled in Moscow, had come to the Soviet Union in large part because that was where Borodin had gone. Madame Sun had followed him out of loyalty to her dead husband; Chen and Prohme, because their stars were tied to his; Strong, because she was writing a book. All had come to depend on Borodin. The Chinese, in particular, felt lost without him. While they waited for him to put in an appearance in Moscow, they wandered about the city, went to the theater, the opera, and ballet, and visited with one another, reliving the past, waiting for something to point the way to the future.

The Wuhan refugees had arrived in Moscow at a time of crisis. The final scenes of the post-Lenin struggle for power were being enacted. The outcome was already clear, but the opposition would make one more last-ditch effort to overturn the verdict. One of the chief causes of the opposition was the "treacherous," "antirevolutionary" mishandling of the China situation by Stalin. The opposition pushed it with vigor. No matter how legitimate his reasons for pursuing his China strategy, Stalin was vulnerable because he had forbade the arming of workers and peasants while cooperating with the bourgeoisie. If the policy had succeeded, all would have been well. But it hadn't. The Chinese revolution—and its representatives—were not only an embarrassment to Stalin but, with the showdown with Trotsky at hand, a possible danger as well. Stalin was tired of China, just as he was tired of the whole international revolutionary game. The opposition, as he saw them, were only Jews and internationalists—what came to be familiary termed "rootless cosmopolitans"—and they and their ideas had brought him nothing but trouble. For the Soviet Union, the wave of the immediate future was not the international, but the domestic revolution.

Madame Sun and Eugene Chen were soon disillusioned by what they saw. One of the hits of the ballet season in Moscow was *Krasny mak* (The Red Poppy), a jingoistic portrayal of the Russian role in the Chinese revolution. All the Russians were tall, clean, and heroic; the Chinese were short, disheveled, and "picturesque," seemingly incapable of accomplishing anything without the Russians.[11] Madame Sun was understandably upset by the ballet. *Krasny mak* added to a steadily growing realization among the Chinese: Moscow was not Wuhan; it did not share Borodin's sensitivity for Chinese feelings. Not even he could change that.

Within days after Chen arrived, he was attacked in *Pravda* as having "learned nothing from the revolutions of the past ten years."[12] And both Chen and Madame Sun were disturbed by rumors of impending executions of oppositionists, by the reorganization of the Comintern, and by a decision to curtail involvement in China. Even more disturbing was the treatment given Borodin. They heard their pillar of strength attacked on every side—for being too Red, for not being Red enough. He was ridiculed and belittled. It was even said that, if Borodin was not actually a Trotskyite, he had a foot in that camp. Was he not both Jewish and an international revolutionary? He must be with Trotsky.[13]

Still, Madame Sun's company waited for and put their faith in Borodin, their friend and protector. As soon as he arrived and got his bearings, he would set things right, as he had done so many times in the past. But they were soon and sadly disappointed. At first, after his reemergence in Moscow, Borodin would not even see them. When they called, he was busy, presumably writing his reports on China. When he was in, he only had a few minutes to spare. Borodin was avoiding them, Madame Sun and Chen correctly concluded. And he was, on orders. China was over, he was told by his mentors, and he had to put that period behind him. Nor could Borodin be too friendly with the CCP people in Moscow, for from among their numbers at Sun Yat-sen University came the *only* echelon to successfully raise a pro-Trotsky banner in Moscow during the demonstration celebrating the tenth anniversary of the revolution. Borodin had better stay away from all Chinese. As a matter of fact, given the turmoil in Moscow and his own long-term involvement with the CI and the international revolution, and Stalin's decision to turn against all this, Borodin had better stay away from all his old compatriots.

That Borodin was resolved to follow this course was indicated at the end of November, when the Wuhan family came together for the last time to attend the funeral of Rayna Prohme. For months, Rayna had had severe headaches; then, in November, she suffered a series of fainting spells. Increasingly, she had difficulty focusing her eyes. After her death on November 21 an autopsy revealed that she had had encephalitis, rather than the tuberculosis for which she was being treated.

Borodin's secretary made the funeral arrangements for Rayna. On the afternoon of November 24, Thanksgiving Day, a group of about a hundred Americans, Chinese, and Russians, walking behind the traditional band—which played revolutionary airs as well as Chopin's and Beethoven's funeral marches—followed the catafalque bearing Rayna's body across Moscow to the new crematorium. Among the mourners was

Madame Sun, who had become reconciled with Rayna only shortly before the latter's death. The two had broken when Madame Sun learned that Rayna had kept from her a *New York Times* story romantically linking Madame Sun with Eugene Chen, hinting that it was love, not revolution, that had brought them both to Moscow. Madame Sun, refusing to ride in the limousine assigned her by the Commissariat of Foreign Affairs, insisted on walking through the snow with the rest of the mourners: Rayna's lover—Vincent Sheean—Anna Louise Strong, the Chens, American journalists assigned to Moscow permanently, such as Louis Fischer; roving journalists there for the tenth anniversary of the revolution, such as Dorothy Thompson; a Russian worker who saw the procession going by and joined it; a number of sovetniki; Fanya—but not Mikhail Markovich.

That night Borodin came to see Sheean in his room at the Metropol to explain why he had not been present at the funeral and to say goodbye to the gifted journalist who was leaving Moscow. He had not gone to Rayna's funeral, said Borodin, because on principle he never went to funerals. "The mind must be kept resolutely on its purposes." Visibly agitated, speaking with difficulty, Borodin told Sheean: "I know what this is. I know exactly. But what is needed is the long view. I have come here to ask you to take the long view—China, Russia ... A wonderful friend and a wonderful revolutionary instrument have disappeared together. But there is no use in anything unless we took the long view. Remember that. China, Russia ..."[14] Then he shook hands with Sheean and left.

Borodin had not gone to the funeral because he was under orders to keep his distance from the Wuhanites. But Sheean, a noted Western journalist and a friend in Wuhan, was now leaving Russia. For Borodin not to have given him some explanation for his failure to attend the funeral of Sheean's great love, and Borodin's own close associate, was too much. Regardless of the cost, he had gone to see Sheean and tried to explain. It was not the last time that Borodin's attachment to his China days would overcome his better judgment.

Following Rayna's funeral, the Wuhan group, realizing that Moscow held little for them and that Borodin's China days were over, began to scatter. Eugene Chen went west to Paris. (Chen remained a stormy petrel throughout his life. He was in Hong Kong in 1941 when the Japanese attacked. Captured, he was taken to Shanghai, where he resisted all Japanese attempts to secure his support of the puppet regime in Nanking. He died in Shanghai in 1944.) Roy left for Berlin. Most of the sovetniki returned to their studies or went on to new assignments. Madame Sun, nervous and unsettled, not knowing what to do with her life, remained in Moscow for a while. Her sister had married the arch-enemy, Chiang Kai-shek, and she couldn't bring herself to return to China. But she too would soon be on her way. (Following the victory of the Chinese communists, Madame Sun occupied high ceremonial offices in the Peking regime. Into her eighties, she was still alive in China at the end of the 1970s.) Only Borodin and a few of his closest Russian collaborators in Canton and Wuhan remained to sweat out the ultimate disposition of the "case of the Chinese Revolution of 1923-1927." Only time would determine how much of the blame Borodin would personally have to shoulder for the "failure" of the Chinese revolution.

Still less than absolutely powerful and ever filled with self-doubts, Stalin could not embrace Borodin as though nothing had gone awry in China. But neither could he cast Borodin aside. Stalin, upon occasion, was capable of loyalty. More important in this case, however, was the common knowledge in higher Soviet political circles that a close relationship had existed between Borodin and Stalin on China. For Stalin to make Borodin a scapegoat now would be an act subject to damaging interpretations. Borodin, therefore, survived, but he was placed in limbo. In this suspended state, Borodin was unnerved. He felt trapped, powerless. Sooner or later the party—Stalin—would take a definitive position on China and his fate would then be decided. While he awaited that decision, all Borodin could do was to pace up and down, play chess, read. He had to be careful whom he saw; they might be the wrong people. Nor would he write the book on China he sometimes talked about—who knew what the party line would be when he had finished it?

It would take Stalin nearly a year to establish the official interpretation of events in China. He must first disprove the accusation that he had been antirevolutionary in China. This he sought to do by ordering a communist uprising in Canton in December 1927, long after it had any chance for success. That debacle caused thousands of Chinese communists and sympathizers to be executed, but it "proved" Stalin's dedication to proletarian action.

Moscow's director of scenario for what happened in China was a young Ukrainian, Mikhail Alexandrovich Fortus, known in party circles as Pavel Mif. In the mid-20s, Mif had been sent by Stalin to keep an eye on Karl Radek, the rector at Sun Yat-sen University. Mif trained himself to become a China specialist, authored a number of anti-Trotsky books and articles on China, and, as we have seen, in 1927 was sent there by the Central Committee of the Russian party. Back in Moscow, after the fall of Wuhan, he succeeded the ousted Radek as head of Sun Yat-sen University and became Stalin's principal spokesman on China at the Fifteenth Party Congress in December 1927.

During the course of late 1927 and the first half of 1928, Mif, in a series of articles that Stalin "coauthored" to authenticate their contents and to embellish his reputation as a theoretician, established the line on China in *Bolshevik*, the leading theoretical journal of the party. Mif maintained that there were no major errors in China until April 1927, when the report of the KMT agrarian commission came in, calling for wide-scale confiscation of land.[15] The CCP at its Fifth Congress in May 1927 made a correct decision, wrote Mif, in favoring confiscation, but it made one major error: it did not remove the adventurist Ch'en Tu-hsiu, the party's general secretary, who was inalterably opposed to confiscation. "Not one hand was raised against comrade Ch'en Tu-hsiu," declared Mif angrily.[16] As soon as the meetings were over, Ch'en, still in power, disregarded the congress' instructions and led the CCP down the path to calamity.

Thus responsibility for the debacle belonged to Ch'en Tu-hsiu and, to a lesser degree, the CCP in general. It could not be placed at the door of the Russians. The Comintern had made the correct decisions and given the proper instructions, wrote Mif. "Only the most evil enemies of the CI will unload all the mistakes of the leadership of the Chinese Comparty on the Comintern. Only people who wish to use the temporary defeat of the Chinese revolution to defeat the CI can think that the Leninist-trained leadership of the CI gave any ground for the . . . Menshevik . . . treacherous and opportunistic activities of the then CC of the Chinese Comparty."[17] Either one accepted Stalin's account of China, or one would risk being labeled a Menshevik or a Trotskyite—or both. The consequences could well be fatal.

The line having been established, Borodin was called upon to confirm it. Until now, Borodin had been forced to be silent when he might have wished to talk. Now he was required to talk, and he would have preferred silence. It would be a psychologically wrenching experience to falsify the facts and deny his role in China. He could still not easily give the lie to what had been accomplished in China and the greatness he had sensed in himself by rearranging the truth. China, at least temporarily, had eroded that Bolshevik discipline about which he had often preached to others.

Throughout 1928, Borodin mostly stayed in his two-room suite at the Metropol, played chess, took an occasional walk, saw hardly anyone except Fanya. Bertram Wolfe, who sometimes exchanged knights and bishops with him, has indicated that Borodin was a very lonely man,[18] out of the stream of things, Pharaoh's butler and baker, awaiting his fate.

Borodin could avoid paying the price demanded of him only if Stalin consented. Stalin's continued sufferance explains why Borodin was not only able to keep his silence but also his large suite in the Metropol, larger than that assigned to any other CI figure at the time. This also explains why Borodin still had influence that could, upon occasion, be used in behalf of old friends. For example, in 1928, M. N. Roy, who had returned from Berlin for the Ninth Plenum of the CI and found himself in Moscow ill and out of favor, feared he would not be permitted to leave the hospital or the Soviet Union. He summoned a girlfriend from Berlin, who obtained Borodin's help in getting Roy out of the hospital and, later, out of the country. Borodin still carried some weight in the Soviet Union—but not enough to save himself the pound of pride demanded.

Borodin maintained his silence for most of 1928. In late 1928 and early 1929, as the campaign against Trotsky's "left" opposition came to include the right opposition as well, the demand for complete and open commitment to Stalin became intense. The time for silence had passed; one must proclaim one's loyalty, openly and enthusiastically, or face the consequences. No one was exempt.

The scenario designed for Borodin's capitulation and affirmation of the Stalinist truth was a scholarly meeting on the topic "The Historical Background of Chentuhsiuism," scheduled for January 25, 1929. The meeting was to focus on a paper by Comrade Kommunar, after which there was to be a discussion by invited guests, of whom Borodin was one. According to the Bolshevik custom, Comrade Kommunar was to give the party line, to be followed by confession from the sinners on the panel. On the 25th, Kommunar made his presentation; on the 29th another meeting was scheduled at which the guilty would express their mea culpas. The days between were to be used to prepare text and attitude for the ceremony.

On the 29th Borodin spoke. "Comrades," he began, "I came here not to participate in the discussion, but in order to listen to comrades who in recent times have been occupied with the history of the Chinese revolution and the Chinese party. But when I arrived, they proposed that I participate in the discussion. I must say that recently I have been working strenuously on the question of the Chinese revolution. The greatest difficulty in the working out of this question appears to be the receiving of Chinese materials, which are not available in Russia. I hope that I will be prepared after a month or two, and I will make a presentation to you."[19]

So Borodin began by declaring, somewhat disingenuously, that he didn't know his participation was expected at the meeting and that he hadn't had adequate time to prepare. He then proceeded to identify with positions taken in Comrade Kommunar's paper. He castigated Chentushuism (the policies ascribed by Stalin to Ch'en) and declared that the latter was an "intervening of Trotskyism and Menshevism on Chinese soil and that in considerable degree Chentushuism is responsible for the defeat which we have received in the past . . . And I underline 'in considerable degree,' because we also—the workers in China and, in particular and especially, I—have made serious mistakes. I have thought about those mistakes a great deal, have studied them and come to certain conclusions about which I will speak

at the right time. I think that this will be soon."[20] One mistake
he had made, which he was prepared to mention now, was not to
have carried his many differences with Ch'en Tu-hsiu "to struggle." If he had, he said, the CCP would not have been in Menshevik hands for so long a time.

But now Borodin took off on his own. Borodin wanted his listeners to understand, he said, that, beginning in 1923, there had
been two different lines in China: the Ch'en Tu-hsiu line
(Shanghai) and the Canton line. The Shanghai line pursued
only the anti-imperialist revolution, but those in Canton realized that either the Chinese revolution would triumph as an
agrarian revolution or it would not triumph at all. Step by step,
they liquidated the roadblocks on the way to the Chinese revolution, but in Shanghai the *Guide Weekly* (the official organ of the
CCP) conducted war only against imperialists and militarism—
and said not a word about social revolution.

When the Canton proletariat, leading the peasants in struggle, rushed to take control of the revolution, they did not receive
Ch'en's support in Shanghai. On the contrary, Ch'en "systemat-
ically paralyzed their enthusiasm" and stood in the way of the
hegemony of the workers and peasants. On all Chinese questions
in those days, Borodin repeated, there were two distinct lines:
that of the Canton leadership and that of the leadership of the
Central Committee in Shanghai, the Menshevik line. Though
the faction in Canton may not always have been right, *it was revolutionary*.

In conclusion, Borodin told the assembled "scholars," that
while they were to remember that Chentuhsuism was chiefly responsible for the defeat in China, *there were other reasons as well
they ought to find out about*. Having made his "confession," followed
by an "explanation" that seemed to modify the official line,
Borodin sat down. He was succeeded on the podium by long-
time CI agent Voitinsky, who then proceeded with his own
breast beating. But Borodin's ordeal was not finished, for after
Voitinsky had finished, G. I. Safarov, a journalist and part-time
Far Eastern specialist, took over. Safarov had been ousted from
the party at the Fifteenth Congress and had just been readmit-
ted to its ranks. He attacked Borodin with ferocity, eager to
prove his own worthiness.

Borodin had tried to be contrite, said Safarov. He had confessed mistakes; he had admitted the existence of Menshevism and Trotskyism in China; he had agreed that he did not oppose Ch'en Tu-hsiu strongly enough. But this was not enough. He was still waffling:

> SAFAROV: Borodin has not taken his confession to heart. The Chinese have corrected themselves so that they might extirpate the Menshevik tendency from their midst. But Borodin, who played not the least role in the events of 1925-1927, when he says that the Chinese revolution can triumph only as a social revolution, and admits that he said that from the beginning, is taking the position of Plekhanov, the father of Menshevism. This reflection of Plekhanov is not without pretense, but it is necessary to say that the next step of the Chinese revolution is not the worker-peasant, but the bourgeois-democratic step.
>
> BORODIN: Correct.
>
> SAFAROV: Comrade Borodin, it is necessary not only to say "Correct," but to say why it is correct. Comrade Borodin presents us constantly with new, incorrect, un-Bolshevik statements. Every confession he makes indicates new errors.
>
> But he really confesses to nothing. He tried to indicate that all errors are explainable in a framework of Shanghai vs. Canton. This is nonsense, a huge historical "confusion," an attempt to explain all in terms of "personality."
>
> Moreover, when he declares that, in Canton, he pushed the idea of the hegemony of the workers and the peasants, he is repeating a Menshevik calumny. The proletariat, more numerous or not, must lead. The Bolshevik way is not "worker and peasant hegemony," but "proletarian hegemony." We must conduct additional struggles against the tendency toward the diminution and Menshevik negation of the idea of proletarian hegemony.

Safarov, having castigated Borodin for insisting on his own explanation and for his assertion of Menshevik principles, now sat down, but he was not yet finished with Borodin. Before the day ended, he would accuse him not only of Menshevism, but also of Trotskyism and social fascism.[21] In the Moscow of the time those were lethal accusations. Borodin, shaken, would ultimately ask that he be permitted to expunge some of his previous statements from the official record.

That was all for January 29. With Safarov's concluding attack on Borodin, and Borodin's request to withdraw his remarks, the meeting adjourned. But another was scheduled for eight days later, and it opened with a resumption of the offensive against Borodin, this time by Comrade Gudkov, another recent penitent restored to party ranks. "It is impossible to be silent about the strange speech with which Comrade Borodin came here," said Gudkov. Borodin had learned nothing; he changed his remarks; he tried to hide behind the historical and geographical fiction of Shanghai-Canton differences. He had only one purpose in presenting this untenable dichotomy, and that was to protect himself.[22] Gudkov had prepared extended remarks and, according to the record, continued for page after page against Borodin. But Borodin did not accept Gudkov's remarks. He counterattacked, and although the copy of the exchange is presumably edited against Borodin, it is clear that Borodin defended himself with vigor against a wide variety of charges, many based on his speech to the Old Bolsheviks on October 23, 1927, when he had just returned from China and did not know how far he would be required to go in denying the past.[23]

After Gudkov had completed his attack and Borodin had answered, Safarov resumed his assault. Employing quotations from Lenin *and Stalin,* he condemned Borodin for having forgotten the lessons of 1905 and, most devastatingly, for having recognized class contradictions in China in 1925-1927 not in a Leninist fashion but according to his own special "Canton" style.[24] The latter was only one of several of Safarov's statements that, according to the stenographic report, brought laughter from the audience. Safarov painted Borodin as an ideological simpleton, even a fool. Safarov, who was working his way back into the party's good graces and would be repaid for this performance by being named editor of the journal *Problemy kitaya,* slashed mercilessly at Borodin, but he did not this time accuse Borodin of Menshevism, Trotskyism or social-fascism. According to the record, Borodin now remained silent.

What happened can only be conjectured. Somehow Borodin received the word that a decision had been made to bring the debate to an end. The party had its position on China, and Borodin would have to conform. Perhaps his protector even allowed him one last word, in answer to Gudkov. But the party, speaking through Safarov, would have the final word. And that final word included ridicule of Borodin. But though Safarov portrayed Borodin as a fool, he did not call him an antiparty person or a Menshevik or a Trotskyite. As a simpleton, Borodin was presumably redeemable, and thus might be rehabilitated and used again.

At this point, a decision on what to do with Borodin had not been handed down (although a deal may have been struck when Safarov made his last statement). Borodin, on orders, met with and was interviewed by Louis Fischer, the American journalist long resident in Moscow. This must have been deeply disturbing. He knew, for example, that Fischer was being permitted to interview a number of prominent people, most of whom were in the opposition. He recognized the interview situation as a kind of test. Could he successfully present the party position on what had happened in China as his own?

When Borodin saw Fischer the first time (his case still undecided), he was so nervous he could hardly speak.[25] He never gave Fischer a definite appointment. He would tell Fischer, "Telephone me Friday evening." When Fischer did so, he would be told: "Comrade Borodin would like you to phone him tomorrow morning at nine." At nine, Borodin would answer the call with: "Call me again in twenty minutes. I may be summoned to a meeting." In twenty minutes, he would either meet the appointment or cancel it. Fischer attributed Borodin's conduct to his natural secretiveness, increased by experiences in Chicago and China, and his desire "to talk and act like an oracle."[26] A more likely reason would seem to be apprehension, brought on by the political ordeal he was experiencing. What was the party going to decide, and what would happen to him and to his family?

Then word arrived that Borodin would not be charged with adherence to the opposition, as Safarov had threatened; he would soon be given a job. Fischer noted that the interviews now became longer and more frequent, that Borodin grew increasingly "interested in the telling," and took on more of his long-view aspect.

By mid-1929, Borodin was over the hump. He would never again, once he had completed the on-order Fischer discussions, allude to China in public.[27] When foreigners approached him on the subject, even during World War II, he would turn away.[28] It was too dangerous. In the late 1920s, it had brought him close to political extinction; later, in the Stalin purges of the 1930s, many of those involved with him in China would be executed, including Karakhan, Blyukher, and most of the miltiary sovetniki. Nothing was to be gained by talking of the dead past.

19

Surviving

The assignment Borodin received in 1929, after the party closed the books on his chapter of revolution in China, was a far cry from those he had previously been given. He was appointed deputy director of Bumprom, the paper and lumber trust. The job seems to have come as a surprise; in his interviews with Louis Fischer, Borodin gave the impression he had been studying the revolutionary potential of India. But Borodin was now too well known to be an effective revolutionary agent there. And the party's attention was drifting further from international revolution. What mattered now was the domestic revolution: collectivization and industrialization. That is where the need for organizational aptitude such as Borodin has displayed in China was to be found.

That Borodin had eventually emerged from the failure-in-China crisis as unscarred as he did suggests that someone on top was in his corner. That he could survive his often-bungled performance in the paper and pulp technology industry further points to his Red guardian angel in the Politburo. Bumprom, of first-rate importance in the Soviet development plan, was in a state of flux when Borodin was appointed its deputy director. Parts of other industries were being drawn into it; it was expanding rapidly and was badly in need of sound management. But managing Bumprom was not the same as managing the KMT or the CCP or running a revolution. Borodin was ill suited to the task and soon was sacked, receiving a reprimand in his party book. Now Borodin was given a lesser job, as a factory director, in the same sector. Here again his performance was unsatisfactory, and he received yet another reprimand.

Borodin was naturally depressed. Was it to run a factory that he had left Chicago? In his heart, he believed there were still great revolutionary deeds to perform. The frustrations and disappointments in China, the massive psychological adjustments of returning to Russia and taking a routine industrial job, were more than he could handle. Borodin was a fearful and an angry man, but he could not express his anger, except perhaps by failure. In spite of failures that might have ended the career of other men, Borodin received another assignment; this time it was in the People's Commissariat of Labor.

By the early 1930s thousands of Westerners were coming to the USSR to work. The depression had brought widespread and prolonged unemployment. But the Soviet Union embarked on a massive program of industrialization and needed labor, especially skilled labor. Soviet labor agents recruited in Britain, Germany, and the United States, and found engineers and technicians eager for well paying jobs, even if they had to go to communist Russia. Other Westerners—refugees from old Russia as well as communists and procommunists—were also returning to Russia, the new land of opportunity. The People's Commissariat of Labor decided that it needed an agency to deal with those coming to the Soviet Union from abroad. Borodin was given the responsibility of dealing with the specialists and immigrants from America.

The job was scarcely a plum, but Borodin was fortunate to get it, considering his recent failures. Apparently he did a competent job, perhaps because it was better fitted to his talents and he was becoming better adjusted to his new milieu. But by mid-1931, the number of specialists being recruited from abroad had dwindled; with the news of famine in the Volga, the trials of Mensheviks, and other negative reports on life in the Soviet Union, the stream of refugees was drying up too. Still only forty-eight, Borodin cast about for another job.

Earlier, in the spring of 1930 while Borodin was in Bumprom, Anna Louise Strong, fresh from her latest jaunt around the Soviet Union (she traveled in the summer and wrote and lectured in the United States in the winter), called on Borodin, as she did whenever she was in Moscow. Certainly not off the cuff, Borodin asked her, "Didn't you once have an idea of starting an American newspaper in Moscow?" And then he told her, on cue from above: "If you tried now, I think you would find support."[1]

Thus was born the *Moscow News,* the "first five-day weekly in the world." (The USSR had embarked on a new work schedule: five days on, one day off, hence the five-day week.) It began publication on October 5, 1930, with Anna Louise Strong as its editor and Borodin as its mentor. Strong intended to make the *Moscow News* a professionally respectable, readable journal for Americans away from home. It carried football and baseball scores from the United States. It helped new arrivals find a place to stay and adjust to their new environment. It told of sightseeing and entertainment possibilities in Moscow and elsewhere, and it organized tours to points of interest. If an American was in town, without a job or useful contacts, he could often find both at the offices of the *Moscow News.* Dozens of United States and British writers who later achieved prominence at home wrote for the *News,* usually to make a few rubles while passing through Moscow.

The paper served not only as a surrogate home for Americans, but also for many of the old Wuhan "family." Eugene Chen's sons, Percy and Jack (the latter as a cartoonist), did part-time work for it. Fanya, who had been engaged as head of the Foreign Language Technical School in Moscow, teaching English to Russians as she and Borodin had done in Chicago, and doing translations on the side to help accommodate the influx of tourists and others from abroad, wrote a congratulatory statement for the first issue. She was present at the reception to celebrate its opening and was frequently mentioned in its columns. Later Millie Billy Mitchell, another Wuhanite, would come to Moscow to become managing editor, and Bill Prohme, Rayna's husband, would also be invited to join the staff.

Like most new enterprises, the *Moscow News* had shakedown problems. It was not getting to readers who wanted it and often went to cities without potential readers. Most of the typesetters didn't know English. Once this led to slave labor in "Liberia" coming out as the slave labor in "Siberia."[2] But the *News* also suffered from more serious difficulties. Bureaucratic rivalries and jealousies abounded. More troublesome still, and not entirely divorced from the battle for control, was antagonism to the basic mission of the paper. Critics disapproved of the English-speaking specialists at whom the *News* was aimed. The specialists, it was said, received high salaries, were frequently incompetent, didn't work very hard, and returned to the United States to write anti-Soviet articles for the *Saturday Evening Post.* Detractors said the *News* made little or no effort to convert the specialists, explain the party line, and give them ideological indoctrination. What was needed was an English-language paper for working men, a paper emphasizing the party gospel and directly serving party interests. On February 4, 1931, such a paper was born, the *Worker's News:* it was written for "mechanics," its lead editorial declared.

For a year, the *Moscow News* and the *Worker's News* fought each other. The *Worker's News* called the *Moscow News* bourgeois and attacked it for minimizing Stalin's speeches, for not emphasizing party and government affairs, and for failing to stress the great industrialization effort going forward in the Soviet Union. For its part, the *Moscow News* accused the *Worker's News* of being illiterate, dull, and wooden.

Anna Louise Strong's job was complicated by the fact that both papers were under a single responsible editor, T. L. Axelrod, whose sympathies lay with the *Worker's News*. Politically, the *Moscow News* was too dangerous—who knew what the freewheeling Anna Louise Strong or the frivolous Milly Mitchell would do next? Strong attended all the congresses in Moscow and hurried back to her *Moscow News* office to try to scoop *Pravda.* Milly Mitchell was always turning out frothy pieces such as "You Can Eat in Moscow" or "May Night in Moscow," hardly appropriate for a party periodical. Fearing that he might be held responsible for what Strong or her staff printed, Axelrod wanted to close the *Moscow News.* But he knew that Strong had support in high places and she was, though hopelessly bourgeois, a respected American writer and Soviet supporter. He didn't dare close her paper, but he might harass her to death. When she went on one of her periodic jaunts, whether to Pittsburgh or the Pamirs, she would return to find that her staff had been bothered, her own articles unused, her orders disregarded. When the situation became intolerable, she would go to see Borodin at the Labor Commisariat and he would commiserate with her.

By early 1932, Strong had about decided to return to the
United States and, she suggested, do an exposé of the *News*. But
before doing so, she found a "sensitive" Russian party member
(Borodin?) to whom she disclosed her frustrations and intent. He
strongly urged her to delay, suggesting that she seek support
directly from Stalin. Her letter to Stalin brought about what she
stated was the high point of her life: a half-hour meeting with
the great man. "Other hours in my life that were marked with
great emotion—when I have adored great men—have all died
out; I cannot recapture their feeling. But that half hour grows
with years. Even today I can feel the atmosphere of that meeting—its sympathetic but unemotional analysis, seeking fundamental lines and relations and acting to set them right."[3] At that
meeting, Strong and her antagonists faced one another in the
presence of Stalin, Kaganovich, and Voroshilov and debated
their positions. All were present when Stalin decreed that the
warring papers should merge into a new paper, the *Moscow Daily
News*, with a new responsible editor: Mikhail Markovich Borodin.

It was thus that Borodin found his niche for the rest of his life,
the editorship of a Moscow-English-language newspaper. He
was not a novice in the printed word. He had been a schoolmaster. In Chicago, he may have written articles for the American
press on Russian socialism. He had written for Comintern publications on a number of occasions. He had drafted an extensive
report on the revolutionary potential in England and, since returning from China, had written two pamphlets on the paper
and lumber industries—one published in 1930, the second in
1931. He had also been involved in the publication of the *People's Tribune* in Wuhan. But literary experience and ability were
not necessarily the critical considerations at the *Moscow Daily
News*.

Being responsible editor of the *Moscow Daily News* was a break
for Borodin, considering his recent reverses. At the *Daily News*,
surrounded by members of his Wuhan family, who respected
him, and in the company of a kaleidoscopic group of young visiting Americans and Britishers, he was in a more congenial environment. If he wasn't making news, he was at least reporting
it. By now, almost five years and several failures after China,

Borodin no longer expected to scale new peaks; most of the time, his goal was to survive. He could afford no more failures. For Fanya's sake, and Fred's (who sought a career in the military), Norman's (still in school), and his own, he needed to succeed here. Fortunately, he had regained his health.

Survival at the *Daily News* was not easy. Dangers beset him on all sides. First, there was the thankless task of trying to get the staffs of the old *Moscow News* and the *Worker's News* to cooperate. Then the Ogonek publishing house, which had formerly controlled both the *Moscow News* and the *Worker's News,* and had now lost control of the *Daily News,* showed its pique by evicting the *Daily News* and its equipment from its offices. Just two days after the first issue of the *Daily News* had appeared, Borodin had to threaten the Ogonek officials: "You saboteurs, keep your paws off our offices or we'll charge you with wrecking."[4] He succeeded in having the typewriters, tables, and chairs moved back in, but only temporarily. His next battle was to find a new location for the newspaper, no small task in space-poor Moscow.

Again using his "Kremlin resources," Borodin was able to get the house at No. 8 Petrovsky Pereulok assigned to the *Daily News.* It was a large, ornate edifice, formerly the home of a Swedish merchant. More recently it had been the Moscow residence of businessman Armand Hammer, once a Russian but now an American citizen, who had secured a number of concessions from the Soviets, including permission to operate a pencil factory. With its elaborate grillwork, its wall paintings, rococo decorations, and carved reindeer heads, the mansion was not an ideal place for a newspaper office, but it had a huge ballroom where the staff could work. The only other real difficulty was that the old Swedish merchant still lived in a sealed-off section of the building. When the babble and banging from the newspaper became too loud, he pounded on the walls. Another part of the building was occupied by Eugene Lyons, correspondent for the *New York Times* and the United Press representative in Moscow. For a year and a half Borodin struggled to get both Lyons and the elderly merchant to leave, complaining about everything from the noise to the small "bourgeois" painting with which Lyons decorated the entrance hall. When at last Borodin succeeded in evicting Lyons, he immediately posted guards to prevent someone else from occupying the liberated space. Such was the nature of the battles Borodin fought as "responsible editor" of the *Moscow Daily News*.

Borodin had two chief tasks: to supervise his foreign staffers and to insure the political acceptability of what they wrote. Neither task was simple, for Borodin reigned over one of the most motley collection of malcontents, misfits, and peripheral journalists ever gathered under one roof. Strong lived in a fantasy world. Borodin saw her as a friend who had shared many experiences, but who needed a tight rein. He had to convince her, for example, not to write about the famine conditions she had witnessed in the Volga. "Our readers know of the food shortage from their own food cards and Stalin's reports . . . Whom would it help to know sensational stories of hunger, or the details of our difficulties? Would it get additional food for anybody? . . . Our friends know the essentials of our struggle; they can wait for details. Our enemies suspect, but they do not really know."[5] On other occasions, he had to discuss with her the nature of the *Daily News*. She wanted it to be lively, breezy, interesting. He knew it had to be dull, pedantic, strictly subservient to the subtleties of the party line. He had to convince her of the correctness of his position again and again. As editor of the *Daily News,* his chief function was to be Strong's nursemaid. But not only hers. He had to prevent the *Daily News* from becoming a trysting place for lonely travelers from New York, Philadelphia, or London, looking for a temporary job; or a haven for homosexuals, as it threatened to beome on at least one occasion.[6] And always he had to beware the dangerous phrase or interpretation.

Borodin's nursemaid service was, of course, supplemented with other activities. He held staff meetings twice a week, during which he passed along the latest nuances of the party line gleaned from that morning's *Pravda*. Sometimes he went to factories and shops to address groups of foreign workers. On May 1 and November 7, he organized the march of the newspaper staff through Red Square, which was followed by caviar and vodka at No. 8 Petrovsky. On occasion and under orders, he would dress up and go to official receptions at the United States embassy as the representative of the *Daily News*.[7] Sometimes there were calls by touring Americans. Borodin would order sandwiches and tea and would talk with the visitors about world affairs. And, from time to time, as a remembrance of the old days, there were visits from the Chen children, from Chiang Kai-shek's eldest son (who had come to Moscow to study in 1925 and was still there a decade later), and from former residents of the United States who, like himself, couldn't go back. For them the *Daily News* was a meeting place where they could relive, discreetly, former days.

Such responsibilities were hardly on a scale with those in China, or even with his CI experiences. He knew his days of glory were over, but he could not alter his style to meet his shrunken role. As editor of a fourth-rate newspaper in the backwater of Soviet journalism, his manner often reflected his past. But where once he had been deferentially listened to and promptly obeyed, the staff now argued with him, disregarded him, even ridiculed him, particularly those who had not known him in the old days. He was the constant butt of the vindictive wit of Charles Ashleigh, the English novelist and a member of his editorial staff. Others, who saw him as pompous, sought to deflate him. In frustration, Borodin demanded, roared, threatened. But to no avail; he was seen as a has-been. Klaus Mehnert, the German sovietologist who observed Borodin during those years, described him as "sad-faced," presenting the "impression of a disused locomotive rusting away on a siding."[8]

In the first months after Borodin took over, the *Moscow Daily News* still gave evidence of the American journalistic style that Anna Louise Strong had tried to instill. She and Milly Mitchell remained as editors and, although their language and material were toned down, they evaded the straitjacket of Soviet journalism. Increasingly, however, the *Daily News* became an English-language repetition of *Pravda*. It dropped American baseball and football scores; it discontinued its coverage of events in the United States unless they had ideological interest; finally, it ceased using original material prepared by its staff. It consisted increasingly—and by 1936, completely—of interviews with any American visiting Moscow who would say something favorable about the Soviet Union; of rebuttals to attacks on Russia by recent returnees from the USSR (critics were usually accused of drunkenness, thievery, or sexual improprieties while in the Soviet Union); and of translations from the official Russian press.

As the *Daily News* became increasingly safe, the hazards to Borodin decreased. So did his workload. There was little to do but explain to Strong what she should be thinking about what she had observed. Borodin was only slightly over fifty, but he was already virtually *v otstavke,* in retirement. When in 1938 the *Moscow Daily News* became the once-a-week *Moscow News* again, his obligations were reduced still further. The rust on the locomotive spread and deepened.

In spite of having been shunted off the mainline of history onto a siding, Borodin was succeeding where many of his contemporaries failed: he was keeping out of jail and staying alive. These were the years of the purges. Millions of Russians were being arrested, sent off to slave labor camps, shot. Almost all of the military sovetniki who had served with him in China were meeting such a fate. Three of his own staff members on the *Moscow News* were arrested, yet he remained free; his wife continued to teach English and German and prepare texts for beginners; his son Fred advanced in his military career, and Norman went to the university.

Borodin knew why he and his famiy had escaped the legendary midnight knock on the door; it was Stalin's doing. Stalin had protected him, arranged his "rehabilitation," given him job after job. In spite of the outcome of the Chinese revolution, Borodin was still known among the cognoscenti as Stalin's man. His continued liberty indicated that Stalin had been right *and* that he could do what he wished. Borodin at large demonstrated Stalin's control, perhaps more to the latter than to others.

With the *News* reduced to a weekly, Borodin in 1939 coedited an English-language volume on the soviet film.[9] It was no credit to him. It was casually and hastily written. He really wasn't interested in the Soviet film; he was concerned with survival and as much tranquility as possible.

World War II now broke out. Fred, a colonel in the Red Army, was killed in the early days of the war. Fanya continued her work in languages. Borodin continued to oversee the *Moscow News.* He also became an official of the Soviet Information Bureau, responsible for meeting the foreign press representatives in Moscow in large number during the war, talking with them, and then reporting to the GPU—the security police—on their conversations.[10] It was a time when most Russians appointed to deal with the Allies sought to give the impression of hail-fellows-well-met. But not Borodin, who was unsmiling and elusive. Engaged in conversation, he revealed little.[11] If questions were asked about his past, he said nothing. He felt vulnerable.

Being an informer was a sorry comedown for the former revolutionary leader of half of China, but the war was on and one must live. China seemed almost like a dream. One was careful, imitated Stalin, grew a moustache like his, dressed like him (remember how Eugene Chen had copied Borodin two decades earlier), and followed the party line scrupulously; one stayed out of trouble. It was the only way to remain alive. For many of his contemporaries, even that was not enough. Borodin's own crucible was just ahead.

Immediately after World War II, Stalin's hand lay heavier than ever on the USSR. His control over the Soviet Union and the new Eastern European empire was absolute—but his fears increased. The addition of new communist states and the imminent advent of a communist China, even though apparently extending Soviet hegemony and influence, created new threats to his and to Soviet authority.

In the postwar period, Stalin had plundered Eastern Europe. Whatever had escaped destruction in the war was carted off to the USSR to hasten its rebuilding. Factories, bridges, railroad tracks, equipment—all were taken. In most of Eastern Europe, no one dared challenge this. The local puppets had, for the most part, spent the war years behind Soviet lines and had been brought to power only by the Red Army. They lacked popular support. In their own lands they were often regarded as Soviet agents.

But in Yugoslavia, the government was headed by Tito, who had organized spirited and effective guerrilla warfare against the Germans and had been personally instrumental in the liberation of the country. Tito could argue, and his countrymen agreed, that his regime had not been placed in power by the Red Army, but through his efforts and those of his fellow guerrillas. He was widely admired. Yugoslav challenges to Stalin grew; the stubbornness they had displayed against Hitler, and the Turks before him, was now turned against Stalin. In June 1948, the Soviet dictator reacted to Yugoslav nationalism by kicking the People's Republic of Yugoslavia out of the Cominform, the postwar successor to the Comintern.

Stalin was trying to curb the cancerous growth of nationalism by warning potential nationalists of the dangers of dallying with it. In particular, he was signaling a message to Mao Tse-tung, who, twenty years after Wuhan, was leading the revolution in China. Mao had been on poor terms with the Russians since 1927. In the early 1930s, they had tried to sidetrack him as long as they could. Moscow felt that Mao, not being Moscow-trained, could not be trusted. Stalin further distrusted his peasant-first doctrines and other anti-Marxist heresies. Stalin had provided the CCP with little aid from the day Mao assumed its control. After the Japanese surrender, Japanese war material was made available to the Chinese Red Army, but the Russians pillaged Manchuria as they had Eastern Europe. Stalin repeatedly urged Mao to go slowly and cooperate with Chiang Kai-shek. Stalin's leadership of the international movement might be jeopardized by a Mao-led China.

Stalin's anxieties increased in 1949 when Golda Meier, the first ambassador to the USSR from the state of Israel, appeared in Moscow and was greeted by 50,000 of her coreligionists. Stalin's antisemitism had long been apparent. Now this outpouring of emotion by a large section of Moscow Jewry proved to Stalin that Jews were disloyal to the Soviet Union. Nationalism was an enemy; Jews were nationalists; hence Jews were enemies.

In the midst of Stalin's mounting determination to stem what he saw as the rising tide of nationalism, Anna Louise Strong returned to Moscow in late 1948, fresh from an eighteen-month tour through Eastern Europe. Previously she had spent most of 1946 and early 1947 in the communist-held portions of China, had visited Mao in Yenan, and had developed a predictable enthusiasm for the Maoist solution to Asia's political problems. Eager as ever, even at seventy, to write about great revolutionary events, she had authored a 125,000 word manuscript on the new China and a series of newspaper articles on Chinese communism and the "science" of Mao. In the most important of the articles, which ran to 10,000 words, she made no mention of any Soviet contribution to the development of Maoism and specifically attacked the dogmatists "who had studied abroad, especially in Moscow, and had the prestige of being able to quote from Marx, Lenin and Stalin in great detail. Their ignorance of the practical problems of China was catastrophic."[12]

Strong then embarked upon a European tour in quest of publishers. However, en route westward through North Korea she was delayed three months, probably at Soviet request, before receiving a North Korean visa. The delay was ominous, but she attributed it to "well-known" bureaucratic bungling. Arriving at last in Moscow, Strong went, as usual, to see her old friend Borodin. She told him of her enthusiasm for what was happening in China, of the accomplishments of his old CCP associates now in power, of the favor her writing was enjoying abroad (including the satellite countries), of her dismay that none of her articles had appeared in *Pravda,* and of the publishing roadblocks in Moscow. Borodin, who had been briefed on what to say, told her of certain "editorial problems in her manuscript" and then, probably by prearrangement, telephoned the State Publishing House in her presence and argued that it should publish the book. As Strong recalled a decade later, Borodin turned aside objections to the manuscript's ideological acceptability with the rejoinder: "The Chinese are winning, aren't they? So their theories can't be all wrong."[13] But Borodin's intercession had no effect; it wasn't meant to. Failing in Moscow, Strong took her book to the Eastern European capitals, where it was accepted for publication. The only exception, interestingly, was Belgrade, her last point of call before returning to Moscow, en route back to China.

In Moscow, Strong renewed her efforts to have the manuscript accepted. Other communist countries were accepting her material, why not Moscow? A morose Borodin told her that the "Kremlin is unhappy with your writings."[14] In talks that followed, she was bluntly informed that the only way to get the manuscript published was to accept certain alterations, which must also be made in all editions published in the communist bloc countries. This she refused to accept.

After months of bickering, Strong decided further efforts would be futile. She requested a visa permitting a return to China to observe and report upon the imminent victory. But

Moscow would not cooperate. Borodin began to realize then, if not before, the trouble she was in. As her contact and intercessor, he might be in trouble too—even though he had cleared with the "authorities" everything he had said and done. For both of them, her enthusiasm for Mao's heretical brand of communism could not have come at a worse moment. Stalin's xenophobic paranoia was at its height. Their predicament was deepened by the eagerness with which the manuscript had been received by satellite editors, by Strong's refusal to permit alterations in the manuscript, by her recent visit to Belgrade, and by Borodin's Jewish origin. In 1949, any one of these would arouse suspicion. Together they spelled deep trouble. Sometime between January 28 and February 4, both Strong and Borodin were arrested—together with the staff of the *Moscow News*, which ceased publication.[15]

After five days in the Lubyanka, Anna Louise Strong was flown to Poland and allowed to leave for the United States. But Borodin, like his newspaper, was never seen again. He had been identified with the enemy, foreign nationalism. That was enough.

On September 3, 1953, Harrison Salisbury, long-time Moscow correspondent of the *New York Times,* was allowed to report that Borodin had died.[16] The place was one of the harshest prison camps, near Yakutsk. The date was May 29, 1951, almost two years before Stalin's death. Borodin was sixty-seven. He had survived imprisonment and concentration camps for two years.

Although news of Borodin's death was allowed to filter out in 1953, it would be another decade before he would be officially rehabilitated, long after others involved in the Chinese revolution had been restored to the good graces of Soviet history. And then he was restored only because the regime, caught up in the politics of the Sino-Soviet split of the 1960s and 1970s, attempted to prove its long-standing concern for the revolution in China. On June 30, 1964, the eightieth anniversary of Borodin's birth, in the closing days of the "liberal" Khrushchev era, an article by General A. I. Cherepanov, who had become the chief chronicler of the Russian experience in China, appeared on an inside page of the Moscow newspaper *Moskovskaya pravda*. Entitled "A Revolutionary Leninist," and printed alongside a small photograph of Borodin in China, the article listed a few facts about Borodin's life and ended: "In February 1949, in the period of Stalin's cult of personality, M. M. Borodin was repressed and in 1951, he died. Now the party has reestablished his good name."[17] Two years later, in a volume of collected articles commemorating the one hundredth anniversary of Sun Yat-sen's birth, Fanya Borodin, who survived Mikhail Markovich by almost two decades, dictated a brief recollection of her husband's early life and his relationship with Sun Yat-sen to their second son Norman, who had become a journalist.[18]

Four years later, the Institute of the Far East of the Academy of Sciences of the USSR published a slim limited-edition volume, *Well-Known Soviet Communists—Participants of the Chinese Revolution*,[19] with chapters on Karakhan, Blyukher, Voitinsky, and Mif as well as Borodin. The Borodin chapter cited statements by Karakhan, Cherepanov, and even a CCP member lauding Borodin's service in China. But it also noted that "in those times, the activity of Borodin had its opponents, who subjected his work to serious criticism, especially in the Wuhan period of the Chinese revolution."[20]

In 1971, presumably in response to numerous unanswered queries about his father, Norman Borodin wrote an article, "Who Mikhail Borodin Was," which appeared in *Otchizna*, a Soviet newspaper directed at Russian expatriates. And in 1977, the introduction to a Soviet volume on the sovetniki in China noted that "unfortunately, the activities of M. M. Borodin and his sovetnik apparat are still very far from being adequately covered in our histories and memoirs."[21]

Even when Borodin has been mentioned, Soviet writers have rarely hinted at the remarkable role he played in the first decade of the international revolution and of the glory that was his when he towered over the Chinese scene: when 300,000 Chinese passed in review before him—Mikhail Markovich Gruzenberg of Yanovichi, Chicago, Canton, Wuhan, the star that glowed so brightly and briefly over China and whose burned-out embers now lie mixed with the soil outside a labor camp in Siberia.

PRINCIPAL SOURCES

NOTES

INDEX

Principal Sources

Archival Materials and Collections

Chicago, Chicago Public Library Omnibus Project (Works Project Administration). "Index to the Foreign Language Press of Chicago 1833–1936." Chicago, 1942.

London. Home Office. File on M. M. Borodin.

New York. Hiram Bingham Collection. Columbia University.

New York. Louis Corey Collection. Columbia Univeristy.

Stanford, California. Collection of Documents, Finnish People's Republic. Hoover Institution on War, Revolution and Peace.

Stanford, California. Jay Calvin Huston Collection. Hoover Institution on War, Revolution and Peace.

Stanford, California. Paris Files on Okhrana. Hoover Institution on War, Revolution and Peace.

Stanford, California. Correspondence of William Morris, 1928–1932. Hoover Institution on War, Revolution and Peace.

Valparaiso, Indiana. Records of Valparaiso University, 1908–1909.

Washington, D.C. Congress. House Committee on Un-American Activities, Hearings.

Washington, D.C. Department of State. "Decimal Archives, 1919–1939."

Articles and Pamphlets

Altshuler, Michael. Articles in *Chicago Daily Socialist*, 5–6 January 1912.

Bio-bibliographicheskii slovar. 1931 ed., s.v. "M. M. Borodin."

Blanshard, Paul. "The Future of the Chinese Revolution." *New Republic*, 7 September 1927: 63–66.

———— "An interview with Karakhan." *Nation*, 23 September 1925: 323–325.

Borodin, M. M. *Kommunisticheskii internatsional*, 18 (October 1921).

———— *Kommunisticheskii internatsional*, 19 (December 1921).

——— "Prichiny porazheniya kitaiskoi revolyutsii." *Izvestiya Ulan-Bator-Khoto*, 28 September 1927.

Borodin, N. M. "Kto byl Mikhail Borodin." *Otchizna*, 8 (1971): 9–11.

Bubnov, A. "O kitaiskoi revolyutsii." *Kommunisticheskaya revolyutsiya*, 8 (April 1927): 3–10.

Bulatsel, A. "Revolyutsionny plakat v grazhdanskoi voine Kitaya." *Novyi vostok*, 12 (1926): 196–201.

Chan, Fook-lam Gilbert. "Liao Chung-k'ai (1978–1925): The Career of a Chinese Revolutionary." *Essays on Chinese Studies*. Presented to Professor Lo Hsiang-lin on his retirement from the Chinese University of Hong Kong. Hong Kong: University of Hong Kong, 1970.

"Changsha under the Terror." *Living Age*, 1 July 1927: 22–25.

Cherepanov, A. I. *Moskovskaya pravda*, 30 June 1964.

Corey, Esther. "Passage to Russia." *Survey*, 53 (October 1964): 23–32.

——— "Passage to Russia, II." *Survey*, 55 (April 1965): 103–115.

Deyateli Revolyutsinnovo Dvizheniya v Rossii, V, part 1–2 (1931), 446–447, s.v. "M. M. Borodin."

Doriot, Jacques. "A French Red in China."*Living Age*, 1 September 1927: 402–407; 15 September 1927: 514–524.

Enloe, Cynthia. "Warlords and Commissars: China's Military Development." *Connecticut College Alumnai News*, Spring 1970: 5–10.

Fischer, Louis. "The Bear's Paw in China." *Independent*, 16 April 1927: 410–412.

——— "China—Seen From Moscow." *Nation*, 30 November 1927: 613–614.

Gannett, Lewis S. "Bolshevism in China?" *Nation*, 25 August 1926: 171–173.

——— "In Red Canton." *Asia*, June 1926: 482–492.

Garushyanits, Yu. "Novyi istochnik po istorii kitaiskoe revolyutsii." *Voprosy istorii*, 5 (1968): 106–108.

——— and E. Teslenko. "Pamyatnaya data v zhivi Kitaya." *Izvestiya*, 31 July 1967.

Godwin, Frank. "On the Scene." *Nation*, 27 April 1927: 475–477.

Gomez, Manuel (pseud.). "From Mexico to Moscow." *Survey*, 53 (October 1964): 3–47.

Hall, Thomas R. "The Russian Community of Chicago." *Papers in Illinois History, 1937*. Springfield: Illinois State Historical Society, 1938.

Ioffe, I. A. *Izvestiya*, 5 January 1923; 22 February 1923.

Iolk, E. "Letter from Hong Kong." *Novyi vostok*, 15 (1926): 278–292.

Jaffe, Philip. "The Strange Case of Anna Louise Strong." *Survey*, 53 (October 1964): 129–139.

Karakhan, L. "Zadachi vostokevedeniya." *Novyi vostok,* 7 (1925): 3-4.

Kartunovo, N. I. "V. K. Blykher v Kitae." *Narody Azii i Afriki,* 5 (1967): 144-147.

Kennan, George. "The Cost of Living." *McClure's Magazine,* March 1908: 639-650.

Keyes, Frances Parkinson. "The Contrasts of Canton." *Good Housekeeping,* June 1927: 66-67.

Khinoy, Mark. *Jewish Daily Forward,* 19 October 1954.

Kobozev, P. A. "Primechaniya k stat'e V. I. Nevskovo 'Yanvarskie dni 1905 goda v provintsii.'" *Krasnaya letopsis,* 2 (1924): 222-224.

Krarup-Nielsen, A. "Borodin's Swan Song." *Living Age,* 1 December 1927: 999-1004.

"Kto takoi Borodin," *Ogonek,* 26 June 1927.

Landis, Richard B. "The Origin of Whampoa Graduates Who Served in the Northern Expedition." *Studies on Asia 1964.* Lincoln: University of Nebraska Press, 1964.

Lau, P. T. "The Aims of Chinese Nationalists." *Annals of the American Academy of Political and Social Sciences,* 132 (July 1927): 72-79.

Lerner, Warren. "Karl Radek and the Chinese Revolution, 1925-1927." *Essays in Russian and Soviet History.* John S. Curtiss, ed. New York: Columbia University Press, 1963.

Little, John S. "The Revolutionary Spirit of the Yangtze." *Asia,* June 1927: 482-486.

McAleavy, H. "China and the War Lords." *History Today,* May 1926: 303-311.

Mann, Tom. "What I Saw in China." London: National Minority Movement, 1927.

"Massacre of Chinese People in Canton China by British and French Armed Men on June 23, 1925." Canton: Euro-American Returned Students Association of Kwangtung Province, 1925.

Meliksetov, A. V. "K otsenke vzglyadov Sun Yat-sena." *Narody Azii i Afriki,* 5 (1969): 80-91.

Murphy, J. T. "Reds in Congress: Preliminary Report of the First World Congress of the Red International of Trade and Industrial Unions." London, 1921.

Nevskii, V. "Yanvarskie dni 1905 goda v provintsii." *Krasnaya letopis,* 4 (1922): 103-113.

Nuorteva, Santeri. "An Open Letter to American Liberals." New York: Socialist Publication Society, 1918.

Ogonek, 26 June 1927.

Osetrov, A. F. "Velikii Oktyabr i kitaiskie rabochie na sovetskoi Ukraine." *Narody Azii i Afriki,* 2 (1967): 81-86.

Powell, John B. "Cleverest Revolutionist in the World Today!" *China Weekly Review*, 16 July 1927: 159–161.

Powers, H. H. "Amenities and Responsibilities." *Atlantic*, April 1927: 466–473.

Radek, K. "Osnovnye voprosy kitaiskoi istorii." *Novyi vostok*, 16–17 (1927): 1–53.

——— "Radek's Criticism of the Communist Party of Great Britain." *Communist Review*, December 1921: 105–106.

"Report of the Commission for the Investigation of the Shakee Massacre, June 23, 1925." Canton, 1925.

Roots, John McCook. "The Canton Idea." *Asia*, April 1927: 285–288.

——— "Chinese Head and Chinese Heart." *Asia*, February 1927: 91–97.

——— "The Moscow End of China-Soviet Affairs." *Asia*, June 1927: 463–478.

——— "The Will Has 150 Characters." *Asia*, May 1927: 362.

Roy, M. N. "Memoirs," *Radical Humanist*, 1953–1954.

Sanger, Richard H. "Life as a Russian Worker." *Foreign Service Journal*, June 1971: 14–19.

Scheffer, Paul. "Borodin's Home-Coming." *Living Age*, 15 September 1927: 503–506.

Shass, M. Review of Cherepanov and Vishnyakova-Akimova. *Novy mir*, 8 (1966): 274–277.

Sheean, Vincent. "Asia at Moscow." *Asia*, March 1928: 221–226.

——— "The Choice of Masters in China." *Asia*, November 1927: 938–942.

——— "The Disruption of the Kuomintang." *Asia*, August 1927: 625–629.

——— "Moscow and the Chinese Revolution." *Asia*, December 1927: 1004–1009.

———"Some People from Canton." *Asia*, October 1927: 812–817.

Sheridan, Clare. "Diary." *New York Times*, 23–27 November 1920.

Shirley, James A. "Control of KMT After Sun Yat-sen's Death." *Journal of Asian Studies*, 25 (November 1965): 69–82.

——— "Factionalism and the Left KMT." *Studies on Asia 1965*. Lincoln: University of Nebraska Press, 1965.

Sokolsky, George. "The Anti-Communist Government in Nanking." *Far Eastern Review*, May 1927: 191–193.

——— "How the Japanese Trouble Started." *Living Age*, 8 August 1925: 304–308.

Sorokin, G. Z. "S'ezd narodov dal'nevo vostoka." *Problemy vostokovedeniya*, 5 (1960): 76–86.

Souvarine, Boris. "Michel Borodine en Amerique." *Contrat social,* 10 (1966): 267–269.

Sovetskaya istoricheskaya entsiklopediya. 1962 ed., s.v. "M. M. Borodin."

"Soviet Plot in China." *Chinese Social and Political Science Review,* 2 (1927): 153–272.

Strong, Anna Louise. "Chang and Feng and Wu." *Asia,* July 1926: 596–601.

———— "Head-High-in-the Wind." *Harper's,* November 1927: 744–749.

———— "Motoring Out from China." *Asia,* September 1928: 708–713.

———— "Mrs. Sun Yat-sen Flees from Victory." *Survey,* 1 October 1928: 34–35.

———— "New Women of Old Canton." *Asia,* June 1926: 493–495.

———— "Old and New Gods in Mongolia." *Asia,* July 1928: 564–569.

———— "Some Hankow Memories." *Asia,* October 1928: 794– 797.

———— "What Canton Learned from Moscow." *Survey,* 7 November 1927: 139–141.

Sun Yat-sen. Interview, March 1924. *Narody Azii i Afriki,* 2 (1966): 138–140.

Sutton, Don. "Nationalism and Party Organization in the Kuomintang before Reorganization: The Communist Influence." London: Royal Institute of International Affairs, September 1965.

"Three Days of Terror at Canton." *Living Age,* 1 April 1928: 603–607.

Tobias, Henry J. "The Jews in Tsarist Russia: The Political Education of a Minority." In *Minorities and Politics.* Henry J. Tobias and Charles E. Woodhouse, eds. Albuqurque: University of New Mexico Press, 1969.

Treint, Albert. *New Militant,* 8 February 1936.

Ustinov, V. M. "Kitaiskie kommunisticheskie organizatsii v Sovetskoi Rossii (1918–1920 gg.)" *Voprosy istorii KPSS,* 4 (1961): 107–115.

"Vi Azoi Ikh Bin Gekumen tsum Bund." *Unzer Tseit,* 3 (1945): 55–63.

Voitinsky, G. *Pravda,* 15 March 1925.

Waln, Nora. "The Rise of the Chinese Nationalists." *Atlantic,* May 1927: 677–690.

Whiting, Allen S. "Mao-Stalin Crunch Caught Anna Louis Strong." *Washington Post,* 12 April 1970.

Wilbur, C. Martin. "Review of Borodin and the Wuhan Regime." *Journal of Asian Studies,* 24 (August 1965): 686–687.

Witkowski, Fritz. "How Canton and the Soviets Got Together." *China Weekly Review,* 8 January 1927: 145–146.

Wright, Quincy. "Bolshevist Influence in China." *Current History,* May 1927: 300–302.

Yurev, M. F. Review of Cherepanov. Narody Azii i Afriki, 2 (1970): 203–224.

Books

Abend, Hallet, *My Life in China, 1926–1941.* New York: Harcourt Brace, 1943.
—— *Tortured China.* New York: Ives, Washburn, 1930.
Addams, Jane. *The Second Twenty Years at Hull House.* New York: Macmillan, 1930.
—— *Twenty Years at Hull House.* New York: Macmillan, 1910.
Adzharov, A. *Klassy i partii sovremennovo Kitaya.* Moscow: Moskovskii Rabochii, 1926.
Akatova, T. N. *Syangan-Guanchshouskaya zabastovka.* Moscow: Izdatel'stvo Vostochnoi Literatury, 1959.
—— ed. *Rabochee dvizhenie v kitae: revolyutsiya 1924–1927. Sbornik dokumentov profsoyuznno dvizheniya i drugikh materialov.* Moscow: Izdatel'stvo Nauka, 1966.
Alsky, M. *Kanton pobezhdaet.* Moscow: Izdatel'stvo Kommunisticheskoi Akademii, 1927.
Asiaticus (pseud.), *Kanton Bis Schanghai, 1926–1927.* Berlin: Agis Verlag, 1928.
Bakulin, A. V. *Zapiski ob ukhanskoi periode kitaiskoi revolyutsii (iz istorii kitaiskoi revolyutsii, 1926–1927).* Moscow: Gosudarstvennoe Izdatel'stvo, 1930.
Balabanoff, Angelica. *My Life as a Rebel.* New York: Harper, 1938.
Beals, Carleton. *Glass Houses: Ten Years of Free-Lancing.* New York: Lippincott, 1928.
Bell, Thomas. *Pioneering Days.* London: Lawrence and Wishart, 1941.
Berkman, Alexander. *The Bolshevik Myth.* New York: Boni and Liveright, 1925.
Blagodatov, A. V. *Zapiski o kitaiskoi revolyutsii, 1925–1927 gg.* Moscow: Izdatel'stvo Nauka, 1970.
V. K. Blyukher v Kitae. 1924–1927 gg. Moscow: Izdatel'stvo Nauka, 1970.
Bonard, Abel. *In China.* New York: Dutton, 1927.
Borkenau, Franz, *World Communism.* New York: Norton, 1939.
Borodin, F. M. *Mirovaya voina, 1914–1918.* Moscow: Gosudarstvennoe Voennoe Izdatel'stvo Narkomata Oborony SSSR, 1939.
Borodin, F. S. *V zastenkakh kitaiskikh satrapov (moi vospaminaniya).* Moscow: Gosudarstvennoe Izdatel'stvo, 1928.
—— *Zhenschiny Kitae.* Moscow: Gosudarstvennoe Izdatel'stvo, 1928.
Borodin, M. M. *Istoriya velikoi izmeny.* Petersburg: Gosudarstvennoe Izdatel'stvo, 1922.
—— *Osnovnye voprosy bumazhnoi promyshlennosti.* Moscow: Gosudarstvennoe Tekhnicheskoe Izdatel'stvo, 1930.

—— ed. *Soviet Photography.* Moscow: State Publishing House for Cinematographical Literature, 1939.

—— *V boi za sovetskuyu bumagu.* Moscow: Gosudarstvennoe Nauchno-politicheskoe Izdatel'stvo, 1931.

Bourguina, Anna. *Russian Social Democracy: The Menshevik Movement: A Bibliography.* Stanford: Hoover Institution, 1968.

Brandt, Conrad. *Stalin's Failure in China.* Cambridge: Harvard University Press, 1958.

—— Benjamin Schwartz, and John K. Fairbank. *A Documentary History of Chinese Communism.* Cambridge: Harvard University Press, 1952.

Browder, Earl. *Civil War in Nationalist China.* Chicago: Labor Unity Publishing Association, 1927.

Bryant, Louise. *Mirrors of Moscow.* New York: Thomas Seltzer, 1923.

Bykov, D. V. *Komkor Pavlov.* Moscow: Izdatel'stvo Politicheskoi Literatury, 1965.

Carr, E. H. *The Bolshevik Revolution, 1917–1923.* 3 vols. New York: Macmillan, 1951, 1952, 1953.

—— *Foundations of a Planned Economy, 1926–1929.* Vol. 1, part 1. New York: Macmillan, 1971.

The Case of Leon Trotsky. New York: Harper, 1937.

Chang Kuo-tao. *Rise of the Chinese Communist Party, 1921–1927: Volume One of the Autobiography of Chang Kuo-tao.* Lawrence: University of Kansas Press, 1971.

Chapman, H. Owen. *The Chinese Revolution.* London: Constable, 1928.

Chen, Percy. *China Called Me: My Life Inside the Chinese Revolution.* Boston: Little Brown, 1979.

Cherepanov, A. I. *Severnyi pokhod natsional'no-revolyutsionnoi armii Kitaya.* Moscow: Izdatel'stvo Nauka, 1968.

—— *Zapiski voennovo sovetnika v Kitae.* Moscow: Izdatel'stvo Nauka, 1964.

—— *Zapiski voennovo sovetnika v Kitae.* 2nd ed. Moscow: Izdatel'stvo Nauka, 1971.

—— *Zapiski voennovo sovetnika v. Kitae.* 2nd ed. *Severnyi vokhod* and 1971 ed. of *Zapiski voennovo sovetnika* combined with a supplement on 1937–1938 campaign. Moscow: Izdatel'stvo Nauka, 1976.

Chesneaux, Jean. *The Chinese Labor Movement 1919–1927.* Stanford: Stanford University Press, 1968.

—— John Lust. *Introduction aux Etudes d'histoire contemporaine de Chine.* The Hague: Mouton, 1964.

Chiang Kai-shek. *Soviet Russia in China.* New York: Farrar, Straus and Cudahy, 1957.

Chiang Yung-ching. *Borodin and the Wuhan Regime, 1926–1927.* Taipei, 1966, in *Synopses of Monographical Studies in Chinese History and Social Science,* vol. 1 (Taipei, 1966).

China Year Book. 1923, 1924, 1925–26, 1926, 1928, 1929–30. Shanghai: North China Daily News and Herald.

Chudodeev, Yu. V., ed. *Na kitaiskoi zemle: vospominaniya sovetskikh dobrovol'tsev, 1925–1945.* 2nd ed. Moscow: Izdatel'stvo Nauka, 1977.

Communist International. *Der I Kongress der Kommunistischen internationale. Protokoll der Verhandlungen in Moskau vom 2. bis zum 19. Marz 1919.* Petrograd: Verlag der Kommunistischen Internationale, 1920.

———— *Der Zweite Kongress der Kommunist Internationale: Protokoll der Verhandlungen vom 19. Juli in Petrograd und vom 23. July bis 7. August 1920 in Moskau.* Hamburg: Carl Hoym, 1921.

———— *Protokoll des III Kongresses der Kommunistischen Internationale (Moskau, 22. Juni bis 12. Juli 1921).* Hamburg: Carl Hoym, 1921.

———— *Piatyi Vsemirnyi Kongress Kommunisticheskovo Internatsionale 17 Iyunia-8 Iyulia 1924g. Stenographicheskii otchet.* 2 vols. Moscow: Gosizdat, 1925.

———— *Rasshirenyi plenum ispolkoma Kommunisticheskovo Internationala 21 Marta-6 Aprelia 1925g. Stenographicheskii otchet.* Moscow: Gosizdat, 1925.

———— *Protokoll: Erweiterte Exekutive der Kommunistischen Internationale. Moskau, 17. Februar bis 15. Marz 1926.* Hamburg: Carl Hoym, 1926.

———— *Vii-e Session du Comite Executif Elangi de l'Internationale Communiste Novembre–Decembre 1926. Compte rendu stenographique.* Paris: La Correspondance Internationale, 1927.

Communist International Executive Committee. Report: "From the Fourth to the Fifth World Congresses." London: CPGB, 1924.

Curtis, Lionel. *Capital Questions of China.* London: Macmillan, 1932.

Dallin, S. A. *Molodezh v revolyutsionnom dvizhenie Kitaya.* Moscow: Novaya Moskva, 1925.

———— *Ocherki revolyutsii v Kitae.* Moscow: Moskovskii Rabochii, 1927.

———— *V ryadakh kitaiskoi revolyutsii.* Moscow: Moskovskii Rabochii, 1926.

Dallin, David. *The Rise of Russia in Asia.* New Haven: Yale University Press, 1949.

Davis, Allen F., and Mary Lynn McCree, eds. *Eight Years at Hull House.* Chicago: Quadrangle, 1969.

Degras, Jane, ed. *The Communist International.* 3 vols. London: Oxford University Press, 1956, 1960, 1965.

Deutscher, Isaac. *The Prophet Outcast: Trotsky, 1929–1940.* New York: Oxford University Press, 1963.

———— *The Prophet Unarmed: Trotsky, 1921–1929.* New York: Oxford University Press, 1959.

————*Stalin.* 2nd ed. New York: Oxford University Press, 1967.

Dipkur'ery. Moscow: Politizdat, 1973.

Domes, Jurgen. *Vertagte Revolution: Die Politik der Kuomintang in China, 1923–1937.* Berlin: Gruyter, 1969.

Drage, Charles. *The Life and Times of General Two-Gun Cohen.* New York: Funk and Wagnalls, 1954.

Draper, Theodore. *The Roots of American Communism.* New York: Viking, 1957.

———— *American Communism and Soviet Russia: The Formative Period.* New York: Viking, 1960.

Dushenkin, V. *Ot soldata do marshala.* 3rd ed. Moscow: Izdatel'stvo Politicheskoi Literatury, 1964.

Ermashev, I. *Sun Yat-sen.* Moscow: Molodaya Gvardia, 1964.

Erdberg, O. *Tales of Modern China.* Moscow: Cooperative Publishing Society of Foreign Workers in Moscow, 1932.

Etherton, P. T. *The Crisis in China.* Boston: Little, Brown, 1927.

Eudin, Xenia J., and Robert M. Slusser. *Soviet Foreign Policy 1928–1934.* Stanford: Stanford University Press, 1966.

Fairbank, John K. *The United States and China.* Cambridge: Harvard University Press, 1958.

Fischer, Louis. *The Life and Death of Stalin.* New York: Harper, 1952.

———— *The Life of Lenin.* New York: Harper and Row, 1964.

———— *Men and Politics.* New York: Duell, Sloan and Pearce, 1941.

———— *Russia's Road from War to Peace.* New York: Harper and Row, 1969.

———— *The Soviets in World Affairs.* Vol. 2. London: Jonathan Cape, 1930.

Fuse, K. *Soviet Policy in the Orient.* East Peking: Enjinsha, 1927.

Gallacher, William. *The Rolling of the Thunder.* London: Lawrence and Wishart, 1947.

Gannett, Lewis S. *Young China.* Rev. ed. New York: Nation, 1927.

Gayn, Mark J. *Journey from the East.* New York: Knopf, 1944.

Getzler, Israel. *Martov.* Cambridge, Eng.: Cambridge University Press, 1967.

Godes, M. *Shto takoe kemalistskii put i vozmozhen li on v Kitae?* Leningrad: Priboi, 1928.

Gompertz, G. H. *China in Turmoil: Eyewitness, 1924–1948.* London: Dent, 1967.

Gould, Randall. *China in the Sun.* New York: Doubleday, 1946.

Green, O. M. *The Story of China's Revolution.* London: Hutchinson, 1945.

Gross, Babette. *Willi Munzenberg: Eine politische Biographie.* Stuttgart: Deutsche Verlags-Anstalt, 1967.

Hahn, Emily. *China Only Yesterday.* New York: Doubleday, 1963.

Harrison, James P. *The Long March.* New York: Praeger, 1973.

Holcombe, Arthur N. *The Chinese Revolution.* Cambridge: Harvard University Press, 1930.

Hull House Year Book. Chicago, 1910, 1913.

Hulse, James W. *The Forming of the Communist International.* Stanford: Stanford University Press, 1964.

Internatsionalisty; Trudyashchiesya zarubezhnykh stran—uchastniki bor'by za vlast sovetov. Moscow: Izdatel'stvo Nauka, 1967.

Isaacs, Harold. *The Tragedy of the Chinese Revolution.* 2nd rev. ed. Stanford: Stanford University Press, 1961.

Itkina, A. M. *Revolyutsioner, tribun, diplomat.* 2nd ed. Moscow: Izdatel'stvo Politicheskoi Literatury, 1970.

Ivin, A. *Krasnye piki.* Moscow: Moskovskii Rabochii, 1927.

———— *Ot Khan'kou k Shankhayu.* Moscow: Moskovskii Rabochii, 1927.

———— *Pis'ma iz Kitaya.* Moscow: Moskovskii Rabochii, 1927.

Kantonskaya kommuna. Moscow: Izdatel'stvo Nauka, 1967.

Kapitsa, M. S. *Sovetsko-kitaiskie otnosheniya.* Moscow: Gosudarstvennoe Izdatel'stvo Politicheskoi Literatury, 1958.

Kazanin, M. I. *V shtabe Blyukhera: vospominaniya o kitaiskoi revolyutsii, 1924-1926gg.* Moscow: Izdatel'stvo Nauka, 1966.

Komintern: Kratkii istoricheskii ocherk. Moscow: Izdatel'stvo Politichoskoi Literatury, 1969.

Komintern i vostok. Moscow: Izdatel'stvo Nauka, 1969.

Konchits, N. I. *Kitaiskie dnevniki, 1925-1926gg.* Moscow: Izdatel'stvo Nauka, 1969.

Kostarev, N. *Moi kataiskie dnevniki.* 2nd ed. Leningrad: Priboi, 1928.

Krarup-Nielsen, A. *The Dragon Awakes.* New York: Dodd Mead, 1928.

Kuo, Warren. *Analytical History of the Chinese Communist Party.* Book 1. Taipei: Institute of International Relations, 1968.

Kuznetsov, N. A., and L. M. Kulagina. *Iz istorii sovetskovo vostokovedeniya, 1917-1967.* Moscow: Izdatel'stvo Nauka, 1970.

Lenin, V. I. *Polnoe sobranie sochinenii.* 5th ed., 55 vols. Moscow, 1958-1965. Citations in notes are to this entry, unless otherwise indicated.

———— *Lenin on Britain.* London: Martin Lawrence, 1934.

Lenin: Istoriko-biograficheskii atlas. Moscow: Institute Marksizma-Leninizma pri TsK KPSS, 1970.

Lenin v vospominaniyakh revolyutsionerov Latvii. Riga: Izdatel'stvo Liesma, 1969.

Leninskaya politika SSR v otneshenii Kitaya. Moscow: Izdatel'stvo Nauka, 1968.

Leninskii sbornik. Vols. 5, 26–36. Moscow: Various imprimatures, 1925–1959.

Lerner, Warren. *Karl Radek.* Stanford: Stanford University Press, 1968.

Linn, James Weber. *Jane Addams.* New York: Appleton-Century, 1935.

Lisochkin, J. B. *Pis'ma za okean.* Moscow: Izdatel'stvo Politicheskoi Literatury, 1965. First appeared in 1963 as *Po zadaniyu Il'icha—za okean.*

Liu, Yang-an, ed. and compiler. *Kitaiskii dobrovol'tsy v boyakh za sovetskuyu vlast (1918–1922gg).* Moscow: Izdatel'stvo Vostochnoi Literatury, 1961.

Lockhart, Bruce. *British Agent.* New York: Putnam, 1933.

Lozovsky, A., ed. *O Kitae: politiko-ekonomicheskii sbornik.* Moscow: Gosudarstvennoe Izdatel'stvo, 1928.

———— *The Pan-Pacific Trade Union Conference, Hankow, May 20–26, 1927.* Moscow: RILU, 1927.

———— ed. *Rabochii Kitae v 1927 godu.* Moscow: Izdanie Profinterna, 1928.

———— *Revolyutsiya i kontr-revolyutsiya v Kitae.* Moscow: Moskovskii Rabochii, 1927.

Lyons, Eugene. *Assignment in Utopia.* New York: Harcourt, Brace, 1937.

McNair, Harley Farnsworth. *China in Revolution.* Chicago: University of Chicago Press, 1931.

Malraux, André. *Anti-Memoirs.* New York: Holt, Rinehart and Winston, 1968.

———— *The Conquerers.* New York: Harcourt, Brace, 1929.

Marguilies, Sylvia R. *Pilgrimage to Russia: The Soviet Union and the Treatment of Foreigners 1924–1937.* Madison: Univeristy of Wisconsin Press, 1968.

Mif, P. A. *Kitaiskaya kommunisticheskaya partiya v kriticheskie dni.* Moscow: Gosudarstvennoe Izdatel'stvo, 1928.

———— *Uroki shankhaiskikh sobytii.* Moscow: Gosudarstvennoe Izdatel'stvo, 1926.

Mirovitskaya, R. A. *Dvizhenie v Kitae za priznanie Sovetskoi Rossii (1920–1924).* Moscow: Izdatel'stvo Vostochnoi Literatury, 1962.

Misselwitz, Henry F. *The Dragon Stirs: An Intimate Sketch-Book of China's Kuomintang Revolution 1927–29.* New York: Harbinger House, 1941.

Mitarevsky, N. *World Wide Soviet Plots.* Tientsin: Tientsin Press, 1927.

Mitgang, Herbert. *The Letters of Carl Sandburg.* New York: Harcourt, Brace and World, 1968.

Murphy, James T. *New Horizons.* London: John Lane, 1941.

—— *Preparing for Power.* London: Jonathan Cape, 1934.

Netosin, Yu. N. *Rabochee dvizhenie v Rige v period stolypinskoi reaktsii.* Riga: Izdatel'stvo Akademii Nayk Latviiskoi SSR, 1958.

North, Robert C. *Moscow and Chinese Communists.* 2nd ed. Stanford: Stanford University Press, 1963.

—— and Xenia J. Eudin. *M. N. Roy's Mission to China: The Communist-Kuomintang Split of 1927.* Berkeley: University of California Press, 1963.

Osetrov, A. F. *Sovetskii narod—revolyutsionnomy Kitayu, 1924–1927.* Moscow: Izdatel'stvo Nauka, 1967.

Oudendyk, W. J. *Ways and By-Ways in Diplomacy.* London: Peter Davies, 1939.

Pelling, Henry. *The British Communist Party: A Historical Profile.* London: Block, 1958.

Pick, Eugene (pseud.). *China in the Grip of the Reds.* Shanghai: North China Daily News and Herald, 1927.

Pis'ma V. I. Leniny iz-za rubezha. Moscow: Izdatel'stvo Mysl, 1969.

Polacy o Leninie: wspomnienia. Warsaw: Ksiazka i Wiedza, 1970.

Politt, Harry. *Serving My Time.* London: Lawrence and Wishart, 1940.

Powell, John B. *My Twenty-Five Years in China.* New York: Macmillan, 1945.

Primakov, V. M. *Zapiski volontera: grazhdanskaya voina v Kitae.* Moscow: Izdatel'stvo Nauka, 1967. Originally published in 1927 with "G. Allen" listed as author.

Rabochii Kitai v bor'be protiv imperializma. Report of the First Trade-Union Delegation. Moscow: VTsSPS, 1927.

Rabochee dvizhenie v Kitae 1924–1927gg.: Sbornik dokumentov profsoyuznovo dvizheniya i drugikh materialov. Moscow: Izdatel'stvo Nauka, 1966.

Rafes, M. *Kitaiskaya revolyutsiya na perelome.* 3rd rev. ed. Moscow: Moskovskii Rabochii, 1927.

Ransome, Arthur. *Chinese Puzzle.* London: Allen and Unwin, 1927.

—— *Six Weeks in Russia in 1919.* London: Allen and Unwin, 1919.

Register of Valparaiso University, 1908–1909. Valparaiso, Indiana, 1910.

Rice, Edward E. *Mao's Way.* Berkeley: University of California Press, 1972.

Roy, M. N. *Kitaiskaya revolyutsiya i kommunisticheskii internatsional: sbornik statei i materialov.* Moscow: Gosudarstvennoe Izdatel'stvo, 1929.

—— *Memoirs.* Bombay: Allied Publishers Private, 1964.

—— *My Experience in China.* Calcutta: Renaissance Publishers, 1945.

———— *Revolution and Counter-Revolution in China*. Calcutta: Renaissance Publishers, 1946.

Salisbury, Harrison. *Moscow Journal*. Chicago: University of Chicago Press, 1961.

———— *War Between Russian and China*. New York: Norton, 1969.

Sapozhnikov, B. G. *Pervaya grazhdanskaya revolyutsionnaya voina v Kitae 1924-1927gg*. Moscow: Gosudarstvennoe Izdatel'stvo Politicheskoe Literatury, 1954.

Schmitt, Karl M. *Communism in Mexico*. Austin: University of Texas Press, 1965.

Schwartz, Benjamin I. *Chinese Communism and the Rise of Mao*. Cambridge: Harvard University Press, 1951.

Schwartz, Solomon. *The Russian Revolution of 1905*. Chicago: University of Chicago Press, 1967.

Serge, Victor. *Memoirs of a Revolutionary, 1901-1941*. New York: Oxford University Press, 1963.

Shamsutdinov, A. M. *Natsional'no osvoboditel'naya bor'ba v Turtsii, 1918-1923*. Moscow: Izdatel'stvo Nauka, 1966.

Shannon, David A. *The Socialist Party of America*. New York: Macmillan, 1955.

Sharmon, Lyon. *Sun Yat-sen. His Life and Its Meaning*. Stanford: Stanford University Press, 1934, 1968.

Sheean, Vincent. *Personal History*. New York: Doubleday, 1934.

Sheridan, Clair. *Mayfair to Moscow: Clair Sheridan's Diary*. New York: Boni and Liveright, 1921.

———— *Nuda Veritas*. London: Thornton Butterworth, 1927.

Sheridan, James E. *Chinese Warlord: The Career of Feng Yü-hsiang*. Stanford: Stanford University Press, 1966.

Snow, Edgar. *Red Star over China*. New York: Random House, 1938.

Sovetskie dobrovol'tsy v pervoi grazhdanskoi revolyutsionnoi voine v Kitae: vospominaniya. Moscow: Izdatel'stvo Nauka, 1961.

Sovetsko-kitaiskie otnosheniya 1917-1957: sbornik dokumentov. Moscow: Izdatel'stvo Literatury, 1959.

Spence, Jonathan. *To Change China*. Boston: Little, Brown, 1969.

Spolansky, Jacob. *The Communist Trail in America*. New York: Macmillan, 1951.

Strietelmeier, John. *Valparaiso's First Century*. Valparaiso, Indiana: The University, 1959.

Strong, Anna Louise. *China's Millions*. New York: Coward-McCann, 1928.

———— *I Change Worlds: The Remaking of an American*. New York: Holt, 1935.

———— *The Stalin Era.* New York: Mainstream, 1956.

Sun Yat-sen, 1866–1966. K stoletiyu so dyna razhdeniya: sbornik statei, vospominanii i materialov. Moscow: Izdatel'stvo Nauka, 1966.

T'ang, Leang-li. *Inner History of the Chinese Revolution.* London: Routledge, 1930.

Tikhvinsky, S. L., *Istoriya Kitaya i sovremennost.* Moscow: Izdatel'stvo Nauka, 1976.

———— *Sun Yat-sen: Vneshnopoliticheskie vozzreniya i praktika.* Moscow: Izdatel'stvo Mezhdunarodnye Otnosheniya, 1964.

Trotsky, L. D. *Problems of the Chinese Revolution.* New York: Pioneer, 1931.

Vidnye sovetskie kommunisty—uchastniki kitaiskoi revolyutsii. Moscow: Izdatel'stvo Nauka, 1970.

Vishnyakova-Akimova, V. V. *Dva goda v vosstavshem Kitae 1925–1927: Vospominaniya.* Moscow: Izdatel'stvo Nauka, 1965.

Vospominanya o V. I. Lenine. 5 vols. Moscow: Gosudarstvennoe Izdatel'stvo Politicheskoi Literatury, 1956.

Wales, Nym. *Red Dust.* Stanford: Stanford University Press, 1952.

Waln, Nora. *The House of Exile.* Boston: Little, Brown, 1933.

Whiting, Allen S. *Soviet Policies in China, 1917–1924.* New York: Columbia University Press, 1954.

Wilbur, C. Martin, and Julie Lienying How, eds. *Documents on Communism, Nationalism, and Soviet Advisors in China, 1918–1927.* New York: Columbia University Press, 1956.

Wolfe, Bertram D. *Three Who Made a Revolution.* New York: Dial, 1948.

Woo, T. C. *The KMT and the Future of the Chinese Revolution.* London: Allen and Unwin, 1928.

Yurev, M. F. *Krasnaya armiya Kitaya.* Moscow: Izdatel'stvo Vostnochnoi Literatury, 1958.

———— *Revolyutsiya 1925–1927 v. Kitae.* Moscow: Izdatel'stvo Nauka 1968.

———— *Rol revolyutsionnoi armii na pervom etape kitaiskoi revolyutsii.* Moscow: Izdatel'stvo Moskovskovo Universiteta, 1952.

Zdes zhil i rabotal Lenin. Moscow: Izdatel'stvo Politicheskoi Literatury, 1966.

Zhukovsky, N. *Posol novovo mira.* Moscow: Izdatel'stvo Politicheskoi Literatury, 1978.

Newspapers and Journals

Asia. 1927–1929.
Chicago Daily Socialist. 1906–1912.

Chicago Evening World. 1912–1918.
Chicago Tribune. 1917–1918, 1925–1928.
China Weekly Review. 1920–1927.
Christian Science Monitor. 1926–1927.
Current History. 1927.
International Press Correspondence. 1921–1928.
Izvestiya. 1923–1927.
Izvestiya Ulan-Bator-Khoto. September–October 1927.
Kommunisticheskii internatsional. 1921–1928.
Living Age. 1927.
London Times. 1922–1927.
Moscow Daily News. 1 May 1932—21 February 1938.
Moscow News. 1930–1948.
New York Times. 1923–1928
Outlook. 1926–1927.
People's Tribune. 12 March—18 August 1927.
Problmy Kitaya. 1929–1935.
Trans-Pacific. 1925–1927.
Workers News. 4 February 1931—28 April 1932.

Unpublished Manuscripts

Bing, Dov. "Revolution in China: Sneevlietian Strategy." Master's thesis, University of Auckland, New Zealand, 1968.

Holubnychy, Lydia, "Michael Borodin and the Chinese Revolution, 1923–1925." Unfinished dissertation, Columbia University, 1979.

Kagan, Richard Clark. "The Chinese Trotskyite Movement and Ch'en Tu-siu: Culture Revolution and Polity, with an appended translation of Ch'en Tu'hsiu's autobiography." Dissertation, University of Pennsylvania, 1969.

Shirley, James A. "Political Conflict in the Kuomintang: The Career of Wang Ching-wei to 1932." Dissertation, University of California (Berkeley), 1962.

Shirtzinger, Dorothy. "Borodin in China, 1923–1927." Master's thesis, University of Southern California, 1964.

Smith, Carlyle A. "Borodin and the Chinese Revolution." Master's thesis, Claremont Graduate School, 1963.

Sorich, R. "Fragments in Biography of M. N. Roy." Hoover Institution on War, Revolution and Peace, Stanford, California, 1953.

Tobias, Henry J. "The Origins and Evolution of the Jewish Bund Until 1901." Dissertation, Stanford University, 1957.

Wilbur, C. Martin. "Forging the Weapons: Sun Yat-sen and the Kuomintang in Canton, 1924." Preliminary Report, Columbia University Seminar on Modern East Asia: China, 19 February 1966.
————— "Sun Yat-sen and Soviet Russia, 1922–1924." Preliminary Report, Columbia University Seminar on Modern East Asia: China, 10 March 1965.

Notes

1. Out of the Pale

1. N. Borodin, "Kto byl Mikhail Borodin," *Otchizna*, 8 (1971), 9–11.

2. R. A. Mirovitskaya, "Mikhail Borodin," in *Vidnye sovetski kommunisty—uchastniki kitaiskoi revolyutsii* (Moscow, 1970), p. 23.

3. N. K. Krupskaya, *Reminiscences of Lenin* (New York, 1970), p. 111.

4. V. Nevsky, "Yanvarskie dni 1905 g. v provintsii," *Krasnaya letopis*, 4 (1922), 112.

5. P. A. Kobozev, "Primechaniya k stat'e V. I. Nevskovo 'Noyabrski dni 1905 goda v provinstii,' " *Krasnaya letopis*, 2 (1924), 222.

2. The 1905 Revolution

1. Krupskaya, *Reminiscences of Lenin*, p. 141.

3. The New World

1. *Daily Telegraph*, 17 October 1906.

2. Much of what is known about the Russian socialist community in Chicago during the decades before World War I comes from the collection of materials and interviews that was assembled in the 1930s by the Chicago Public Library, using the facilities of the University of Chicago and under the sponsorship of the Works Projects Administration. In an article in *Papers in Illinois History, 1937* (Springfield, Ill., 1938) the director of the project, Thomas Randolph Hall, recalls the great difficulties the project had in locating materials. Investigators were sent into "damp basements and dusty attics" only "to find the junkman had been there before them, or that carelessness, aided by fire and dampness, had destroyed records which could not be replaced" (p.

102). Even when the researchers were able to find clippings, letters, and such, they had to convince their owners they would not be used against them. Probably the most valuable source of materials for the project came from the scrapbooks of, by then, Dr. Henry Krasnow, Borodin's old friend.

3. *Eighty Years at Hull House,* Allen F. Davis and Mary Lynn McCree, eds. (Chicago, 1969), p. 142.

4. Jane Addams, *Twenty Years at Hull House* (New York, 1910), p. 402.

5. Hyman Bolotin, interview, "Index to the Foreign Language Press of Chicago, 1833–1936," Chicago Public Library Omnibus Project (Works Projects Administration; Chicago, 1942); hereafter cited as Chicago Public Library–WPA Project; II B2f/IV.

6. Henry Krasnow, interview, Chicago Public Library–WPA Project, II B2g/IV.

7. Anna Bourguina, *Russian Social Democracy: The Menshevik Movement: A Bibliography* (Stanford, 1968), p. 337. That the *Rabochii* is listed in the 1960s as a Menshevik publication proves little about Borodin's affiliations in 1908–09 since party distinctions were blurred at this time, though it does indicate willingness to cooperate with a variety of revolutionary groups. It seems unlikely, however, that he would have mentioned it in the 1920s if he had recalled it as being Menshevik.

8. *Chicago Daily Socialist,* 5 January 1912.

9. Mark Khinoy, *Jewish Daily Forward,* 19 October 1954.

10. Henry Krasnow, interview, Chicago Public Library–WPA Project, II B2g/IV.

4. On the Brink of Decision

1. Henry Krasnow, interview, Chicago Public Library–WPA Project, II B2g/IV.

2. Ibid.

3. L. D. Trotsky, *My Life: An Attempt at an Autobiography. (New York,* 1930), p. 278.

4. A. M. Itkina, *Revolyutsioner, tribun, diplomat.* (Moscow, 1970). p. 109.

5. V. I. Lenin, *Polnoe sobranie sochinenii,* 5th ed. (Moscow, 1964), XLIX, 163n**.

6. Trotsky, *My Life,* p. 277.

7. *Russkaya pochta,* 28 April 1917, Chicago Public Library–WPA Project, IE/IV.

8. *Russkaya pochta,* 26 May 1917, Chicago Public Library–WPA Project, IE-IC/IV.

9. *Novyi mir* (New York), 6 July 1917, Chicago Public Library–WPA Project, IE/IC/IIIC.

10. *Russkaya pochta,* 14 July 1917, Chicago Public Library–WPA Project, IE.

11. *Chicago Tribune,* 5 August 1917.

12. *Novyi mir,* 15 August 1917, Chicago Public Library–WPA Project, IE/IV.

13. *Chicago Tribune,* 5 August 1917.

5. Back in the Fray

1. V. I. Lenin, *Collected Works* (Moscow, 1965), XXVIII, 52–53.

2. Ibid., p 62.

3. Ibid., pp. 72, 74–75.

4. Herbert Mitgang, *The Letters of Carl Sandburg* (New York, 1968), pp. 134–135.

5. Ibid., p. 144.

6. Ibid., p. 145.

7. Letter from Nuorteva to Granville McFarland, 28 January 1919, in the collection of Finnish People's Republic Documents, Hoover Institution on War, Peace, and Revolution, Stanford, California.

8. U.S. Department of State, *Diplomatic Dispatches from USSR,* telegram 1544, to the Secretary of State from the American Embassy in Christiana, 30 January 1919.

9. Great Britain, Home Office, File on M. M. Borodin, document 436.947/11.

10. Angelica Balabanoff, *My Life as a Rebel* (New York 1938), p. 222.

6. Comintern Agent

1. Jane Addams, *The Second Twenty Years at Hull House* (New York, 1930), p. 149.

2. Spolansky's memory is very bad on some points, and he writes with great license. Much of what he states is not to be trusted, but what is related here seems plausible. Jacob Spolansky, *The Communist Trail in America* (New York, 1951).

3. U.S. Congress, House, Committee on Un-American Activities, Hearings, 76th Cong. 1st sess., 1939, vol. 8, pp. 5157–5159.

4. Theodore Draper, *The Roots of American Communism* (New York, 1957), pp. 240–241n25, pp. 434–435. Draper got the story from Max Eastman.

5. Manuel Gomez (pseud.), "From Mexico to Moscow," *Survey,* 53 (October 1964), 35.

6. M. N. Roy, *Memoirs* (Bombay, 1964), pp. 170–175.

7. Ibid., p. 195.

8. Manuel Gomez, *Survey,* p. 36.

9. Roy, *Memoirs,* p. 195.

10. Ibid., p 215.

11. Manuel Gomez, *Survey,* p. 38.

12. J. T. Murphy, *New Horizons* (London, 1941), p. 89.

7. Apparatchik

1. Murphy, *New Horizons,* p. 118.

8. Assignment in England

1. Karl Radek, "Radek's Criticism of Communist Party of Great Britain," *Communist Review* (London), 2 (December 1921), 105–106.

2. Ibid., p. 105.

3. *Komunisticheskii internatsional,* 18 (18 October 1921), and 19 (21 December 1921).

4. M. M. Borodin, *Istorii velikoi izmeny* (Petrograd, 1922).

5. V. I. Lenin, *Lenin on Britain* (London, 1934), p. 271.

6. Great Britain, Home Office, File on M. M. Borodin, documents 436.947/2 and 436.947/11.

7. Ibid., 436.947/2.

8. Ibid., 436.947/8.

9. Ibid., 436.947/11.

10. Ibid., 436.947/4.

11. Ibid 436.947/11.

9. To Canton

1. N. Borodin, *Otchizna,* p. 10.

2. M. F. Yurev, "Ustanovlenie sotrudnichestva mezndu KPK i Sun Yat-senom v 1921–1924 gg.," in *Sun Yat-sen, 1866–1966: K stoletiyu so dnya rozhdeniya,* S. L. Tikhvinsky, ed. (Moscow, 1966), p. 147.

3. Dov Bing, "Revolution in China: Sneevlietian Strategy" (Master's thesis, University of Auckland, New Zealand, 1968), p. 73.

4. Lenin, *Polnoe sobranie sochinenii,* XXI, 406.

5. R. A. Mirovitskaya, "Pervoe desyatletie," in *Leninskaya politika SSSR v otnoshenii Kitaya* (Moscow, 1968), p. 26. Mirovitskaya had access to the archives of the Military Section.

6. Ibid.

7. N. Borodin, *Otchizna*, p. 10.

8. "Kto takoi Bordin?" *Ogonek*, June 26, 1927.

9. N. Borodin, *Otchizna*, p. 10.

10. Ibid.

11. S. L. Tikhvinsky, *Sun Yat-sen: Vneshnepoliticheskie vozzreniya i praktika* (Moscow, 1964), p. 278.

12. M. S. Kapitsa, "Lev Karakhan," *Vidnye*, pp. 12–13.

13. Allen S. Whiting, *Soviet Policies in China, 1917–1924* (New York, 1954), p. 243. From Louis Fischer's personal files.

14. Great Britain, Home Office, File on M. M. Borodin, document 436.947/21.

15. N. Mitarvesky, *World Wide Soviet Plots* (Tientsen, 1927) p. 131.

16. Ibid.

17. Ibid., p. 133.

18. Ibid., p. 137.

19. A. I. Cherepanov, *Zapiski voennovo sovetnika v Kitae* (Moscow, 1964), p. 37; hereafter cited as Cherepanov, I.

20. Ibid., I, 36.

21. Mitarvesky, *World Wide Soviet Plots*, p. 137.

22. Cherepanov, I, 38.

23. Ibid., I, 42.

24. M. I. Kazanin, *V shtabe Blyukhera: vospominaniya o kitaiskoi revolyutsii, 1924–1926 gg.* (Moscow, 1966), p. 127

25. I. Ermashev, *Sun Yat-sen* (Moscow, 1964), p. 270.

26. A. I. Kartunova, "Komintern i nekotorye voprosy reorganizatsii gomin'dana," *Komintern i vostok* (Moscow, 1969), p. 309.

27. Cherepanov, I, 57–58.

28. Ibid., p. 59.

29. Kartunova, *Komintern i vostok*, p. 310.

30. Chang Kuo-t'ao, *The Rise of the Chinese Communist Party, 1921–1927*, I (Lawrence, Kansas, 1971), 329.

31. Kartunova, *Komintern i vostok*, p. 309.

32. Glunin, *Komintern i vostok*, p. 261.

33. Cherepanov, I, 71.

34. Ibid., I, 77.

35. Yurev, *Sun Yat-sen, 1866–1966*, p. 164.

36. Cherepanov, I, 78.

10. Setting the Stage

1. V. V. Vishnyakova-Akimova, *Dva goda v vosstavshem Kitae, 1925–1927: Vospominaniya* (Moscow, 1965), pp. 179–180.

2. Kartunova, "Sun Yat-sen i russkie sovetniki po dokumentam, 1923–1924 gg.," *Sun Yat-sen, 1866–1966,* p. 176.

3. Kartunova, *Komintern i vostok,* p. 306.

4. Kartunova, *Sun Yat-sen 1866–1966,* p. 180.

5. Kartunova, *Vidnye,* p. 55. The statement is by Blyukher.

6. Cherepanov, "Pod znamenami Sun Yat-sena," *Sun Yat-sen, 1866–1966,* p. 316.

7. Nora Waln, *The House of Exile* (Boston, 1933), p. 204.

8. C. Martin Wilbur, "Forging the Weapons: Sun Yat-sen and the Kuomintang in Canton, 1924" (Preliminary Report, Columbia University Seminar on Modern East Asia, China, 19 February 1966), p. 47.

9. Lewis S. Gannett, "In Red Canton," *Asia,* June 1926, p. 42.

10. André Malraux, *The Conquerors* (New York, 1929), p. 234.

11. First Steps

1. Blyukher's cover name was taken from the first syllables of his wife's Christian name and patronymic.

2. *China Weekly Review,* 29 November 1924.

3. Chang Kuo-t'ao, *The Rise of the Chinese Communist Party,* pp. 391–392.

4. Glunin, *Komintern i vostok,* p. 280.

5. Chang Kuo-t'ao, *The Rise of the Chinese Communist Party,* p. 394.

6. *Peking Leader,* 23 October 1925, in the Jay Calvin Huston Collection, Hoover Institute on War, Peace and Revolution, Stanford University.

7. N. Borodin, *Otchizna,* p. 11.

8. T'ang Liang-li, *Inner History of the Chinese Revolution* (London, 1930), p. 197n.

9. Lyon Sharman, *Sun Yat-sen, His Life and Its Meaning* (New York, 1934), p. 307.

10. Ho Hsiang-ning, *Vospominaniya o Sun Yat-sene* (Moscow, 1966), p. 98; first published in China, 1957.

11. M. S. Kapitsa, *Sovetsko-kitaiskie otnosheniya* (Moscow, 1958), p. 144.

12. Cherepanov, I, 152.

13. Ibid., I, 146.

12. Victory Without Success

1. Chang Kuo-t'ao, *The Rise of the Chinese Communist Party,* p. 455.

2. Ibid., p. 448.

3. O. M. Green, *The Story of China's Revolution* (London, 1945), p. 95.

4. Jean Chesneaux, *The Chinese Labor Movement, 1919–1927* (Stanford, 1968), p. 293.

5. Mirovitskaya, *Leninskaya politika SSSR v otnoshenii Kitaya*, p. 34.

6. Cherepanov, I, 246.

7. C. Martin Wilbur and Julie Lien-Ying How, *Documents on Communism, Nationalism and Soviet Advisors in China, 1918–1927* (New York, 1956), p. 212.

8. A. Kimileff, "Journey to Canton in October, 1925," in the Jay Calvin Huston Collection.

13. Holding On in Canton

1. A. I. Cherepanov, *Severnyi pokhod natsional'no-revolyutsionnoi armii Kitaya* (Moscow, 1968), pp. 9–16; hereafter cited as Cherepanov, II.

2. It may seem unusual for a Russian revolutionary to call his sons Fred and Norman, but it shows the extent of Borodin's Americanization prior to his decision to return to the revolution in 1918.

3. Cherepanov, II, 24

4. Ibid., II, 26.

5. Ibid., II, 28.

6. Mirovitsakaya, *Leninskaya politika SSSR v otnoshenii Kitaya*, p. 34.

7. Ibid., p. 36.

8. Wilbur and How, *Documents on Communism, Nationalism and Soviet Advisors in China*, p.251.

9. Cherepanov, II, 106.

10. Ibid., II, 66.

11. Ibid., II, 64.

12. Ibid., II, 60.

13. Ibid., II, 69.

14. Wilbur and How, *Documents on Communism, Nationalism and Soviet Advisors in China*, p. 220. Chiang Kai-shek, *Soviet Russia in China* (New York, 1957), p. 39. Vishnyakova-Akimova, *Dva goda v vosstavshem Kitae, 1925–1927*, p. 240.

15. Cherepanov, II, 84–85.

16. Wilbur and How, *Documents on Communism, Nationalism and Soviet Advisors in China*, p. 252.

17. Ibid., p. 254.

18. Cherepanov, II, 58.

19. Chang Kuo-t'ao, *The Rise of the Chinese Communist Party*, p. 506.

20. Ibid., pp. 511–512.

21. Cherepanov, II, 127–128.

22. V. K. Blyukher, "Perspktivy dal'neishei raboty na yuge ili bol'shoi plan voennoi raboty gomin'dana na 1926 g.," *V. K. Blyukher v Kitae, 1924–1927 gg.* (Moscow, 1970), pp. 161–171.

23. Ibid., p. 170.

24. Cherepanov, II, 142.

14. The Northern Expedition

1. A. Bulatsel, "Revolyutsionny plakat v grazhdanskoi voine Kitaya," *Novyi vostok,* 12 (1926), 200.

2. Louis Fischer, *Russia's Road from War to Peace* (New York, 1969), p. 128.

3. S. A. Dalin, *Ocherki revolyutsii v Kitae* (Moscow-Leningrad, 1927).

4. Ibid., p. 95.

5. Ibid., p. 151.

6. Ibid., p. 153.

7. Chang Kuo-T'ao, *The Rise of the Chinese Communist Party,* p. 558.

15. The Wuhan Experience

1. Chang Kuo-t'ao, *The Rise of the Chinese Communist Party,* p. 566.

2. Cherepanov, II, 208.

3. A. V. Bakulin, *Zapiski ob ukhan'skom periode kitaiskoi revolyutsii* (Moscow-Leningrad, 1930), p. 41.

4. A. V. Blagodatov, *Zapiski o kitaiskoi revolyutsii, 1925–1927 gg.* (Moscow, 1970), p. 162.

5. Cherepanov, II, 295.

6. Blagodatov *Zapiski o kitaiskoi revolyutsii, 1925–1927 gg.,* pp. 43–44.

7. Ibid., p. 50.

8. Cherepanov, II, 218.

9. A. Lozovsky, *Revolyutsiya i kontr-revolyutsia v Kitae* (Moscow, 1927), p. 70.

10. M. E. Shass, "God raboty v revolyutsionnom Kitae (iz vospominanii finansovo sovetnika)," *Na kitaiskoi zemle, Vospominaniya sovetskikh dobrovol'tsev, 1925–1945,* ed. Yu. V. Chudodeev (Moscow, 1977), p. 140.

11. *People's Tribune,* 1 April 1927.

12. Ibid., 19 March 1927.

13. Ibid., 15 March 1927.

14. Ibid., 16 March 1927.

15. M. F. Yurev, *Revolyutsiya 1925–1927 v Kitae* (Moscow, 1968), p. 471.

16. Harold R. Isaacs, *The Tragedy of the Chinese Revolution,* 2nd rev. ed. (Stanford, 1961), p. 163.

16. The Hard Truth

1. Warren Kuo, *Analytical History of the Chinese Communist Party,* I, (Taipei, 1968), 313.

2. *People's Tribune,* 17 April 1927.

3. Ibid., 24 April 1927.

4. Chang Kuo-t'ao, *The Rise of the Chinese Communist Party,* p. 590.

5. Quoted in Isaacs, *The Tragedy of the Chinese Revolution,* p. 502.

6. Eugene Pick, *China in the Grip of the Reds* (Shanghai, 1927), p. 28.

7. Vincent Sheean, "Some People from Canton," *Asia,* October 1927, p. 812.

8. Kazanin, *V shtabe Blyukhera,* p. 127.

9. Vincent Sheean, *Personal History* (New York, 1934), p. 231.

10. Randall Gould, *China in the Sun* (New York, 1946), p. 69.

11. Kazanin, *V shtabe Blyukhera,* p. 125.

12. Ibid.

13. Shass, *Na kitaiskoi zemle,* p. 135.

14. Kazanin, *V shtabe Blyukhera,* p. 125.

15. *People's Tribune,* 29 April 1927.

16. *Guide Weekly,* quoted in Dalin, *Ocherki revolyutsii v Kitae,* p. 190.

17. Tom Mann, *What I Saw in China* (London, 1927), p. 24.

18. Chang Kuo-t'ao, *The Rise of the Chinese Communist Party,* p. 604.

19. Ts'ai Ho-sen, "History," in Wang Chien-min, *Draft History of the CCP* (Taipei, 1965), I, 494, quoted in James P. Harrison. *The Long March to Power* (New York, 1972), p. 109.

20. Vishnyakova-Akimova, *Dva goda v vosstavshem Kitae,* p. 354.

21. Isaacs, *The Tragedy of the Chinese Revolution,* p. 185.

22. J. V. Stalin, "The Revolution in China and the Tasks of the Comintern," *Works* (Moscow, 1946), IX, 300.

23. Albert Treint, *New Militant,* 8 February 1936.

24. Chang Kuo-t'ao, *The Rise of the Chinese Communist Party,* p. 637.

25. Ibid., p. 638.

26. Jay Calvin Huston, "Sun Yat-sen, the Kuomintang and the

Chinese-Russian Political Economic Alliance," Hoover Institute on War, Peace and Revolution, Stanford University, p. 187.

27. M. N. Roy, *Revolution and Counter-Revolution in China* (Calcutta, 1946), p. 552n.

28. Ibid., pp. 552–553n.

29. Ibid., p. 520n.

30. M. N. Roy, *My Experience in China* (Calcutta, 1945), p. 49.

31. Ibid., pp. 53, 51.

32. T'ang Liang-li, *Inner History of the Chinese Revolution*, p. 281.

17. Going Home

1. Mitarevsky, *World Wide Soviet Plots*, p. 22.

2. Chang Kuo-t'ao, *The Rise of the Chinese Communist Party*, p. 647.

3. *People's Tribune*, 14 June 1927.

4. James E. Sheridan, *Chinese Warlord: The Career of Feng Yü-hsiang* (Stanford, 1966), p. 227.

5. A. Krarup-Nielsen, "Borodin's Swan Song," *Living Age*, 1 December 1927, p. 1001.

6. Ibid., p. 1003.

7. Anna Louise Strong, *I Change Worlds: The Remaking of an American* (New York, 1935), p. 254.

8. *People's Tribune*, 8 July 1927.

9. Ibid., 2 July 1927.

10. Anna Louise Strong, "Some Hankow Memories," *Asia*, October 1928, p. 794.

11. J. B. Powell, "Michael Borodin, 'Cleverest Revolutionist in the World Today!'" *China Weekly Review*, 16 July 1927, p. 159.

12. Percy Chen, *China Called Me: My Life Inside the Chinese Revolution* (Boston, 1979), p. 121.

13. Edgar Snow, *Red Star over China* (New York, 1938), p. 147.

18. Reality

1. Anna Louise Strong, *China's Millions* (New York, 1928), p. 280.

2. Ibid., p. 234.

3. Ibid., p. 262.

4. Cherepanov, II, 64.

5. Strong, *China's Millions*, p. 242.

6. Anna Louise Strong, "Motoring Out from China," *Asia*, September 1928, p. 713.

7. Ibid.

8. Ibid.

9. Ibid.

10. *Izvestiya Ulan-Bator-Khoto,* 28 September 1927.

11. Vincent Sheean, "Moscow and the Chinese Revolution," *Asia,* December 1927, pp. 1008–09.

12. *Pravda,* 18 September 1927.

13. Louis Fischer, interview, 27 March 1969, Princeton, New Jersey.

14. Sheean, *Personal History,* p. 302.

15. P. A. Mif, *Kitaiskaya kommunisticheskaya partiya v kriticheskii dni* (Moscow, 1928), pp. 66, 75.

16. Ibid., p. 66.

17. Ibid., p. 100.

18. Bertram Wolfe, interview, 25 April 1969, Stanford, California.

19. "Istoricheskie konni chendusyuizma," *Problemy Kitaya,* 3, (1930).

20. Ibid.

21. Ibid., pp. 214–217.

22. Ibid., p. 217.

23. Unfortunately, the speech of 23 October 1927 is not available, though Cherepanov, II, 101–103, does paraphrase it at length.

24. *Problemy Kitaya,* pp. 227–228.

25. Louis Fischer, interview, 27 March 1969, Princeton.

26. Louis Fischer, *Men and Politics* (New York, 1941), pp. 138–139.

27. Borodin would not write the book on China to which he alluded in 1927 (Vishnyakova-Akimova, *Dva goda v vosstavshem Kitae, 1925–1927: Vospominaniya,* p. 373), though it is possible that at the time he did produce a manuscript of his memoirs—see Jean Chesneaux and John Lust, *Introduction aux etudes d'histoire contemporaire de Chine* (The Hague: 1964), p. 72. If so, it has never been cited in any Soviet source.

28. Harrison Salisbury, interview, 11 August 1970, New York; George Moorad, *Lost Peace in China* (New York, 1949), p. 206n.

19. Surviving

1. Strong, *I Change Worlds,* p. 300.

2. *Moscow News,* February 6, 1931.

3. Strong, *I Change Worlds,* p. 341.

4. Ibid., p. 351.

5. Ibid., pp. 373–374.

6. Leon Dennen, interview, 12 August 1970, New York.

7. John N. Hazard, interview, 1 June 1980, New York.

8. Klaus Mehnert, *Peking and Moscow* (New York, 1962), p. 240.

9. M. M. Borodin, ed., *The Soviet Film* (Moscow, 1939).

10. Louis Fischer, interview, 27 March 1969, Princeton, New Jersey.

11. Moorad, *Lost Peace in China*, p. 206n.

12. Phillip Jaffe, "The Strange Case of Anna Louise Strong," *Survey*, 53 (1964), 133.

13. Allen S. Whiting, "Mao-Stalin Crunch Caught Anna Louise Strong," *Washington Post*, 12 April 1970.

14. Ibid.

15. Harrison Salisbury, interview, 11 August 1970, New York.

16. *New York Times*, 3 September 1953.

17. *Moskovskaya pravda*, 30 June 1964.

18. F. S. Borodina, "Sovetnik Sun Yatsena," in *Sun Yat-sen, 1866–1966*, pp. 286–288.

19. Mirovitskaya, "Mikhail Borodin," *Vidnye sovetski kommunisty*.

20. Ibid., p. 39.

21. *Na kitaiskoi zemle*, p. 7.

Acknowledgments

The old, but nonetheless real, fear of leaving someone out, and the risks involved in naming people in communist countries who have helped, lead me to express my gratitude for assistance in preparing this volume, except in some instances, to categories rather than to individuals by name. This in no way diminishes the depth of my appreciation. Thanks, then, to:

The librarians in Oxford, Berkeley, Palo Alto, Washington, Chicago, New York, Cambridge, Bloomington, London, Paris, Oslo, Moscow, and a dozen other places, who have demonstrated concern, persistence, ingenuity, and courtesy in carrying out the tasks with which I burdened them.

The colleagues and associates at the Hoover Institution, the University of California (Berkeley), Miami University, Valparaiso University, the University of Illinois, Columbia University, in the Department of State and the Home Office, who have gone out of their way to help me in my search for Borodin materials.

The graduate students who have ably and carefully carried out the research I assigned them.

Those who over more than a few years have sustained my conviction that Borodin deserved a biography and that a sound one was possible.

Miami University, which provided funds for travel and typing, and to Viola Webster, Alice Lafuze, Dotti Pierson, and Jil Rubin, who painstakingly took my scratchings on yellow pads and converted them into well-typed copy.

Finally, Ruth Limmer and Reo Christenson, without whose superb skills and beyond-the-call efforts this project would never have been realized.

Dan N. Jacobs

Oxford, Ohio

Index

Addams, Jane, 27, 28, 60–61
Alexander II, tsar, 1
Alexandrescu, Mr., 66, 73. *See also* Borodin, Mikhail
All-China Labor Federation, 282
Allied blockade, 57–58, 78
Altshuler, Michael, 32–33. *See also* Borodin, Mikhail
Antisemitism, 6, 10, 324
Ashleigh, Charles, 321
Austro-Hungarian Empire, 56
Axelrod, T. L., 317

Bakhmetiev, Boris, 42–46, 48, 105
Balabanoff, Angelica, 57
Barrabas, 262
Bavaria, 59, 60
Bellamy, Edward, 31
Berg, 45, 55. *See also* Borodin, Mikhail
Berg Progressive Preparatory School, 30, 37–38
Berliln: general strike, 77; left wing in, 78; illegal practices, 78; CI center, 78; literary salons, 79; underground headquarters, 86
Bingham, Hiram J., 283
Black Friday, 98
Blanshard, Paul, 169, 258
Bloody Sunday, 7–9
Blyukher, Vasily Konstantinovich (Galin), 184, 186, 198, 229, 327; sovetnik, 164, 171–172; military plans, 171, 176, 210; propaganda use, 171; adviser to Chiang, 205, 209, 232–233, 240–241; Northern Expedition and, 209, 210, 215;

Borodin split, 259–260, 270; execution, 313. *See also* Northern Expedition
Bokharan nationalist movement, 90
Boland, Harry, 65
Bolotin, Hyman, 26, 30
Bolsheviks, 6, 8; organization, 9; opposition in Riga, 11–12; at Stockholm conference, 19; in power in Russia, 46–47, 57; in Norway, 55; in Russia (1920), 80; interest in China, 108–111; support, 191. *See also* Lenin; Menshevism
Bolshevism, 310. *See also* Menshevism
Borodin, Fanya (wife) 24, 38, 54, 153, 194, 300; jewels, 62, 64, 72, 97; capture, 237–239, 256, 262, 276, 291; appearance, 239; trial, 281, 283; escape, 283, 292; in Moscow, 301, 304, 316, 322; memoir of husband, 327
Borodin, Frederick (son), 26, 194, 237, 319, 322
Borodin, Mikhail: youth, 1–3; languages, 4, 7, 10; education, 4–5; Lenin's use of, 7–10; in Riga, 9–12, 15; at Tammersfors, 14–15; "Forest Brotherhood," 15–16; at Unity Congress, Stockholm, 16–20; to U.S., 21; teacher of English, 21–22, 28–30; in Boston, 22, 23; in Chicago, 24, 26, 37, 70; Valparaiso University, 24–26; activities in Chicago, 29–30, 37–38; socialist, 32–36; Lenin and, 35, 49–50, 81–82; interest in Russian revolution, 38–39,

DATE DUE

16 Dec 82			
GAYLORD			PRINTED IN U.S.A.